Reanimating Shakespeare's
Othello in Post-Racial America

For Gabriel, Levi, and Jasmine, my true loves,
and the reason for *la lucha*.

Reanimating Shakespeare's *Othello* in Post-Racial America

Vanessa I. Corredera

EDINBURGH
University Press

Edinburgh University Press is one of the leading university presses in the UK. We publish academic books and journals in our selected subject areas across the humanities and social sciences, combining cutting-edge scholarship with high editorial and production values to produce academic works of lasting importance. For more information visit our website: edinburghuniversitypress.com

© Vanessa Corredera 2023, 2024

Edinburgh University Press Ltd
The Tun – Holyrood Road
12(2f) Jackson's Entry
Edinburgh EH8 8PJ

First published in hardback by Edinburgh University Press 2023

Typeset in 11/13 Adobe Sabon by
IDSUK (DataConnection) Ltd

A CIP record for this book is available from the British Library

ISBN 978 1 4744 8729 0 (hardback)
ISBN 978 1 4744 8730 6 (paperback)
ISBN 978 1 4744 8731 3 (webready PDF)
ISBN 978 1 4744 8732 0 (epub)

The right of Vanessa Corredera 2023 to be identified as the author of this work has been asserted in accordance with the Copyright, Designs and Patents Act 1988, and the Copyright and Related Rights Regulations 2003 (SI No. 2498).

Contents

Acknowledgments	vi
Permissions	ix
Introduction	1
1. Images of Objectification: Othello as Prop in *Kill Shakespeare*	29
2. Colorblindness on the Post-Racial Stage: Hip Hop, Comedy, and Cultural Appropriation in *Othello: The Remix*	77
3. *Othello*, Race, and *Serial*: The Ethics of a Shakespearean Cameo	117
4. "No tools with which to hear": Adaptive Re-Vision, Audience Education, and *American Moor*	156
5. At the Intersection of Gender, Race, and White Privilege: A Case of Three Desdemona Plays	206
6. Resisting Lobotomized Shakespeare: Whiteness and Universality in *Key & Peele* and *Get Out*	253
Epilogue	299
Bibliography	320
Index	344

Acknowledgments

Any book that takes a non-traditional academic route toward existence accrues significant thanks, and this one is no exception. The (professional) beginning is, indeed, a very good place to start, and I appreciate the professors at Northwestern University who laid the foundation for my current academic life, particularly the early modernists comprising my committee, Wendy Wall, Jeffrey Masten, and William N. West. I am also so grateful for the cohort that kept me going: Hugh Grady, Greg Laski, Carissa Harris, Anne McCarley, Jackie Murdock, Rachel Nelms, Laura Passin, Wanalee Romero, and Michael Slater. I especially appreciate Michael's input on early versions of this work, and Greg's and Carissa's feedback during the proposal stage.

I am indebted to the various academic communities shaping this book, particularly the warmth and generosity of the Shakespeare and race community. Patricia Akhimie, Ruben Espinosa, Kim F. Hall, Carol Mejia LaPerle, and Ayanna Thompson were exceptionally helpful, offering vital direction, insight, and encouragement as I developed this project. The arguments here were refined and strengthened through the feedback provided by conference colleagues at the *Borrowers and Lenders* Conference, Ohio Valley Shakespeare Conference, the World Shakespeare Congress, and most frequently, the Shakespeare Association of America, especially when those colleagues subsequently became editors, as did Sujata Iyengar, Christy Desmet, and Miriam Jacobson, Kim F. Hall and Peter Erickson, Kim F. Hall and Patricia Cahill, and Nora J. Williams and Sally Barnden. I also appreciate those who provided me with materials enriching specific chapters, including Keith Hamilton Cobb's generous dialogs with me and the Chicago Shakespeare Theater, which offered me access to their archives. My gratitude also extends to the editors at Edinburgh University Press, Michelle Houston and Susannah Butler, for both their patience with all of my questions and excellent guidance in shaping this book. Support has also come in less formal but no less meaningful ways.

I am grateful to Kristin N. Denslow, Nedda Mehdizadeh, Kathryn Vomero Santos, Urvashi Chakravarty, Letty García, and Emily Shortslef for being friends, constant sounding boards, and cheering me on. Debapriya Sarkar, you are proof that meaningful friendship can grow both by checking in and through collaborative silence. To Valerie M. Fazel, Louise Geddes, and Geoffrey Way, you are advisors, colleagues, friends, and collaborators extraordinaire, and I thank you for the daily uplift. And Brandi K. Adams, Ambereen Dadabhoy, and Kim, you embody the fierceness and passion of Cleopatra, with an intelligence and generosity that enriches my life every day.

I am also deeply grateful to my Andrews University community, particularly the Department of English and my encouraging, supportive colleagues there. I especially recognize my long-term chair, Meredith Jones Gray, who helped me carve out research time when it was neither easy nor convenient for her to do so. That time was also significantly supported by vital Faculty Research Grant funding awarded by Gary Burdick and the Office of Research and Creative Scholarship. I am likewise extremely thankful for my intelligent, generous, and engaged students. Without them, I may not have found *Othello: The Remix*, and I certainly would not have watched a horror film like *Get Out*! They make me sharper and more passionate. Thanks too for the research assistance undertaken by my student readers, Danni Thaw, Alexi Decker, and most especially, Alyssa Henriquez. Alyssa, I am *so* appreciative of your extensive editorial feedback and overall, sanity-saving help! Special gratitude goes to my research group, L. Monique Pittman and Karl Bailey, faithful interlocutors and unstinting counsellors who have incisively guided the project and my professional life in deeply meaningful ways. Monique, I am specially and profoundly grateful for you, *hermana*. What a privilege to write our books alongside each other. In the best way, your fingerprints are all over this project and every part of my life, making it richer and lovelier.

More than anything, this book would not exist without my family. I appreciate Brenda and Oscar Montes for providing generous childcare so I could fulfill professional obligations. Titi Moe and Tio Pablo, thank you for your steadfast love and being our chosen family. My sister, Eileen McMillen, thanks for always helping me process how to achieve a healthy work/life balance. My loving parents, Ivette and Wilfred Corredera, you valued my education from the start, and you truly meant it when you said I could be whatever I wanted. Thank you for so lovingly shaping who I am and unwaveringly helping me find my voice. Levi and Jasmine, thank you for the love and joy you bring to each day of this life. You make me want to make the world a better place. To Levi specifically, I am grateful for your patience over the years it took to write this book. I will never forget how you asked me every day, 'Mama, did you get to research today?' Thank you for valuing my joy in my work, even at such a tender age. And to Gabriel Montes, words cannot express the love and gratitude I have for who you are, who you help me to be, and for the journey we are on together. In so many ways, this labor of love would never have happened without the abundant support you provided: financial, mental, emotional, and more. You literally made me a room of one's (my) own! *Te quiero con todo mi corazon.*

Permissions

Permission to use the cover image was graciously granted by Glenda Richardson, President of the African American Quilters of Baltimore. Her quilt, "Paul Robeson as Othello," is part of Dr. Carolyn Mazloomi's collection.

Portions of Chapter 3 have appeared previously in *The Routledge Handbook of Shakespeare and Global Appropriation* and *Shakespeare Quarterly*. Portions of Chapter 6 have appeared previously in the *Journal of American Studies* and *Borrowers and Lenders: The Journal of Shakespeare and Appropriation*. All pieces are reprinted with permission.

Introduction

Speak of me as I am
                        —*Othello* (V, ii, 352)

Reanimating *Othello* in Post-Racial America

Three panels—that is all artist Mya Lixian Gosling uses to distill the essence of the Shakespearean plays she reimagines through the stick-figure comics on her site *Good Tickle Brain*. In the *Othello* three-panel play, originally crafted in 2014, the first panel emphasizes Iago's deceitfulness, the second stresses how Othello subsequently becomes "insanely" jealous, and the third focuses on the ultimate deaths of Desdemona, Iago, and Othello. In these panels, race in *Othello* is both present and absent. The stick-figure drawing of Othello depicts his Blackness, for unlike the other characters, Gosling darkly shades his face. Yet any direct discursive reference to Othello's singular Blackness in an all-white Venice does not make the cut in Gosling's three panels. As such, his jealousy can be framed as insane rather than legitimately paranoid, stemming, it seems, from a character flaw, with no external nor sympathetic reasoning gestured toward. Perhaps it may seem I expect too much from a three-panel comic intended to offer up each play as having a "beginning, a middle, and an end" so as to introduce people to Shakespeare in an accessible way (Reid 48, 49).[1] Nevertheless, I turn to this three-panel version of Shakespeare's famous Venetian tragedy

---

[1] Admittedly, Gosling more intentionally addresses race in other, sustained engagements with *Othello*, such as her Character Spotlight on Desdemona, where she mentions Brabantio's racism and suggests that Othello may have "self-esteem issues," as well as in her Stick Figure Iconography of Othello, wherein she notes the performance tradition of applying burnt cork and/or cosmetics to perform the role, while also gesturing to Ian Smith's reading of the handkerchief as black.

because it illustrates what creators deem worthy of emphasis—and, just as importantly, what they do not—when they reinterpret *Othello*.

Some, such as Gosling, choose not to "see" or emphasize race, thereby leaving a fundamental element of the play unspoken and therefore uncommented upon. Yet other times, race makes surprising yet equally vexed appearances. Take the *Sassy Gay Friend* (2010) send-up of the play. Comedian and actor Brian Sullivan created the *Sassy Gay Friend* web series, which consists of short clips that imagine how the titular Sassy Gay Friend (SGF), played by Sullivan, would have intervened in the narrative, thereby creating a different outcome for classic literary tales. Regarding *Othello*, according to the ninety-second clip, Desdemona would not have died if she'd had a sassy gay best friend. Why? Not only would he have warned her to stop moping in her bed because Othello was coming to murder her over a handkerchief, but just as significantly, he would have disabused her of her compassion for Othello. When the SGF explains that Othello has seen Cassio with the handkerchief and now thinks Desdemona is unfaithful, she replies, "I can understand why Otello would think that." He retorts that she not only needs to stop her pretentious use of "Otello," but also points out the error in her thinking with the incredulously articulated question: "What? Some guy ends up with your handkerchief, so your husband gets to murder you? No." He is, of course, correct. Nothing excuses Othello's behavior. Yet the clip leaves no room to explore any potential empathy for Othello that might result from recognizing his outsider status or Iago's abuse of him. Such considerations distract from the comedy. What does Sullivan deem funny, however? Apparently, racist, stereotypical jokes. A direct reference to race appears at 1:11, when Desdemona mentions that Othello called her "false as hell." SGF replies, "False as hell? Wow, he *is* black. Speaking of which, does Moor mean more [gestures toward his penis]? Oh, okay, now I'm being racist." Yes, of course he is, through both a reference to Othello's Blackness that stresses how the Black man, not the white gay friend or the white Desdemona, uses racialized epithets, but also through his admitted stereotypical reference to Black male virility, with Desdemona's delighted, open-mouthed laughter belying the SGF's acknowledgment of his racism. If Gosling's approach of muting race is one version of the problematic interpretive coin, Sullivan's thoughtless repetition of racist caricature employed for entertainment is another.[2]

---

[2] Not only do these examples illustrate the problems present in reinterpretations of *Othello* that I want to address in this book, but they also merit consideration because they are precisely the type of brief, accessible reimaginings that can and do frequently appear in the classroom.

These examples illustrate the dynamics present in half of the engagements with *Othello* I explore in this book. All too often, as these instances indicate, when creators across mediums speak about and for Othello, they do so in ways that suggest their affinity might be to Shakespeare's great tragedy or perhaps the innocent Desdemona, but not the titular character himself. Ian Smith poignantly confronts this same dynamic in Shakespeare studies, questioning why "The Horatian assignment to tell Hamlet's story has become the business of literary criticism" ("We Are Othello" 106), while scholars have been much more reluctant to do the same for Othello, despite a similar invocation. Smith explains that this "general absence" regarding *Othello* stems from a "lack of identification" because he "is black while the cadre of critics in Shakespeare studies have been predominantly white" (108). Due to the "cultural desire to distance oneself from the abjection that is blackness" (108), there is a "racial distinction that affects the telling" of Hamlet's and Othello's respective stories (109). What happens when these scholars, who decidedly do not identify with Othello, teach the titular play? Likely, they run the risk of passing on this disidentification to their students, students who may one day craft Shakespearean retellings very much like *Good Tickle Brain* or the *Sassy Gay Friend* series.

One cannot deny that the perspective from which someone articulates or rearticulates Othello's story proves crucial not only to the reiteration's very existence, but also to how the tale gets retold. The distinction can be crystallized as simply as this: is the storyteller willing to consider Othello's point of view, including pieces of his paradigm informed by his race, or is the storyteller inclined to deny his point of view instead?[3] Concerns about who will tell Othello's story and how they will tell it are not simply the purview of modern criticism. Othello famously gives voice to this same anxiety when he movingly supplicates near the play's conclusion, "Speak of me as I am," as Venetians congregate and pass judgment, subsequently pleading that they "nothing extenuate" (V, ii, 352).[4] People may frequently understand "extenuate" as a synonym for excusing, reading the moment as Othello desiring that those left behind assign him full responsibility for his actions. Yet the *Oxford English Dictionary*

---

[3] Francesca Royster also notes the importance of perspective in Shakespearean retellings when she inquires, "What could we see if we took the point of view of Cleopatra instead of Antony?" (*Becoming Cleopatra* 15).

[4] All quotations from *Othello* are taken from *Othello: Texts and Contexts*, edited by Kim F. Hall (Bedford, 2017).

illuminates that here, "extenuate" instead takes on a meaning more common in the Renaissance but almost lost today—to leave out, to make thin, to "lessen in representation."[5] Othello's apprehension thus arises from disquiet about narrative accuracy, laying bare his fear over the fate of his story and the possibility that it will misrepresent the singular Black person in the Venetians' midst.

Reanimating Shakespeare's Othello in Post-Racial America takes up this question of retelling Othello's story, turning to a particular mode and time that seemingly hold out unbounded possibility for reinterpreting this famous—perhaps some would argue infamous—race play. I use the term *reanimation* to encapsulate the varied engagements with *Othello* in this book. The works present across my six chapters each bring *Othello* back to life in and for the twenty-first century, revivifying this early modern play for new audiences and thereby creating the possibility of reenergizing age-old themes and ideas associated with the play, or inspiring fresh ones. Reanimations of *Othello* thus need not be committed to a straightforward retelling of it.[6] As I move across works, each merits its own precise terminology, which I develop to varying degrees in the respective chapters.[7] Some works I categorize as adaptations, pieces where *Othello* changes genres and/or modes (Sanders 22). Others I designate appropriations, where creators couple movements across mode with a perspective ostensibly distinct from the one Shakespeare appears to take in *Othello*; in other words, works that signal a shift from one "interpretive frame to another," thereby invoking questions of power, property, ownership, and control (Lanier, *Shakespeare and Modern* 5). Using Peter Erickson's formulations, in some works, I suggest that *Othello* functions as a source for allusion or citation, fragmentary references invoking characters, plot lines, and language, so that the allusive "part stands for the whole from which it is excerpted," but no forthright retelling is aimed for (Erickson, *Citing Shakespeare* 6). Yet despite these important distinctions, the aforementioned categories nevertheless share the potential to reimagine rather than simply duplicate *Othello*'s narrative, for they are not circumscribed by the expectation of authenticity or fidelity that delimits "traditional," "authentic," and "faithful" instantiations of the play. As Douglas M. Lanier remarks, "any claim to the 'authentic' or

---

[5] *OED*, "Extenuate," v. (I, 3a, II).
[6] *OED*, "Reanimate," v. (1, 2, 3).
[7] In using *work*, I borrow from M. J. Kidnie's use of the term "to describe the play as process" (5). While my object of study is not always a play, I share her commitment to thinking through the object as constituted by process.

'essential' Shakespeare—the 'real thing'—carries with it considerable cultural power" (*Shakespeare and Modern* 9). Conversely, reanimations, especially those that exist in the realm of popular culture, are not "so strictly governed by notions of authoritative meanings or 'proper' respect" (7). Or as Joyce Green MacDonald asserts in regard to adaptations, "Adaptation's freedom and multiplicity of address may thus have at least the potential to dislocate the power of the Shakespearean text, since it shows that in its reception and consumption Shakespeare is subject to endless processes of interpretation, that he is never just one thing, despite the majoritarian political uses to which he has been put. They imagine a way forward" (*Shakespearean Adaptation* 6, 7). This is why, whether using the terms *adaptation*, *appropriation*, or *citation*, people often view Shakespearean reanimations as especially capacious regarding their narrative boundaries.

Reanimations work as sites of concomitant identification and resistance to Shakespearean authority, whether "in the sense of truth, validity, and reliability (authorised, authoritative)" or "in the sense of power, control, and enforcement (authoritarian)" (Williams). Crucially, because they can safely distance themselves from various elements of *Othello* by their very nature as reanimations, they also have the possibility of moving in a new direction regarding the ideological race work the play undertakes. Put differently, they can lean in to the idea of reviving and reinventing, not just the characters or narrative, but also the racial representation advanced by *Othello*. Nonetheless, as the well-known example of the Monster in Mary Shelley's *Frankenstein* (1818) reminds us, in the wrong hands and for the wrong purposes, that which is reanimated can and likely will be detrimental. As MacDonald acknowledges, "adaptation itself . . . holds out no automatic guarantee of re-presentation" (*Shakespearean Adaptation* 167), and Ayanna Thompson concurs, affirming, "the outcomes of appropriation are never guaranteed" (*Passing Strange* 15). Reanimations thus hold out the potential for reimagination, but neither this aim nor result can ever be taken for granted.

Moreover, as the sites of Shakespeare's most far-reaching cultural circulation—from commercials to novels to memes—reanimations are more accessible and therefore potentially more influential than almost any other Shakespearean archive, making the vision of race, power, and justice they disseminate especially impactful. Thus, just as the work of Kim F. Hall, Thompson, MacDonald, Virginia Mason Vaughan, Celia R. Daileader, and Robert Hornback demonstrates how *Othello*'s performance history has provided fruitful ground for understanding both how the play has been (re)conceived and also how it has manifested particular conceptualizations of race across places and time, so too do contemporary reanimations of the play merit rigorous scrutiny.[8] With the exception of a chapter or two in Daileader's, Thompson's and MacDonald's scholarship and the most sustained engagement in Peter Erickson's *Citing Shakespeare: The Reinterpretation of Race in Contemporary Literature and Art*, this scrutiny has so far not been undertaken as fully as have engagements with *Othellos* of the past. Yet modern reanimations of the play likewise expose the racist, specifically antiblack cultural fantasies that *Othello* challenges, but even more frequently, advances.

Reanimation is thus the mode. The time? I should more accurately say a specific time and place, one imagined as having overcome racial injustice: post-racial America (2008–16). I will elaborate on the concept of post-racial America shortly. For now, it is sufficient to understand that even if only eight years long, this important period in American history and culture invites profound engagement with both the USA's past and its future. Law scholars, political scientists, and philosophers alike observe how President Barack Obama's historic elections suggested that America had entered an era of racial equality in which people saw merit rather than race as the most important factor for determining one's identity and therefore place in American society. Post-racial America thus held out on a broad social scale a promise like the one offered by reanimations of *Othello*—the possibility of letting go of painful vestiges from the racial past then using the American sociopolitical imagination to create not just a better story, but even more vitally, a better society.

In the case of post-racial America, promise did not manifest into reality. Indeed, in hindsight, the warnings against embracing such a naive view of race in America seem achingly obvious. The failed dream of post-racial America thus casts a wide historical scope, raising questions about which ideologies from America's racial history lay obfuscated, bubbling under the surface until exposed most pointedly with Donald Trump's 2016 election and its societal aftermath. Similarly, the imaginative possibilities afforded by reanimations of *Othello* likewise

---

[8] See Hall, *Othello: Texts and Contexts* (Bevington, 2007); Thompson, "Introduction" to the Arden Shakespeare *Othello* (Bloomsbury, 2016), 1–116; MacDonald, "Acting Black: *Othello, Othello* Burlesques, and the Performance of Blackness," *Theatre Journal* 46 (1994): 231–49; Vaughan, *Othello: A Contextual History* (Cambridge University Press, 1997); Daileader, *Racism, Misogyny, and the Othello Myth: Inter-racial Couples from Shakespeare to Spike Lee* (Cambridge University Press, 2005); and Hornback, *Racism and Early Blackface Comic Traditions: From the Old World to the New* (Palgrave, 2018).

do not necessarily come to fruition. Both *Good Tickle Brain*'s *Othello* and the version of the play created by the *Sassy Gay Friend* series are post-racial American creations. But neither presents a forward-thinking approach to race. As Lanier cautions, Shakespeare in popular culture "is often bound up with specific cultural interests and ideologies of its own, not all of them progressive" (*Shakespeare and Modern* 18). Post-racial America thus not only failed to craft a more racially just society, but its values could not even ensure more racially thoughtful reimaginings of Shakespeare's most famous Black character and his tale. In other words, post-racial American reinterpretations of *Othello* do not necessarily break with but often reify the problems inherent in Shakespeare's tragedy, thereby troubling the narrative of racial progress.

It is no wonder, then, that Thompson calls *Othello* "toxic" and suggests that it may resist recuperative appropriation ("All That Glisters"). *Reanimating Shakespeare's Othello in Post-Racial America*, however, demonstrates that the play does not defy ethical appropriation entirely. Take the poster uploaded on the site *DeviantArt* in 2014 by user Bubba-Buu. They explain that their class assignment had them "make a fake movie poster for our final."[9] Bubba-Buu chose to "Disney-fi" *Othello* by employing a Disney visual aesthetic to promote an imagined Disney film version of the play, a project chosen because *Othello* is their "favorite Shakespearean play." The poster has a wine-red background and in the foreground stand Iago, Othello, and Desdemona, positioned almost like Russian nesting dolls, but one in front of the other. Iago looms large over Othello, whose arms encircle a Desdemona, eyes closed, holding a white handkerchief to her breast.

What I find most notable about this image is its express depiction of Iago, not Othello, as the villain of the story, while it at the same time invites viewer sympathy for both Othello and Desdemona. In the tradition of numerous Disney villains, Iago's physiognomy signifies his moral perfidy. Bubba-Buu colors his skin in an ashy purple similar to the sea witch Ursula from *The Little Mermaid* (1989). His eyes are a deviant red, and his extremely arched eyebrows invoke *Aladdin*'s (1992) nefarious Jafar.[10] Together, these signifiers, easily

---

[9] User Bubba-Buu does not designate whether they are in high school or college, nor the class, only that it was "last quarter."

[10] Popular culture observers note that Disney villains' visual and characterological depictions tend to employ both queer and racialized coding to communicate their immorality. For representative examples of these discussions online, see Meghna Chatterjee, "The Problematic Representation of Queer Masculinity in Disney Films," *Feminism in India* (2020), and "The Color of Evil: How American Media Racializes Villains," *Sociology Lens* (2013).

identifiable to any Disney fan and most popular culture consumers, position Iago as the inarguable villain of Bubba-Buu's *Othello*. Just as significant, however, is the single prop Iago holds. Each hand lifts up black-handled puppet strings that connect directly to Othello, providing a visual, metaphorical shorthand for Iago's manipulation of Shakespeare's protagonist. Thus, even as the white handkerchief signals Desdemona's purity while it "conjures the specter of racial otherness" in the poster, as it often does in the play's performance (Mehdizadeh 13), this time, there is another image that demarcates the play's moral logic. In this version, visual representation communicates to the viewer that blame falls on Iago.

Additionally, Othello receives very sympathetic treatment from Bubba-Buu. Of the three characters, Othello's gaze is the only one that meets the viewer's line of sight. His face looks plaintive, with his arms partially encircling Desdemona yet at the same time outstretched toward the viewer. Just as Othello reaches out for assistance by the end of Shakespeare's play, so too does he seem to gesture for understanding in the poster. That said, the drawing nonetheless raises questions about the artistic choices made, such as why Othello's eyes are green, or what interpretive possibilities Desdemona's lack of gaze and diminutive stature open up. Even so, I use this image as a twofold illustration: reanimations of *Othello* can re-envision the tragedy in more ethical (even if imperfect) ways, and significantly, that re-envisioning depends on the potential for identification. After all, *Othello* is not only Bubba-Buu's favorite play, but they share that Othello is "one of my all time favorite Shakespeare characters ever."[11] And while a random image on a fan website may not have the same reach as *Good Tickle Brain* or the *Sassy Gay Friend* series, interestingly, a commentor tells Bubba-Buu that "my English teacher actually pulled this picture up in class after we finished reading Othello." This poster therefore not only supports my point about the unexpected and surprising reach of *Othello*'s modern reanimations, but just as significantly, it indicates that these reanimations can strive to achieve the reimaginative potential that the concept of reanimation offers.

If, as I have indicated, *Good Tickle Brain* and the *Sassy Gay Friend* exemplify half of the works addressed in this book, then at its most basic, Bubba-Buu's poster represents the other half: antiracist postracial *Othello*s that sidestep racial misrepresentation by, even more

---

[11] For an incisive discussion of race and fandom, see Rukmini Pande, *Squee from the Margins: Fandom and Race* (University of Iowa Press, 2018).

so than the poster, grappling with the complexities of Black experience in an America still mired in racial injustice. In other words, by offering modern iterations of Shakespeare and race the same precise, responsible engagement as given to constructions of race in the sixteenth and seventeenth centuries, *Reanimating Shakespeare's Othello in Post-Racial America* exposes the pervasiveness of *Othello* in twenty-first-century culture as a means of circulating competing racial representations: to echo Ibram X. Kendi's formulation, depictions that are either antiblack or antiracist. At its core, *antiblackness* describes "an accretion of practices, knowledge systems, and institutions designed to impose [the ontological status of] nothing onto blackness and the unending domination/eradication of black presence *as* nothing incarnated" (Warren 9). Conversely, *antiracism* fundamentally entails "locat[ing] the roots of problems in power and policies" and honestly, committedly "confront[ing] racial inequities" (Kendi, *How to Be* 9). Distinguishing between antiblack and antiracist representational frameworks proves especially important in an era with rising calls for social justice and increasing considerations of Shakespeare's potential role within such social aims. Antiracist appropriations counter antiblack ones by highlighting strategies that do not succumb to the all-too-easy desire to universalize *Othello* or reimagine it as a story of racial uplift. Rather than extenuating or making thin, antiracist appropriations speak for Othello. They shed light upon the distinct and what Erickson and Hall term "cross-historical" racial oppressions lurking underneath the veneer of both Shakespeare's Venice and America's post-racial society (7).[12]

Post-Racial and Colorblind

I use the metaphor of shedding light intentionally because its imagery of allowing a person to gaze upon what has been obscured contrasts pointedly with one of the most common mainstream racial ideologies in post-racial America: the concept of no longer seeing race. Though scholars complicate the timeline of the post-racial as a concept, for most people, November 4, 2008 seemed to usher in America's post-racial era. As Julius Bailey observes, "The massive wave of optimism that accompanied Obama's election was premised on the belief that

---

[12] The terms *post-racial*, *antiblack*, and *antiracist* can variably appear hyphenated or not. I use the terms as designated here unless quoting others' differing versions of them.

something had finally changed, that America had rounded a corner and was, at long last, putting its checkered racial past to bed. The moment was felt to hold national (even global) significance: this was the long-awaited rebirth of America as a post-racial society" (23). Obama's election thus popularized the idea of America's "repudiation of racial discrimination and racism, indeed of racial categories themselves as meaningful" (Banet-Weiser, Mukherjee, and Gray 1). Michael Tesler reports on just how widespread this assurance was, noting, "Public opinion polls taken shortly before and after the 2008 election showed that citizens of all races were optimistic about the effect of Barack Obama's presidency on American race relations. Black and white citizens alike were also more upbeat about racial progress in the United States after Barack Obama's election than they had been in recent years" (4). With this historic election, Americans seemed to have accomplished the aim of Obama's 2008 campaign slogan: "Hope and Change."

Surprisingly, both the political and cultural right and left embraced the concept of the post-racial, often for distinct aims but with results that nevertheless "foreclos[ed] alternative and more democratic paradigms for antiracist reform" (Banet-Weiser, Mukherjee, and Gray 9). Even as it appeared to invite racial progress, the "slippery" and ambivalent concept of post-race opened the door not only to "older cultural logics of white racial grievance but also [to] articulating new and distinct formations of whiteness, racial discrimination, and anti-black racisms" (2). Post-race amplified these ideologies because the assertion that race is no longer meaningful "[obscures] the relations of structural racisms, concocting a heady palliative against the continuing resonance and necessity of progressive antiracist struggle" (4). To identify a specific example of this reasoning, note how Republicans argued that "Racism . . . is no longer something that produces social or economic inequalities of any kind" (Bailey xxv). Rather, the poor must not have worked hard enough, often even desiring government aid. Bailey explains that this language carries with it "covert racism that reframes our national discussion about race into one about economics" (xxv). One can therefore recognize how "postrace renders racial grievances by people of color an anachronism while amplifying white grievance, the former surviving as little more than tedious investments in long-ago crimes and fetishizing a victimhood that no longer exists" (Banet-Weiser, Mukherjee, and Gray 9).

If the right used post-racialism to argue that claims of racial injustice across social spectrums were anachronistic, neoliberals employed the idea of the post-racial to maintain and repackage a preferred racial strategy: colorblindness, an erasure of race "in which individuals are asked to not consider race, gender, and other kinds of difference" (7). Tesler explains how by the 1990s, Republicans wanted to appeal to conservative white voters without turning off centrists by being "overtly racist" (14). To do so, they used "implicit racial appeals like ... race-coded language." Democrats had a different political problem. They needed to maintain their attractiveness to African American voters without "alienating racially conservative swing voters." Their answer was "benign neglect or racial silence," essentially choosing not to recognize or "see" race. By the 2000s, however, "the divisive bent of these [political] campaigns entangled the racial projects of color blindness with the transparent racial-subordination agendas of the Racial Right, injuring the brand for moderate-to-liberal voters" (Banet-Weiser, Mukherjee, and Gray 9). Thus, as Sarah Banet-Weiser, Roopali Mukherjee, and Herman Gray reveal, the idea of post-race allowed for a repackaging of colorblindness "but without so much of its retro-regressive baggage" (9). Though used differently by the right and left, one can see how post-race became the "'racial common sense' in the United States" (Banet-Weiser, Mukherjee, and Gray 5), making evident Stuart Hall's assertion that "diametrically opposed political positions can indeed be derived from the same philosophical formulations" (*The Fateful Triangle* 36). Banet-Weiser, Mukherjee, and Gray's use of "common sense" in fact highlights how and why post-race would effectively become the new package for a colorblind approach to race. As Hall argues, "common sense does not require reasoning, argument, logic, thought: it is spontaneously available, thoroughly recognizable, widely shared. It *feels*, indeed, as if it has always been there ... " ("Culture, the Media" 310). If applied to a post-racial perspective, one grasps how positioning the post-racial as common sense would encourage people to hold on to their preferred feelings of racial hope or racial resentment by not "seeing," i.e. analyzing, issues of racial injustice.

Such an interrelated relationship between colorblindness and the post-racial invites a deeper consideration of colorblindness, an element of the post-racial most frequently woven throughout this book either as manifested in reanimations of *Othello* or challenged by them. Meghan Burke provides a clear, accessible definition when she explains, "Colorblind racism typically refers to an assertion of equal opportunity that minimizes the reality of racism in favor of individual or cultural explanations of inequality" (2). This approach thereby allows those who harbor racist views to merely utter, "I don't see race" as "protection" for their racist ideologies (3).[13] It is no wonder, then, that colorblind racism results in what the title of Eduardo Bonilla-Silva's influential book calls *Racism without Racists*. This type of racism emerged most strongly in the wake of Jim Crow racism. Tesler describes how, beginning after World War II and continuing until the 1960s and 1970s, particularly post–Civil Rights Movement, Jim Crow racism receded from public view, especially its belief in a biological distinction between races (19). Historian Carol Anderson traces the strategic nature of this deemphasis on Jim Crow racism. In order to minimize the achievements made by the Civil Rights Movement, white Americans rescripted racism by transforming "damning images of white supremacy"—such as pictures of KKK rallies—"into the sole definition of racism" (100). Anderson argues that this transformation was not only "soothing" but also "allowed a cloud of racial innocence to cover many whites" and their racial resentment. Racism thus started to be conceived as an individual problem rather than a systemic one. Ultimately, Anderson contends, "The objective was to contain and neutralize the victories of the Civil Rights Movement by painting a picture of a 'colorblind,' equal opportunity society whose doors were now wide open, if only African Americans would take initiative and walk on through" (101). As a tool for maintaining and advancing racial inequity, then, colorblind racism has a significant history, meaning that its re-popularization in the 2000s as part of America's supposed post-racial era illuminates how the post-racial carried with it "formidable and enduring national scripts" (Banet-Weiser, Mukherjee, and Gray 7), scripts that "[unmask] the cyclical nature of oppression that simply morphs into new iterations of itself over time" (Mehdizadeh 13).

In his foundational work on colorblind racism, Bonilla-Silva traces a similar historical shift, detailing more extensively how Jim Crow racism did not disappear, but rather took on different socially acceptable forms. Specifically, colorblind racism replaced Jim Crow racism by offering "racism lite" (3). As Bonilla-Silva elaborates, 'Instead of relying on name calling . . . color-blind racism otherizes softly" (3). In other words, "Practices have emerged that are more sophisticated and subtle than those typical of the Jim Crow era . . . [but] are as effective as the old ones in maintaining the racial status quo" (25) through

---

[13] Burke explains how colorblind racism can be situated within the "collective body of scholarship on symbolic racism, modern racism, covert racism, new racism, and *laissez-faire* racism" (6).

a "blaming the victim" approach (Bonilla-Silva 73). Tim Wise unpacks precisely how and why victims get blamed when he observes, "if the rhetoric of racial transcendence gives the impression—as it does, almost by definition—that the racial injustices of the past are no longer instrumental in determining life chances and outcomes, it will become increasingly likely that persons seeing significant racial stratification in society will rationalize those disparities as owing to some cultural or biological flaw on the part of those at the bottom of the hierarchy" (18). Or as Tesler puts it, "racially resentful whites cite deficiencies in black culture, rather than innate inferiority, to explain the ongoing racial inequality in America" (20). Put simply, by articulating such deficiencies while claiming not to see race, indeed by suggesting that seeing race is in and of itself racist, colorblind racism allows whites to "enunciate positions that safeguard their racial interests without sounding 'racist'" (4). Ultimately, then, by shifting attention away from institutions and systems, colorblind racism functions as a "defense of the status quo" (Burke 1).

Colorblind racism carries with it particular methods and themes that both Burke and Bonilla-Silva helpfully delineate. Rather than tracing all their contributions, I emphasize the elements of colorblind racism that appear most frequently across my six chapters, either as reiterated or disputed. Burke, for instance, details how, in a seemingly paradoxical move, the "ongoing use of racial stereotypes" functions as one of colorblind racism's core features (5). However, rather than signaling the direct racial hierarchies of the past, stereotypes instead represent "an objective measure of presumed reality," such as the "fact" that many African American communities suffer from absent fathers. In this way, "racial myths, racial codes, and racial storylines are deployed as a commonsense understanding of the contemporary racial landscape . . ." Though colorblind racism can apply across disadvantaged groups of people (i.e. the model minority myth applied to Asians), Burke explains how it is most frequently employed to discuss Black Americans by emphasizing their "often-imagined traits" (9). Colorblind racism thus carries with it deep-seated antiblackness. But such features can be hard to see because of what Burke calls colorblind racism's covert nature, or "racially loaded topics where specific racial imagery supports racist ideas about who these categories of people are understood to be," but with no direct racial references made, such as the cultural implications in the word "terrorist" (10, 11). Bonilla-Silva's discussion of what he terms colorblind racial frames is largely sociological, but he too identifies a particular facet of colorblind racism applicable here, namely the racial frame of naturalization, through which white people can "explain away racial phenomena by suggesting they are natural occurrences" (Bonilla-Silva 76). I will discuss how *Othello*s of the post-racial era manifest these features of colorblind racism below. For now, what I hope to stress is how Burke's and Bonilla-Silva's theorizations helpfully illustrate colorblind racism's slippery and multifaceted nature.

In outlining the contours of and interrelationship between colorblind racism and post-racialism, it becomes clear that these concepts most often fall under the purview of sociologists and political theorists. Yet even if both colorblind racism and post-racialism manifest most significantly in sociopolitical arenas, they nevertheless make their way into culture more broadly through racial ideologies— *"the racially based frameworks used by actors to explain and justify* (dominant race) *or challenge* (subordinate race or races) *the racial status quo"* (Bonilla-Silva 9). Inherently, racial ideologies move one in the direction of media, art, and popular culture. Though these directions are not identical, they may all be considered a form of mass media, which Stuart Hall argues

> have progressively *colonized* the cultural and ideological sphere. As social groups and classes live ... increasingly fragmented and sectionally differentiated lives, the mass media are more and more responsible (a) for providing the basis on which groups and classes construct an "image" of the lives, meanings, practices, and values of *other* groups and classes; (b) for providing the images, representations, and ideas around which the social totality, composed of all these separate and fragmented pieces, can be coherently grasped as a *"whole."* ("Culture, the Media" 327)

Essentially, Hall explains that mass media provides the frames for understanding outside groups or "*other* groups and classes," as well as the representations supporting these frames, which in turn creates inside groups. Frames that function to prop up power differentials, such as racial distinctions, essentially *"set paths for interpreting information"* (Bonilla-Silva 74) and are reiterated and strengthened through "communicative interaction" (11). Thus, whether considered more or less accessible, popular culture or art, low status or high, cultural works essentially depend upon and facilitate interpretation and communication, thereby reiterating or contesting particular racial ideologies, or frames.

Indeed, Robert M. Entman and Andrew Rojecki address the importance of race and framing in relation to media, noting how people use "mental shortcuts" like schemas and frames to make meaning (40). They clarify, "A schema is a set of related concepts that allow people to make inferences about new information based on already organized prior knowledge" (Entman and Rojecki 48), while "Frames are very much like schemas, except they reside within media texts and public discourse," thereby "tell[ing] more or less coherent stories that define problems, diagnose causes, make moral judgments, and suggest remedies" (49). In other words, if the schema were colorblindness or post-racialism, then the frame would be the particular manifestation of those concepts in and across media. For instance, given the way colorblindness depends on the moral and cultural pathology of Blackness (the schema), it explains "the tenacious survival of racial stereotypes despite a social norm that dampens public admission of prejudice [the frame]" (49).[14] Thus, as important as it is for scholars to address the schema of the post-racial and colorblind in US history, politics and society, so too is it vital to consider their specific regressive or resistant articulations in more humanistic cultural domains.

The Post-Racial and the Colorblind in Cultural Works

Moving across more traditional media and works likely categorized as "art," treating both "low" (or "mass") and "high" culture, *Reanimating Shakespeare's Othello in Post-Racial America* builds upon these arguments that stress the importance of how culture communicates particular racial frames. My shift between modes—from a comic series to a podcast to stage performances to a comedy show to film—is not meant to collapse distinctions among genres and forms. In each chapter, I carefully attend to the cultural status of the work at hand: its perceived social capital, structural expectations, methods for delivery, predominant audience, and above all, racialized dynamics. Moreover, as this list indicates, as chapters confront varying conceptualizations of the term *Shakespeare*, whether the man, the written works, or the term as communicating the concept of "*the* icon of high or 'proper' culture" (Lanier, *Shakespeare*

---

[14] It is thus no wonder that Banet-Weiser, Mukherjee, and Gray stress how "the postracial manifests not in electoral politics alone but equally in poplar cultural realms ... It shapes media productions and offers ready alibis to rationalize increasing rates of inequality across a range of social arenas ..." (5). Indeed, they contend that "The concept of postrace ... has gained in discursive legitimacy in part through its mediations in culture and, specifically, via ideological consolidations of the analytic gaze it engenders" (10).

and Modern 3), *Shakespeare* is not my predominant concern per se. Rather, *Shakespeare* "as a principle of categorization and interpretation" becomes the tool for thinking about the racialized nature of the qualities, themes, and interpretations considered "essential" to post-racial reanimations of *Othello* (Lanier, *Shakespeare and Modern* 9).

Ultimately, then, the multifaceted signifier *Shakespeare* becomes a conduit for reexamining the equally complex concept of *race*. Stuart Hall aptly calls race "a discursive construct, a sliding signifier," moving back and forth between biological and cultural conceptions (*The Fateful Triangle* 32). This book rejects the concept of race as biological while acknowledging the concept's very material effects. *Race*, as I use it here, especially in the context of post-racial America's supposed rejection of biological race/biological racism, is "*a structural relationship for the articulation and management of human differences, rather than a substantive content,*" a "blank that is contingently filled under an infinitely flexible range of historical pressures and occasions" (Heng 19, 20), essentially "a social construct that is fundamentally more about power and culture than it is about biological difference" (Hall, *Things of Darkness* 6). As Harvey Young contends, "To conjure a racial label and project it across another person in an effort to categorize that person is an exercise of power. It is a demonstration of the capacity to control and manipulate others: to divide them, to sort them, to mark them, and even, to name them" (10, 11). Young helpfully elaborates on the various elements that allow people to establish and shore up this power, explaining:

> The concept of race exceeds physical appearance. It uses the look of a person as an indicator of expectations of background, history, status, and behavior. These expectations are set by first-hand observation, an awareness of the social and legal rights available to specific populations, and the consumption of a variety of media representations—television, film, and theatre, among others—that model examples of racial behavior. Together, these elements racialize the everyday act of looking. (5)

By turning to diverse works across cultural registers and the precise media Young identifies, I thereby more effectively illuminate the dynamic nature of both *Shakespeare* and *race*, as well as the complex interrelationship between the two. In other words, I uncover how post-racial America uses Shakespeare as a form of cultural power in order to fill in the blank that is race during a historical period where race is especially blank because it is supposedly unseen.

I therefore aim to continue Valerie M. Fazel and Louise Geddes's consideration of Shakespeare's use in appropriations, the way "user agency and authority" play a role as Shakespeare "is continuously being reimagined and reconstructed" ("Introduction" 2). Fazel and Geddes's work takes up questions raised by digital culture and Web 2.0 to frame their examination of Shakespeare's use across "heterogeneous platforms" (4). I am less interested in user agency and authority than I am in the ways Shakespeare users use Shakespeare to advance or contest specific racial frames. Thus, even as I too turn to heterogeneous platforms, racial ideologies rather than the digital world function as my framework for considering how and why Shakespeare is used. Put differently, I take up the important question of Shakespeare's use that Fazel and Geddes address, but by focusing on the purpose of the used rather than the user. In this way, I couple the topic of use with Alexa Alice Joubin and Elizabeth Rivlin's important call for scholars to consider the ethics of Shakespearean appropriation. For, as Sara Ahmed reminds us, "The moral stakes of use are high," often tied to issues of injustice, the subject's slippage into an object, and questions of purpose and power (*What's the Use?* 5). To trace Shakespeare's use in post-racial *Othello*s thus means addressing Shakespeare's imbrication in antiblack injustice, the objectification of Black individuals both within and through his tragedy, and the purpose and power the great signifier *Shakespeare* holds in works that advance ideologies of racial oppression or resistance.

Shakespeare and America's Racecraft

Examining Shakespeare's racialized use across cultural registers thereby exposes the *racecraft* undertaken in post-racial America, racecraft that carries with it legacies of the US's racial past, and that shapes the possibilities for America's racial future, for "it is impossible to understand what 'post-racial' might be without first understanding more profoundly than we do at present just what 'racial' is" (Fields and Fields 20). Coined by Karen E. Fields and Barbara J. Fields, racecraft positions modern America's belief in race as analogous to the pre-scientific belief in witchcraft. Race may not have an ontological reality; nevertheless, people understand it to be real in a way parallel to the pre-scientific belief in witchcraft, which was likewise a fiction conceived of as actual and with genuine material consequences. Furthermore, neither the belief in witchcraft nor race should be dismissed as mere superstition. Though untrue, both are based on seemingly rational arguments. Racecraft thus "highlights the ability of pre- or non-scientific modes of thought to hijack the minds of the scientifically literate" (5, 6).

The concept of racecraft therefore undertakes the project of offering up an explanation for one of the most important ideological puzzles raised by the post-racial. Scholars of the post-racial agree that staunch beliefs in biological distinctions between races have mostly disappeared in modern America, so much so that Bonilla-Silva contends, "Today only white supremacist organizations spout things such as this [beliefs in biological racial hierarchies] in open forums" (77). So then why do a belief in race and manifestations of racism remain? Significantly, it is important to note that biological racism has by and large been replaced by cultural racism, which focuses on "presumably learned differences" (Burke 17). Typically, as Tesler elaborates, cultural racism pits these differences as distinct from and a threat to important cultural values, like a strong work ethic or an emphasis on family (20). Racial inferiority therefore develops from "customs and folkways" (Kinder and Sears 820), with racial narratives "draw[ing] artificial essentializing lines that organize and justify the power relations of a multicultural society . . ." (Ndiaye 163).

I especially put pressure on this turn to the cultural because it continues to dismantle the "tendency to view race as a 'special topic' rather than as a construction that undergirds *all* identities" (Royster, *Becoming Cleopatra* 22), particularly, the specious assertion that threatened to derail academic work on premodern race in the 1990s and that lingers to this day: that it is anachronistic to address race in early modernity since in the premodern world "race" was not a concept based on biology (see Chapter 3). These arguments give the Enlightenment focus on biological race primacy, positioning it as the singular, monolithic type of racial formation. But how can such contestations stand when racism clearly remained in post-racial America in spite of widespread denunciations of biological racial hierarchies? How can *race*'s capacious, flexible nature in modernity be denied when one can see "Definitions of race in practice today at airport security checkpoints, in the news media, and in public political discourse [that] flaunt ethnoracial categories decided on the basis of religious identity ('Muslims' being grouped as a de facto race), national or geopolitical origin ('Middle Easterners'), or membership in a linguistic community (Arabic-speakers standing in for Arabs)" (Heng 20)? In light of the racist rhetoric pervading Donald Trump's 2016 election, his subsequent presidential tenure, and the attempted coup on January 6, 2021, in which Confederate flags were raised alongside antisemitic signs held by people wearing antisemitic t-shirts, it would be preposterous to assert that just because it is understood fluidly, race does not exist in the present. How, then, can scholars continue to make such assertions about race in the past?[15]

This is not to say that conceptualizations of race in early modernity are entirely equivalent to conceptualizations of race now. Yet, as I elaborate in Chapter 3, it is erroneous to suggest that race in modernity is a more stable concept than in the premodern era. As Arthur L. Little Jr. contends, "We come up short, I would argue, when we fantasize that our contemporary construction of race—through our well-honed technologies of racism—offer us proof of a real racial ontology more truly embedded in individual subjects than arbitrarily embodied in and across an infinite number of our cultural discourses. Race, then and now, is not a discrete subject" (Little Jr., *Shakespeare Jungle Fever* 1). Indeed, in both epochs, "Race is envisioned as something fundamental, something immutable, knowable, and recognizable yet visible only when its boundaries are violated; thus race is also, paradoxically, mutable, illusory, and mysterious [. . .] Race is ideology; race is ontology. Race is all this and nothing: a shaping fantasy" (Hendricks, "Obscured" 42). To embrace Margo Hendricks's formulation of race as fantasy returns one to Fields and Fields's concept of racecraft, which they contend manifests not only through "human action," but most significantly here, through human "imagination" (18). Racecraft therefore references the imaginative fictions, the fantasies, created about race that are nevertheless deployed as truth both "then" and "now."

The fantasies delivered through specific racial frames most present across the first three chapters of *Reanimating Shakespeare's Othello in Post-Racial America* are ones, to use Fields and Fields's evocative metaphor, that expose the fingerprints of post-racial America's colorblind racism. Prevalent elements of colorblind racism appear and reappear in both obvious and more surreptitious ways. They can easily be seen in decidedly stereotypical and therefore antiblack depictions of Othello, and easily overlooked in covert racialized depictions where Othello's shortcomings appear naturalized—in other words, stemming not from his alienation in Venice nor from Iago's exploitation, but rather from his nature. Specifically, these chapters uncover how those

---

[15] It is no wonder that Ruben Espinosa contends, "My unvarnished take on this [claims of anachronism] is that such views regarding race and early modern literature are facile and idle ways to evade not necessarily the topic of race but the topic of racism" (*Shakespeare on the Shades* 4).

who create Shakespearean reanimations frequently deploy antiblack strategies as varied as the caricaturing of black identity popular in the Jim Crow era, and the emphasis on the moral failings of Black individuals more common in the neoliberal 1980s and 90s, which took firm hold by America's post-racial epoch, to the racialized humor present in *Good Tickle Brain* and the *Sassy Gay Friend* series. In the post-racial era, such frameworks were especially easy to overlook, for "liberal colorblind racism" encourages "white audiences ... to celebrate [a reanimation's] artistic achievements, edgy sensibilities, and witty interpretation of Shakespeare rather than to scrutinize the way it re-centers and affirms whiteness" (Gillen). Though Katherine Gillen speaks here of Michael Almereyda's *Cymbeline* (2014), her observations equally apply to all supposedly post-racial retellings of Shakespeare. This book thereby uncovers the frequently overlooked racial extenuations—stereotyping, whitewashing, and racial minimizing—in post-racial *Othello*s that occur despite the broad imaginative possibilities post-racial reanimations seem to promise.

Chapter Overviews

As I have clarified thus far, Chapters 1 through 3 each illuminate different forms of antiblackness (antiblack racial frames) present in post-racial reanimations of *Othello*. Chapter 1 turns to the comic series *Kill Shakespeare* (2010–14) to demonstrate how modern *Othello*s still succumb to the most obvious and perhaps long-standing method for shaping antiblack narratives: stereotyping Blackness, specifically Black masculinity. I read Othello's caricatured depiction through comic books' vexed history of representing Blackness, Patricia Hill Collins's concept of "controlling images," and Ebony Elizabeth Thomas's theorization of "the dark fantastic" to argue that the controlling images in *Kill Shakespeare* are both metaphoric and literal, working together to depict a minimized, pathologized, and therefore particularly colorblind version of Othello. A combination of textual and visual close reading illustrates how flattening Othello through stereotyped representation normalizes his supposed pathologies while ultimately positioning him as a prop for the white protagonists' self-actualization. By addressing the recurring ideas of both antiblack stereotyping and the positioning of Blackness as a foil for whiteness, Chapter 1 thus establishes the foundation for all subsequent chapters.

Questions of stereotyping persist in Chapter 2 because of the colorblind narrative approach to *Othello* taken in the Q Brothers' "ad-rap-tation" *Othello: The Remix* (2012). This production serves as a complex site displaying the friction caused when employing hip hop for reimagining Shakespeare. I situate *Othello: The Remix*'s use of hip hop through Imani Perry's, Tricia Rose's, and Michael Asante Jr.'s respective discussions of the genre's history as a Black, polemical art form. This history clashes with the Q Brothers' decision to highlight comedy within *Othello* so as to appeal to conservative white theatregoers. The merging of these genres results in two forms of racial distortion: a colorblind approach to race paired with supposedly comedic racial stereotyping. The Q Brothers thus create a toothsome version of hip hop, which mirrors white society's cultural appropriation of the genre. Paying homage to but methodologically extending conversations about colorblind casting and Shakespeare, I conclude that countering appropriative, colorblind Shakespearean reanimations entails an emphasis on the idea of the color-conscious, not only as applied to casting, but just as importantly, at the narrative level.

NPR's hit podcast *Serial* (2014), which invokes *Othello* as an interpretive lens, serves as Chapter 3's focus, which treats subtler strategies for centering whiteness. This chapter considers the importance of narrative framing through Joe Feagin's concept of the white racial frame. The white racial frame not only shapes the covert, Iago-like focus on whiteness host Sarah Koenig undertakes in the series, but also informs how whiteness frames the topic of race in premodern studies by insisting on the fluidity of race in the Renaissance while ignoring it in modernity. Scholars can thus conveniently argue for the anachronism of studying race in the premodern. By using *Serial* to illustrate race's fluidity in the modern era, the chapter prompts a reconsideration of the resistance to locating race in early modernity as well as a more nuanced understanding of how racial history shapes the present's racial imaginary. Read together, these chapters demonstrate that it is only with a holistic commitment that reanimations of *Othello*, and Shakespeare more broadly, can tackle racial inequity.

In the face of the pernicious racial frames these post-racial *Othellos* advance, one must remember that even within the post-racial US, true antiracist commitments still flourished. Banet-Weiser, Mukherjee, and Gray remind readers that post-race "is conditioned too by antiracist movements like Black Lives Matter, support of immigrant rights, LGBTQ rights movements, and the emergent promise of the student-led gun control movement, which work against the power and allure of postracial race in the United States" (21). My interest here is not in the specific progressive movements they pinpoint but rather in their identification of post-race's ambivalent nature, for my last three chapters demonstrate that alongside antiblack post-racial reanimations of *Othello* coexist antiracist post-racial reanimations of the play. These versions of *Othello* truly speak for him, resisting racial extenuation by employing racial frames that directly contest the antiblack ones demarcated above.

Chapters 4 through 6 therefore articulate antiracist racial frames that compete with common antiblack post-racial frames: complex racial representation, an intersectional approach to racial identity, and the willingness to embrace a non-white narrative perspective. In Chapter 4, Keith Hamilton Cobb's play *American Moor* (2012) powerfully brings together the concerns of the first three chapters by confronting how the white gaze stereotypes and therefore delimits Black masculinity's relationship to Shakespeare and American culture. The play uses *Othello* as a touchstone, for as the actor auditions to play "the Moor" for a young, white director, overlaps appear between his experience and Othello's. I thus build on the work of Erickson and Margaret Jane Kidnie to contend that *American Moor* champions a turn to what I call adaptive re-vision. This term expands on Kidnie's important assertion that "adaptation" is the standard against with "authentic" or "original" performance is established. Adaptive re-vision pushes back against the racialized nature of this commitment to authenticity by describing a performance that may approximate whatever is deemed "original" but that intentionally takes a critical point of view, embracing instead of rejecting adaptation as a mode for critiquing the white-oriented perceptions, traditions, and standards shaping Shakespearean theatre. This recuperative adaptation thus embraces Erickson's concept of re-vision, accepting adaptation at the level of perspective, namely, a perspective that does not need to conform to the right/white one that has so long shaped the authoritative standard for performance. Importantly, Cobb models how to undertake this journey through what I call audience education; essentially, strategies that strive to help audiences be receptive to the racial adaptive re-vision that *American Moor* poignantly encourages.

While Chapters 1 through 4 only discuss Desdemona briefly, she functions as the focus of Chapter 5's comparative analysis of three Desdemona plays: Ann-Marie MacDonald's *Goodnight Desdemona (Good Morning Juliet)* (1988, Canada); Paula Vogel's *Desdemona: A Play about a Handkerchief* (1994); and, most centrally, Toni Morrison's *Desdemona* (2011). MacDonald's and Vogel's respective plays step outside of this monograph's boundaries of time and place. Nonetheless, they provide an important site for comparison, one that exhibits the significance of an intersectional perspective for reinterpreting *Othello* by considering race alongside gender. These feminist reinterpretations of *Othello* powerfully reimagine the play's gender dynamics, yet in ways that manifest white feminism's marginalization of persons of color. Conversely, Morrison's *Desdemona* launches a feminist critique of Othello's toxic masculinity but avoids antiblackness by taking what Kimberlé Crenshaw terms an intersectional approach, a view examining multiple dimensions of oppression. *Desdemona* thus posits that recuperating *Othello*'s broken relationships entails honest reconciliation, one that only occurs when Desdemona confronts her white privilege and complicit subordination of both Barbary and Othello. *Desdemona*'s uneasy conclusion therefore reveals how feminist appropriations of *Othello* do not necessitate racial misrepresentation even as it raises questions about audience reach and access.

I conclude with a chapter that demonstrates how disrupting white audience expectations depends on approaching narratives through an interpretive perspective contesting the idea of universal storytelling, which is very often, as Richard Dyer argues, de facto white storytelling. Situating my analysis within discussions about universality as whiteness across storytelling modes, I demonstrate how comedy show *Key & Peele*'s sketch "Othello 'Tis My Shite" (2013) and horror-thriller *Get Out* (2017) defy whiteness's perspectival dominance. The sketch upends the myth of Shakespearean universality through two "Moors" who watch *Othello* at the Globe, their reactions indicting Shakespeare's representation of Blackness. The sketch's twist ending, however, imagines appropriations that take a Black perspective seriously as potentially rehabilitating this caricaturing. Jordan Peele makes real the challenge posed by the sketch in his film *Get Out*, a direct response to America's post-racial fantasy. In its reimagining of both the horror genre and *Othello*'s basic narrative structure, *Get Out* literalizes the "necropolitics" (Achille Mbembe)—the physical and psychological violence and threat of literal and metaphorical death—enacted on Othello. Specifically, the film confronts America's necropolitics through its emphasis on microaggressions, the concept of the coagula, and the idea of the sunken place. These two examples thus provide powerful frameworks for transforming *Othello* into a story about white supremacy's alienation and appropriation of Blackness, a gesture that resists the universal white perspective in favor of a particular Black one. Ultimately, then, to echo Francesca Royster's words, "The central crux for me in writing this book is the tension between being and becoming, between history and reinvention" (*Becoming Cleopatra* 17). As such, the book's concluding chapters not only speak back to the racial frames addressed in the first half, but more importantly, they provide frames that help readers undertake "the monumental task . . . to render visible, and enable ways of seeing, race," which can in turn fuel "critical resistances" to the presence of racial injustice across art, media, and culture at large (Banet-Weiser, Mukherjee, and Gray 13).

Conclusion: Shakespeare, Race, and Habitus

What I am stressing here is that even as I emphasize the value in bringing care, ethical consideration, and an intentional critical analysis to the process of reanimating *Othello*, what is at stake is not simply the advancement of a particular reading of any of the works I analyze, nor really, any one reading or reimagining of *Othello*. Rather, each of these six case studies uncovers pieces of America's racial habitus. Pierre Bourdieu outlines the concept of *habitus*, or the "structuring structures" governing cultural dispositions, practices, and representations (72). A habitus functions most effectively through its hiddenness, for the structure is made to seem objective and inevitable, without any recognition of either "aiming at ends" or "the orchestrating action of a conductor." In other words, habitus should appear objective and regular, perceived as one among many potential options (73). This approach entails "the production of a commonsense world endowed with the objectivity secured by consensus on the meaning (*sens*) of practices and the world," a consensus which brings individuals into a homogenizing collective that is taken for granted, with no reference to a particular norm or standard (80). The dispositions and practices advanced by habitus are not only grounded in history, but also shape the future via perpetuation, even if the practices and dispositions disseminated are unable to be granted "a rational basis" (82). Thus, "the habitus is the product of the work of inculcation and appropriation necessary in order for those products of collective history, the objective structures (e.g. of language, economy, etc.) to succeed in reproducing themselves more or less completely in the form of durable dispositions, in the organisms (which one, can, if one wishes, call individuals) . . ." (85). Habitus, therefore, "is both unconsciously built—the result of the influences that have surrounded us since birth and frame the way that we think and behave—and the consciously sculpted" (Young 14).

Race is a structuring structure, a habitus. It is made to seem normal, naturalized, and supported by common sense. It shapes systems, ways of thinking, and relationships based on seemingly objective ideas.

Indeed, Bourdieu's conceptualization of habitus overlaps with the dynamics prevalent in post-racial and colorblind ideologies I delineated above: seeming objectivity, a dependence on common sense, no need for rationality or analysis. Royster draws connections between habitus and Shakespeare when she remarks on habitus as "our modes of distinction, the ways that we exercise our social power in public space and the ways that our identities are interpolated by others." (*Becoming Cleopatra* 12) She continues, "The tactics by which we choose to use cultural icons are influenced by these outside forces" (12*)*. Of particular interest to me, then, is identifying the great cultural icon, Shakespeare's, function or use in the proliferation of racial habitus.[16] This leads, therefore, to the overarching questions guiding my analysis: What roles does Shakespeare play in America's racial habitus, and what role might he play in transforming it? To delve further into these questions—Why does American culture keep returning to and reimagining *Othello*? What racial frames can be identified in these post-racial reanimations? Are these racial frames antiblack or antiracist, and how can one tell? What racecraft or racial fantasies do these frames disseminate as truth? What are the interpretive and representational choices that articulate these racial frames and fantasies to a particular audience? Who is the audience imagined to be? And what cultural and theoretical contexts can help us more meticulously engage with these racialized Shakespearean reanimations? In other words, what tools does one need in order to identify, analyze, and potentially reshape the relationship between Shakespeare and America's racial habitus?

This book is therefore indebted to the groundbreaking scholarship that grapples with the role Shakespeare performs in developing and maintaining a racial habitus from the premodern to modernity. Especially influential on my thinking has been the work of the earliest scholars to take on what Twitter calls #ShakeRace, voices from the 1990s and 2000s that broke the ground of Premodern Critical Race Studies (PCRS). I take seriously Hendricks's admonition that

---

[16] Scholars have long noted Shakespeare's influence on American culture, its habitus, for both academic and popular audiences. See Michael D. Bristol, *Shakespeare's America, America's Shakespeare* (Routledge, 1990); Frances Teague, *Shakespeare and the American Popular Stage* (Cambridge University Press, 2006); Alden T. Vaughan and Virginia Mason Vaughan, *Shakespeare in America* (Oxford University Press, 2012); James Shapiro (ed.), *Shakespeare in America: An Anthology from the Revolution to Now* (The Library of America, 2016); James Shapiro, *Shakespeare in a Divided America: What His Plays Tell Us about Our Past and Future* (Penguin Press, 2020); and Kevin J. Hayes, *Shakespeare and the Making of America* (Amberley Publishing, 2020).

these voices should not be relegated to the footnotes. Thus, even though this scholarship predominantly treats race in the premodern era, I nevertheless weave the contributions of Kim F. Hall, Hendricks, MacDonald, Erickson, Smith, Ania Loomba, and Little Jr. across my chapters. And, alongside these foundational voices, one will also find voices representing the very best of what Erickson and Hall, building on Derrick Bell (who himself is invoking W. E. B. Dubois), call PCRS's "new scholarly song" (13).[17] I therefore situate this book as part of PCRS's legacy and future, striving to move this field toward the goals for 2025 so rigorously delineated by Erickson and Hall (3–11).

Much more closely aligned to my methods, questions, and approaches is criticism by scholars undertaking in-depth explorations of Shakespeare's role in the twentieth and twenty-first centuries' racial habitus, particularly in performance and popular culture—namely, that of Royster, Daileader, Erickson, Thompson, and MacDonald. Royster, Daileader, and Erickson all model the richness possible even when examining a singular character or text across place, time, and genres. Erickson's work in *Citing Shakespeare* on *Othello* as employed by artists of the African diaspora in the twentieth- and early twenty-first centuries has been particularly influential. *Reanimating Shakespeare's Othello in Post-Racial America* expands the important archive Erickson develops, extending much further into the twenty-first century and examining works by artists with more varied backgrounds, many of whom create more antiblack versions of *Othello* than Erickson discusses. Though its scope goes beyond present-day versions of *Othello*, just as instrumental to this book is Thompson's landmark *Passing Strange: Shakespeare, Race, and Contemporary America*, the first monograph to tackle at length contemporary race studies and contemporary Shakespeare studies in order to interrogate "how well and how comfortably Shakespeare and race fit together in the American imagination" (5). The legacy of Thompson's vital monograph can be seen in MacDonald's more recent book, *Shakespearean Adaptation, Race and Memory in the New World*, which examines twentieth- and twenty-first-century Shakespearean adaptations that to varying degrees recover Black women's long-silenced voices.

Reanimating Shakespeare's Othello in Post-Racial America complements this scholarship, further expanding the archive of modern

---

[17] For a meditation on where PCRS scholarship stands in relation to this scholarly song, see Vanessa I. Corredera, "Where Are We in the Melody of the New Scholarly Song? A Reflection on the Present and Future of Shakespeare and Race," *Exemplaria* 33.2 (2021): 184–96.

Shakespearean appropriations that invite questions about race. At the same time, however, it does so by focusing specifically on post-racial America, an era thus far overlooked, perhaps because it is part of our immediate past. This book also draws together unique methodological and theoretical strands of inquiry, joining scholarship on PCRS, Critical Race Theory, and Shakespearean performance studies with a deeper attention to Shakespeare adaptation and appropriation studies, especially its work on popular culture, as well as more extensive engagement with scholarship exploring race in media and cultural studies outside of Shakespeare. In other words, I rigorously contextualize the reanimations I study not just through the more common lens of performance studies, but also through the less frequently employed media studies and popular culture contexts pressuring and pressured by Othello. *Reanimating Shakespeare's Othello in Post-Racial America* therefore enriches existing scholarship on the intersection of Shakespeare, race, and the modern world. But its interdisciplinary approach also contributes to the inquiries of media and race studies, and even American cultural studies, by providing a method for ethical engagement with and judicious consumption of popular culture.

On the surface, a book tackling only American works, and furthermore, only works created between 2008 and 2017, the frequently cited start of the post-racial era and just after its decisive close, may seem somewhat narrow in scope. I hope, however, that my extensive contextualization of the intertwined concepts of the post-racial and the colorblind signals how the racial dynamics, frames, and fantasies they carry reach far into the past, even at times all the way to premodernity. And as Fields and Fields contend, without recognizing racisms' cross-historical paths, the steps toward a more liberatory racial future cannot fully take shape. Moreover, while each work I address has been created in the US, most, if not all, have an international scope. For instance, each of the performances I examine toured internationally, while a film like *Get Out* certainly reaches non-American audiences. Recognizing the potential of this breadth means identifying the wide-ranging applicability of *Othello*'s narrative, the racial frameworks used to tell and retell it, and the racial fantasies these frameworks widely disseminate.

Ultimately, despite claims that *Othello* is not about race, this book rejects colorblindness by exposing that no version of the play, whether straightforward or reinterpreted, is ever ideologically neutral when it comes to race. Whether antiblack or antiracist, the frames used to reinterpret *Othello* not only shape the nature of the tragedy's reanimations, but also how audiences engage with the contested issue of race, both in *Othello* and in American society, and likely even further. This monograph thus challenges white supremacy's eras-long shaping of *Othello*, thereby affording disparate audiences new critical, theoretical, and interpretive apparatuses for engaging with *Othello*—and identifying with Othello—through a more ethical racial consciousness. By elucidating the presence and function of competing antiblack and antiracist frameworks, *Reanimating Shakespeare's Othello in Post-Racial America* illuminates the more or less ethical ways to wrestle with *Othello* and race in appropriations, scholarship, the classroom, and beyond.

Even as this book's focus on *Othello* directs attention to America's Black/white racial divide, the notable, recent increases in both anti-Asian and antisemitic hate crimes serve as painful reminders of the racism pervading American society even in the post-post-racial.[18] More frequent and more thoughtful representation of racial identities across American culture is not the entire path toward rectifying these painful and pervasive injustices, but it is a part. Consider the fact that during a poll conducted by the nonprofit Leading Asian Americans to Unite for Change (LAAUNCH) during 2021's Asian American and Pacific Islander Month, "42% of respondents couldn't name a prominent Asian American" (Jones). A 2020 survey by the Claims Conference found that "Almost two-thirds of millennials and Gen Zers don't know that 6 million Jews were killed in the Holocaust, and almost half can't name a single concentration camp, an alarming new survey on Holocaust knowledge has found" (Miller). Such surveys raise the questions—which racialized identities, and their histories, is US culture centering, which are being marginalized, even silenced, and of course, why? Put differently, what role is racialized representation currently playing in forming America's racial habitus? And for both scholars and fans of Shakespeare, what is his function in that process? Answering these questions, I hope, allows us to begin "locat[ing] through the varied experiences a sense of solidarity that cuts across color lines in an effort to challenge racist ideologies and white supremacy" (Espinosa, *Shakespeare on the Shades* 3). My aim is therefore that in some small way, this book offers theoretical and methodological insights that can be employed broadly in order to continue thinking more ethically through the tangled web of Shakespeare, race, and representation in and beyond American culture.

---

[18] For recent books considering Shakespeare and other racial identities, see Alexa Alice Joubin, *Shakespeare and East Asia* (Oxford University Press, 2021) and the collection *Shakespeare and Latinidad*, edited by Trevor Boffone and Carla Della Gatta (Edinburgh University Press, 2021).

Chapter 1

Images of Objectification: Othello as Prop in *Kill Shakespeare*

Depicting Othello: Visual and Ideological Distortions

What does *Othello* look like? Here, I mean not the character, nor the play, but rather the material text of *Othello* itself, specifically the cover images of popular editions. When one pauses to examine these images, which function as first impressions of the play, one finds that, disturbingly, many of them contain long-circulating antiblack conceptualizations about both Othello and Black masculinity more broadly. The Oxford *Othello*, for instance, displays the 1826 James Northcote portrait of Ira Aldridge entitled *A Moor*. While the title evokes the play's performance history—Aldridge was the first Black actor to perform Othello in England—it also operationalizes the racist, colonizing move of eschewing singularity in favor of grouping people into "an anonymous collectivity," what Albert Memmi calls "the mark of the plural" (129). The portrait's title, *A Moor*, conflates Aldridge with the role, creating an overlap that instantiates the collapsing of individuality into racial collectivity so commonly enacted by and articulated through white supremacist structures and ideologies. In other words, the vague title not only applies an anachronistic appellation to Aldridge but does so in a way suggesting that the distinction between the actor and the part he performed is of no consequence. Indeed, Aldridge was not identified as the portrait's subject until 1983 (British Library). This is the same ideological turn to group identity underpinning Iago's assertion that "These Moors are changeable in their wills" (I, iii, 339): apparently, the portrait suggests, also in their names, their very identities. The Aldridge image thus indicates how problems related to race and representation remain ever present in *Othello* before a page has even been turned.

The Norton Critical Edition shifts from an antiblack ideological construction to the reification of an antiblack stereotype applied to Othello as it too looks to the stage for its imagery. It depicts Adrian Lester as Othello, dressed in tan military fatigues against a tan wall, peeking out from behind it or perhaps a curtain. The indeterminacy of this object matters, for it suggests a thematic emphasis before the reader opens the text. Initially, it seems as if one is seeing Lester's image reflected on a translucent white wall or perhaps showing through a transparent curtain. But upon closer inspection, the perspective makes it clear that the body seen behind the wall or through the curtain cannot simply be either Lester's reflection nor an obscured other half. Rather, it is a modified composite image, one in which Lester's covered body depicts Othello looking off into the distance, concealed behind something white, as his more visible half looks off to the side with a much more consternated look upon his face. Such an image suggests a duality in Othello, two parts—perhaps competing parts—of the same person, one clear, the other almost inaccessible. Is this image a racialized one? Perhaps not overtly. But given that the division within Othello has long been conceived of as "noble vs. savage," that the portion of Lester's face which is readily visible carries a look of disquiet, maybe even menace, and that he is both unseen yet clearly appears as if looming around a corner, this is certainly not a race-neutral depiction of Othello. Rather, it invites instead of discourages stereotypical understandings of both Othello and Black masculinity by suggesting deception, anger, and potential threat.

Even in abstract form, depictions of Othello can tap into an antiblack racial imaginary, as occurs with the invocation of Black monstrosity on the cover of No Fear Shakespeare's *Othello*. No Fear Shakespeare's covers are all evocative, deconstructed images representing key figures or moments from each play. Though this abstractness challenges precise description and analysis, an examination of *Othello*'s cover suggests its image likely invokes a monstrous Othello for the reader. The image is split down the middle with a white line. On either side, identical wavy and dotted white lines loosely form the shape of a head outlined against a dark purple background. What would otherwise be interpreted as green ovals crystallize into eyes with the help of a somewhat white triangle "nose." All in all, the disconcerting visual approximates a skeleton head, yet not quite. Why do I read this as Othello? As mentioned above, though the duality associated with identity in *Othello* could easily be applied to Iago's Janus-like self-presentation, more often than not, the split becomes associated with Othello, as he does with himself during his closing speech. Patricia Akhimie explains this duality, asserting, "In comparing himself to the base Indian/Judean, Othello becomes a local and an insider, subjectively evaluating the relative merits of other cultures, while at the same time he is the unfortunate and vaguely human object of this xenophobic gaze, too backward to be aware that his behaviour is being judged, too ignorant to behave in another, more acceptable way" (*Shakespeare* 78). Further signaling Othello are the darkness of the purple associated with the head's "skin" and the green eyes. After all, it is Othello, not Iago, who turns into the "green-eyed monster" (III, iii, 180). This cover thus depicts an inhuman Othello, one who threatens the reader with the unsettling green gaze directed precisely at them. The cover's indeterminacy therefore capitalizes upon readers' potential fears and presuppositions about Black identity, opening up the possibility of a monstrous Othello even as it leaves enough plausible deniability that upon first glance, such a cover could seem unproblematic regarding its racial representation.

Finally, the Signet Classic cover of *Othello* taps into one of the most virulent stereotypes of Black masculinity—its threat to white femininity. This cover depicts a black and white pencil sketch of Othello and Desdemona that has not been completely colored in. Othello takes up much of the cover as he bends over Desdemona, both of his hands upon her neck as he straddles and strangles her. The black and white sketch emphasizes Othello's Blackness, for while Desdemona is totally white—not even her sprawled-out hair is colored in—Othello's hair and face are all painted black. He is also exoticized by his earrings and the pattern on his robe, upon which a gold-colored Persian Manticore stands out prominently. This cover thereby depicts one of the most disturbing moments in the play and directly heightens Othello's Blackness and difference while doing so. By tapping into elements of Orientalized Othellos so popular in the nineteenth century through his exotic clothes and accoutrements, the image signals Islamophobic concerns about Muslim men's attitudes toward women. At the same time, it taps into antiblackness as it connects fears of domestic violence with Black masculinity, reinscribing long-held stereotypes about the threat Black men pose to white women. This cover, then, provides readers with a buffet of stereotypes from which to choose in their interpretive framings of Othello.

I spend time considering these covers because, as Ian Smith's argument about Othello's black handkerchief demonstrates, any culture's visual representations of the play reveal much about that culture's understanding of the drama, its protagonist, and the role race plays in his tragic fall.[1] Pursuing this premise invites a turn to other visual representations, especially those that, like book covers, may circulate more widely than a painting. Namely, this chapter asks, what do comic book depictions of Othello reveal about how post-racial American culture perceived both Othello and, through his representation, Black masculinity? What presuppositions about his racial identity does a medium so dependent on visual depiction capitalize upon?

To answer these questions, I turn to the comic book series *Kill Shakespeare*.[2] Co-created and written by Anthony Del Col and Conor

---

[1] Smith's contribution to rethinking the handkerchief cannot be overstated, as he is one of the few to discuss the way it takes up issues of racial difference, as well as the creation of race on the early modern stage. For different readings of the handkerchief's meaning, see Lynda E. Boose, "Othello's Handkerchief: 'The Recognizance and Pledge of Love,'" *English Literary Renaissance* 5 (1975): 360–74; John Hodgson, "Desdemona's Handkerchief as an Emblem of Her Reputation," *Texas Studies in Literature and Language* 19 (1977): 313–22; Dympna Callaghan, "Looking Well to Linens: Women and Cultural Production in *Othello* and Shakespeare's England," in *Marxist Shakespeares*, ed. Jean E. Howard and Scott Cutler Shershow (Routledge, 2006), 53–81; Edward A. Snow, "Sexual Anxiety and the Male Order of Things in *Othello*," *English Literary Renaissance* 10 (1980): 384–412; Peter Stallybrass, "Patriarchal Territories: The Body Enclosed," in *Rewriting the Renaissance: The Discourse of Sexual Difference in Early Modern Europe*, ed. Margaret Ferguson et al. (University of Chicago Press, 1986), 123–42; Karen Newman, "'And wash the Ethiop white': Femininity and the Monstrous in *Othello*," in *Shakespeare Reproduced: The Text in History and Ideology*, ed. Jean Howard and Marion O'Connor (Routledge, 1987), 143–62; Robert Hornback, "Emblems of Folly in the first *Othello*: Renaissance Blackface, Moor's Coat, and 'Muckender,'" *Comparative Drama* 35.1 (2001): 69–99; and Michel Neill's response to Smith's article, "Response to Ian Smith," *Shakespeare Quarterly* 64.1 (2013): 26–31.

[2] Some scholars refer to *Kill Shakespeare* as a graphic novel even though it was originally released as a monthly, serial comic book. The first volume is now available in the authoritative *Kill Shakespeare: Backstage Edition*, which is bound in a hard, dark brown cover gilded with gold, paginated, and annotated by early modern scholars. All subsequent volumes can be purchased as trade paperbacks, collections that reprint a particular arc of a series (in this case, a volume) in book form after their run has been completed. This may be where some of the confusion between considering *Kill Shakespeare* as a comic book series or as a graphic novel arises. Nevertheless, I am using the term *comic book* because it pushes back against the high culture/low culture distinction often signaled by the term *graphic novel*. As Marc Singer observes, "Comics artists and critics have long used the term with some uneasiness, however, viewing it as an attempt to bestow dignity on comics or simply as a misnomer" (*Breaking the Frames* 19), the misnomer coming from people referring to trade paperbacks as graphic novels.

McCreery and published by IDW, *Kill Shakespeare*'s four volumes ran from 2010 until 2014, with Andy Belanger as the artist, Ian Herring as colorist, and Kagan McLeod creating the cover art.[3] Each volume ranges from four to six issues that follow the story of a wide range of Shakespeare's characters—Hamlet, Juliet, Othello, Falstaff, Richard III, Lady Macbeth, The Weird Sisters, Iago and more—as they battle each other for ascendancy, with the Prodigal Rebellion opposing Richard III's forces. The missing William Shakespeare initially hovers as an absent presence over the narrative, as characters debate whether he is the world's creator, a prophet, more, or nothing at all. Hamlet eventually decides to find an answer. Subsequently, a number of misadventures occur, including an ill-fated trip to Prospero's island and a pirate escapade involving Cesario, Viola, and a cannibalistic Lucius. *Kill Shakespeare* thus provides generative ground for considering the intertwining of narrative, images, and the American racial imaginary.

As my narrative overviews make clear, *Kill Shakespeare* demonstrates a capacious understanding of and revelry in Shakespeare, but also absolute irreverence for both his oeuvre and the vision of Shakespeare as a great, universal author. Yet as so often happens, the creative, ideological limits of reimagining and critiquing Shakespeare appear when one carefully considers racial representation, in this case, Othello's highly caricatured visual and narrative depiction. This limited imaginative vision regarding race has dual implications. First, it allows readers to situate *Kill Shakespeare*'s position in the vexed history of representing Black identity in comics. Second, it reveals the racist, and more specifically antiblack, fault lines informing just how far people are willing to push Shakespeare in post-racial America, even when unencumbered by expectations of genuineness and authenticity that frequently inform conversations about Shakespeare, race, and performance. Is it the cultural capital of Shakespeare and his works, a capital that depends so much on whiteness, that stymies the transformative imagination by making a fully reconceptualized understanding of race in Shakespeare one step too far? Or, does the restrictive sway come not from Shakespeare but rather the white supremacist American racial imaginary? Both this chapter and *Reanimating*

---

[3] While some of *Kill Shakespeare*'s creators are Canadian, some are also from the US, and the series was published by IDW Publishing, an American publisher. My chapter covers the original three series released between April 14, 2010, and June 25, 2014. However, IDW released *Past Is Prologue: Juliet* on April 5, 2017, which this chapter does not cover.

Shakespeare's Othello in Post-Racial America as a whole demonstrate the interwoven relationship between these forces. One may exert more pressure than the other depending on the reinterpreter, the time, or the mode of Shakespearean reconsideration. But they nevertheless remain fully inseparable.

In exploring the nuances of *Kill Shakespeare*'s post-racial, stereotypical representation of Othello, this chapter establishes a foundation for the rest of the book by delineating the common stereotypes associated with Othello in antiblack reanimations of the character (and play) and challenged in antiracist ones. These stereotypes are the controlling images Patricia Hill Collins identifies, i.e. cultural representations meant to subordinate Black people, ones this book reveals, all too often disseminated via *Othello*, even in its most neoliberal, colorblind, post-racial reinterpretations. As a comic book, in *Kill Shakespeare*, the controlling image is both literal and figurative: literal in an Othello drawn as a visual manifestation of Black male brutality, just one more caricature of Black identity so prevalent across comic book history, and figurative in that Othello's simplified narrative turns him into one of the least reimagined and indeed most abject characters in *Kill Shakespeare*.

Importantly, these controlling images appear in a world of almost limitless possibility—a fantasy world involving ghosts, magic quills, and a godlike Shakespeare among other fantastical elements. Ebony Elizabeth Thomas calls this type of speculative fiction—"stories-about-worlds-that-never-were"—"the fantastic," for that term "captures the wonder of stepping into a world-that-never-was, and immersing yourself in it in a way that speculative fiction does not" (7, 8). Put differently, worlds like those in *Kill Shakespeare* can be anything, for they are defined as what the real world is not. Yet despite being fantastic, Thomas identifies how, frequently, these worlds suffer from an "imagination gap" in their depiction of characters of color (5). These characters are frequently altogether missing, or if present, "are often problematic," depending on "Stereotyping, caricature, and marginalization of people of color, poor and working-class children and families, gender and sexual minorities, immigrants, and other minoritized groups." Though not a villain in the story, as a character embodying controlling images, *Kill Shakespeare*'s Othello exemplifies this type of stereotyping, positioning him as the threatening "Dark Other"—the figure whose purpose is to "disturb, to unsettle, to cause unrest" (19)—at the heart of what Thomas calls "the dark fantastic": "the role that racial difference plays in our fantastically storied imaginations" (7). Though Thomas considers the

Dark Other specifically in fantasy literature, without using the same term, Arthur Little Jr. nevertheless notes that this trope also appears in early modern literature, in which "blackness figures as the ocular sign of a cultural need to create and destroy monsters: create them so that they may not create themselves; destroy them so that they may not procreate or multiply" (*Shakespeare Jungle Fever* 86). *Kill Shakespeare* mixes the early modern and the fantastic, and in this convergence, the Dark Other reappears in Othello, whose race has a very clear role in the fantasy, an antiblack one. For by its conclusion, the series positions him as narratively subservient, ultimately turning him into a prop, an object serving the white protagonists' self-actualization.

This chapter thus casts a critical eye on race's ideological work within and the white supremacist racial imaginary supported by *Kill Shakespeare*, using this nuanced textual and visual close reading to further lay the groundwork for the five forthcoming chapters. Notably, scholars writing on *Kill Shakespeare* have not commented on Othello's violent, animal-like, and one-dimensional characterization, choosing instead to turn their critical attention to Hamlet and/or Shakespeare. Chapter 1 thus continues the meditation begun in the Introduction on point of view and identification, a meditation that carries across this book's six chapters. Further establishing the foundation for subsequent chapters, by placing Collins's concept of controlling images in conversation with Thomas's of the dark fantastic, I demonstrate how even with the creative latitude afforded the most fantastical reanimations of *Othello*, antiblack stereotypes, and with them, the centering of whiteness, persist, stereotypes that either get reinscribed or confronted by engagements with *Othello* addressed in chapters to come. Finally, as the chapter closes, I argue that *Kill Shakespeare*'s Othello works as a prop and then employ the concept of fandom to consider the implications and possible acceptance of this dynamic. Chapter 1 thus concludes with a reflection on another of this book's significant through lines: the audience's relationship to and role in the antiblack or antiracist approaches taken by post-racial *Othello*s. Analyzing race within *Kill Shakespeare* thereby creates a compelling dialogue between the use of Shakespeare in post-racial America's racecraft and the complex history of race in comic books. But just as significantly, it powerfully illustrates the racial tapestry created by the interwoven threads of racial representation (both narrative and visual), perspective, racial framing, and potential reception to which *Reanimating Shakespeare's Othello in Post-Racial America* repeatedly returns.

Controlling Images and Stereotyping of Black Men

Collins addresses controlling images as a way of discussing the oppression of Black women. As such, her argument serves as an important reminder that in a patriarchal culture, Black women in America must resist their marginalization in raced, gendered, and classed spaces all at once. Even so, I apply the term more broadly to discuss what antiblack stereotypes do, the work they undertake for white supremacy. According to Collins, controlling images are essentially "stereotypical images" that uphold the "ideology of domination" (*Black Feminist* 69). These images are based on overly simplistic yet seemingly rational, hierarchical binaries that result in "political economies of race, gender, and class oppression" (71). These binaries may be made to seem inherent but are in fact unstable, thereby necessitating that the divisions they uphold—between, for example, white/Black or male/female—depend upon subjugation for their reification. Collins ties this subjugation to objectification, explaining that objectification encourages whatever comes to be viewed as the object to be "manipulated and controlled" (70). This is why "Domination always involves attempts to objectify the subordinate group," which can be achieved through numerous means, such as enforced labor, characterizing those objectified as "less capable beings," or even through erasure entirely (71).[4] Ultimately, their purpose is to "make racism, sexism, poverty, and other forms of social injustice appear to be natural, normal, and inevitable parts of everyday life" (69), which is why, "Even when the initial conditions that foster controlling images disappear, such images prove remarkably tenacious" (69, 70).

While Black men certainly have fewer "intersecting oppressions" than Black women, (69, 70), Collins's argument remains helpful in that it elucidates the function of stereotypical racial characterizations. In other words, the controlling images may differ for Black men than for Black women, but they nevertheless serve the same purpose: subjugation, objectification, and oppression. Of the numerous stereotypes associated with Black masculinity, overwhelmingly, scholars across disciplines focus on the "criminalization of the

---

[4] Collins discusses how controlling images of Black women have included the mammy, the matriarch, the welfare mother/breeder, the Black Lady, and the Jezebel/hoochie. For additional discussion of these stereotypes, see Melissa Harris-Perry, *Sister Citizen: Shame, Stereotypes, and Black Women in America* (Yale University Press, 2013).

black male image" (Tucker 4), or the characterization of Black men as inherently violent and/or criminal. William T. Hoston catalogs these painful stereotypes, noting,

> The stereotypical depictions of members in the Black male subculture are as "niggers," "who are subhuman," "who are angry," "who are aggressive," "who are hyper-sexual," "who are thugs," "who are criminals," and "who are violent," which makes it difficult to be free in their own Black bodies. These stereotypes are so racially driven and intertwined that Black males are constantly in a daily struggle to shed them for their own human survival and mental well-being. (5)

Athena D. Mutua illuminates how even as these are raced stereotypes, "the historical stereotype of Black men as violent, sexually aggressive, and lazy employs not only racialized images" but also "images that are classed, sexualized, and gendered" (24). Just as Collins notes, these images create objects, dehumanizing Black masculinity by reinscribing it as animal-like instead of human.[5]

These various caricatures of Black masculinity may appear as broadly held assumptions (Black men are lazy, Black men cannot maintain romantic relationships, etc.) or take on distinct names—the brute (the violent Black man), the Black buck (a version of the Black male rapist), the thug (the gangster of hip hop culture)—but they nevertheless grow out of the same history. While the most popular stereotypes in the antebellum South stressed "black male docility" in figures such as Uncle Tom, the aftereffects of emancipation changed the controlling images deployed by white supremacy (Richardson 58). George M. Fredrickson traces how, in the post–Civil War South, the threat of the "negro vote" as well as the faltering Southern economy led to the creation of "the [Black] degeneracy myth," which included not only accounts of Black indolence, but also of murder and rape, especially of white women (266). Thus, Black people "became the scapegoat[s] for the political and economic tensions of the period. The result was legal disfranchisement, the passage of rigorous Jim Crow laws, new and more horrible forms of lynching, and a series of one-sided race riots which took a heavy toll on defenseless blacks"

---

[5] In *Becoming Human: Matter and Meaning in an Antiblack World*, Zakiyyah Iman Jackson argues that though resistance to this dehumanization has been "a plea for human recognition," this plea only props up "liberal humanism as an antidote to racialization" (1). Jackson thus calls for "rethinking ontology," advocating for a vision that rejects both "liberal humanism as the authority on being (human)" as well as "animal abjection" (2).

(Fredrickson 266). In short, the white supremacist fantasy of the "Negro as beast" was formed as a means of justifying Black oppression, especially through lynching (275). A particular subset of this supposed bestiality came in the form "of the rapacious black buck whose sexual pathology and depravity were an ever-looming threat to white female purity in the South" (58), Riché Richard explains. It is no wonder that Mark Anthony Neal argues "That the most 'legible' black male body is often thought to be a criminal body and/or a body in need of policing and containment—incarceration—is just a reminder that the black male body that so seduces America is just as often the bogeyman that keeps America awake at night" (*Looking* 5).

These stereotypes do not simply reverberate historically; rather, they have real, material effects on the way that contemporary society treats Black men. In other words, though the US may have moved so far from Reconstruction that by 2008 many believed it had become post-racial, these lingering stereotypes remind us of the all too real ways vestiges of enslavement remain. Since white supremacy imagines and then re-presents Black men as criminal, the racist ideology insists the Black male body must in turn be surveilled and controlled. Hoston movingly makes the connections between America's anti-black past and present evident when he asserts:

> . . . the lives of many black males are spent attempting to avoid institutional and systemic forces that use modern-day slave methods as a form of social and racial control (for example, being slaves = limited productive opportunities and quality resources; whippings = racial profiling, arrests, wrongful convictions, unarmed deaths, the devaluation of black male life; noose = life in prison and eventually death by incapacitation). (5)

Beneficiaries of white supremacy, according to Hoston, create a family of racist practices in order to sustain the benefits of Black suppression, for "your great-grandfather (slavery), grandfather (systemic racism and discrimination), father (institutional racism and discrimination), and brother (individual racism and discrimination) passed this vile mentality down through the generations" (17).[6] Put differently, whereas slavery turned into Jim Crow oppression, Jim Crow oppression has now turned into what Michelle Alexander terms "the new Jim Crow," or the carceral system writ large in America.

---

[6] The opening of Alexander's book moves beyond the family as a metaphor, tracing how the methods used to create the new Jim Crow affect a real Black family.

Building on Foucault, Linda Tucker helpfully explains the logic undergirding the system that Alexander so carefully discusses. The stereotypical images of criminal, deviant, pathological Black masculinity position Black men as a group "innately inclined toward criminal behavior and thus deserving of control via disproportionate levels of incarceration and surveillance" (5). Alexander elaborates on what happens next: these Black men become part of what she terms "a new racial caste system" (3). In a post-Jim Crow era, "it is no longer socially permissible to use race, explicitly, as a justification for discrimination, exclusion, and social contempt" (2). Thus, society turns to the criminal justice system, so that "Like Jim Crow (and slavery), mass incarceration operates as a tightly networked system of laws, policies, customs, and institutions that operate collectively to ensure the subordinate status of a group defined by race" (13). To bring the argumentative pieces together—the phantasmagoric controlling images of Black masculinity result in the very real social responses of increased scrutiny, discrimination, and ultimately, incarceration. The data on the racial nature of America's carceral system is staggering, and starts from youth, for Black children "are 61 percent more at risk of being conscripted into the school-to-prison pipeline," while "Latinos were nearly twice as likely—and African Americans a staggering five times more likely—to be incarcerated than whites" (Banet-Weiser, Mukherjee, and Gray 3). To put these numbers into perspective, "The United States imprisons a larger percentage of its black population than South Africa did at the height of apartheid" (Alexander 6). The "racial dimensions" of mass incarceration in turn position Black men (and women) as what Alexander calls a racial undercaste, "individuals who are permanently barred by law and custom from mainstream society" (6, 13). Thus, the controlling images disseminated in *Kill Shakespeare* have implications beyond a critique of a particular Shakespearean reanimation. Rather, it is imperative to recognize that they are part of a larger insidious system that strives to use whatever ideological and social means necessary to strip Black men of their citizenship.

Representing Blackness in Comic Book History

In part, controlling images effectively advance white supremacy's aims because of their pervasiveness. They move across media, for as Collins observes, "The growing influence of television, radio, movies, videos, CDs, and the Internet constitute new ways of circulating controlling images. Popular culture has become increasingly important in promoting these images, especially with new global technologies that allow US popular culture to be exported throughout the world" (*Black Feminist* 85). In the US, "racial isolation heightens the importance of the messages Whites receive about Blacks from the mass media," so that stereotypes in media not only reflect American culture but also "act as a causal agent: they help to shape and reshape the culture" (Entman and Rojecki 2, 3). Comics are part of this media. Frantz Fanon identifies comic books specifically as "an outlet whereby the energy accumulated in the form of aggressiveness [collective catharsis] can be released" (124). Because these are stories "written by white men for white children," evil and savagery are always associated with "Blacks or Indians" (124, 125). As a result, both little white children and little Black children identify with the white explorer and hero. In other words, the Black child takes on the perspective of the "civilizing colonizer," thereby "adopt[ing] a white man's attitude" (126). In short, the Black child "invests the hero, who is white, with all his aggressiveness—which at his age closely resembles self-sacrifice: a self-sacrifice loaded with sadism" (126). Just as the comic books read by Antillean children mirror and perpetuate the colonizer's beliefs and interests, so too do "superhero comics and popular culture reflect, produce, and contest changing—if not always evolving—attitudes toward race within US culture" (Austin and Hamilton 11). In their reflection and production of antiblack views, comic books have, like much of popular media, turned to and spread controlling images of Black masculinity to the (predominantly white) masses (see Chapter 4).

Comic books in fact prove to be a particularly fruitful site for considering racial stereotyping because the very nature of the medium depends on stereotyping. In their discussion of Black comics (both comics representing Black characters and comics by Black artists), Frances Gateward and John Jennings explain how "Comics traffic in stereotypes and fixity. It is one of the attributes at the heart of how the medium deals with representation. Comics abstract and simplify" (2). Though he uses the language of formulas rather than stereotyping, Bradford W. Wright elaborates on the same idea when he notes, "Audiences turn to formulaic stories for the escape and enjoyment that comes from experiencing the fulfillment of their expectations within a structured imaginary world . . . Put simply, formulas that appeal to audiences tend to proliferate and endure, while those that do not, do neither . . . Formulas, therefore, are essentially historical constructions, and they are central to understanding comic book history" (xvi). Wright's point bears emphasizing, for when stereotypical racial narratives circulate within comics, it means that this "formula" must appeal to audiences, suggesting that both comic creators and comic readers play important roles in the "stereotypes and fixity" that Gateward and Jennings stress.

Rebecca Wanzo traces how stereotyping is not just a matter of the stories to which comics turn, but also the visuals they include. Wanzo explains that

> Comic art evolves from the tradition of caricature: exaggerated representations of the human face and form . . . Not necessarily recognizable likenesses of people, caricatures were not only exaggerated faces or body types, but also fantastic depictions of inanimate objects or humans. The latter clearly were a precursor to anthropomorphic characters in many popular comics. (4)

Caricatures became popular enough to earn their own name in Britain by the eighteenth century, so that "caricature and scientific racism emerged in roughly the same period," no accident according to Wanzo, given that they were both a form of what she terms "visual imperialism—the production and circulation of racist images that are tools in justifying colonialism and other state-based discrimination" (4). Racial caricatures thus literalize Collins's concept of the controlling images; they were actual images deployed to advance racial discrimination. It is no wonder, then, that the terms *caricature* and *stereotype* are synonymous, for even though the visual medium of a caricature often focuses on the individual and excess while stereotypes focus on a group and simplification, both depend on reducing others "in order to represent something understood as essential about their character" (5).[7]

Given that comics derive from caricatures, as Wanzo details, and that caricatures so deftly participated in advancing imperial racial ideology, it should come as no surprise that comic books too participated in crafting and continue to shape America's racial imaginary during the twentieth and twenty-first centuries. I use the term *imaginary* purposefully, for comics are a genre deeply invested in the imagination. Sheena C. Howard and Ronald L. Jackson II explain, "Comics have functioned to sustain our imaginations. They have

---

[7] Laura Lehua Yim provides an incisive analysis of the ways caricature, racialization, and settler colonialism work in tandem, thereby demonstrating how "indigeneity is part of understanding race and Shakespeare in 'black America'" (39), in "Reading Hawaiian Shakespeare: Indigenous Residue Haunting Settler Colonial Racism," *Journal of American Studies* 54.1 (2020): 36–43.

aided readers, artists, and general consumers in stepping outside of themselves to become something beyond what is real. They have also been quite adept at taking what is real and turning it topsy-turvy to demonstrate the idiosyncrasies or wrong-headedness of our thinking" (1, 2). Because of this imaginative turn, comic books are typically understood as the purview of children, which means that they are often disregarded. But precisely because of their youthful appeal, they "fortify at an early age what we have been taught about right and wrong, justice and evil, as well as friends and enemies" (Howard and Jackson 2). Perhaps most famously, superheroes function as the comic book characters communicating these social justice concepts, and "For decades young readers have encountered a defining and idealized image of heroism that was explicitly honest, law abiding, chaste, excessively masculine, and above all, white" (Brown 3). As such, comic books advance what Howard and Jackson II identify as "White patriarchal universalism. In other words, oftentimes comics tell a story about White heroes and minority villains, White victors and minority losers, White protagonists and perhaps a minority sidekick" (3). This clear binary establishes "a concealed residue of minority inferiority" that "imprint[s] on young impressionable readers' imaginations a sense of minority incapacity, incompetency, and impossibility" (2). Wanzo adds more specificity to the history of Black comic book characters, noting how:

> In many comics and cartoons, blackness is the villainous threat to the state, but in a large number of other early important comics, the Africanist presence facilitates white adventure ... Such caricatures demonstrated the view of black people as less human than white citizens while also functioning as a consistent means of pleasure. (11)

Wanzo's assertions thus mirror Gateward and Jennings's claim that "The first images of Black people in comics were loosely based on the stereotypes generated in blackface minstrelsy, stereotypes mired in the notion of fixity . . . dim-witted buffoons who needed the white male either to save them or to guide them in their lives" (3). From their beginnings as eighteenth-century caricatures to their flourishing in what is known as the Golden Age of comics (1930s–1940s) and beyond, it is clear that the history of comics has concomitantly been a history of antiblack (mis)representation.

While Black characters were eventually integrated into both comic strips and comic books, especially in what is known as the Modern

Age of comics (1985 to today), integration did not necessarily solve the racial representational problems. All too often, comics depended on "black characters who showed little difference from white characters, or black characters who still referenced some essentialist understanding of black people" (Wanzo 12, 13). This essentialist gesture was especially notable in depictions of Black superheroes. In a "post-racial" world where the superhero film *Black Panther*, based on the eponymous comic book series, shattered box office expectations in part because of its progressive representation of Black identity, claims asserting Black essentialism in comic book culture perhaps seem to ignore the importance and popularity of famous Black superheroes such as Blade, Luke Cage, Falcon, and of course, Black Panther himself. Yet as frequently happens, qualities valorized when enacted by white bodies become denigrated when enacted by Black bodies. As Gateward and Jennings elaborate:

> The genre of the superhero is very much a white-male-dominated power fantasy that is itself very much based on ideas around physical performance and power in relation to the negotiation of identity. Because the Black body has historically been linked to physicality and not intelligence, the depictions of Black superheroes already have inherent issues built into the very conventions of the genre. (4, 5)

This is not to downplay the importance of Black superheroes in comics. As Jeffrey A. Brown observes, the most "contemporary superhero model" works differently than those of the past "by emphasizing brains over brawn" (13). This "reversal . . . is especially powerful and progressive because it is written on the bodies of black men, who have historically been aligned with the unthinking, bestial side of Western culture's nature-versus-civilization dichotomy" (13). Adilifu Nama likewise argues that Black figures in Marvel and DC comics "frequently challenged conventional and preconceived notions concerning black racial identity by offering a futuristic and fantastic vision of blackness that transcended and potentially shattered calcified notions of blackness as a racial category and source of cultural meaning" (6). Even so, the overwhelmingly valorized white presence and long-standing misrepresentation of Black characters within comic books cannot and should not be easily discounted, for they manifest Thomas's concept of the imagination gap—how even a medium so dependent on expanding the imagination frequently cannot stretch far enough when it comes to reconceiving race.

Kill Shakespeare's Othello and the Complexities of the Black Superhero

Kill Shakespeare both does and does not fit within the typical expectations associated with comic books. On the one hand, there are no traditional superheroes in *Kill Shakespeare*. While Hamlet does have supernatural powers that make him the "shadow king," meaning the only figure able to find the missing Shakespeare, these powers are limited to his experiencing supernatural sensations that navigate him toward his creator. All other supernatural characters, such as Lady Macbeth and Prospero, practice magic. The series likewise upends expectations in that it is decidedly *not* for children. Belanger depicts significant violence and gore across *Kill Shakespeare*'s pages, including beheadings, eyes being gouged out, and cannibalism. Marina Gerzic and Helen Balfour similarly note:

> Belanger's comic art . . . has a detail and complexity about it that does not exactly fit the house styles of the larger comics' publishers, such as Marvel and DC. Belanger's art is "vibrantly exaggerated, and unflinching in the violence department . . ."

McCreery and Del Col's story also includes sufficient sexual innuendo and even a discussion of bestial rape (between a wolf-like Caliban and an emotionally disturbed Miranda) to make it evident that this series is not the typical purview of youth.

Kill Shakespeare nevertheless follows in the comic imaginative tradition. Certainly, the characters inhabit a world originated by Shakespeare, yet his world also shifts in McCreery and Del Col's hands. For instance, rather than dying, Juliet is saved by the apothecary; Hamlet Sr. transforms into a jealous father fearful of his son's usurpation; Lady Macbeth learned her magic from Prospero when under his care, while Viola is now a pirate and Cesario her pirate king. Furthermore, famous Shakespearean lines are tweaked and reassigned, giving them new meaning and context. What remains constant amid these various retellings is the moral demarcation of the characters who inhabit a world governed by clear good and evil (at least in the first two series), with the righteous Prodigals led by Juliet on the side of good, and the Black Army and other competing forces under, varyingly, Macbeth's, Richard III's, and Lady Macbeth's control, on the side of evil. As Peter Holland concurs:

> The narrative unmoors Shakespeare's characters from their plays and their plots, allowing them to interact freely across a canvas of a

world that is peopled by Shakespeare's creations but without being constrained by his concept of action. They are instead constrained by a pre-determinate—that is, Shakespearean—character so that the action pits the expected forces of evil (Lady Macbeth, Richard III, Don John, Iago) against the equally predictable forces of good (Hamlet, Falstaff, Othello, Juliet) in a quest to find Shakespeare himself, the hidden god of a prophetic myth, in order to gain control of the magic quill (think: the pen as phallus, the penis mightier than the sword) in a world in which one swears "by Will."

McCreery and Del Col thus undertake a playful form of worldbuilding. They use what Shakespeare already created but transform those elements through inventive reconstructions, all while providing sufficient constancy to keep audiences oriented through their moral delineations.

Yet even as the series' creators craft clever (and not so clever) Shakespearean reinterpretations, they cannot seem to conceive of a different version of Othello, either in regard to his traditional Shakespearean trajectory nor his moral ambiguity as an unredeemed domestic murderer. This fact is especially notable given that he is the only character of color depicted in the entire series. Othello thereby parallels the 1980s dynamic in which "Single or 'token' nonwhite—and most often black—members added to established teams remained largely marginalized both within the team and literally on the page" (Austin and Hamilton 16, 17). On the surface, however, Othello's inclusion in *Kill Shakespeare* may instead seem to be a nod to the multicultural potential of comics, for as Michelle Ephraim observes, the Prodigals "are a band of institutional outsiders and rebels: Hamlet, Juliet, Falstaff, Puck, and Othello – a heterogeneous jumble united by their loyalty to their father and protector, Shakespeare. While most certainly of the 'alternative comic' genre, *Kill Shakespeare*'s superheroes also evoke the Golden Age of American comics and thus also the ethnic American melting pot of its creators" (Ephraim). To return to Holland's description, Othello clearly appears to be one of the "forces of good," a hero serving as an important general for Juliet's righteous rebels. Ultimately, however, both his visual representation and his role across *Kill Shakespeare*'s various storylines traffic in stereotypical controlling images that visually and narratively overwhelm any positive interpretation of Othello. For Othello does not receive the redemption arc afforded to white characters like Hamlet and Juliet. *Kill Shakespeare*'s depiction of Othello thus not only exemplifies the representational dangers of attempting a race-neutral or "colorblind" perspective when reimagining Othello, but also vividly manifests the prevalent stereotypes that haunt and flatten out Shakespeare's most famous Black character, even when divorced from the limiting expectations of Shakespearean fidelity.

Othello's representational problems begin from the series' conceptualization, a detail that signals the importance of attending to race from any work's outset, but especially reanimations that carry with them Shakespeare's cultural authority. Gerzic and Balfour argue that "Every comic book and graphic novel version of a Shakespearean play offers an interpretation by the artist and the adapter, and thus a reader must be conscious and critical of the ways in which these texts 'make meaning.'" In the case of *Kill Shakespeare*, this critical eye must attend to the racialized meaning of Blackness made through Othello. The *Kill Shakespeare Backstage Edition*, an annotated collection of *Kill Shakespeare*'s first and second volumes (*A Sea of Troubles* and *The Blast of War*), includes the pitch art for the series, which provides insight into how Belanger initially imagined the characters. Belanger explains that Othello "was my favorite character to draw" for he understood Othello as "my Shakespearean Incredible Hulk." Belanger's comment indicates how the superhero conventions so tied to comic books influence *Kill Shakespeare* in subtle ways. But how is Othello like Hulk when he is neither green, invincible, nor transformed by gamma rays? Belanger explains the connection, for like the white Bruce Banner and his alter ego, Othello is "this big guy who can flip from being clever, gentlemanly, and calm into a violent, brutal raging soldier in the blink of an eye." In his explanation, Belanger does not mention race at all. This racial silence is part and parcel of a colorblind approach, one that does not see race by refusing to acknowledge its importance to identities both real and imagined. As Beverly Daniel Tatum observes, there is no American generation

> living in a postracial, color-blind society. Instead, we may be living in a color-*silent* society, where we have learned to avoid *talking about* racial difference. But even if we refrain from mentioning race, the evidence is clear that we will notice racial categories and that our behaviors are guided by what we notice. (24)

Indeed, as Thomas argues, in the dark fantastic, readers notice race, for "Darkness is personified, embodied and most assuredly racialized," leading to the generic expectation of the Dark Other (20). Thus, Belanger's inattention to race, particularly in this genre, creates a tension in Othello's depiction. Belanger clearly has fondness for

Othello, who he perceives as "the most traditional action hero" of all of *Kill Shakespeare*'s protagonists. Yet in being inattentive to race, Belanger does not consider how Othello's race makes him markedly different from Hulk, even if they share certain qualities.

Take, for instance, the fact that according to Belanger, Othello has "such huge sways in his personality." Even if one agrees with his characterization, it is different for Othello to manifest this sway than it is for Hulk. One key distinction between the two depends on the "central convention of the split identity," which establishes a contrast between the extraordinary hero and the hero's everyday self (Singer, "'Black Skins'" 114). Even dabblers in superhero culture know this convention: Clark Kent/Superman, Bruce Wayne/Batman, or turning to one of Hulk's fellow Avengers, Tony Stark/Iron Man. Hulk too exemplifies this split identity, for he "alternates between two entirely different bodies" (Singer, "'Black Skins'" 113). In other words, reserved, weak, introverted scientist Banner transforms into Hulk, but they are different personalities manifested in distinct forms. The depiction of Hulk in the Marvel Cinematic Universe (MCU) film *Avengers: Infinity War* (2018) clarifies the dynamic I describe here. In the movie, Banner repeatedly wants to transform into Hulk, but Hulk never acquiesces to Banner's supplications regardless of the danger at hand. Directors Anthony Russo and Joe Russo visually distinguish the two, with actor Mark Ruffalo's head signaling Banner; his head enlarges and turns green when Hulk refuses Banner, which then changes back as Banner must accept Hulk's rejection. My point here is to emphasize how Banner/Hulk are often two distinct beings, each designated by an easily differentiated body.

This split identity is not the case with Othello. Marc Singer argues that the split identity has the potential to explore compellingly the complexities of race in comic books, for it "perfectly mimics the dialectical, existential, or differential split which [W. E. B.] Du Bois, [Frantz] Fanon, and [José] Muñoz ascribe to racial and other categories of minority identity" ("'Black Skins'" 114). Singer elaborates:

> Superhero comics can literally personify the otherwise abstract ontological divides of minority identity, assigning each self its own visual identifier, its own body, and then charting the effects as these bodies house and are housed by the same mind. Those few comics writers who already use the superhero split identity to portray this aspect of minority identity generally present race and sexuality with richness and complexity, free of the tokenism and erasure which have dominated the genre. (116)

Singer thus articulates why the split identity afforded to Hulk would be especially helpful for processing Othello's racial identity, including what Belanger describes as his emotional swings.

Crucially, however, Othello is denied this comic book convention. He manifests one ragingly varying personality in a single form rather than in two clearly demarcated forms like Hulk. In other words, Othello does not have an alternate identity like so many superheroes. This decision implies a singularity and therefore innateness to Othello that would be ameliorated by the duality afforded to other traditional comic characters. He is therefore not afforded any explanation for his widely varying changes in mood. A scientific experiment gone wrong transformed Banner's body and therefore his character. With no comparable reasoning provided, Othello's emotional deviations appear to stem from his nature, exactly the individual pathology dynamic so favored by both colorblind and cultural (post-racial) racism. Moreover, Belanger does not account for the fact that brutality and violence signify differently for a large Black man than they do for an affable, white, scientific genius who turns into a bright green monster of monumental proportions. Stated differently, Othello is still a regular though strong man, and a Black man at that, while Banner becomes the paranormal Hulk. Thus, precisely when embodying the characteristics Belanger valorizes—strength, power, rage—Othello fits within the quotidian expectations that stereotypes establish for Black men while Hulk breaks all expectations associated with mild-mannered scientists who hold multiple PhDs. Clearly, in this instance, whether by choice or by inattention, not seeing race creates rather than rectifies representational issues by reinscribing stereotypes.

In a seemingly less vexed vein, Othello's visual depiction may also be an homage to the Black comic book heroes who have preceded him. After all, as Brandon Christopher explains:

> Within the industry, creators have often crafted their work as homage (both ironic and not) to earlier comics creators and eras. This backward-looking tendency, unsurprising in an industry built in large part on reworking the same stories, themes, and characters for decades, has had the effect of establishing a canon of recognizable gestures and styles, of creating a hierarchy of influences whose signs were deployed for the benefit of a subset of readers who could be counted on to recognize and decode them. (153)

Unpacking Othello's representation thus necessitates situating his depiction in relation to Black superheroes of comics past. Allan

W. Austin and Patrick L. Hamilton address this significant piece of comic book history. In an "effort to diversify," they explain, "black heroes led the way, with the Black Panther playing the pioneering role in 1966. Others—including the first African American hero, the Falcon (1969), and the first headlining Black superhero, Luke Cage (1972)—arrived soon after at Marvel" (Austin and Hamilton 127).[8]

These historical and famous Black comic book figures clearly inspire Othello's visual depiction. In *Kill Shakespeare*, Othello stands taller than every other character, with a smooth pate, manicured eyebrows and goatee, as well as a gold hoop earring in his left ear. He is also incredibly strong, as signaled by his rippling muscles, almost always on display beneath his cloak given that his costume has no sleeves. Perhaps the most obvious inspiration for Othello's visual depiction is the superhero Luke Cage, known for his incredible strength. Like most comic book characters, Luke Cage takes on several different visual manifestations, but even a cursory Google Image search makes clear that his most common modern characterization mirrors Othello's: an incredibly large build, bald head, bulging muscles pushing against tight clothes, a fastidiously manicured goatee, and in some cases even pierced ears. A more recent character may also be invoked here—Nick Fury as re-envisioned in 2002 by comic book author Mark Millar and artist Bryan Hitch in the Marvel series "The Ultimates." In an almost tautological approach, Millar and Hitch used Samuel L. Jackson as an inspiration for Fury; inspired by Millar and Hitch's Fury, Jackson would later go on to play that very character in the MCU films (Lubin). As those familiar with Jackson know, this reinterpreted Nick Fury is likewise bald and, in the comics, very muscular, though less broad than Belanger's drawing of Othello. Fury and Othello also share very serious dispositions compared to their comrades. Othello may also reference Nick Fury Jr., Fury's son, who looks almost exactly like his father, but taller and larger, muscles more akin to Captain America's, and therefore more like Othello. The point is not to identify one particular

---

[8] Austin and Hamilton provide even more details, noting that "DC introduced Mal Duncan in 1971; the Green Lantern John Stewart in 1972; Tyroc, the first black member of the Legion of Super-Heroes, in 1976; and then its first headlining black superhero, Black Lightning, in 1977. Other notable black superheroes to debut include Marvel's Blade (1973), Brother Voodoo (1973), and Black Goliath (1975)" (127). They also stress the importance of Black women, such as Marvel's Misty Knight (1975), the X-Men's Storm (1975), DC's villain Nubia (1973), and DC's "first black female hero," Karen Beecher, who become Bumblebee (1977) (Austin and Hamilton 127).

visual influence for Othello but rather to demonstrate how Othello visually aligns with a tradition of Black masculinity in comic books: burly, bald, and strong.

Yet like these characters, Othello becomes a complicated visual depiction of heroism on the one hand, but of caricatured Black male physicality on the other. This mirroring of the Black comic tradition (meaning Black characters in comics) is not inherently problematic. In the white-dominated world of superheroes, these Black crusaders serve as vital figures who extend the very idea of who gets to be a hero and what those heroes look like. The $1.347 billion made by the 2018 MCU *Black Panther* film signals the still-present hunger for precisely this type of representation. Yet it is important to note that Black superheroes "have proven fertile ground for stereotyped depictions of race" (Singer, "'Black Skins'" 107). Singer identifies a tension in representations of Black superheroes. There are those that "still perpetuate stereotypes, either through token characters who exist purely to signify racial clichés or through a far more subtle system of absence and erasure that serves to obscure minority groups even as the writers pay lip service to diversity" (118). On the other hand, "superhero comics also possess a highly adaptable set of conventions," with some comics presenting "race and sexuality with richness and complexity, free of the tokenism and erasure which have dominated the genre" (116). In general, then, Black superheroes resist either a simply celebratory or purely critical reading.

Austin and Hamilton contextualize the history of this dynamic, pointing to two periods in comic book history that illustrate competing approaches toward racial representation. In the 1970s, inclusion in comic books was typically seen as a "numbers game," they argue, so that simply adding more racially and ethnically diverse characters seemed sufficient (126). Even if unintentional, this superficial engagement with inclusion led to "new ethnic superheroes of this era ... mired in persistent stereotypical representations" (129). Regarding Black characters specifically, Austin and Hamilton identify a recycling of cultural primitivism—"valuing of the natural and nature over the man-made or artificial," including the lives of the primitive over those who are civilized (130)—and with it, an emphasis on physical violence over mental acuity, as well as the domination of the Black buck stereotype (addressed above) as the most pervasive racial caricatures. While 1980s comics often deployed racial tokenism and retained hierarchal partnerships (17), by the 1990s and early 2000s, thoughtful reinterpretations "directly engaging with their problematic pasts" at times transcended them, according to Austin and Hamilton, therefore successfully crafting updates containing "human and empathetic characters that gestured toward a growing tolerance in the early twenty-first century" (17, 18). Given this complex history, Black superheroes function as knotty sites of racial representation that must therefore be carefully considered, not entirely dismissed nor simply valorized.

The challenge, as Singer recognizes, is depicting the complexity of these Black characters, for they carry the legacy of primitive, hyperphysical, and violent stereotyping. Brown likewise addresses this difficulty, explaining that "If comic book superheroes represent an acceptable, albeit obviously extreme, model of hypermasculinity, and if the black male body is already culturally ascribed as a site of hypermasculinity, then the combination of the two—a black male superhero—runs the risk of being read as an overabundance, a potentially threatening cluster of masculine signifiers" (178). Brown's caution sheds further light on the problems created by equating Othello with Hulk. He also adds clarity and a more nuanced attention to race to what Austin and Hamilton call "guises"—comic book tropes that when applied to ethnic superheroes, "overpower the perception of the [racial] type," thereby "repackaging it insidiously" (129). What Austin and Hamilton do not frankly acknowledge but what Brown articulates without hesitancy is this fundamental fact: characteristics that make one body, a white male body, heroic, signify differently when applied to a Black male body. This is the case with Othello. He resides in a liminal space between hero and menace, his superhero-like physique occupying the difficult representational place of the Black comic book superheroes who have come before him.

Othello: The White Protagonists' Foil

The challenge with interpreting Othello did not get addressed as pitch art turned into the final published product. Instead, it remains with his introduction in *Kill Shakespeare*, which further demonstrates the divide between intent and effect. It is evident that on the surface, Othello's physical strength should function as a boon rather than a drawback, for Belanger's discussion of Othello makes it clear that even as his physical representation signals his capacity for violence, the story presses this capacity into appropriate service as a potential threat to Richard III's powerful forces. Othello's first appearance in the series (aside from the character introduction page) furthers this characterization. On the cover image of Issue Four, "So Wise So

Young Never Do Live Long," drawn by Kagan McLeod, Juliet and Othello appear alongside each other, with Juliet in the foreground and Othello in the background. Juliet holds a staff, looking off to the side, much larger on the page than Othello. She has blonde hair, blue eyes, and a traditional feminine physique, but her ponytail and muted clothing communicate her more typically masculine role as the leader of the Prodigals. Othello stands in a half crouch behind her, looking directly at the viewer. He holds a bloody serrated knife in one hand and what looks like a sword, edges only just visible, in the other. This complicated image introduces readers to Othello's friendship with Juliet and his martial role in the story. If Juliet communicates uncertainty about the battle to come, as her facial expression suggests, then Othello exudes confidence through his bold gaze. He is both ready to fight and defend, the battlefield hero to the political Juliet. This reading of him would indicate his valorized status as a formidable general within *Kill Shakespeare*'s world and his role as a character following in the heroic footsteps of famous Black comic book characters like Luke Cage.

Yet the power dynamics of this visual depiction trouble such a simple understanding, reminding readers how race remains despite attempts not to see it. In many ways, this image mirrors the premodern "double portraits" Kim F. Hall examines in *Things of Darkness* (209). Hall traces how "colonizers in the mid-seventeenth century heightened the juxtaposition of black and white [previously depicted in] the cameo by representing themselves with African children" (226). These portraits therefore commodified the Black body, which occupied the edges and corners of the visual plane, and which functioned as "figures for the exotic or foreign" (227). Othello may not be a child, and he may not quite be on the margins of the cover, but he too serves as a symbol of difference in contradistinction to Juliet. Juliet and Othello's dimensions and positioning make clear his function as a foil for Juliet. She takes up most of the cover, extending over half of it. And because she takes up the foreground, she is much larger in perspective despite her diminutive size in comparison to Othello throughout the rest of the series. Her positioning therefore denotes her significance. Othello remains behind her, mostly visible, but somewhat to the side so that the frame cuts off the drawing of his sword. Comic book paratexts (including covers), Christopher argues, "[work] out questions of influence and authority" (153), and thus is the case with this cover, which decidedly designates influence and authority as Juliet's purview. In other words, while both Juliet and Othello work as key figures in the Prodigal movement, this cover image leaves no doubt that the narrative focus will be on Juliet. As such, readers begin to develop a sense of the ways that *Kill Shakespeare*'s numerous plots consistently emphasize white characters while giving much less attention to—and in fact developing very vexed storytelling about—the one character of color, a dynamic I will elaborate on further below.

Not only does Othello highlight Juliet's important narrative status, but like the painted enslaved children, his visual depiction also heightens her whiteness through his Blackness, especially as the Black/white dynamic becomes associated with her sexuality. Hall explains that "The 'black skin' of both male and female attendants becomes a key signifier in such portraits: associated with wealth and luxury, it is the necessary element for the fetishization of white skin, the 'white mask' of aristocratic identity" (*Things of Darkness* 209). The correlation here is not exact, for *Kill Shakespeare*'s story does not expressly associate Juliet's white skin with aristocratic wealth. Even so, Othello's Blackness nonetheless assists in the fetishization of whiteness, Juliet's to be precise. Specifically, the male characters in Issue Four fetishize Juliet's whiteness most especially when she comes under threat, including sexual assault. They do so by contrasting her skin with Othello's or with other forms of blackness, all while suggesting a sexual relationship between her and Othello. Though disturbing, such rhetorical moves reflect what Richard Dyer notes as the emphasis whiteness places on female sexuality, and the threat interracial, heterosexual sex poses to racial purity. Such union

> breaks the legitimation of whiteness with reference to the white body ... if white bodies are no longer indubitably white bodies, if they can no longer guarantee their own reproduction as white, then the "natural" basis of their dominion is no longer credible. If races are conceptualised as pure (with concomitant qualities of character, including the capacity to hold sway over other races), then miscegenation threatens that purity. (25)

This is why white artists often turn to the "motif of rape in white race fiction," for it upholds the white patriarchy. Thus, "Inter-racial (non-white on white) rape is represented as bestiality storming the citadel of civilisation, itself achieved and embodied by whites" (26). Celia Daileader in fact argues that it is precisely this dynamic that accounts for *Othello*'s cultural longevity in America; she explains, "the historical popularity of *Othello* on American stages—even despite squeamishness about inter-racial marriage—makes perfect sense. Whatever might have been Shakespeare's point in telling the story, it has served well as a cautionary tale for white women who might besmirch either their own (sexual) 'purity' or that of their race" (9). To be clear, *Kill Shakespeare* does not contain instances of interracial sex nor interracial rape. It is worth keeping in mind, however, that "in early modern drama the black man frequently stands in this place, at least the *symbolic place*, of the rapist" (Little Jr., *Shakespeare Jungle Fever* 4). Such is also the case in *Kill Shakespeare*. When the white male characters repeatedly reference Othello having sex with Juliet as they discuss harming or actually attempt to injure her, or when the text and visuals stress the imagery of darkness in these same moments, they tap into the concatenation of Blackness, whiteness, rape, and racial purity that Dyer and Daileader articulate and visualize them through the binary codification of Black objectification and white superiority that Hall identifies.

Othello's Blackness therefore sits alongside rhetorical and visual forms of blackness to stress Juliet's whiteness, as well as the importance of whiteness overall in *Kill Shakespeare*. In the same issue with Juliet and Othello on the cover, for instance, Parolles hits Juliet after she calls him a coward (87, panel 4). Othello appears for the first time in the series as he subsequently emerges from the crowd to defend Juliet, to which she tells him, "No, no Othello. Let him strike me if he wishes. Let him cast his reputation in iron" (87, panel 5). Interestingly, Juliet's iron imagery echoes the associations of immorality with blackness so common in the early modern era, an association the series reiterates across characters. Parolles retaliates further when he declares to Othello, "It seems your taste in women has not changed. I had heard you bedded both Desdemona as well as Iago's wife . . . and now I suspect you ride another pale horse" (88, panels 1 and 2). In this moment, Parolles makes clear his belief in a sexual relationship between Othello and Juliet, and he does so by stressing Juliet's whiteness, for she is a "pale horse." His remarks denigrate Juliet's humanity, but key here is that this devaluation comes precisely because of her supposed sexual union with Othello. According to Parolles's logic, Othello's Blackness contrasts with her whiteness, thereby diminishing her personhood through their sexual relationship, or as Daileader puts it, "Pitch defiles" (5). It would be easy to dismiss Parolles's insinuations as the articulations of a misogynistic, racist villain. But ultimately, he only repeats and extends the moral logic of whiteness with goodness and purity and darkness with badness and impurity that Juliet herself already began.

This racialized moral linkage appears once again with Don John so that *Kill Shakespeare* develops a tissue of verbal and visual references that racialize Othello in an otherwise ostensibly colorblind presentation. When Don John soon arrives as a general in Richard III's army seeking to destroy the Prodigals, he too implies a sexual relationship between Othello and Juliet, remarking after setting the inn on fire, "Soon Moor, your lady will be as black as you" (94, panel 5). For Don John, Othello's Blackness transfers onto Juliet, literalized by the smoke he believes will soon consume her, the appropriate consequence for her transgressive political and sexual alliances. When Juliet escapes, Don John finds her, telling her that "No smoke can shield thy radiance" (96, panel 8). Once outside of Othello's company, it seems that for Don John, Juliet's whiteness returns, as signaled by her "radiance." The contrasting smoke is not an explicit reference to Othello, but the imagery of the smoke as it wafts in shades of gray and black around Don John and Juliet invokes the Blackness of Othello's skin that Don John has only just referenced. The smoke thus makes Juliet seem all the whiter even as the blackness he just associated with her engulfs them. In a borderless splash panel, which functions to emphasize the image, Don John looms over Juliet, his face covered in shadows so dark they obscure his white face and blond hair as his intention to rape her becomes clear when he commands, "No, lady Capulet, don't get up," and when she responds, "I shall fight thee with every breath I possess," he replies, "I count on it" (101, panel 1). Once again, blackness connects to immorality, for the panel's coloring darkens the white Don John so much that one can barely discern his features just as he is about to enact his most nefarious deed yet. By this point, Othello no longer appears anywhere near Juliet, and no one references him. Nonetheless, Parolles's comments about Othello's Blackness and his relationship with Juliet, Don John's similar remarks, and the spoken and visual references to blackness that appear at moments where Juliet is most endangered all work together to associate blackness with corruption while invoking if not explicitly referencing white supremacist concerns regarding Blackness and the peril it creates for white female sexuality.

The issue's narrative structure only strengthens this dynamic by providing no moment in which Othello's identity serves as salvific for Juliet despite the fact that he is her protector. It is worth noting, for example, that even though Othello supposedly guards Juliet, when Don John moves to assault her, it is the white hero, Hamlet, who intervenes. This decision therefore eradicates the hovering menace of

Blackness, and thus begins Hamlet's redemption arc. To return to the cover image of this same issue, one can see that even if it is not evident upon first glance, its composition signals how blackness both literally (through Othello) and symbolically functions in *Kill Shakespeare* just as it did in the double portraits: as a tool for highlighting whiteness's primacy. Thus, while Othello may not be a commodity in the same sense as the attendants in the double portraits since he does not function as a material resource of accumulated wealth, he nevertheless works as a commodity in a different sense, for he is put to "use" to reaffirm whiteness's importance in *Kill Shakespeare*.

Othello's depiction on the cover also adds another complicating factor that further undermines attempts to easily position him as a hero in the series, that of his visually explicit association with violence. Othello's more threatening, blood-soaked weapons in comparison to Juliet's intensify his aggressive nature, and his direct gaze at the reader opens up the question of to whom he is directing that aggression. Presumably, this is not a problem because he is one of the "good guys." Indeed, the scholarly annotations that are only part of the *Backstage Edition* give insight as to how this image might be received. Anna Wolosz-Sosnowska remarks in her annotation of this cover that "Juliet plays against her Shakespearean type in the image, as she brandishes a weapon, while Othello is interpreted more classically as one of his knives is visibly bloody." This annotation carries with it a number of assumptions that have implications for Othello's racial representation. What does it mean for Othello to be "interpreted more classically"? Is this referring to classic warriors, or alternately, does this reference traditional understandings of Othello himself? And if it is the latter, by whom—artists, directors, actors? Whatever her unspecified meaning, of importance to Wolosz-Sosnowska seems to be the martial status of both Juliet and Othello and how that status reveals something about their characters fitting with or going against "type." But as I have detailed, the "type" for Black men is a litany of stereotypes that imagine them as violent and subsequently tie that violence to an innate inhumanity.

Othello's significant contribution to Issue Four's storyline in fact only advances this interpretation of him. After he and Juliet escape the burning inn, Othello goes on a rampage against the invading soldiers. While McCreery and Del Col provide Juliet with actual dialogue, Othello instead gets, "Raaah!" and "Gaaah" as he kills soldiers while wide-eyed and open-mouthed in rage (96, panels 4 and 5). Even as this characterization heightens his martial prowess, it also depicts him as animalistic, violent, aggressive, and physical, precisely the types of associations Austin and Hamilton trace in the stereotypical 1970s comic book representations of Blackness. Belanger visually associates this primal characterization with foreignness through Othello's curved sword, the only one in the series. All other characters carry a rapier, "an elegant slender, sharply pointed sword" associated with "fencing and dueling" in the traditions of sixteenth- and seventeenth-century Italy and Spain (Niayesh). Othello, on the other hand, holds the scimitar, "an equally refined sword of South West Asian origin, with its crescent-shaped blade frequently connected with Islamic traditions, and which in our time adorns the flag and coat of arms of Saudi Arabia" (Niayesh). While such a sword functions metaphorically to designate "qualities like manliness," building off Frances Teague's analysis of props, Ladan Niayesh contends that when juxtaposed visually with a rapier, as done in *Kill Shakespeare*, it also functions metonymically, representing the "East" and "Orient" agonistically opposed to the Western Occident. Thus, Othello's valorizing tool also distances him from the other characters by indicating an Otherness that, as Edward Said famously notes, Western culture has historically associated with uncontrolled emotions, violence, and irrational cruelty.

McCreery's, Del Col's, and Belanger's primitive portrayal only heightens when Othello believes he is hallucinating visions of Iago during the battle. Othello attacks such a vision in a particularly crazed way. In this perspectivally complex splash page, the reader first sees Iago and two soldiers from Othello's point of view, a view which is overlaid with two panels that shift perspective by showing Othello running through smoke and Iago looking back toward him. But the most dominant image, one that seems to mirror Iago's line of sight, is that of Othello, which takes up more than half of the page. Othello looks forward, directly at the reader. He runs out of the smoke with eyes once again wide, his rage inflamed, and mouth open in a seemingly primal yell of "Iaaaagggooo!" (99, panel 4). Othello's right hand raises his serrated knife above his head ready to strike, while his left hand reaches out to grab the figure before him. Yet who is this figure? Ostensibly, it is Iago as Othello's yell designates. Belanger's drawing, however, places readers in Iago's supposed position; Othello's gaze looks at them, his sword seems as if it will strike them, and his hand looks as if it will reach out of the frame to grasp them. The gaze Othello casts at the reader on the cover of the issue thus returns in this panel, manifested in a version of Othello only *just* human. As he reaches for Iago, who is in fact alive and present, Othello—in another attention-grabbing borderless splash panel—once again casts his eyes upon the reader. Belanger depicts him with blood spattered across his body, especially his face, his eyes wide, and mouth once again agape in a guttural "Hrrraaaarrrr!" (100, panel 9). In the first issue introducing his character, then, readers confront a stereotypically atavistic Othello, one drawn so that even as he threatens Richard III's forces and Iago, he disturbingly also turns the same danger toward them. Interpreted alongside Othello's commodified characterization in relationship to Juliet's whiteness, it becomes clear just how many narrative, visual, and thematic elements work against understanding Othello as a heroic character, having him instead "substantiate and resolve what the audience suspects it already knows about the essence of blackness as the savage and libidinous Other" (Little Jr., *Shakespeare Jungle Fever* 75). Thus, even if McCreery, Del Col, and Belanger intend for Othello to pay homage to a number of Black comic book heroes, and even if his moral status within *Kill Shakespeare* should ameliorate his intimidating nature, he nevertheless reifies the controlling image of Black masculinity as inherently physical, ferocious, and menacing in ways directed not just to Iago, but also to the reader. In other words, he functions as the Dark Other. This degrading racialized vision is authorized by no less than Shakespeare's cultural power.

On the Story's Margins: Othello's Narrative Limitations

Othello's visual characterization is only exacerbated by what McCreery and Del Col *do not* do with Othello in their retelling, for in comparison with other characters, Othello plays a limited, one-dimensional role across *Kill Shakespeare*'s various storylines. Notably, Othello is one of the only protagonists not to undergo some sort of transformation within *Kill Shakespeare*'s first volume. Perhaps most striking in contrast are the changes in the central heroes, Hamlet and Juliet. Hamlet follows in the footsteps of famous literary questers, having lost himself and now seeking redemption and a sense of identity. He explicitly conveys, "I . . . I have lost my true self somewhere along this journey and I will not find it amongst you," as he doubts his role among the Prodigals (113, panel 3). The series makes it clear from the outset that Hamlet's turmoil derives from an unsettled relationship with his father, one that figuratively and literally haunts Hamlet. While Hamlet walks through a graveyard, blue smoke surrounds him, then he hears a voice calling "Hamlet," to which he responds "Father?" (7, panels 1 and 2). It is thus the seeming voice of Hamlet Sr. (which readers learn actually comes from the Weird Sisters) that almost lures Hamlet from his home. Furthermore, Richard III's promise that once Hamlet finds Shakespeare's quill, he will restore Hamlet Sr. back to life serves as the provocation that convinces Hamlet to embark upon the journey to find Shakespeare, thereby leading Hamlet to embrace his role as the shadow king. The graveyard scene also exposes how Hamlet's murder of Polonius likewise plagues him as revealed when he declares to the smoke, "I am no killer!" (8, panel 6). Though less explored than Hamlet's relationship with his father, this too serves as a means of complicating Hamlet's story, for he carries not only shame over his father's death, but also guilt over Polonius's demise.

A literal haunting that brings together Hamlet's double guilt emphasizes how much attention the series gives to his personal struggles. As Hamlet reclines on a bankside, Hamlet Sr.'s decaying body rises out of a river. Belanger draws Hamlet Sr. in shades of blue and gray, skin rotting, which he literally begins to pull off from his own face. Hamlet Sr. hurls abuses at a cowering Hamlet, declaring, "Yours will be the hands that kill me. Thy cowardly nature will doom me, Hamlet" (116, panels 2–4). As Hamlet Sr. tears at his face, his features transform into Polonius, mouth open with pestilent flies coming out, and whose own clawing at his visage reveals squirming maggots escaping from his bodily orifices. Polonius likewise exclaims, "Ye steal my life and still deny me? Ye murder your friend's father but leave the wizard Shakespeare alive? Oh, Dull Hamlet. Thou truly believes thou seem a saint when most thou plays a devil?" (117, panels 1, 3, 4). The specters' respective comments make explicit Hamlet's emotional struggles. Gerzic and Balfour remark of the moment, "This nightmare sequence literally illustrates Hamlet's guilt over his inaction regarding his father's murder (a guilt absent from Shakespeare's playtext), but also over his earlier murder of Polonius; Hamlet's harried expression is palpable." Taking this observation a step further, the grotesque imagery allows readers to share Hamlet's affective reaction of disgust, though he is not just repulsed by the ghosts before him, but also by himself. I emphasize the recurring nature and intensity of these moments because they establish how McCreery and Del Col strive to create a multilayered Hamlet who, as Gerzic and Balfour similarly observe, deviates from his Shakespearean counterpart as he grapples with his relationship with his father while confronting his misdeeds against Polonius.

Juliet likewise carries psychological and emotional burdens that pave the way for her character development. In some ways, the moment that introduces Juliet's struggles prefigures her relationship with Hamlet, for she too is haunted. As she attempts to gain more followers for her cause, she confesses:

> I am haunted by a ghost . . . he reminds me that I was once a spoiled young girl, fated to become a woman who would turn her head at the stories of a tyrant's cruelty to others as long as my own plate was full . . . but then because of that narrow vision, because of those selfish concerns, I lost . . . I lost someone more precious to me than gold. And I swore—I swore to William—that never again would I blind myself to the world around me. That while I stood, I would stand for justice. (140, panels 5, 6)

Without naming him, Juliet references Romeo here, the figurative ghost who reminds her of her girlhood and therefore her selfishness. While Hamlet Sr. and Polonius only appear as conjurations of the Weird Sisters' or Lady Macbeth's magic, Romeo actually returns, fully alive, a devout soldier in the service of William Shakespeare. Though the series explores Hamlet's personal journey more than Juliet's, even amid the final, bloody confrontation between the Prodigals and the Black Army, Juliet's past life reappears, for it is in this moment that she discovers that Romeo is alive (284). Juliet does not experience the same conflict Hamlet does. She swiftly chooses her romance with Hamlet instead of pursuing a relationship with Romeo once more. Nevertheless, McCreery and Del Col write both Hamlet and Juliet with narrative layers that add complexity to their characterizations.

In fact, the commencement of their romantic relationship functions as the apotheosis of their respective character growth. *Kill Shakespeare* contains a scene that includes a version of the Murder of Gonzago. Rather than showing the conscience of the king, it reveals the conscience of the shadow king, Hamlet. The play creates flashbacks for Hamlet, who then runs off the stage into, inexplicably, a hall of mirrors (166–67). There, he confronts his own reflection, which visually replicates the ghostly Polonius as flies come out of Hamlet's mouth, as well as the ghost of Hamlet Sr., for Hamlet's face similarly stretches and seems to rot. Juliet follows him, and as she begs for him to tell her why he has fled, he confesses his murder of Polonius, for which he asserts his "reflection" to be "now worthless, barren, forsaken" (171, panel 5). At the same time, Hamlet acknowledges for the first time, "My father was not a wise king. He was rash, suspicious, and like the miser, he grew to believe that all sought to steal what was [*sic*] he felt was his" (172, panel 2). Thus, this confrontation amid the mirrors, in which Belanger interpolates flashbacks to Hamlet with Hamlet Sr. in the mirrors' frames, functions as the key moment in Hamlet's personal transformation as he admits and articulates his personal demons. Juliet does so too, responding, "Hamlet, thou art not alone in your errors" (173, panel 1). Juliet's story generally follows Shakespeare's version except that ultimately, the apothecary saves her, though not Romeo. As such, like Hamlet, Juliet carries a sense of personal shame, declaring that "Romeo died that day, killed by the callowness and selfishness of my youth. I have woken for nobody since . . . Sometimes I wonder if I would be happier in Romeo's dead arms—his corpse bride" (173, panel 16). Juliet thus struggles with her own self-worth after Romeo's demise. The reiteration of their personal challenges serves to remind readers of where they have been in their narrative trajectories, all in preparation for where they will be by the end of the issue.

Ultimately, this interchange in the mirrored room works to move these characters forward, to signal their transformation to readers both individually and as a pair. Just as Juliet offers up comfort to Hamlet, he likewise consoles her, reminding her, "Your brave voice inspires others to bravery, to hope. Your words struck the blow that won yesterday's battle" (173, panel 17). As each provides solace to the other, readers are likewise invited to perceive these characters in new, more complicated ways. At the same time, the characters in the series with the most narrative focus unite romantically, suggesting that the romance serves as a reward for their personal growth. The visuals of the moment signal their mutual affection. While dialoguing about their struggles, in Pyramus and Thisbe fashion, they stand on either side of a dividing mirror so large it appears almost like a wall, then they slowly lower down to sit upon the ground in a visual that confirms their shared trajectory. Finally, Juliet asserts, "I propose, Hamlet, that we pledge to learn to live with these pale visions. To draw strength from them," to which he responds, "Both the damned and the blessed . . ." (174, panel 5). Stressing their increased agency, Juliet closes by replying, "How they are seen is ours to decide . . ." (174, panel 6). The interchange ends with a rare-for-the-series full-length splash page containing no layered panels. Stage curtains border and therefore frame a largely black page in which Juliet and Hamlet sit on either side of the mirror, hands reaching toward each other, enshrined in a gold light. While Hamlet must yet fully realize his role as shadow king and find Shakespeare, and Juliet still needs to embrace her role as general, leading the Prodigals into a final battle, this scene propels the characters forward, both as leaders within their world and as soon-to-be lovers. I stress this moment because it is important to grasp the attempted narrative layers granted to both Hamlet and Juliet, as well as the very express ways in which the story and visuals work together to communicate their personal and interpersonal transformations.

In a pointed distinction, however, the series denies Othello this same complexity and opportunity for characterological development. Indeed, McCreery and Del Col offer such a cursory engagement with Othello's story that it relies on a previous reading of Shakespeare that is not the case with either Hamlet's or Juliet's arguably more familiar tales. While McCreery and Del Col's story allows Hamlet and Juliet the ability to articulate their own pasts, the writers do not provide Othello the same opportunity. Instead, in a move that mirrors the Iago-centric problems that so plague Shakespeare's *Othello*,[9] Iago voices Othello's murder of Desdemona, and he does so in ways much less clear than either Hamlet's or Juliet's retellings. Othello's history comes to light for readers as he and Iago work together to train soldiers for the final battle. These potential soldiers are ill prepared, so Othello and Iago duel in front of them to "again demonstrate the technique" (180, panel 3). As they do so, Iago offers up martial advice, words overlaid on red-shaded panels that reveal his past with and psychological conquest of Othello. For instance, he advises, "It is also important to plant the seeds of doubt in your opponent" in a light-yellow text box over a

---

[9] *Othello* has long had an "Iago problem," in which productions quickly turn Iago-centric. Frequently, the Iago role becomes the marquis performance, so that relative newcomers like Laurence Fishburne or André Holland are cast against more seasoned performers like Kenneth Branagh (for the 1995 film) and Mark Rylance (for the 2018 Globe performance), to name but two contemporary examples. This tension between an emphasis on Othello or on Iago in fact has long been part of *Othello*'s performance history. In the nineteenth century, for instance, the actors playing Othello and Iago would switch roles every night so that each would get the spotlight, as undertaken by Edwin Booth and Henry Irving at the Lyceum Theatre in London. As Ayanna Thompson explains, "By alternating the roles, these actors were able to show the versatility required to master both parts" ("Introduction" 77). In more contemporary productions, the Iago problem may arise as a result of Iago's relationship to an audience that "knows more than the titular tragic hero" and is thereby "positioned as distinctly different from Othello" ("Introduction" 41). Iago thus has a more direct, aligned relationship to the audience, a dynamic intensified by his ability to make them laugh. Moreover, as Thompson observes, "The notion that Iago is somehow more adaptive, socially spontaneous and improvisational has gripped scholars and performers alike as a unique quality that differentiates him not only from everyone else in the play, but also from the standard early modern constructions of identity" ("Introduction" 58).

red-shaded panel in which readers see Iago peering behind a stone wall as a crazed Othello points an accusatory finger at a Desdemona weeping with her hand over her mouth on one side of him, and a confused Cassio backing away from Othello's other outstretched arm (181, panel 2). In the next flashback panel, a "close-up" style drawing shows Othello strangling Desdemona with, ostensibly, the handkerchief, as he cries, teeth gritted, while she struggles with a look of pain upon her face. Yet no narrative information accompanies these images. While Juliet and Hamlet fill in important details of their stories, the only information readers get about Othello is visual. They must provide the specifics themselves and can only do so if they have read Shakespeare's play. In this way, Othello's story is doubly mediated, first, by Iago's reframing of it, and second, by the knowledge readers can or cannot bring to bear as they interpret Belanger's drawings.

The fact that Othello is sidelined in his own story could not be clearer. As Iago finishes his advice, so do the red flashback panels conclude, and readers see that Iago has defeated Othello in the duel, for Iago stands over Othello, sword handily pointed at Othello's neck. Certainly, this overthrow mirrors Iago's earlier one in Venice. My point, however, is that Othello does not get to overcome his past in the ways that Hamlet and Juliet do. Aside from living, McCreery and Del Col do not afford Othello the same narrative changes they provide for Hamlet. Neither do they allow him the self-actualization that both Hamlet and Juliet achieve, nor a new romantic relationship mirroring the one Hamlet and Juliet find with each other. In fact, this moment creates further self-doubt for Othello. He shares with Juliet, "For years—*years*—I have blamed Iago for my downfall . . . But he has returned and done no wrong. He is not as I remember. And this makes me wonder . . . perhaps *I* am the villain of my history? Did *I* not deny Iago what he most wanted—to serve me as my most trusted lieutenant? Did *I* not doubt that this old black form was worthy of Desdemona's eternal love? Perhaps it is I that should not be trusted?" (183, panels 2–3). Readers already have much less understanding of Othello than they do of other characters into whose histories the series delves. Thus, for those unfamiliar with his original story, and therefore Iago's Machiavellian machinations, Othello's doubt about himself may become their own uncertainty about him as a character. In fact Juliet tries to assuage his concerns, but she does so in a way much less reassuring than the support she provides for Hamlet. She admonishes Othello: "But to blame thyself for everything that has happened is as foolish as putting all villainy on Iago. You are not perfect. But you're not a villain" (183, panel 4). An easily missed contradiction resides in Juliet's words. On the one hand, she asserts that Othello is not a villain. But on the other, she implies that he has been foolish in placing all "villainy" on Iago; is Othello therefore not a villain as well, for where else would castigation lie? Lynne Bradley's annotations for this exchange are also complicit in this unsympathetic approach to Othello's backstory, for she asserts, "His [Othello's] persistent second-guessing of his own judgment in *KS* corresponds to a key feature in Shakespeare's play: to what extent is Othello to blame for murdering Desdemona? Was he the villain of the play or simply a dupe of Iago's?" Rather than fostering reader empathy for Othello, *Kill Shakespeare* goes in the opposite direction by combining an omission of any details that would properly contextualize Othello's past behavior for readers with Juliet's and Bradley's comments that in fact suggest he is the villain of his own story rather than the infamously malignant Iago. In fact, even when Iago's villainy in the series is revealed, it is Hamlet, not Othello, afforded the opportunity to confront Iago's evil. Ian Smith powerfully chastens how Shakespeare scholars do not speak for Othello because his Blackness does not invite a still predominantly white professoriate to identify itself with and therefore develop an affinity for Othello. A similar dynamic appears in *Kill Shakespeare* (and also, as noted here, in the scholarly apparatus of the *Backstage Edition*). Even if ostensibly a hero, Othello's character ultimately remains a flat, stereotypical manifestation of crazed Black masculine violence whose story and therefore character never garners sympathy, never changes, and never receives true closure for the abuse enacted upon him in his former life.

Tellingly, the final two moments in which Othello appears in the foreground of *Kill Shakespeare*'s first volume only solidify this one-dimensional representation of him. The second of the two is the least significant narratively, but it nonetheless promotes the image of a singularly violent Othello. Othello encourages Hamlet to "go to Shakespeare. Leave this [battle] to me" (285, panel 3). Yet as he does so, Othello does not face Hamlet but rather his oncoming foes. Even as he encourages the shadow king, Othello also ably flings his sword in the face of one of Richard's most evil soldiers, as designated by the opponent's black, spiked armor and his skull-shaped helmet (285, panels 2, 6), an appearance that continues the series' blatant association of evil with blackness. Thus, as Hamlet turns to the more emotional, intellectual task of grappling with Shakespeare's true status in their world, Othello remains on the battlefield to function as the key figure in physical, martial conquest. In this way, *Kill Shakespeare* aligns these characters with the common white supremacist division of whiteness as associated with intellectual, philosophical pursuits, and Blackness as associated with corporeal, even violent activities.

The first moment chronologically, and the most important to Othello's narrative trajectory, occurs as Hamlet attempts to ascertain Iago's motivation, and it too solidifies Othello's simplistic characterization. As the two fight each other, Hamlet asks a bruised, battered, and exceedingly bloodied Iago, "Why Othello? I saw you earn his trust back. I saw your admiration for him. It was real, Iago" (277, panels 4, 5). It is therefore Hamlet, not Othello, who tries to dig deeper in order to resolve the wounds of the past. As Iago begins to answer, a bold, black, all-caps "SHHKKK" against a bright red background consumes the frame of the final panel (277, panel 6). Iago thus remains as silent about his motivations in *Kill Shakespeare* as he does in *Othello*. In the latter, he chooses his silence. In *Kill Shakespeare*, it comes at Othello's hands, for the "SHHKKK," we learn, signals the sound of Othello's sword severing Iago's head, a head that flies off Iago's form as blood and gore trail its arc from his body to the ground (278, panel 5). The first image readers see after Iago's decapitation is Othello, kneeling in the field, gazing forward at the reader, with the still blood-soaked scimitar in his hands (279, panel 1). Othello then helps Hamlet rise, encourages him to resume fighting, and the two men walk away as the final panel focuses on Iago's dismembered visage, blood flowing like drool from his open, torn mouth, one eye swollen shut, his gaze likewise facing the reader (279, panel 5). Several details stand out here. First, once again, in an especially violent moment, Othello's gaze turns to the reader. This decision on Belanger's part certainly captivates the reader's attention. At the same time, however, it continues the pattern of extending Othello's threat not just to the Prodigals' foes, but also to *Kill Shakespeare*'s audience. Second, it takes until the end of the first series for Othello's story to achieve this significant revision. While, as I have argued, McCreery and Del Col afford Hamlet and Juliet important narrative changes early in the story, the same cannot be said for Othello. His narrative thus receives limited emendations to help distinguish his trajectory in *Kill Shakespeare* from the one established by Shakespeare. Yet even in *Kill Shakespeare*, Othello's final, truly significant moment ends with death—his murder of Iago—this time, more visceral and gory than what Shakespeare imagined. There may be no "unproper bed" in *Kill Shakespeare*;[10] nonetheless, Othello still offers up a vision that offends sight in Iago's repulsive severed head.

---

[10] For a discussion of the "unproper bed," see Michael Neill, "Unproper Beds: Race, Adultery, and the Hideous in *Othello*," *Shakespeare Quarterly* 40.4 (1989): 383–412.

Certainly, there can be no doubt that Iago receives his comeuppance in *Kill Shakespeare* in a move that provides at least a degree of closure for Othello. The challenge, however, resides in Othello's depiction. Ultimately, McCreery and Del Col do not craft an alternative side of Othello—the duality afforded so many heroes across comic book series—in order to add layers to his character. Thus, despite any attempts to salvage vexed perceptions of Othello by positioning him both narratively and visually on the side of heroism, Othello remains trapped by *Kill Shakespeare*'s unimaginative storytelling, its "imaginative gap" (Thomas 5), when it comes to its only Black character. The story therefore trades in both figurative and literal controlling images, ones that place Othello in a long line of Black men imagined by culture at large as one-dimensional—a dimension simplistic, violent, and therefore always threatening to the white status quo whether in the fantastic or the very real day-to-day.

When a threat exists, it must be contained. As Collins contends, this is the purpose of controlling images: domination of Blackness reified through objectification, erasure, and subjugation. The same dynamic exists in the dark fantastic, for as Thomas explains, "the dilemma created by the presence of the Dark Other must be resolved with *violence*" (26). It should perhaps come as no surprise, then, that as *Kill Shakespeare*'s stories continue, so too does the antiblack depiction of Othello, one that ends with him undergoing "a form of ritual sacrifice, purging the very source of darkness" (Thomas 25), in this case, both metaphorical and literal darkness. In fact, all the strategies that Collins identifies for the domination of Black identity exist across the series' four volumes. Volumes 1 and 2 comprise *Kill Shakespeare: The Backstage Edition*, which objectify Othello both visually and narratively. Volume 3, *The Tide of Blood*, manifests Othello's erasure. While he appears in the series, his presence is significantly sidelined in comparison to volumes 1 and 2. The character description explains that despite his revenge on Iago, "the Moor is still haunted by his past." In addition to using an objectifying terminology for Othello instead of his proper name, the description foreshadows Othello's only narrative purpose. He, Juliet, Hamlet, and Romeo travel to Prospero's island to assist a woman they believe to be Miranda, and are eventually followed by Shakespeare himself. Miranda (in fact Lady Macbeth in disguise) warns them that the island "can hold a mirror to thy soul and cast upon thy deepest fears and regrets. Do not allow it" (27, panel 1). Despite this warning, they drink the island's water, which makes each of them go mad. For Othello, this reveals that the fear consuming his soul is his murder of Desdemona. He continually hears her voice indicting his murder of her by declaring, "At your hand" (31), which appears repeatedly across panels. After this, Othello is never the same. While Juliet, Romeo, and Hamlet all recover from their mental and emotional anguish, Othello does not. If readers take Miranda at her word, this lack of mental and emotional healing suggests that Othello has a darker soul than the others, a soul that once unleashed, prevents his selfhood from being recuperated.

This implication proves not all that dissimilar from the suggestions about his character made in the thoughtless comparison between him and Hulk: there is something inherently, essentially different about Othello in comparison to the other (white) characters, a weakness that, given the similar circumstances they experience (i.e. he does not drink more water than the others), can only stem from an indelible distinction in his more susceptible nature. Ultimately, however, the reader never has an opportunity to explore further the problems plaguing Othello. *The Tide of Blood*'s story focuses on the love triangle between Juliet, Romeo, and Hamlet on the one hand, and a magical contest for authority between Prospero and Shakespeare on the other. Thus, after turning Othello into the weakest character on Prospero's island, McCreery and Del Col erase him, never allowing him dialogue after the second chapter of the volume, a man spoken of in racialized terms like "Moor" (20) and called the man with an "ebony form" (108), yet never speaking.

Othello's silent madness in fact extends into the fourth and final volume of the series, *The Mask of Night*, which takes *Kill Shakespeare*'s antiblack treatment of Othello to the extreme imagined by both controlling images and the dark fantastic—the absolute subjugation of Black identity. This volume turns to pirate lovers Viola and Cesario, the former who relishes the freedom she has as a female pirate, and the latter who longs for a quieter, more traditionally domestic life with Viola. As their ship struggles to flee the pirate ship *The Lavinia*, captained by the cannibalistic Lucius, they come upon castaways, who turn out to be Juliet, Hamlet, Shakespeare, and Othello. Juliet and Hamlet's domestic tension takes center stage, for while under the island's spell, she slept with Romeo and in an implausible plot development, knows she is pregnant a mere day later even if she does not know the father. Amid this drama, Othello barely speaks. His most sustained dialogue comes early on in order to establish the degree of his madness. He only speaks to demand where Desdemona is, and when people cannot comply with his request to see her, he throws them through windows. He accuses others of lying, hiding her, and deceiving him (9, 10). Othello has thus lost his mind, his sense of self, and his community. In this complete alienation, he becomes the manifestation of long-standing white fears as he attacks white femininity. When Viola wants to forcefully subdue Othello, Juliet responds, "It is a fever of the mind. I can calm it" (11, panel 1). Yet when she attempts to do so, an enraged Othello accuses her of lying and begins choking her. This moment thus reiterates Othello's strangulation of Desdemona, keeping the supposed threat Blackness poses to white womanhood at the forefront of readers' minds. While Juliet eventually calms Othello, there can be little doubt that the limited humanity afforded to him earlier in *Kill Shakespeare* disappears by *The Mask of Night*. This Othello is barely human, objectified so as to suppress.

Indeed, the final image of Othello provided to readers renders him entirely oppressed. Viola has thrown all her captives into the brig, where Shakespeare now lies deathly ill. As he experiences something like a seizure, Hamlet and Juliet attempt to assist him. In the last panel of the series in which Othello appears in the foreground, Shakespeare, Hamlet, and Juliet occupy the left side of the panel as the two protagonists hover over Shakespeare's convulsing body. Othello takes up the right side of the cell. He hangs, shackled to the ceiling with his arms above his head, shirtless, eyes cast down on the ground (48, panel 2). Now that circumstances have subdued Othello, in what should be his most empathy-inspiring moment, his gaze no longer meets the reader's. This same image appears twice more. In each instance, Othello takes up only a small portion of the left side of the panel as Hamlet and Juliet argue. His helplessness thereby offsets their fervid dispute. Speaking of what it feels like to read fantasy as a person of color, Thomas observes, "Very often, when you appear on the page or on the screen, you are a slave, a servant, or a prostitute—your body is not your own. If you have words, your speech serves only to support the narrative, never to subvert it" (24). This description encapsulates Othello's role across *Kill Shakespeare*. His main function is to serve Juliet specifically as well as her Prodigal forces more generally. He cannot describe his own story, so ultimately, his words simply advance Juliet's and Hamlet's respective plots. When he cannot serve that role, he no longer speaks. And by the end, his body is not his own, bound to save others from physical peril at his hands.

The threat posed by the Dark Other "is most often resolved by enacting symbolic and/or actual violence against [them]" (Thomas 24). This too fits Othello as he epitomizes the role of the racialized individual in the dark fantastic, closing the story enchained and, for all intents and purposes, enslaved. Thus, by *Kill Shakespeare*'s conclusion, Othello, the stereotypical yet still potentially heroic Black warrior, hangs limply in the bowels of a ship, an image grotesquely invoking the transatlantic journey of hundreds of thousands of stolen people that comprised the African diaspora. As Juliet and Hamlet achieve reconciliation, while Viola temporarily becomes captain of her ship, sacrifices herself, and then defeats the vile Lucius, Othello hangs, a true abject. These closing moments depict him controlled visually and narratively to such a degree that he emblematizes not only how white supremacy employs metaphoric and literal controlling images in order to reify its authority, but also the multifaceted yet equally destructive ways these images subjugate Black selfhood in spaces both fantastical and quotidian.

Othello as Prop

Othello's inarguably objectified status by *Kill Shakespeare*'s conclusion positions him as not a true character. Paul Yachnin and Jessica Slights observe that fundamentally, functioning as a character means being "capable of autonomy and change, and possessed of some measure of inwardness and inscrutability . . . " (5). Yet as already established, *Kill Shakespeare* does not afford Othello narrative change, nor do McCreery and Del Col allow him to articulate any inwardness. Othello may thus appear to be a contemporary version of the one-dimensional, villainous Moor so popular on the mimetic English stage (Barthelemy 72, 73). On this stage, the villain did not need to be signaled physically, for his character, his "dissembling . . . ranting . . . [and] histrionics" made him known (75, 76), descriptors not all that different from the Othello in *Kill Shakespeare*. This villainous archetype was associated with Moors through Muly Mahamet in 1589, and this characterization lingered as "the archetype for most black Moors for over a century" (76). The Othello in *Kill Shakespeare* seems to carry on this characterological legacy.

I would like to propose, however, if conceptualized through his narrative function, Othello is not so much a character but more accurately a prop. Such terminology is fitting, for at its outset, *Kill Shakespeare* invokes the genre underlying it: Shakespeare's dramas. The story is broken into acts, for example, blending the comic form with that of the stage plays from which *Kill Shakespeare*'s creators draw. Props undoubtedly play a vital role in Shakespearean theatre, but even as Teague notably addresses stage properties' complexity, she also acknowledges their primary function: to "establish a character or forward action" (17). Jonathan Gil Harris and Natasha Korda explain how this utility has resulted in the term *prop* taking on connotations of "an object placed beneath or against a structure," thereby leading stage properties to be seen "as theatrical prostheses, strictly ancillary to and 'beneath or against' the main structure, the play-text" (1). Significant scholarly work has pushed back against this devaluation of stage properties. As such, my argument may seem a return to diminishing the importance of theatrical practice's material culture. By asserting that Othello functions as a prop in *Kill Shakespeare*, however, I instead want to stress a fundamental tension. Not all props are literal *things*. In a white supremacist, heterosexist, patriarchal, capitalist world, many props are actually human beings thingified. Stated differently, what society employs as ideological props are actually subjects transformed into *things*—"a catchall, inherently paradoxical term that both limits and delimits, categorizes while simultaneously nullifying the value of the category" (Gamboa and Switzky 1)—then strategically placed beneath or against societal and ideological structures in order to support inequities of power.

Thus, even as scholars elevate the importance of objects, with critics turning to object-oriented ontology as perhaps the most notable example, such efforts must never lose sight of how objectifying human beings has long been a vital tool for white supremacy, whether in the form of white settler colonialism or the white racial imaginary from which the antiblack stereotypes present throughout *Kill Shakespeare* derive. Shakespeare may therefore "routinely [deploy] the term 'thing' to blur lines between subject and object," thereby "lend[ing] agency to objects and to make objects of agents" (Gamboa and Switzky 3), yet scholars must acknowledge that the ideological consequences of such an elision manifest very differently for the high-status, white, male characters populating Shakespeare's plays such as Claudius, Julius Caesar, or even Edgar as Poor Tom than they do for a Black character like Othello. Take, for instance, Brett Gamboa and Lawrence Switzky's consideration of things in Shakespeare's drama. In their persuasive discussion of the relationship between New Materialism and Shakespeare studies, they trace how New Materialism not only has roots in the works of academic, philosophical voices, but also in speculative fiction, for "The odd features of thing-life—peripheral yet pervasive, inscrutable yet insistent—seem to find purchase in a corresponding set of counter-canonical exempla, proposals by twilight prophets who write in or at the edges of science fiction, fantasy, and horror" (11).

They proceed to assert that "Marginalized persons have, perhaps, been most attentive to other forms of marginal existence: oddly compelling bars of soap in hotel rooms, out-of-place pieces of string that excite quizzical conjectures . . ." (Gamboa and Switzky 11). To position non-canonical yet wildly successful and/or influential voices like Kafka, Philip K. Dick, and H. P. Lovecraft as "marginalized" disturbingly risks overlooking those truly marginalized—human beings that society deems, to varying degrees, less than human.

Gamboa and Switzky themselves explain, "Things are fugitive with respect to knowledge. The simultaneous precision and deflection of the 'thing' indicates an evasive if commonplace feature of experience: a desire to name something (or some thing), an object, an atmosphere, or a sensation, that refuses to settle within anthropocentric parameters" (5). As both Collins's discussion of controlling images and Thomas's of the dark fantastic expose, anthropocentric parameters get stripped away from Black subjects, positioning them instead, as Hall's title makes clear, as things of darkness. Gamboa and Switzky's acknowledgment, via Andrew Sofer, that "we are in danger of thing-fatigue" may be true. But the seemingly universal "we" in that sentence does significant obfuscating work. The still predominantly white field of Shakespeare studies may be fatigued by new materialist turns to things. But persons of color, and most pertinent here, Black people specifically, are fatigued by being turned into things for centuries, their objectified plight long sidestepped or ignored in Shakespeare studies even as the things in Shakespeare's culture and on his stage have been elevated to the status of almost human.

To read *Kill Shakespeare*'s Othello as a prop, then, means recognizing the strategies for antiblack objectification present in the series but simultaneously representative of tactics used across American culture to which I return in subsequent chapters. To restate them clearly here:

1. Employing and thereby recirculating long-held stereotypes associated with Black identity.
2. Creating narratives that uncritically apply generic conventions in supposedly race-neutral ways.
3. Using persons of color for the main purpose of advancing whiteness's subjectivity.
4. Positioning Blackness as a foreign, exotic foil to normalized whiteness.
5. Creating a pathological Black identity that ultimately justifies its violent suppression.

Whether in Shakespeare's play or in *Kill Shakespeare*, Othello does not choose to turn himself into a thing. It is a dynamic foisted upon him, one that reappears over and over in supposedly post-racial versions of the eponymous play, and one which creators of color vitally, potently resist in their antiracist reimaginings of this centuries-long toxic tragedy.

Conclusion: Audience, Othello, and Limits of Re-Presentation

Even as Othello's depiction in *Kill Shakespeare* draws attention to creators who reanimate this well-known race play, it also raises questions about the relationship between the revivified work and the audience. *Kill Shakespeare* sits at the intersection between at least two types of fans—fans of Shakespeare and fans of comic books, audiences traditionally holding very different expectations for the respective genres to which they devote themselves. Del Col and McCreery could easily be positioned as Shakespearean fans given that *Kill Shakespeare* shares many similarities with the *fanfic* genre. Regarding Shakespearean fanfic, Valerie M. Fazel and Louise Geddes explain, "The loose explanation that Shakespeare fanfic is a form of literary appropriation that is created by fans of a given Shakespearean text, character, or setting is almost as far as any unmitigated description can run. Fanfic posits alternative endings, improvised 'off-stage' lives, sequels, and prequels, to name but a few examples. Fanfic can be presented in Shakespearean-styled verse, or modern prose, and can fuse together, or crossover, characters, texts, and genres, both within and beyond the Shakespearean corpus" ("Give me" 3). Though Fazel and Geddes develop their argument in relation to online communities that rewrite Shakespeare's canonical plays, their description nevertheless fits *Kill Shakespeare*, for it too creates a narrative that alternates from yet continues Shakespeare's works. In this regard, the series could be categorized as what Kavita Mudan Finn and Jessica McCall identify as the alternative universe, "a genre that, on the surface, radically alters the source texts, but is in fact intended to illustrate the flexibility and adaptability of that source text to different contexts" (30). Key to understanding the vitality of fanfiction is the very possibility of transformation exemplified in *Kill Shakespeare*. Jonathan Pope observes, "While it is common for fan fiction writers to seek to spend more time in these worlds and with these characters, it is also quite common for fan fiction to demand more from these worlds and characters, recognizing faults and seeking to address or fix them. In this sense, fan fiction sometimes does work that runs parallel to scholarly criticism, often by repudiating, for example, the lack of diversity in a text by making it more diverse" (Pope 12). Likewise discussing online fanfic communities, Finn and McCall expand on Pope's assertion by noting that this revision derives from fanfic's predominant audience identity. Fandom, they explain, "is a community overwhelmingly driven by marginalized readers: women, members of the LGBTQIA+ community, and readers of color who are actively agitating against white patriarchal epistemologies that have historically defined which texts have cultural value and how those texts should be interpreted" (32). As a reanimation verging on fanfiction, then, *Kill Shakespeare* held much imaginative promise for the very types of revision mentioned above by increasing the diversity of its world and by providing an alternate, antiracist ending for Othello. Fanfiction, in other words, reveals the promise of what *Kill Shakespeare* could have been.

Yet *Kill Shakespeare*'s failures in this regard rest not only with its creators, but also with its audience. For while fanfic readers desire transformation, comic book readers are often less flexible in the narratives they will accept. Like fanfic, as a genre often associated with fantasy, superheroes, and youth culture, comic books are intimately tied to fandom. Fans in fact play a crucial role in the narratives comic books produce. Wright explains that comic book audiences expect, indeed demand, formulaic narratives. He elaborates:

> Audiences turn to formulaic stories for the escape and enjoyment that comes from experiencing the fulfillment of their expectations within a structured imaginary world. While I do not perceive the market as a purely free exchange in which producers simply give the audience "what it wants," there is a certain democratic, or Darwinian, axiom in the entertainment industry that leads popular ideas to prevail over unpopular ones. Put simply, formulas that appeal to audiences tend to proliferate and endure, while those that do not, do neither. As a means through which changing values and assumptions are packaged into mass commodities, formulas are the consequence of determining pressures exerted by producers and consumers, as well as by the historical conditions affecting them both. (xvi)

When it comes to racial representation, what is the narrative formula that audiences expect and through their consumption authorize? As the history of race in/and comic books I have traced demonstrates, the unfortunate answer is that the formulas audiences desire are still all too often ones that do not truly reimagine the racial injustice that plagues everyday life. It is to this ideologically limited fandom that *Kill Shakespeare* capitulates. And its creators are not really held accountable for such a decision. Not a single scholarly article on *Kill Shakespeare* to date addresses the issue of race at all. This raises yet another question: are Shakespeareans more like the fans who create fanfic, open to change and transformation, or are they more like comic book fans who take comfort in the formulaic, a formula that does not as strongly challenge the inequitable status quo?

This question, however important, is very difficult to answer. Just as music, television, and film fandoms are not monolithic, neither are the Shakespeare "fans" that comprise Shakespeare studies. Yet one can venture toward an answer when considering a facet vital to various types of fandom: subjectivity. Finn and McCall note how "approaches to texts and prizing these qualities [emotions, self-interiority, and subjectivity] places a premium in fandom on rewritings that are grounded in a reader's subjective response to a text and encourages remythologization of historically enforced readings of those texts" (28). Fazel and Geddes observe that fanfic authors "frequently [insert] themselves into the content of the piece" ("Give me" 5). Pope likewise acknowledges the central role of subjectivity in regard to fandom when he explains his monograph's focus, concluding his introduction thus: "Such is fandom. We all possess a unique and sometimes overlapping constellation of media interests and passions that constructs and reflects us as readers and audiences" (29). Put simply, our interests reflect our subjectivity.

The disinterest in reimagining Othello in *Kill Shakespeare*, and the attendant scholarly disinterest in calling out the antiblackness *Kill Shakespeare* depicts, indicates a subjective disidentification with Othello. There is no speaking about and for him, as Smith notes, because whoever comprises the "we" that has crafted *Kill Shakespeare*, read it, and critiqued it cannot see itself in him. As Finn and McCall vehemently remind us:

> Gender, sexuality, race, and disability remain some of the most pressing and complicated areas of cultural theory and lived experience. Our ability to theorize and critically discuss these issues is also tied to *our ability to represent and explore them through fictionalized representations*. The continued relevance of Shakespeare's text and the possibility for critical conversation remain limited by the discursive

boundaries created through imaginative possibilities and perpetuated through mythic discourse. (31, emphasis added)

What Thomas calls the imagination gap thus not only results in a denigrating misrepresentation of Black masculinity in *Kill Shakespeare*, but in fact extends further, creating an ideological boundary that makes it all the more difficult to use Shakespeare as a tool that challenges an antiblack norm. Crucially, the responsibility for this imagination gap falls not just on the creators but also on audiences who sanction their work through a powerful combination of discursive and monetary approbation.

Yet just as not all creators nor characters are equally privileged, neither are audiences, for the effect of this imagination gap affects readers of color very differently. To understand this is to remember that Shakespearean reanimations are part of a popular culture that places these works not just in conversation with Shakespeare's plays, if that conversation occurs at all, but also with other narratives likewise explicitly and tacitly but nonetheless ubiquitously advancing antiblackness. For *Kill Shakespeare*, this means positioning this text not only within comic book history, but also within the dynamics of fantasy. Like Shakespeare, fantasy too "is often positioned as universal in our culture" (Thomas 24). But just as with discussions of Shakespeare, it becomes critical to resist this universalizing gesture. In the dark fantastic, narratives are racialized so that "the implicit message that readers, hearers, and viewers of color receive as they read these texts is that *we are villains. We are the horde. We are the enemies. We are the monsters*" (23). What is the result? A reification of the imagination gap, for this consistent misrepresentation frequently means that "*even when those who are endarkened and Othered dream in the fantastic, the Dark Other is* still *the obstacle to be overcome*" (23). Put differently, "it is not only history that has been irrevocably inscribed by its victors, but also memory and imagination itself" (25). Henry Jenkins may thus understand fandom as "an imagined community . . . constructed through the *collective imagination*" (xxix), but when one considers the ways racial inequity shapes this imagination, one understands how hard it is to free narratives from the racialized limits this imagination and its gaps impose.

It takes, as Thomas contends, a "radical rethinking of everything that we know" in order to emancipate ourselves and the fictions we create from this dark fantastic (28). By exposing the ideologies and strategies that led to complacent post-racial perspectives as manifested through various reimaginings of *Othello*, and by concomitantly challenging them by turning to powerful antiracist reconceptualizations of this same play, my hope is that this book brings to the fore the tools necessary for this imaginative emancipation. Doing so means not only reshaping the ways many Shakespearean reanimations—as well as popular culture more broadly—undertake racial representation, but also how audiences, including scholars, receive them and hold them accountable for the racial imaginary they disseminate.

Chapter 2

Colorblindness on the Post-Racial Stage: Hip hop, Comedy, and Cultural Appropriation in *Othello: The Remix*

"I know what you're thinkin'": Hip Hop, Shakespeare, and Audience Expectations

"Good story/tellers borrow/But great/ones steal" (2).¹ So begins the Q Brothers' *Othello: The Remix* (2012), which was commissioned for and debuted as the US entry and "only self-proclaimed [Shakespearean] adaptation in the 2012 Globe to Globe Festival" (Della Gatta 78). The production subsequently toured internationally in the UK, Germany, Australia, New Zealand, and Abu Dhabi, then ran twice at the Chicago Shakespeare Theater (CST), which co-produced the "ad-rap-tation," and again off Broadway, where it was presented by John Leguizamo. This modernized, 90-minute reinvention transforms Othello into an on-the-rise rapper destroyed by Iago, now a jealous member of his crew. From its sparse, graffitied set and limited props to its pulsating 4/4 hip hop beat to the four jumpsuit-wearing men who bound upon the stage, the production signals its untraditional approach by invoking classic elements of hip hop culture: "graffiti writing, deejaying, break dancing, [and] rap music" all at once (Pough vi).² Upon first consideration, the Q Brothers—who wrote the

---
¹ All quotes unless otherwise designated are taken from the Dramatists Play Service script.
² I only discuss the aesthetics and artistic choices of the performances at Shakespeare's Globe Theatre and at the Chicago Shakespeare Theater. A number of production choices changed as the performance moved off-Broadway, including costumes, props, and scene design.

script, composed the music, and directed the performance—appear to emulate the confident posturing often central to hip hop through the logic of their opening lines. Because they do not mention Shakespeare throughout the "Oh Snap Intro," their opening song focuses on *them* as storytellers, highlighting the ways that they have taken the narrative from Shakespeare's *Othello* but transformed it by updating context, changing language, excising characters, and most obviously, by adding a hip hop framework. Put succinctly, they have borrowed, or perhaps stolen, from the Bard. Indeed, the argument advanced by "Good story/tellers borrow/But great/ones steal" rests on the logic of degree so that the greater the intensity of the derivation, the more authorial weight garnered (Q Brothers 2). Thus, in stressing the Q Brothers stealing from someone as famous as Shakespeare, *Othello: The Remix*'s opening echoes the bravado often associated with hip hop as it introduces the appropriation to theatregoers.

Yet as the first song slips into the second, their juxtaposition exposes anxiety over the imaginative hip hop approach taken in order to retell Shakespeare.[3] The articulation of this apprehension reveals the audience to which the Q Brothers envision speaking: an audience concerned with the treatment of Shakespeare but unconcerned with the treatment of hip hop, and along with it, issues of race. As they open their self-described operetta,[4] the Q Brothers position the importance of hip hop as a genre discursively, for after the second "Good story/tellers borrow/but great/ones steal," the actors comprising the Q Brothers Collective chant "hip hop, hip hop," asserting, "So believe me the thievery is how we keep it real" (3).[5] The repeated attention to hip hop within the intro signals the uniqueness of the Q Brothers' approach. The second song, however, swiftly exposes concern about audience reception when they rap, "Now I know what you're thinkin'/'Hold on just a minute,/That's a tragedy [said in a faux British voice]'/Yep/but there's comedy in it" (3). The aside

---

[3] Most of the songs are not given a proper name, with a few exceptions. I will thus reference them by their order in the performance/on the soundtrack, and provide a title as indicated by the script and/or promptbook.

[4] According to the brothers, the production would best be characterized as "more of an opera than . . . a traditional musical" because once the music starts, it does not stop until the performance's completion, meaning that actors are "rap-ting," or acting while rapping ("Episode 64", *Shakespeare Unlimited*). Promotional materials also often call their works Shakespearean "ad-rap-tations."

[5] I use the designation "Q Brothers" when discussing GQ and JQ, the writers, composers, and directors of *Othello: The Remix*, while I use the designation "Q Brothers Collective" when discussing all of the performers: the brothers as well as Postell Pringle and Jackson Doran.

present in "Hold on just a minute" points to the type of audience the Q Brothers imagine—one clearly skeptical about the production. In fact, on the official CST soundtrack, the voice used to represent the audience is male with a British accent. This characterization suggests that the Q Brothers conceived of themselves speaking back not only to Shakespeare, but also to theatregoers who may not be receptive to their project, ones they believed to be more traditional regarding Shakespeare, as the stuffy male British voice signifies.

The prologue prefacing the Globe performance but absent in later versions reveals even more about those the Q Brothers pictured attending their production. In it, they reference Shakespeare directly, with, "Willy Shakes was a master/no one can ignore that/But he borrowed his stories from the Greeks before that . . ." (Globe Script). They go on to stress that they are keeping "this tradition alive" through their repackaged "latest version . . . in rhyme," which they emphasize gets to the "essence of the story" while putting a "new twist/on an old allegory." What they are providing, then, is a Shakespeare that takes audiences "Straight to a place that/we can relate to . . ." Similar to the "Oh Snap Intro," the prologue exposes a desire for relevancy to the audience ("we can relate to") while also displaying concern about how the audience will perceive the performance. This projected incredulity informs the defensive and offensive posturing that the Q Brothers articulate as they set themselves alongside Shakespeare's literary tradition while simultaneously conveying and justifying the attraction of their chosen interpretive methods. In essence, most especially in the space of Shakespeare's Globe as signaled by the purpose-written prologue, the Q Brothers communicate anxiety about hip hop as the means for retelling Shakespeare.

This concern over hip hop's reception when applied to Shakespeare's works creates a different resonance for the Q Brothers' assertions of borrowing and stealing all in the name of good (or great) storytelling. Borrowing suggests mutuality, an exchange of sorts between parties; stealing, quite the opposite. The Q Brothers directly invite a consideration of whether they have borrowed or stolen from Shakespeare, and whether Shakespeare himself borrowed or stole. But as *Othello: The Remix*'s opening makes clear, hip hop serves as the other significant cultural force in this production. This genre also ought to invite similar questions about borrowing and stealing given that the use of hip hop in adapting Shakespeare entails a cross-cultural exchange, an exchange often at the heart of concerns surrounding cultural appropriation. Though now global, hip hop has long been associated with Black America, where both the musical form and its attendant cultural symbols took root. As M. K. Asante Jr. lyrically explains, "With its sands scattered to the winds of the world, hip hop joins scores of other vibrations that are born in the Black community, but that live, thrive, and reproduce all over the world" (2). Even more emphatically, Imani Perry insists, "Hip hop is an iteration of black language, black style, and black youth culture" (2). The Q Brothers thus take a predominantly Black, pop-status cultural symbol and deploy it to recast the decidedly white, high-status Shakespeare.[6]

Queries about the deployment of hip hop remain unarticulated by the Q Brothers, however. This decision tells us even more about the audience that the Q Brothers envision: the audience may *very much* care about their ad-rap-tation of Shakespeare, but it *will not* care about the ways with which they engage hip hop. Yet hip hop's force within *Othello: The Remix* and cultural resonance outside of it cannot be ignored; in fact, it is the very thing fostering the anxiety so prevalent across *Othello: The Remix*'s first two songs. Nevertheless, the Q Brothers choose not to interrogate the racial dynamic at the heart of hip hop, focusing instead on the low-status/high-status, hip hop/Shakespeare binary. The fact that questions about the use of hip hop remain unasked and unanswered, in part because they assume the audience does not care about this issue, signals what I argue is both the cultural borrowing and prevailing blindness toward matters of race (i.e. colorblindness) pervading this production.

In large part, this blindness comes as a result of a third, less obvious element highlighted in *Othello: The Remix*'s introduction: comedy. The fourth hip hop reimagining of Shakespeare by brothers Gregory and Jeffery Ameen Qaiyum (known as GQ and JQ), *Othello: The Remix* is their first attempt at tackling a Shakespearean tragedy.[7] However, in song 2, the actors expressly state the significance of comedy to the operetta, indicating that they perceive it as a central ingredient to their success. Remember, the fussy British voice insists of *Othello*, "That's a tragedy," while the Q Brothers Collective rebuts, "Yep/but there's comedy in it" (3). In other words, the first two minutes of the show make it evident that it is the combination of hip hop with an emphasis

---

[6] Arthur Little Jr. argues that Western culture insists on positioning "Shakespeare as both universal and white" (*Shakespeare Jungle Fever* 20).

[7] Previous Shakespearean ad-rap-tations include *Dress the Part* (*Two Gentlemen of Verona*), *The Bomb-itty of Errors* (*The Comedy of Errors*), and *Funk It Up About Nothin'* (*Much Ado About Nothing*). Subsequent to *Othello: The Remix*, the Q Brothers have returned to Shakespearean tragedy with *I Heart Juliet* (*Romeo and Juliet*).

on comedy that the Q Brothers locate in Shakespeare's original tale which becomes their principle means of crafting a production engaging to audiences; the hope is that this strategy will successfully quell possible audience concerns about their fairly unorthodox approach to Shakespeare.

The specific mixing of hip hop and comedy, however, creates an audience appeal based on a problematic ideological foundation. The Q Brothers' use of hip hop may seem obvious, as the genre often signals an edginess and coolness not typically associated with Shakespeare. But why use comedy as a second strategy for audience engagement, especially when trying to adapt a tragedy? I suggest that the use of humor functions as a way of creating a colorblind approach to hip hop, and by extension, toward race. Comedy distracts from or even strips away the racial tensions inherent in *Othello*, tensions only heightened by the hip hop milieu. By colorblind here, I pay homage to and expand upon the scholarly tradition of considering color in the casting of Shakespeare's plays; I use colorblind to mean not an approach to casting but rather the creation of a racial narrative that manifests a blindness toward color, specifically in this case Blackness, as anything more than a mere symbol of identity instead of a crucial factor motivating and justifying systemic injustices.

Indeed, a careful analysis of key moments within the production reveals that ultimately, the comedy skews toward stereotyping, thereby muting the performance's exploration of racial identity and representation. The Q Brothers therefore provide the audience with a fun, vibrant production irreverent in its Shakespearean appropriation but that says little about race. They thus neuter the hip hop framework's ability to critique contemporary constructs of and systemic imbalances against Black identity; rather, the framework functions simply to uphold common critiques of hip hop as a genre—namely, an emphasis on violence, glorification of gangster culture, and rampant misogyny—without the dialectic of its most valued feature: its ability to potently reframe and communicate the cultural experiences of Blackness. This dynamic thus raises the question that *Othello: The Remix*'s first moments refuse to consider: when it comes to hip hop, do the Q Brothers borrow or steal? To use more theoretical language, do they culturally appropriate as they deploy hip hop culture? I argue that the answer to the question is yes, they do by sacrificing the power of racial polemic in favor of colorblindness. They create this colorblindness through both an erasure of Blackness and comedy's distractions, all in service of garnering white audience appeal.

Reconsidering Colorblind Shakespeare

At first glance, *Othello: The Remix* does not seem to merit a typical discussion of colorblind Shakespeare given that there is no extensive colorblind casting in the most common sense but rather colorblind (and gender-bending) doubling. The white actor Jackson Doran plays Cassio and Emilia, African American Postell Pringle plays Othello, part-Indian GQ and JQ—who characterize themselves as "aliens" in the north side of Chicago, where they "were [called] camel jockeys and dot heads" (Feliciano)—perform the roles of Iago and Brabantio and Roderigo, Loco Vito, and Bianca respectively, while all four men intermittently function as the ad-rap-tation's chorus. The updated context of *Othello* complicates a reading of this casting as "colorblind" in any customary sense, for there is no primary role that "the race nor the ethnicity of an actor should prevent her or him from playing," save Othello (Thompson, "Practicing a Theory" 6). In this regard, the production better fits within a practice "in which the best actor [is] hired for the best role, except when the race of the character [is] identified and significant within the corpus of the text."[8] In the case of *Othello: The Remix*, Othello's race signifies not only within the history of Shakespeare's text but also the hip hop milieu the Q Brothers deploy. Thus, the Q Brothers do not make any casting decisions that would signal as colorblind aside from the now common practice of eschewing a blackface Othello.

Yet as discussed at length in the Introduction, when removed from the realm of casting, colorblindness takes on different theoretical underpinnings, ones that shift the focus to the ways that white America purposefully turns a blind eye to issues of color—essentially, issues of race.[9] To review briefly, sociologist Eduardo Bonilla-Silva outlines the contours of "color-blind racism," explaining:

> This ideology, which acquired cohesiveness and dominance in the late 1960s, explains contemporary racial inequality as the outcome of nonracial dynamics. Whereas Jim Crow racism explained blacks' social standing as the result of their biological and moral inferiority, color-blind racism avoids such facile arguments. Instead, whites

---

[8] According to Ayanna Thompson, this approach to casting "is an admission that socio-political and cultural-historical factors influence an audience's viewing abilities" (7).

[9] Colorblind is also often spelled color-blind. I will be using the former spelling in order to signal the continuity between my discussion and that of colorblind casting. However, *color-blind* will appear in quoted passages.

rationalize minorities' contemporary status as the product of market dynamics, naturally occurring phenomena, and blacks' imputed cultural limitations. (2)

Through this approach, whites can "enunciate positions that safeguard their racial interests without sounding 'racist,'" especially because this logic invests in the idea of meritocracy so that systemic injustices against minorities can be argued away as individual shortcomings (Bonilla-Silva 4). This emphasis on meritocracy proves especially important, at least in the unfolding of colorblind racism in the US, for it explains how colorblind racism became wedded to the idea of the post-racial after President Obama's election in 2008 and reelection in 2012. A Black man achieving the most elite position in the country allowed whites to point to the validity of meritocracy in America's racial order, leading them to affirm that the US was now post-racial. Journalist and cultural critic Touré observes:

> During Obama's presidential campaign you could see a self-congratulatory glee in many of his white supporters: they were proud of themselves for being so far beyond racism that they could support a Black man for president and proud of their nation for being open-minded about having a Black man lead ... This was a far different vibe than when Reverend Jackson ran for president in 1984 and 1988, when tropes in his self-presentation reminded whites of the guilt they felt about the past. He seemed to be the president whom Blacks were owed for our suffering. Obama was the president whom America, in its multiracial glory, had created ... someone who some whites saw as the harbinger of the end of racism or at least the first light at the end of the tunnel. (176)

Yet taking up the distinction Touré notes between Reverend Jackson and President Obama, in his trenchant critique of Obama's political self-fashioning, Bonilla-Silva argues that Obama achieved political success precisely because he presented himself as the type of minority candidate palatable to colorblind racists, one who "is not a race rebel" (260). Most important for my argument here is Bonilla-Silva's assertion that colorblind America accepted Obama because he invoked race in symbolic ways, invocations sanitized in order to make him more acceptable to white America.

The defanged approach to race that Bonilla-Silva claims characterizes acceptance of Obama mirrors Charles A. Gallagher's explanation of the dynamics informing colorblindness and cultural consumption. Gallagher contends that in a colorblind America, "Color as a cultural style may be expressed and consumed through music, dress, or vernacular but race as a system which confers privileges and shapes life chances is viewed as an atavistic and inaccurate accounting of US race relations" (3). To use language that more directly invokes Bonilla-Silva's argument about Obama, Gallagher notes that it is not that whites ignore race but rather that they accept "racial symbols" that can circulate regardless of identity so that "race becomes nothing more than an innocuous cultural signifier" (5). As such, whites can assert their progressivism and racial tolerance because this approach acknowledges race while muting attention to racial inequalities.

Cultural Appropriation, Colorblindness, and Hip Hop History

Particularly salient for a discussion of *Othello: The Remix* is the way that hip hop becomes affected by colorblind borrowing that recognizes race but is made toothsome by ignoring forms of injustice. This dynamic dovetails with a concurrent discussion regarding hip hop and cultural appropriation, namely, the ways whiteness erases key facets of hip hop as a genre. Jason Rodriquez notes how the type of colorblind ideology outlined above affects the ways white youth interact with the hip hop scene. Because they disconnect racial identity from their cultural consumption, they "take the racially coded meanings out of hip-hop, and replace them with color blind ones . . . for their own purposes" (647). In other words, "the mass marketing of racially coded cultural symbols such as hip-hop allows whites to experience a felt similarity with communities of color. Whites who pick up on African American styles and music do not necessarily want to be black; they seek to acquire the characteristics of blackness associated with being cool" (649). While Rodriquez calls this cultural appropriation, he does little to theorize the concept. Yet the dynamics he identifies indeed fit within the theoretical framework of cultural appropriation.

At its most basic, cultural appropriation entails borrowing from a culture not one's own. If defined solely in this way, then cultural appropriation appears to be the most essential and pervasive of human activities. Yet the term more often than not applies to cultural borrowing that lacks mutuality (i.e. not cultural exchange) and that reifies either historical or contemporary imbalances of power (i.e. not assimilation), such as American pop singer Gwen Stefani using the Indian bindi or celebrity Kim Kardashian wearing cornrows to make a fashion statement. The issue, then, is one of dominance by one culture, typically hegemonic, over another, most often not so. Especially relevant for this discussion is the dominance enacted through erasure of a marginalized culture by a hegemonic one. Erasure is precisely the power imbalance that both Bonilla-Silva and Gallagher identify as central to colorblind approaches to American culture and that Rodriquez locates more narrowly in his analysis of whiteness and hip hop. But discussions about cultural appropriation of hip hop by white Americans extend beyond the youth Rodriquez studies to American society's use of hip hop more broadly, and within it, the music industry's role in reconfiguring what hip hop looks and sounds like.

While scholars may differ on the details, by and large they agree that the history of hip hop is concomitantly a history of cultural appropriation. Asante Jr. recounts hip hop's radical, political beginnings, explaining:

> Although West African in its derivation, hip hop emerged in the Bronx in the mid-seventies as a form of aesthetic and sociopolitical rebellion against the flames of systemic oppression. This rebellion, on the one hand, was musical because rap music was a radical alternative to disco, which excluded many Blacks and Latinos in inner cities. (9)

Patricia Hill Collins likewise comments on rap's role in speaking back to America's racially stratified social norms:

> Crafted in the South Bronx, an urban landscape that had been abandoned by virtually everyone, African American, Latino, and Afro-Caribbean youth created rap, break dancing, tagging (graffiti), fashions and other cultural creations . . . With few other public forums to share their outrage at a society that had so thoroughly written them off, Black youth used rap and hip-hop to protest the closing door of opportunity in their lives and to claim their humanity in the face of the dehumanization of racial segregation and ghettoization. (*Black Sexual* 92)

From the 1970s to the 1980s, then, hip hop had a socially progressive presence and function.

This form of socially conscious hip hop may be unfamiliar to many, however, because of the genre's appropriation by dominant white cultural forces. Asante Jr. traces the story of hip hop's corporatization. As hip hop artists sought commercially viable careers with the major record companies in the late 1980s and early 1990s—Universal Music

Group, Sony, BMG, EMI Group, and Warner Music Group (11)—their music underwent a change in order to appeal to the masses via radio and music video play, play controlled by even more "multinational corporations like Viacom, Clear Channel, and Vivendi" (6).[10] At the hands of white executives running these companies, artists experienced "censorship through intimidation, budget-cutting, refusing to advertise or allow airtime, and via other legal channels," which resulted in a "[restriction of] the sociopolitical voices of commercially viable artists" (Asante Jr. 109).[11]

Take a particularly infamous example of hip hop history that explains the rationale behind the executives' choices: the furor over rapper Ice-T's 1992 song "Cop Killer," distributed by "one of the widest, and Whitest, labels in the world," Warner Bros. Records (Charnas 370), and whose release resulted in boycotts by police in Texas. As Dan Charnas explains in his extensive history of the hip hop business, Ice-T's album *Original Gangster* (1992) sold "nearly one million" copies, whereas his subsequent *Home Invasion* (1992) "slow[ed] down around 500,000 copies. What the hell was going on? ... Many large retail chains would no longer stock Ice-T's record" (400). Thus, as a direct result of what happened to Ice-T's sales, "Fear of another 'Cop Killer' was spreading to other major labels, and rap releases were being affected across the board ... Now, as all the righteous rage about racial oppression was making its way to wax via hip-hop, suddenly rap was under attack. The more political and rebellious the song, the more likely it was to be suppressed" (392). Significantly, "party, political, afrocentric, and avant-garde" forms of rap did not cease to exist; instead, they were "driven out of the corporate-promoted mainstream," Tricia Rose explains (2). In other words, it is not that hip hop with a sociopolitical message disappeared entirely. Rather, it was less promoted, often sidelined on the radio or relegated to album cuts. Rose asserts

---

[10] For an engaging, detailed overview of the business of hip hop, see Dan Charnas, *The Big Payback: The History of the Business of Hip-Hop* (New American Library, 2010).

[11] Asante Jr. explains how such assertions may seem to stand in contradiction to the popular idea of the black rap mogul. However, "Despite the perception that Black entrepreneurs like P. Diddy, Russell Simmons, Jay-Z, Cash Money are moguls, they're, in actuality, the children of their respective parent companies. P. Diddy's Bad Boy Records is owned by Warner Music Group; Suge Knight's Death Row by Interscope is owned by Universal Music Group; Def Jam is also owned by Universal ... What's worse is that, despite popular perception, there are no Blacks—none [in 2008]—in top executive positions of the parent companies" (111).

that even in the 1990s, the spirit of hip hop as seen in the 1970s and 1980s remained significant, with hip hop serving as "compelling music dealing with the pleasures and pains lived by those with the least" (x). But one had to work harder to access this form of hip hop, for white corporate America attempted to make it "a conservative instrument" (Asante Jr. 10).

Claims of conservatism may seem antithetical to anyone who has even a passing familiarity with the violence, homophobia, and misogyny present in much of what has come to be known as "gangsta rap." But these characteristics reflect white conservatism in that they reinforce and re-code America's long-held stereotypes about Black masculinity (see Chapter 1). Rose notes how hip hop "has increasingly become a playground for caricatures of black gangstas, pimps, and hoes" (1). She pinpoints the flourishing of these now familiar hip hop tropes to the early-to-mid 1990s with the "meteoric rise" of West Coast rappers Dr. Dre and N.W.A., who crafted a West Coast rap that "solidified and expanded the already well-represented street criminal icons—thug, hustler, gangster, and pimp—in a musically compelling way" (3). As a result, "This grab bag of street criminal figures soon became the most powerful, and to some, the most 'authentic' spokesmen for hip hop and, then, for black youth generally." Miles White more specifically locates this shift to "hardcore styles of hip-hop performance" in the commercial success of Dr. Dre's 1992 album, *The Chronic* (61). White contends that Dr. Dre minimized "aggressive beats and much of the vitriol" theretofore associated with rap in order to keep its street content but in a less aggressive form. What followed was a "shift to more profane and obscene language, explicit sexual content, graphic depictions of casual violence, drugs, and representations of urban masculinity" (59). As a result, "The use of profane language containing pornographic and misogynistic content and narratives of gangbanging and drug dealing" became the central characteristics of hardcore or gangster rap "as hip-hop culture, street gang culture, and the epidemic of crack cocaine collided" (59), a collision which provided the blueprint for success of well-known hardcore performers such as Notorious B.I.G., Tupac, and Jay-Z, artists who "retained violent and drug-laden themes with sing along choruses" (61). These artists, Rose explains, took figures such as the "gangsta and street hustler," which were previously socially, artistically, and politically important, "[devolving them] into apolitical, simpleminded, almost comic stereotypes" (2). Conservatism, then, came not in the form of language or content but rather in the racial imaginary strengthened by the rap personas deployed for commercial viability.

Rose remarks on the importance of this version of hip hop for economic success, arguing that "This consolidation and 'dumbing down' of hip hop's imagery and storytelling took hold rather quickly in the middle to late 1990s and reached a peak in the early 2000s. The hyper-gangsta-ization of the music and imagery directly parallels hip hop's sales ascendance into the mainstream record and radio industry" (3). She provides figures, noting that between 1990 and 1998, rap accounted for 9 to 10 percent of US music sales, rising to its "peak" of 13.8 percent in 2002, and settling at 12 to 13 percent in 2005 (4). She contextualizes these sales through comparison:

> To put the importance of this nearly 40 percent increase in rap/hip hop sales into context, note that during the 2000–2005 period, other genres, including rock, country, and pop, saw decreases in their market percentage. The rise in rap/hip hop was driven primarily by the sale of images and stories of black ghetto life to white youth. . . . Indeed, between 1995 and 2001, whites comprised 70–75 percent of the hip hop customer base. (4)

To pull the threads of hip hop's history, cultural appropriation, and erasure together, what these narratives of hip hop's past reveal is that the cultural appropriation of hip hop by white-run corporations resulted in the erasure of the "link between Black music and the politics of Black life" that characterized hip hop in the 1970s and 1980s (Asante Jr. 4), promoting in its stead a version of hip hop often critiqued for its emphasis on materialism, sexism, homophobia, and racial caricatures but enthusiastically consumed by white youth because of these very qualities.

The connection between hip hop's history and its cultural consumption in regard to race informs the Q Brothers' use of the genre in *Othello: The Remix*. Particularly noteworthy is the duality taken when approaching race and hip hop. On the one hand, the music industry's cultural appropriation of hip hop sees race by using an understanding of white racism in order to appeal musically to white youth (Asante Jr. 114). On the other hand, as Rodriquez notes, marketing strategies encourage the same youth to remain colorblind by inviting them to employ the markers and enjoy the seemingly transgressive nature of hip hop culture without considering the social burdens of Blackness upon which the genre was built. This relationship between cultural appropriation and colorblindness likewise exists in *Othello: The Remix*. Mirroring the divesting of racial polemic from hip hop, the Q Brothers strip the operetta of inquiry into racial injustice. Their use of hip hop is thus the stance that Dwight Conquergood identifies as "The Enthusiast's Infatuation." In his discussions of the ethics of ethnographic performance, Conquergood identifies five approaches to performance, outlining the ethical dimensions of each. Conquergood defines the Enthusiast's Infatuation in this way: "Too facile identification with the other coupled with enthusiastic commitment produces naive and glib performances marked by superficiality ... this performative stance is unethical because it trivializes the other. The distinctiveness of the other is glossed over by a glaze of generalities" (6). While Conquergood uses the language of glossing over, one could easily substitute erasure, an erasure *Othello: The Remix* enacts by advancing a particular racial form or identity without substance. Instead, the Q Brothers craft a colorblind performance through casting practices in concert with costuming, mise en scène, troping, and characterization—performance elements employed in dangerously colorblind ways to craft and disseminate a colorblind narrative. In other words, *Othello: The Remix* turns a blind eye to color—namely Blackness—in any meaningful way by highlighting comedy instead of the social issues surrounding Blackness and identity. In doing so, even if inadvertent, *Othello: The Remix* potentially functions as an antiblack appropriation of *Othello*, for it offers up caricatured and superficial depictions of race masked by the edginess of Shakespeare performed to a hip hop beat.

Racial Erasure: *Othello: The Remix* and the Flattening of Racial Identity

Before turning to *Othello: The Remix*'s use of comedy to deflect from the racial politics of hip hop, it is useful to recognize how easily one may mistake the play as confronting race and racial identity, for *Othello: The Remix*'s narrative includes scenes that explicitly reference race. But they do so, I argue, in shallow ways. These moments register the production's unachieved potential—what might have been. They signal passing acknowledgments of race as an important factor to both *Othello* and hip hop as a genre, which only heightens the subsequent blindness when these gestures toward the complexities of racial identity and injustice remain unpursued, providing instead stereotypical depictions of pathological Black masculinity that mirror the colorblind dynamics favored by post-racial America.

Expectedly, *Othello: The Remix*'s superficial consideration of race appears most frequently in its exploration of Othello, as highlighted by both the script's character description and the production's first song. The character description does not mention Othello's African American identity expressly, but it does provide background, which includes the fact that he has "escaped the pitfalls of the ghetto he was raised in," with "ghetto" here functioning as racially coded language for the Black inner city (Q Brothers 1). This familiar socially mobile rap persona fits within the personal narratives articulated by real-life MCs including The Notorious B.I.G., Fat Joe, 50 Cent, and the rappers directly inspiring Othello in *Othello: The Remix*, Jay-Z and The Game. In Othello's first song, "Never Comin Down," Othello expounds on these details in ways that explore the "hard knock life" so often attributed to rappers—one that acknowledges the challenges of growing up Black, urban, and poor—yet in ways also potentially recirculating stereotypes. He and his backup vocalists, or hype men, relay his rise "to the top." As they do so, it becomes clear that the Q Brothers felt the rise would be more compelling if Othello came from rock bottom (5). His rap begins, "I never knew my pops, moms was a junkie," and then proceeds to explain that he was "Raised in the streets" as a "child of the ghetto" filled with "people smokin rocks." On these streets, "Either ya slang crack or ya got a wicked jump shot." The language of escape used in the character description only clarifies as he elaborates: "I survived the impossible./Caught in gang crossfire and crawled to the hospital." And returning to his family life, he reveals, "Momma so cracked out, she don't recognize me./I had to get out for my life and my sanity,/'Stead o' gettin' high waitin' to die like my family . . . Now I'm a mothafuckin' millionaire!" (6). In fact, unlike real-life rappers known for maintaining close relationships with family, such as Tupac and Jay-Z, Othello's kinship ties prove to be a detriment rather than a boon. He makes it clear that he had to "get out for my life, and my sanity,/'Stead o' gettin' high waitin' to die like my family" (6). It is no wonder, then, that Othello declares, "I made it to the top . . . And we're [Othello and his crew] never coming down." The song's narrative momentum makes it evident that its goal is to celebrate Othello's economic success, which markedly contrasts with his humble beginnings. This depiction of Othello's past, a common rap trope, thus inhabits the tense space that many hip hop personas do: on the one hand inviting a true, gritty exploration of some of the most marginalized African American voices, on the other hand invoking prominent stereotypes of drugs, absent fathers, and welfare queens that circulate in the US about Black communities and the families within them.

Yet most rappers can create an entire oeuvre through which they may craft a counternarrative that contextualizes and interrogates their seemingly stereotypical backgrounds. Perry notes the importance of this dialectic, contending:

> The narratives of gangsterism, drug dealing, and other violence often explain these practices with poverty, desperation, lack of educational opportunity, or a conflicted relationship to a father. This expands on the narrative, shifting the interpretive paradigm of outlaw activity to a sociological analysis. (108)

It is through these multifaceted narratives that artists push back against stereotyping. They may, as Perry suggests, adopt "thug mimicry," embodying American stereotypes of Black masculinity, but they do so in order to "[give] a voice to the stereotypical figure" through "an indictment of white supremacy" which entails "a critique of the sociological conditions—poverty, police brutality, and joblessness—that contributed to his or her becoming this person" (109). For "thug mimicry" to work, then, the artist must intentionally create a counternarrative to the stereotypical persona he (and more rarely, she) taps into.

This extended narrative possibility and attention to sociological structures is not the case for the Q Brothers' Othello, for across the performance's 90 minutes, he does not provide an alternative view or thoughtful interrogation of his drug-addled family and neighborhood. For example, when Othello contemplates the reasons behind his seeming alienation—he notes "it's lonely when you're up at the top"—racial identity does not play a role (7). He and his crew respond to his alienation by stating, "Mo money, Mo problems." This direct quote comes from The Notorious B.I.G.'s 1997 posthumous hit single "Mo Money, Mo Problems." The song celebrates the wealth and materialism of hip hop success through rappers Mase, Puff Daddy, and The Notorious B.I.G. In each verse, the rappers address those who would hold them back or drag them down as they reach the apex of their success: Mase rebukes the "PhD" or playa hater degree people, the ones who "didn't know me in '91" but now "can't hold me down"; Puff Daddy defies those who would "rather see 'em die than to see me fly," reminding them that "I call all the shots" from his "yacht" with "money much longer than yours/ And a team much stronger than yours "; and The Notorious B.I.G. tackles the DEA, boasting, "Federal agents mad cause I'm flagrant," though when they attempt to catch him, "My team supreme, stay clean . . ." The Q Brothers lift lyrics from the chorus, which goes, "I don't know what they want from me/It's like the more money we come across/The more problems we see."[12] The song most clearly explores conflict that arises mostly from economic status, which mirrors Othello's claim that he cannot trust others because he is now a millionaire. The choice to highlight this particular song is surely at least in part due to its recognizability. But deploying it as an intertext for *Othello: The Remix* is simply one more way that the Q Brothers choose to overlook race. For instance, instead, they could have referenced Biggie Smalls's "Juicy," (1994), which likewise focuses on social mobility but also nods to race's presence in this newly achieved success with the lines, "Considered a fool 'cause I dropped out of high school/Stereotypes of a black male misunderstood." Or more potently, they might have pulled lines from "Things Done Changed" (1994), which narrates how "Back in the day," neighborhoods were characterized by "Lounging at the barbecues, drinking brews/With the neighborhood crews, hanging on the avenues." But "Turn your pages to 1993/Niggas is getting smoked, G, believe me/Talk slick, you get your neck slit quick . . ." In fact, in this song, The Notorious B.I.G. makes an assertion very similar to Othello's in "Never Comin Down" when he relates, "If I wasn't in the rap game/I'd probably have a key knee-deep in the crack game." The distinction is that he provides a complementary picture of Black neighborhoods, those involving cookouts, sitting on the porch on a summer day, and importantly, community, which invokes images more commonly associated with white suburban America. This more positive view of Black communities never appears in *Othello: The Remix*. Here, the Q Brothers decide to echo the ghetto fabulous hip hop narrative, the one advanced by white corporate America, with no other version of Black life presented as an alternative. Thus, the choice to pull from "Mo Money, Mo Problems" becomes one in a catalog of the Q Brothers' representational decisions that, intentionally or not, sidelines issues of racial inequity even as they deploy the racialized discourse and beats of hip hop to retell Shakespeare's classic tragedy.

Indeed, as former residents of Chicago, the Q Brothers seem almost willfully to disregard the history of racial disparity in their home town; this history, which characterizes many urban cities, contextualizes the ghetto invoked in *Othello: The Remix* by providing an alternative explanation to claims about Black moral failings, that

---

[12] The chorus of "Mo Money, Mo Problems" is a sample of Diana Ross's "I'm Coming Out."

of the socioeconomic inequities potently crafted by white supremacy. In his lauded essay "The Case for Reparations," Ta-Nehisi Coates uses Chicago as an exemplum of the various means of disenfranchisement experienced by African Americans that have led to the creation of the ghetto, and subsequently, to assertions about Black pathology. Coates explains, "From the 1930s through the 1960s, Black people across the country were largely cut out of the legitimate home-mortgage market through means both legal and extralegal," means including predatory contract sales instead of traditional mortgages, redlining, the refusal of loans by the FHA, restrictive covenants, and even physical violence. African Americans were positioned as undesirables, people who would lower existing home values, thereby destabilizing a neighborhood. Redlining and the creation of public housing in particular explain the ghettoization of African Americans. Coates describes how the FHA would give neighborhoods with in-demand locales—signaled by green on a map—an "A" rating, which made them "excellent prospects for insurance." These green neighborhoods "lacked 'a single foreigner or Negro.'" Neighborhoods in which Black people lived were given a "D" rating, often making them "ineligible for FHA backing." These neighborhoods were colored red. People in these communities were often at the mercy of predatory lenders and had little to no legal protection. The wage gap between Blacks and whites intensified as a result. In trying to pay inflated housing prices, Black men and women worked more jobs, longer hours, and made difficult choices about how much to spend on their families' needs. In other words, the dynamics of the housing market created by white supremacy and imposed on Black America shaped the structures of Black home life. An alternative to these exclusionary housing options, public housing was often restricted in white neighborhoods and built in all-Black neighborhoods instead. This was just one more way of limiting African American access to home ownership, a key feature of the American dream. It is for these reasons that Coates argues against the common belief that the problems within African American communities "stem from cultural pathologies that can be altered through individual grit and exceptionally good behavior," avowing, "The kind of trenchant racism to which Black people have persistently been subjected can never be defeated by making its victims more respectable," for the perceived dysfunctions are racism's "grim inheritance." *Othello: The Remix* thus readily invokes the results of this "grim inheritance" without acknowledging the concept of inheritance itself—the racial legacy forming the ghetto from which Othello emerges.

This decision to eschew a counterexample to the pathological and stereotypical Black narrative Othello invokes differs from Shakespeare's tragedy, in which Othello communicates the abjectness "Of being taken by the insolent foe/And sold into slavery" (I, iii, 140), yet also comments on the success of his subsequent "redemption" as well as his high-status lineage "From men of royal siege" (I, ii, 22). This is not an issue of fidelity but rather of possibility. If Renaissance Othello was a slave of literal warfare, could not twenty-first-century Othello be framed as a casualty of socioeconomic warfare? If Renaissance Othello's ancestry made him some form of prince, could not twenty-first-century Othello embody a similar high-status lineage? No such counterpoint in Othello's identity exists within *Othello: The Remix*. Moreover, in the production, even though Othello comments on his past, it does not seem to affect him in his present. Othello's remarks about his youth provide striking opportunities to explore the ways that his background would make him feel alienated as he achieves the status of the "greatest emcee" (Q Brothers 3). Just as Othello's past in Shakespeare's play informs how he negotiates his confrontation with the Duke and the Venetian senators, so too could Othello's ghetto upbringing serve as important contextualization for his navigation of a predominantly white and culturally appropriative music industry. However, because of the Q Brothers' adaptive choices, ultimately, culpability for his financially and emotionally destitute childhood rests with the moral failings of his family and neighborhood—precisely the argument for Black pathology Coates convincingly defies—rather than with any institutional force. As such, the reference to Othello's background ultimately seems extraneous because it does not help the audience understand how it informs Othello's present circumstances and decisions. Othello's ghetto childhood therefore serves as mere window dressing at best and stereotypical representation at worst. This opening characterization thereby provides a missed opportunity for turning a critical eye toward the way racial and socioeconomic inequalities shape Othello's identity.

These moments expose the blindness toward and subsequent erasure of race in the production. Instances that raise the possibility of interrogating racial inequalities, racism, and alienation exist within *Othello: The Remix*; the Q Brothers can, in fact, see race as it applies to *Othello*. They simply choose not to interrogate it. Audiences may easily overlook this disregard for delving into racial inequity, however, thanks to a key distraction at the heart of the performance: the Q Brothers' emphasis on comedy.

Comedy and Colorblindness

By erasing the possibility of racial polemic in favor of sidelining or ignoring the cultural significance of Othello's Blackness, *Othello: The Remix* manifests a colorblindness, one in large part created through the strategic use of comedy, much of it racial if not racist in nature. Simon Weaver notably defines racist humor as "[drawing] on dichotomous stereotypes of race and/or [seeking] to inferiorise an ethnic or racial minority" (538).[13] Scholars who engage with racial and/or racist humor through a Critical Race Theory lens remain divided in their assessment about its effects, though most agree that this form of humor is a difficult genre because of its ability to cause personal and social harm.[14] Using the terminology provided by Donald A. Saucier, Conor J. O'Dea, and Megan L. Strain, one can categorize racial humor as "prosocial," a term describing humor that subverts the political, economic, and social dominance of whites (78). For instance, using the comedy of Stephen Colbert as an example, Jonathan P. Rossing argues that humor "talks back" to America's post-racial ideology (46), thereby serving as "a site for racial meaning-making that may provide a corrective for impasses in public discourse on race and

---

[13] Weaver insists that the term *racist humor* be used, for "not labelling the humour racist is a form of ideological denial" (538).

[14] Academic responses to racial humor vary widely across a range of fields. Those who study the ethics of humor, for instance, tend to focus on audience reception, such as what it says about a person if they laugh at a racist or sexist joke. In this vein, Ronald de Sousa argues that if a person laughs at a racist or sexist joke, that person can only do so because they share the racist or sexist assumptions underlying the joke. David Benatar admits that jokes can harm, "especially so against a background of sustained prejudice and discrimination against certain groups" (192); but he does not go as far as de Sousa, instead concluding that "we need not endorse gender and racial stereotypes in order to appreciate humor that turns on them. Racial and gender jokes do not necessarily express prejudice and thus are not necessarily morally defective" (202). Even so, Benatar acknowledges that his "very limited conclusion should not obscure the unpleasant fact that racial and gender humor often do express, inculcate, or reinforce prejudice, or cause people to be insulted or demeaned." Aaron Smuts takes a stronger stance, for even though he acknowledges that humor has ethical dimensions—"Telling jokes, encouraging jokes, and laughing at jokes are actions with clear ethical significance—they are capable of producing harms" (346)—he nevertheless staunchly rejects the premise that telling or laughing at a joke makes one immoral. He counters common philosophical positions on humor, contending, "The proposed necessary conditions for getting and subsequently finding a joke funny—incongruity, cognitive shifts, error perception, attitudinal endorsement of beliefs—all fail to tell us enough about any given case to say that it is wrong to find it funny" (345).

racism" (45).¹⁵ Rossing admits that racial humor has the potential to reinforce the very stereotypes that it attempts to critique. Even so, he stresses "the possibility of multiple readings," "incongruity," and "polyvocality," found in racial humor, which he contends allows for it to serve as a destabilizing force (53, 54).¹⁶ Despite the *potential* for these competing intents regarding racial humor, scholars by and large note the difficulty of racial humor serving a prosocial function, especially when it is articulated by a white performer about a person belonging to one of America's many outgroups.

Thus, returning to Saucier, O'Dea, and Strain's categories of racial humor, rather than prosocial, one can characterize racial humor as "antisocial" in both intent and effect, meaning that this disparaging humor attacks certain groups, with the result that it "not only [targets] outgroups but also [impacts] subsequent evaluations of those groups' members by individuals who are exposed to the joke" (76). Raúl Pérez's work on racial humor argues for its antisocial effects, particularly as he traces its long history in America as a tool for racial division, from blackface to the present. Pérez deploys the same framework I have been using here, colorblind racism, in order to consider humor's role in discussing race. He argues that "in a supposedly 'color-blind' society, racist humor continues to be used as a social pleasure that reinforces racist sentiments and ideologies" (957).¹⁷ Pérez explains that while laughter creates "social affiliation," its "dark side" divides social groups by "generating and reinforcing social boundaries, social distance and inequalities" (958). When this humor comes at the expense of the moral, intellectual, and ethical representation of someone from an outgroup, such as a racial or ethnic Other, it creates a bond among those comprising the in-group, so that "humor aids in reproducing and popularizing notions of racial superiority and inferiority."¹⁸

---

[15] Rossing acknowledges Colbert's white male privilege, which he sees as an asset, something that will appeal to and draw in more cynical viewers. In this article, he only discusses Colbert during his tenure on Comedy Central.

[16] As a result, Rossing advocates, "Rather than dismissing racial humor because it may confirm some racist ideologies or because it fails to address an issue in its full complexity, critical communication scholars should carefully consider the educative and transformative potential of humor" (57).

[17] Pérez notes the paradox here: "While such activity challenges the very notion, the myth, that we live in a color-blind society, many deny that such humor is socially harmful and insist that these are 'just jokes'" (957).

[18] In this way, humor can reflect society's power imbalances, which is "why white ridicule of blacks and people of color is different from people of color ridiculing whites, as the insult and ridicule of whites by people of color has not carried the same social, political and historical *weight* and consequences" (Pérez 958, 959).

Thus, Pérez contends that in a colorblind society, humor recreates and disseminates "racial stereotypes, narratives, imagery, and emotions, while fostering racial affiliation, reinforcing racial boundaries and ideologies, and aiding racial formation" (959). In other words, in a colorblind society, racist humor allows a public racist discourse, especially by whites, that would not be utterable otherwise, and does so in a way that positions racism as "unserious" and therefore far removed from "racial hatred" (970). Pérez's compelling argument sheds light on the difficulty that comedians face when attempting to perform prosocial racial humor; whatever their intent, their consideration of race may simply reinforce same-race affiliations as well as different-race boundaries.

In fact, the work of Brendon Barnes, Ingrid Palmary, and Kevin Durrheim on the use of racial humor in commonplace racial dialogues reaches conclusions that support Pérez's claim about humor as a means of discussing race while seemingly distancing oneself from racist ideology. In their discourse analysis of secretly taped individuals in South Africa, they note that humor was often used as a way of introducing race into a conversation (327). Moreover, within a given exchange, white speakers dialoguing about sensitive racial topics with an interracial couple also deployed humor as a rhetorical strategy to shield themselves from accusations of racism and, particularly important to a discussion of *Othello: The Remix*, to dispel "the tension associated with racial discourse, that is, to ease the atmosphere when a person touches on an especially sensitive topic" (328). Humor is therefore transactional, for it "invites humorous responses in other speakers, thus preventing a hostile response to the comment given that the atmosphere is lighthearted rather than confrontational" (329). Ultimately, Barnes, Palmary, and Durrheim conclude that humor deployed during racially challenging moments invites laughter in order to "[discourage] others from inferring racism due to the inappropriateness of anger as a response to [humor]," and as a way for the speaker to "mock racist beliefs and individuals" even as the speaker "[reproduces] racist stereotypes" (331). Barnes, Palmary, and Durrheim's study is significant in that it shifts focus away from a person's beliefs and attitudes toward the use of humor as a strategy for navigating race in an interpersonal context. Their conclusions thus shed light on the Q Brothers' use of humor, which does not need to depend on racist assumptions and beliefs in order to perpetuate vexed racial dynamics. For a close examination of humor in *Othello: The Remix* reveals that the Q Brothers mirror the very dynamics the study identifies: the deployment of humor as a means of minimizing racial tension through distraction *and* as a way to distance themselves from any suggestions of racism even as they restage and therefore reinscribe racial stereotypes.

"But there's comedy in it": Comedy as Racial Balm

The Q Brothers' decision to highlight comedy proves puzzling, especially in light of their chosen Shakespearean play. Audience laughter already causes problems regarding both the presentation and reception of *Othello* even when creators do not emphasize it. In a plenary at the 2016 World Shakespeare Congress in which Ayanna Thompson interviewed actor Adrian Lester, he addressed the tension audience laughter creates, remarking, "I don't like the play . . . I worry for Desdemona. I'm disgusted at that kind of behavior. I'm disgusted at the fact that Iago makes people laugh" (17). Lester explains that in the 2013 National Theatre production, in which he played Othello, director Nicholas Hytner attempted to calibrate the performance in order to eradicate audience laughter: "Nick came in again and said, 'We haven't got it yet. We got it when they shut up and don't laugh at it.' And we worked, and worked, and worked. I don't think we ever got rid of all of the laughs, but we reduced them" (17). This is not simply an issue with Hytner's production, however. Ruben Espinosa recounts watching *Othello* at Shakespeare's Globe with Mark Rylance playing Iago and André Holland playing Othello. In this 2018 performance, "The audience leaned into the laughter that Rylance provoked, and then they leaned into the racism and misogyny by laughing at it instead of expressing repulsion at the racist and sexist language. Looking up at the gifted actor, André Holland, it was difficult not to imagine that this laughter weighed heavy on him" (*Shakespeare on the Shades* 18). Laughter at *Othello* may function for some as a reaction to nervousness, but even so, these examples signal the work any production of the play must undertake. Those staging *Othello* must be aware of laughter's presence and work to reduce it when possible. The Q Brothers take the opposite approach, however. They cater to laughter. By incorporating heightened comedic elements into the *Othello* narrative, and emphasizing them accordingly, *Othello: The Remix* therefore exacerbates the tension between laughter and *Othello*'s narrative that Lester identifies.

Within the operetta, comedy often abates the racial tension inherent in *Othello*'s narrative. Nowhere is this dynamic clearer than in the production's depiction of Brabantio confronting Othello after learning about the elopement. Ironically, though the Q Brothers' overall narrative approach sidesteps the nuances of racial identity and dynamics of racial prejudice, with their depiction of Brabantio—specifically, his concerns about Desdemona's interracial relationship—the production comes closest to a thoughtful consideration of the complexities surrounding the construction of race and the manifestation of racism. It does so as Brabantio conflates gendered sexual purity with nationalistic purity. An extended analysis of this moment's racialized ideological potency exposes just how much the Q Brothers' deployment of humor undermines true inquiry into racial injustice. Wearing a red smoking jacket and a cravat, Brabantio enters center stage and exclaims, "This [the relationship between Desdemona and Othello] has to be a joke./You're a good girl, crazy 'bout Elvis, true./You love horses, of course, and America too" (Q Brothers 13). These are slightly revised lines from the opening stanza of rocker Tom Petty's 1989 hit "Free Fallin'":

> She's a good girl, loves her mama
> Loves Jesus and America too
> She's a good girl, who's crazy 'bout Elvis
> Loves horses and her boyfriend too.

In service to Desdemona's backstory, the Q Brothers excise references to "her mama," and "Loves Jesus." More significant, however, is the fact that "and her boyfriend too" no longer follows the line about horses. The reference to loving horses serves as a slant invocation of Iago's "you'll have your daughter covered with a Barbary horse" (I, i, 113). Yet this allusion to the Shakespearean Desdemona's sexuality only stands out all the more because Brabantio attempts to erase Desdemona's sexuality in *Othello: The Remix*. Petty's mention of a boyfriend no longer exists; Brabantio thereby subtly establishes Desdemona's supposed sexual purity by leaving no trace of romantic affection. He then connects sexual purity with national devotion in a rhetorical move that echoes the language and thinking comprising the "self-preserving instinct of Shakespeare's Venice, or Shakespeare's England, [where] a white woman's marrying a black man . . . amounts to nothing less than a violation of national proportions" (Little Jr., *Shakespeare Jungle Fever* 87). In Brabantio's lines, America replaces "her boyfriend" as the object of "She's" affection, becoming, "You love horses, of course, and America too." While the overall purpose remains the same—to convey an all-American girl—these lyrical adaptations create a different logic, one that rests on female purity in which desire is displaced from a romantic object of affection onto a patriotic ideal embodied by the great signifier that is "America."

The racial assumptions underpinning America's signification become clear as Brabantio opines that he cannot "understand how he [Othello] attracts a child so innocent,/Perfect and pure, sweet and lily-white" (Q Brothers 13). Here, the racialized language of whiteness invoked through "pure" and "lily-white" morphs Desdemona's supposed American patriotism into Brabantio's white nationalism. The language of innocence and Desdemona's infantilization once again reveal anxiety about female sexuality. But soon Brabantio's logic moves in a different direction. His reference to purity and her "lily-white" skin functions just as what Kim F. Hall has termed the "poetics of color" in the Renaissance did (*Things of Darkness* 67), signifying morality, beauty, and race all at once (70, 71). Brabantio's logic implies the illogicality of Desdemona's attraction because of the distinction between her and what she supposedly desires, a distinction only heightened when he asserts that "bunnies don't befriend big bears" (Q Brothers 13). Furthermore, Brabantio dismisses the belief that "we can all just get along," calling it "silly." If Brabantio's disbelief at the relationship rests on his rejection that seeming opposites cannot attract, then one can only assume that if Desdemona is pure, Othello is not pure; if she is lily white, he must be black as "pitch" (II, iii, 320). What does this mean about the America Desdemona supposedly loves? If one unpacks the assumptions underlying Brabantio's assertions, for it to be acceptable to him, this must be an America also pure, also idealized, and though he never says it outright, also white. For if we *cannot* all get along, then the ideal he seems to embrace and espouse can only be achieved once all that embodies the opposite of this romanticized, unsullied whiteness—the "big bear," so to speak—is removed. Intended or not, because of its exploration of interracial relationships, Brabantio's speech exposes the complex, competing, and complementary ways America constructs race. It also reveals how Americans articulate exclusionary, racist ideologies through coded, indirect rhetoric that nevertheless depends on the ideology of white supremacy and superiority.

It should perhaps come as no surprise, then, that as Brabantio continues, he articulates the racial nightmare held historically by white America (and beyond) of Black male rapacity. As his speech builds, it climaxes with his assertion, "You're so small, he's so much bigger,/I just don't see you with that . . . that . . . (pause)" (13). Though not as explicit as it could be, in invoking Othello's size in relation to

Desdemona after emphasizing her color, Brabantio invokes the trope of the Black male rapist while stopping one step shy of using virulent racist language. At this moment, Othello, who has bemusedly stood beside Brabantio, looks shocked. Clearly, the need to complete the rhyming couplet leaves the unspoken word "nigger" hanging over the theatre, only filled in by the audience. Up until this scene, the Q Brothers have sanitized the racial conflict in the narrative by never having Brabantio—and Iago before him—utter the vile racist language made so famous in Shakespeare's play. Their omission thereby elides the violent language of racism. In the pause, however, the discourse exists as an absent presence. This powerful decision therefore makes the audience complicit in Brabantio's racist musings by filling in the discursive gaps. The resonance of the moment looms over the rest of the interchange, so that when Brabantio insists, "I was gonna say rapper, you didn't let me finish" (13), the line comes across as disingenuous not only because of his tone but also because of the slant rhyme created by "rapper." What one is left with, then, is a speech that begins with coded racial messaging but that ultimately becomes much more explicit. It is, therefore, *Othello: The Remix*'s most sustained engagement with race.

I stress this moment's potential for provocatively interrogating race because understanding its significance for scrutinizing racial identity and race relations raises the question: why would the Q Brothers back away from the difficulties that make this exchange between Brabantio and Othello so rich? Yet they defuse the tension raised by the interchange through a strategic deployment of humor as an antidote to the bitter racial reality articulated by Brabantio. GQ's take on Brabantio in fact depends on humor, for he affects a quavering, high-pitched voice that makes Brabantio sound like a cranky old man, a characterization only heightened by his costuming and the fact that GQ plays him as hunched over, walking with a cane. The choice to have Pringle play Othello with a bemused smile during Brabantio's complaint only heightens the comedic details seemingly meant to alleviate the thematic tension of the encounter by making his racist points come across as "no big deal." Furthermore, the choice to have Brabantio deliver his rebuttal that he meant "rapper" in a whiny, almost toddler-like voice likewise adds levity to the moment. Indeed, if there were any doubt as to the Q Brothers' desire to evacuate the moment of the racist characterization at the heart of its conflict, one need look no further than the Chorus's response after Brabantio declares, "I have no daughter!" (14). The Collective narrates, "He turned his back on her,/But not out of hatred./He was stuck in the ways of a/different generation" (14). These lines shed light on the use of Petty's song to introduce Brabantio, as well as on GQ's choice to play Brabantio as aged through styling, posture, and tone of voice. The Q Brothers' discomfort with race comes through in this clear disavowal of racism. Brabantio has no "hatred"; rather, his issue is generational. He is stuck in the old ways. But what ways are these? The production wants to play Brabantio both as racist and yet not, a bigot yet a well-meaning one. Comedy serves as the distracting factor that can help an audience ignore the contradictions inherent in the production's characterization of Brabantio, and within it, the Q Brothers' reluctance to engage with racism seriously as a motivating factor for Othello's alienation.

The Q Brothers deploy the same distraction-through-comedy strategy in a confrontation between Iago and Othello. In this scene, however, comedy works not to defuse racial tension but rather to distract from its absence, by, paradoxically, depending on stereotypical racialized humor. This instance occurs as a part of the interchange between Othello and Iago in what serves as *Othello: The Remix*'s equivalent of Othello's psychological seduction in III, iii. Iago jumps almost immediately to telling Othello about Cassio's behavior during his inebriated dream. As Othello's jealousy mounts, Iago advises, "Cassio's a screw up and it's bad for business. You just gotta axe him" (50). The context makes Iago's comment clear; Othello must fire Cassio. But this comment turns into racialized humor when Othello responds, "Axe him what?" to which Iago retorts, "No, axed from the line-up . . ." (51). During his reply, Othello's face registers his confusion. He interprets "axe" as "ask," thus necessitating the clarification from Iago. I characterize this as racialized humor because as journalist Shereen Marisol Meraji observes, "The most common stereotype of black vernacular is the pronunciation of the word 'ask' as 'ax.'" Linguist John Rickford identifies this as one of the "Distinctive phonological (pronunciation) features of AAVE [African American Vernacular English]" (4), which includes, "Metathesis or transposition of adjacent consonants, as in *aks* for SE [Standard English] 'ask' (one of the biggest shibboleths of AAVE, often referred to by teachers, personnel officers, and other gatekeepers in the course of putting down the variety) . . ." (5). People have said or written "ax" for centuries—it was even used by Chaucer—Jesse Sheidlower, the president of the American Dialect Society, explains (qtd. in Meraji). Yet today, "Pronounce 'ask' as 'ax' and immediately many will assume that you're poor, black, and uneducated." Despite its history, then, *ax* functions as a widely recognized racialized pronunciation. Parallels thus exist between Othello's speech in the ad-rap-tation and what Robert Hornback traces as "early constructions of black characters via a broken speech pattern," which "enacted proto-racist stereotypes in racial impersonation that helped to rationalize African slavery across Western Europe and across the Atlantic" (143). He elaborates, "When such constructions continued in later antebellum minstrelsy, they merely solidified a preexisting paternalistic image of a stereotypical black speaker as inherently ignorant, inseparable from foolish mental debility, and as a result, above all, as exhibiting a child-like dependence." With this historical representation of Blackness and speech in mind, one can see how "axe's" use in *Othello: The Remix* serves several purposes. It heightens the power imbalance between Iago and Othello by having the former correct the latter during one of Othello's most vulnerable moments. Furthermore, for the length of the exchange, it positions Iago as more intelligent than Othello through his discursive facility, one which signals as white in opposition to both the recurrent hip hop lingo influencing *all* characters' speech patterns and more narrowly, in distinction to Othello's Black speech.

It also follows the Q Brothers' pattern of inserting moments of humor, even if ever so brief, during confrontations. The use of this humor not only reduces the interpersonal tension within the exchange, but it also shifts attention away from the adaptive change the Q Brothers make. In *Othello*, Iago famously echoes Brabantio's assertions about Desdemona's erring nature as he emphasizes her rejection of matches "Of her own clime, complexion, and degree/ Whereto we see in all things nature tends" (III, iii, 47, 48). As scholars have long noted, Othello picks up on the racial assumptions underlying Iago's (and Brabantio's) allegations as he echoes the racialized language that opened the play, applying it to himself for the first time. In *Othello: The Remix*, however, Iago never once mentions race nor exploits racial difference as a means of attacking Othello's sense of self. This decision changes the reasons prompting Othello's descent into violence, for it removes the possibility of racial abuse as a motivating factor for Othello's mental deterioration. Concomitantly, it heightens the possibility of interpreting the pathology as lying within Othello, and more insidiously, within his Blackness. With this comedic deployment of "axe," however, race makes an appearance, though for very different purposes. Yet to the casual observer, it might just be enough to make one believe that race remains central to this crucial dialogue between villain and protagonist. Ultimately, then, this emphasis on comedy creates audience amusement, which in turn blinds the audience to both the vexed racial presence *and* pointed racial absences within *Othello: The Remix*.

The comedy within *Othello: The Remix* merits critique not only because it distracts from *Othello*'s more serious elements, but also because it depends on stereotypes in order to do so as exemplified by the "axe/ask" linguistic confusion. Such stereotypes become most visible through the depictions of Bianca and Loco Vito (both played by JQ). Bianca, here less a prostitute and more Cassio's devoted fangirl, embodies the caricature of the urban Latina. Clown-like in her neon-pink afro, Bianca sashays her way across the stage, hands on hips, with oversized hoop earrings joined with her speech and attitude marking her as a woman of color. Bianca speaks in something akin to a Nuyorican accent, most notably when she exclaims over Cassio, "oh what a maing [man]!" (Q Brothers 25). As part of the hip hop framing, Bianca signifies in the vein of an unpolished Jennifer Lopez, a Latinx woman "from the block" with attitude to match, coded as such in the script description which calls her "fiery and feisty" (1). Certainly, Bianca's comedic depiction does not rest solely on stereotypes. Her obsession with Cassio—as signaled when she recounts, "it's been so long Cassio, like a week!/ . . . But that's 7 days, 168 hours!/10,080 minutes, has our love soured?" (25)—serves to elicit significant audience laughter. But her Latina stereotyping works alongside her romantic fixation as a way of adding stereotypical humor to the ad-rap-tation.

Loco Vito, the production's equivalent to the Duke, is also a Latinx side character, and his ethnicity too serves as comedic relief. Described by the narrators as "a hard core gangster" (26), Loco Vito talks in a Chicano accent, a characterization heightened by his distinguishing props: dark sunglasses and a lime green bandanna tied around his head. As the character description notes, "He is a West Coast Chicano gangster who loves tennis" (1). Unlike Bianca, Loco Vito's accent does not directly create humor within the production. Rather, like Bianca, he derives laugh lines due to an obsession, in his case, with tennis. For instance, when describing the difficulty of a tour consisting of seventy-eight shows in eighty-one days, Loco Vito declares, "It's the toughest job most of you will ever see!/ Like tryin' to beat Bjorn Borg, you know, in the Seventies" (27). Similarly, when praising Othello's marriage to Desdemona, he notes, "Marriage requires trust, discipline, and patience./Like a good tennis volley, it's a beautiful thing./Like Boris Becker had—a beautiful swing" (28). These repeated allusions to tennis, however, depend on

Loco Vito's ethnicity and hip hop persona in order to prompt laughter. Humor exists due to the irony inherent in this "hard core" gangster's fixation with tennis, a game much stuffier than the cool world of hip hop, and much whiter too, particularly emphasized by Loco Vito's references to Scandinavian and German players. As Claudia Rankine reminds the reader in *Citizen: An American Lyric*, tennis is a white sport, a fact especially highlighted by the presence of sisters Serena and Venus Williams. She observes, "They win sometimes, they lose sometimes, they've been injured, and they've been happy, they've been sad, ignored, booed mightily, they've been cheered, and through it all and evident to all were those people who are enraged they are there at all—graphite against a sharp white background" (26); more succinctly, she notes how in Serena's case, "[nothing] could shield her ultimately from people who felt her black body didn't belong on their court, in their world." In other words, the Williams sisters, and Serena's ascendancy to arguably the greatest player of all time, have through their contrast exposed the whiteness of tennis. Thus, the humor residing in Loco Vito's lines depends on ethnic distinctions— the fact that a gangster, inner-city Latinx man articulates his passion for a decidedly and overwhelmingly white sport. One may counter that tennis functions here as a means of cultural exchange. But Loco Vito's comments are entirely played for laughs based on the friction between his interests and his Chicano persona. Exchange thus proves uneasy at best. Certainly, stereotypes function much less obviously with Loco Vito than they do with Bianca. Even so, both of these secondary characters veer into caricature as the Q Brothers attempt to inject the comedy they recognize in Shakespeare's original tale into *Othello: The Remix*. The humor, however, fosters a levity in response to these racial and ethnic stereotypes, thereby creating another means of achieving audience colorblindness through stereotyping in the performance's engagement with ethnic and racial Others.

Stereotypes and Their Aftereffects

This dependence on stereotypes is a problem in and of itself, for it only perpetuates common caricatures of persons of color for a predominantly white audience. After all, "The more frequently we encounter people whose appearance and behavior corresponds with our previous observations, the easier it is to create classification systems to contain them" (Young 4). Though not as extreme, this decision echoes the power dynamics inherent in the humor associated with minstrel shows. Whether played to American audiences or those abroad, and whether performed as originally done by white men in blackface or as embodied much later by African American performers, minstrel shows depended on parodic burlesque versions of Black men and women. In other words, they derived audience appeal from simplified and amplified representations created to elicit laughs from the audience. This is not to say that *Othello: The Remix* is, as Douglas M. Lanier calls the Q Brothers' earlier *The Bomb-itty of Errors*, "an updated minstrel show" (Lanier, "Minstrelsy"). But in choosing to emphasize humor over careful racial representation, the production creates an interpretive dynamic for the audience that fosters, almost paradoxically, a colorblind perspective *and* racial prejudice. When stereotypes come packaged through comedy, audiences may literally be able to laugh them off. As such, stereotyping becomes acceptable, enjoyable even, rather than pernicious. Put differently, easily digested stereotyping rejects nuanced racial representation, thereby eschewing a finessed audience interpretation. These repeated racial and ethnic caricatures thus prime the audience to further identify and associate stereotypes not only with the racial and ethnic Others on stage, but also those around them in day-to-day life. As such, audiences can more readily attribute characters' failings to pathologies stemming from their Otherness rather than with the systemic social issues the Q Brothers so noticeably ignore, and they can in turn repeat this racialized attribution when they leave the theatre.

This ability to simplify and pathologize a character most especially affects viewers' potential perception of Othello, particularly as jealousy consumes him, for he turns into an embodiment of a long-held American stereotype of Black masculinity. In Shakespeare's *Othello*, Othello's trajectory from "noble Moor" to "savage" mirrors early modern concerns about Otherness and barbarity.[19] As a modern retelling, *Othello: The Remix* similarly taps into racial concerns, but those with a more recent historical resonance, namely, the angry Black man or brute. As I explain in Chapter 1 and elsewhere, historians note that the brute stereotype was a caricature developed by white supremacists arguing for the innate viciousness of Black masculinity as a means of justifying lynching, especially during Reconstruction. The gangster rapper functions as a twentieth- and twenty-first-century

---

[19] For discussions of barbarity and race in the early modern period, see especially Ian Smith, *Race and Rhetoric in the Renaissance: Barbarian Errors* (Palgrave 2009) and Lara Bovilsky, *Barbarous Play: Race on the English Renaissance Stage* (University of Minnesota Press, 2008).

subset of this historical stereotype (Corredera, "Far More Black"). In some ways, Postell's Othello mirrors this gangster rapper with his gold chains, backward baseball cap, and references to his "hood" upbringing. His beats and flow never echo the hard-hitting style of most gangster rappers, but aural considerations likely fall by the wayside as Othello turns to violence. Othello thereby embodies the critique so often launched against Black masculinity as represented in hip hop.

Further exacerbating Othello's one-dimensionality is the fact that Desdemona's absence from the production omits a sustained complimentary view of Othello. The decision to exclude all but Desdemona's disembodied voice from the operetta in many ways mirrors the prop-like use of women in hip hop culture, though with a crucial difference: Desdemona is white, while the women often demeaned in hip hop are Black. Before addressing the significance of this distinction, however, one must understand critiques leveled against hip hop's use and representation of women. It is now fairly commonplace knowledge that "Hip hop as a genre has received a great deal of criticism of misogynist lyrics and sexist representations of women ... Too often, hip hop portrays women as gold diggers seeking only to take advantage of men, as disease carriers and self-hating, hypersexualized animals who shake their stuff for the camera, and as symbols of capitalist acquisition" (Perry 128). Alesha Dominek Washington too notes the prevalent image of women in hip hop: "materialistic, promiscuous, and sexually available" (80). Rose draws the connection between these depictions and the way Western culture at large depicts women, arguing, "The most visible representations of black women in hip hop reflect the hallmarks of mainstream masculinity: They regularly use women as props that boost male egos, treat women's bodies as sexual objects, and divide women into groups that are worthy of protection and respect and those that are not" (119). Mark Anthony Neal adds further specificity, arguing that hip hop is "a world best described as having a 'bitch/queen' complex," in which women can be sexually exploited yet at the same time praised for their "spiritual grounding" (*New Black Man* 130). In *Othello: The Remix*, Desdemona's corporeal exclusion from the production makes her the prop-like woman Rose identifies. She never speaks, only sings or moans, so that even as *Othello: The Remix* makes room for her role in Othello's narrative, it never allows for a shift in attention away from the performance of masculinity enacted by the all-male Q Brothers Collective. Furthermore, Othello's move from ardent love to fiery jealousy mirrors the dichotomy Neal identifies concerning women's role in hip hop. Desdemona starts off as the "queen" who provides Othello with meaning, purpose, and artistic success but eventually transforms into the sexually unfaithful "bitch" who must be destroyed. Othello therefore embodies the hip hop misogyny so often railed against in criticisms of the genre.

What audiences of *Othello: The Remix* may not realize, however, is that typical hip hop artists direct their misogyny against Black women rather than white women. Hip hop, in other words, often enacts what Moya Bailey developed as the concept of *misogynoir*, a term addressing "the specific violence of representational imagery depicting Black women ... particular kind[s] of racist, sexist tropes" (341, 342). Further reenacting the erasure endemic to cultural treatments of and engagements with hip hop, however, the Q Brothers mute the genre's misogynoir by focusing on misogyny directed against white women. This is not to say that such misogyny does not merit critique, but it does direct attention to women who already most often garner societal sympathy. As such, *Othello: The Remix* obfuscates the true recipients of hip hop's sexist structures by excising Black women from hip hop's narrative rather than pushing the audience to recognize the particular forms of racialized and sexist abuse Black women face. Yet this distinction will likely not matter for an audience that can find its expectations about the treatment of women in hip hop verified by the performance, a confirmation likely only heightened by having a white woman as the victim of this Black male misogyny. What the audience is left with, then, is an Othello that in no way challenges stereotypical expectations about Black masculinity; rather, he fully embodies them.

These performance choices take on heightened significance because of the minimal discourse on race within *Othello: The Remix*, which if present could serve as a counterpoint to the violent, misogynistic version of Black masculinity the Q Brothers otherwise depict. In fact, though race and its importance to the play has some presence at the start of the production, however humorously and limitedly addressed, as the ad-rap-tation unfolds, race virtually disappears from the production until *Othello: The Remix* concludes. Performance reviews across locales mirror *Othello: The Remix*'s thematic and discursive erasure of race. Certain reviews do not remark on race, such as Lawrence Bommer's in *Stage and Cinema* who claims that "Nothing's lost in this deft translation or delirious presentation." Others instead use euphemistic phrasing onto which one *could* read critique of race's absence, but certainly would not need to. The *Chicago Tribune*'s Chris Jones, for instance, notes *Othello*'s "undercurrent of racial complexity," then points out, "The piece could, for sure, go further down the rabbit hole of jealousy in a world that still has sharper lines of division. It shies away at some junctures." Kieran Yates from the *Guardian* observes that "many of the play's themes of power and betrayal remain," but does not mention race, and further comments, "The play's brutality felt largely missing." Only two note the way the production ignores race. Elizabeth Kipp-Giusti remarks in her review for *Theater is Easy*, "the show almost avoids talking about race entirely, a strange erasure of one of the most complicated themes in the original," while Raven Snook for *Time Out: New York* observes, "bizarrely, racial strife is practically ignored." These reviews signal the importance of what happens on stage. Ideally, Thompson contends, "Performance reviewers must be more attentive to the way in which a production makes race semiotically (ir)relevant. Thus, it should never be a mere matter of noting an actor's race in a review; rather, it should be a matter of assessing what and how a production renders the semiotic value and meaning of that actor's race" ("To Notice or Not to Notice"). When a production attempts to ignore race, however, it is easy to see how this type of "critically engaged" review fails to manifest (Thompson "To Notice or Not to Notice"). Stated differently, colorblindness in the production permits colorblindness outside of it. It is not a stretch, then, to suggest that, like the reviewers, audiences might not *see* race. But if they do, what they are left with is the stereotype of the violent, sexist gangster rapper, hip hop's long-held cultural whipping boy.

Colorblindness and Cultural Appropriation Revisited

This colorblind approach to race—created by minimizing race's presence and by deploying comedy—limits the potency of *Othello: The Remix*'s hip hop framing. For the interrogation of racial identity and inequity is one of hip hop's most powerful social and generic contributions. Rose reminds readers that even though mainstream hip hop may have diminished this particular resonance, at one time, "hip hop was a locally inspired explosion of exuberance and political energy tethered to the idea of rehabilitating community" (ix). Asante Jr. explains the stakes of this shift in the genre, "When we consider hip hop's origins and purpose, we understand it is a revolutionary cultural force that was intended to challenge the status quo and greater American culture. So, its relegation to reflecting American culture becomes extremely problematic if one considers the radical tradition of African American social movements—which have never been about mirroring dominant culture" (8). This inventive, polemical form of hip hop is once again on the rise, challenging the materialistic gangster rap made prevalent and commercially viable during the 1990s and 2000s. As a result of the Q Brothers' decision to re-present only the most readily attainable forms of hip hop—an interesting choice made by men claiming how formative hip hop was for them growing up—they foreclose the possibility of tapping into hip hop's vibrant political potential. It thus becomes difficult to articulate antiracism when there is little acknowledgment of racism in the first place. The Q Brothers' racial colorblindness, then, comes at a cost, both by limiting the thematic resonances in their reinterpretation of *Othello* and by circumscribing the power of the generic form they use to deliver their retelling.

With the Q Brothers' colorblind production in mind, one can return to their unasked question: when it comes to hip hop, do the Q Brothers borrow or steal? Do they or do they not culturally appropriate hip hop? Admittedly, even with the evident colorblindness pervading *Othello: The Remix*, it is difficult to answer this question. As persons of color, the Q Brothers are not members of America's dominant culture. Furthermore, the key to cultural appropriation is the lack of acknowledgment regarding the culture from which an artifact is borrowed. Across *Othello: The Remix*, the Q Brothers repeatedly pay homage to great hip hop performers and songs through their lyrics, which sample from artists such as Common and Erykah Badu ("The Light"), Jay-Z ("99 Problems"), A Tribe Called Quest ("Electrical Relaxation"), and 50 Cent ("In Da Club") (Hutchinson). It is actually Shakespeare that introduces the power imbalance inherent in cultural appropriation. For, despite its joy in hip hop, this production still reflects the dynamics of cultural appropriation by using a marginalized culture (hip hop, predominantly associated with Blackness) in order to advance a dominant culture (Shakespeare, predominantly associated with whiteness). The erasure of identity central to cultural appropriation also exists here, for the Q Brothers erase the Black racial politics of hip hop to achieve this advancement. That is the question here: is hip hop Shakespeare only palatable without a racial polemic? For the Q Brothers, the answer seems to be "yes." And this silencing leaves the image of the stereotypical, pathological Black man in its wake. Being part-Indian does not inoculate the Q Brothers from reflecting the dynamics of white supremacy, even if inadvertently. Ibram X. Kendi reminds readers, "Racist ideas are ideas. Anyone can produce them or consume them ... Anyone—Whites, Latina/os, Blacks, Asians, Native Americans—anyone can express the idea that

Black people are inferior, that something is wrong with Black people" (*Stamped from the Beginning* 10). Unsurprisingly, the silencing of Blackness results in antiblackness in the performance's representation of Black masculinity—the cost of making hip hop Shakespeare palatable to the white, middle-class patrons who frequent the theatre.

The muting of racial polemic, and with it an interrogation of white supremacy, is in fact a broader issue when it comes to deploying hip hop in high-status venues. Consider Lin-Manuel Miranda's Broadway sensation, the hip hop historical musical *Hamilton* (2015), to which *Othello: The Remix* has been frequently compared in interviews.[20] *Hamilton* is arguably even more radical in its aesthetic project in that it casts America's founding fathers (and more nominally, mothers) with persons of color and has key US documents and philosophies delivered through rapping. Unlike *Othello: The Remix*, *Hamilton* does acknowledge racial issues. For instance, across several songs, Alexander Hamilton mentions that his good friend John Laurens is fighting for the abolition of slavery. Moreover, the musical directly confronts the limitations of America's racial progressivism during the Enlightenment in the song "Yorktown (The World Turned Upside Down)" when, after the important victory that signals the end of revolutionary conflict within the musical, Laurens raps, "Black and white soldiers wonder alike if this really means freedom," to which George Washington replies with an emphatic, "Not yet" (122). A reference note Miranda includes in *Hamilton: The Revolution*, written by him and Jeremy McCarter, makes it evident that Washington's response applies across racial lines, for Miranda comments, "Washington, of course, owned hundreds of slaves, and did not emancipate them until his death at the end of the century" (note 7). The production also references slavery directly in "Cabinet Battle # 1" when Hamilton

---

[20] People frequently reference *Hamilton* when discussing *Othello: The Remix*. For instance, in an interview for the podcast *Shakespeare Unlimited*, Barbara Bogaev remarks to the brothers, ". . . *Hamilton* has happened, and *In the Heights*, and it seems like those shows, I would imagine, would make it both easier and maybe harder to get the word out about a new hip hop show." The brothers respond, regarding *Hamilton*, ". . . one awesome thing that we can point to that *Hamilton* and Lin-Manuel has done for our work is that people now have less of a preconceived notion, something they can let go of. The public now perceives hip hop as accessible in theater" ("Episode 64", *Shakespeare Unlimited*). Briefer examples include the title of a 2016 *Playbill* article on the Q Brothers, which employs the headline, "16 Years Before *Hamilton*, The Q Brothers Were Bringing Hip Hop to the Stage," and a 2015 *Chicago Tribune* article promoting *A Q Brothers' Christmas Carol*, which opens with the line, "Long before the world had 'Hamilton,' Chicago had the Q Brothers and their 'ad-rap-tations' of classic plays."

reminds Thomas Jefferson, "Your debts are paid cuz you don't pay for labor . . . We know who's really doing the planting" (161). These details suggest that despite frequent comparisons between *Hamilton* and *Othello: The Remix*, the former strives to be much more radical in its artistic vision for and engagement with race.

Yet even as *Hamilton* reimagines American history by centralizing the voices of persons of color, the musical also mutes the racial inequities both plaguing and shaping the foundation of the United States. Consider the cut song "Cabinet Battle #3," which *Hamilton: The Revolution* also titles "The Slavery Debate." This song did not make the final version of *Hamilton* because, according to Miranda and McCarter, it "didn't shed new light on the characters—the point after all, is that none of the Founding Fathers did anything to stop it—so the song had to go" (223). Yet the song would have been a "fierce" reminder of our "national shame" (223, 206), one only otherwise gestured toward through brief references in the lyrics and through a moment near the end of the show where "Chris [Jackson], as Washington, bows his head in shame" while acknowledging Eliza Hamilton as "[Jackson's] way of having Washington accept responsibility for what he did and didn't do" (208). Thus, even a production like *Hamilton* that decentralizes whiteness through its use of hip hop and of performers of color struggles to fully confront the horrors of America's racial past and to stridently indict traditional views of whiteness, whether those held by the white heroes of our national mythology or the white inhabitants of modern day. Because *Othello: The Remix* is not comprised of the creative choices that afford *Hamilton* the potential for the benefit of the doubt in regard to ameliorating its racial blind spots, the production has that much more difficult a task when it comes to this confrontation.

Othello: The Remix, a Post-Racial Product

Rather than being groundbreaking, *Othello: The Remix* is very much a product of its 2012 post-racial time. In its evacuation of race from both *Othello*'s narrative and from its hip hop framing, *Othello: The Remix* encapsulates the post-racial dynamics of an America that "doesn't see race." Consider what this national entry says to a global audience about race and the United States as a result. Essentially, it writes small at least three of America's pervasive racial problems, namely the marginalization of the racial Other, the reification of racial stereotypes, and the appropriation of Black culture (as well as systemic sexism), all while distracting the audience from these issues with good beats and well-timed ripostes. First, even as *Othello: The Remix* attempts to present a version of America that ostensibly celebrates its diversity, it inadvertently stresses the sustained Othering of Black culture by the white hegemonic powers that be—in this case, the Globe Theatre. Carla Della Gatta explains how "language restrictions [were] integral to the design of the festival. Only the Globe players were given the freedom to claim the stage by employing the use of spoken English, as the festival mandated that all other theatre companies translate Shakespeare's plays" (76). Thus, amid versions of Shakespeare performed in British Sign Language, Maori, Urdu, Yoruba, and Hebrew, the Globe's rules positioned hip hop's discourse as a foreign language. One might argue that the presence of different forms of Spanish (Mexican, Castilian, and Argentinian) as well as Arabic (Juba and Palestinian) suggest that the hip hop language in *Othello: The Remix* could be interpreted as a different form of English. However, as Della Gatta elaborates, "Hip hop was deemed a 'language,' although it was the only language in the festival that is not recognized by linguists as such" (77). While Spanish or Arabic are preceded by regional clarifiers, one can take no such approach to describe the English used in *Othello: The Remix*. The unstated subtext here is that this English differs because of its racialized history, or put more frankly, its Black history. Race may not be acknowledged, but it is certainly seen, or in this case, heard.

Second, as elaborated on above, *Othello: The Remix* reinscribes the following racial caricatures: the sassy Latina, the gangster Chicano, the victimized white woman, and relatedly, the violent, ghetto Black man. It is difficult to know the demographic makeup of the audience attending *Othello: The Remix* at the Globe. But whether these were international tourists, curious locals, or a mix of the two, they left the performance with common American racial stereotypes re-presented, and for some, reaffirmed. In his discussion of hip hop and stereotypes, White illuminates how the stereotypes that comprise hip hop culture work, especially for non-Black audiences and particularly regarding Black masculinity:

> The Black body and representations of Black masculinity in hardcore styles of hip-hop performance are socially constructed kinds of gender and racial performance that are historically marked by notions around criminality, deviance, and pathology and that are deeply implicated in the construction of an African Americanized white masculinity mediated through popular culture media. (23)

Even if the rap artist may intend this type of caricature as a form of speaking back to (white) power, as Perry contends, White argues that the problem often lies with the audience. He maintains:

> Whites and other racial and ethnic groups who may have had little contact with black males except through such representations may find it difficult to see beyond the persona of the hardcore gangsta as performance, or in any case, as one kind of performance of black maleness that may be part real and part artifice. (23)

I cannot answer how much contact the Globe's audience previously had with Black males. But the mere possibility that this authoritative Shakespearean race play, performed in an authoritative space during a festival ostensibly celebrating both Shakespeare's global appeal and the richness of diverse national identities, presented caricatured racial personas that subsequently *could have* been perceived as real is enough to expose the pitfalls of performing race while refusing to truly see it.

Third, the Q Brothers' cultural appropriation of hip hop mirrors the neocolonial attitude toward African American culture, and hip hop more specifically, taken by the American nation. Asante Jr. helpfully draws the connection between neocolonialism and hip hop. Neocolonialism essentially functions as a series of "economic arrangements" based upon exploitation which maintain the power structure of the former colonizing force over those formerly colonized (110, 111). For instance, "raw materials are taken from places like Ghana and sold to the citizens of the mother country" (113). Though hip hop may not seem to have direct ties to the colonial world of the colonizer and colonized, as Asante Jr. explains:

> Blacks in the inner cities share many of the characteristics of the colonized ... So essentially, the ghetto—with poverty, poor schools, drugs, police terrorism, et cetera—provides raw materials needed to produce rap. Then, just as the gold and diamonds that are taken from Africa are primarily sold in the mother countries (Europe and the United States), rap is mainly purchased by a white audience, the parent companies' citizens, if you will. (113)

Neocolonialism, then, shares many of the qualities of cultural appropriation with the addition of an economic component. Thus, just as white American culture has appropriated hip hop culture—both within the music industry and in society at large—in order to adopt it without carrying the burden of the racial marginalization that inspired much of the genre's early artists (and many even today), so too do the Q Brothers utilize a sanitized form of hip hop for amplified artistic exposure via the Globe, and therefore also for financial gain. Indeed, it is this tempered version of hip hop that allows them to access the authorizing space of the Globe in the first place, a space that has served as representative of a Eurocentric culture. Furthermore, the humor, fun, and carefree engagement elicited from the audience in the Q Brothers' perpetuation of hip hop's cultural appropriation only encourages viewers to do the same. It is therefore perhaps apropos that this was the American national entry in the Globe to Globe festival. By taking a colorblind approach to race and encouraging the audience to do so as well, *Othello: The Remix* functions as a synecdoche of American sociopolitical approaches toward race, those that candy-coated the US's racial divisions to such a degree that the idea that the US is *not* post-racial in the wake of the 2016 elections came to many people, especially neoliberal white ones, as a shock.

In fact, this much more virulent tenor of racial conflict in the US post-2016 only makes *Othello: The Remix*'s whitewashed deployment of hip hop more noticeable. As racial subtext became explicit racist context, articulated virulently everywhere from social media to the press briefings of the Trump administration, accordingly, hip hop likewise turned political once more. Take artists like Kendrick Lamar, who in his song "Fear" (2017) tackles verbal and physical abuse as he discusses his fear of his mother with lines like "I beat yo' ass, keep talkin back" and "you gon' fear me if you don't fear no one else," yet in the second verse also addresses oppressive powers outside of the Black home when he wonders if he will "die from one of these bats and blue badges/Body-slammed on black and white paint, my bones snappin'"; Jay-Z, who in "The Story of OJ" (2017) tackles racial wealth disparity, noting that whether a Black man or woman is a "Light nigga, dark nigga, faux nigga, real nigga/Rich nigga, poor nigga, house nigga, field nigga" for white America, he or she is "Still nigga, still nigga," to which he responds by noting the importance of investments in property, art, and establishing "credit"; and Childish Gambino, whose Grammy-winning "This is America" (2018) warns Black artists, "This is America/Don't catch you slippin' now" while noting that "Police be trippin' now" amid a song that over 3 minutes and 46 seconds grapples with topics ranging from African American artistry and complicity in white supremacy to gun violence to the marginalization of Black artists and more. These are but a few examples of hip hop tracks that hearken back to the antiracist message of 1970s–80s rap while shedding the trappings of gangster violence from the 1990s and 2000s. They show what *Othello: The Remix* could have been: a deployment of hip hop that speaks not for Shakespeare but rather for Othello—for his Black identity and for the hip hop persona the Q Brothers have him represent—by focusing on the systemic racial injustices of the American nation.

Despite the myriad problems created by the Q Brothers' colorblind approach to race in *Othello: The Remix*, their production also provides possibility: the possibility of seeing what could make a more ethical, thoughtful engagement with hip hop and Shakespeare. Even as Conquergood takes the enthusiast to task for "a facile identification with the other," he notes that what he terms the immorality of this approach can be rectified by the creation of a dialogic performance: "This performative stance struggles to bring together different voices, world views, value systems, and beliefs so that they can have a conversation with one another. The aim of a dialogical performance is to bring self and other together so that they can question, debate, and challenge one another" (9). The creation of this type of performance necessitates speaking to and with the Other instead of about them, which in turn depends on three key qualities: "energy, imagination, and courage" (10). Anyone who has seen *Othello: The Remix* can recognize that the Q Brothers and the Q Brothers Collective have energy and imagination. But energy and imagination are not enough. These qualities did not prevent them from a colorblindness that extends beyond issues of casting to the themes highlighted, the adaptive choices made, and the structural decisions implemented that work together to strip race from a play with the potential to speak potently to the trauma of racial marginalization. Their production therefore reminds one of the importance of courage. Specifically, it directs attention to the courage needed to challenge white supremacy by creating a narrative that acknowledges its abuses. Artistic courage must also place this narrative in a performance crafted so that its adaptative, theatrical choices awaken the audience to its potential complicity with this supremacy in a way that cannot be shrugged, or laughed, off, once the house lights come on.

Chapter 3

Othello, Race, and *Serial*: The Ethics of a Shakespearean Cameo

Frame, n. I. Advantage, benefit, profit. *Obsolete*.
Frame, n. II. Something that has or confers structure.
—*Oxford English Dictionary*

The White Racial Frame

In an article discussing the importance of frames to works of art, Emma Crichton-Miller characterizes them as the "Cinderellas of the art world" due to their multifaceted functions. As Crichton-Miller elaborates, frames

> protect the artworks they support; they show off the qualities of a picture, drawing attention to its formal structure, its patterns and colours, enabling them to resonate fully with a viewer; they mould the response of the viewer to the work by suggesting the value we should attach to it; they accommodate a painting to its setting, acting as a liaison between the dream world of art and the decorative scheme of the museum, gallery or private home the work inhabits.

For instance, she observes how, when considering Raphael's portrait of Lorenzo de Medici that was up for auction at Christie's London, "The eye of the viewer was attuned to the exaggerated curves of the Duke's costume by the lively sinuous pattern of scrolling vine and foliage carved on the frame's frieze, which also echoed the leaf pattern on the duke's torso." Frames, in other words, create various forms of emphasis. Yet despite this work, "anomalously, to all but certain connoisseurs and collectors, museum curators and auctioneers and the artists and dealers who depend upon [frames], they are practically invisible" (Crichton-Miller). Thus, except perhaps to those with expertise, a frame's function remains crucial—shaping the viewer's relationship to the art work—yet largely imperceptible.

Despite their vastly different contexts, ideological frames function similarly, as illustrated by sociologist Joe R. Feagin's concept of the "white racial frame." Feagin moves away from sociological studies of race focusing on individual racial prejudices, instead examining a cultural system of racial meaning.[1] Though people use multiple frames, the white racial frame is hegemonic and therefore "More than just one significant frame among many; it is one that has routinely defined a way of being, a broad perspective on life, and one that provides the language and interpretations that help structure, normalize, and make sense out of society" (Feagin 11).[2] In creating the nation, Feagin argues, white Americans have crafted a "white worldview" that positions whites as racially superior by stressing "positive" characterizations of whiteness and "negative" understandings of various racial Others; this binary depends upon conceptions of superior white intellect, rationality, modernity, emotions, and values (10). White Americans combine various methods and elements to advance the white racial frame, including: beliefs (stereotypes); cognitive facets (racial narratives); the visual and auditory (racialized media and accents); feelings (racialized emotions); and actions (discrimination). Moreover, the frame positions white-controlled institutions as the norm and establishes stereotyping as a means of reinforcing this ideological and institutional normalcy. The white racial frame is so systemic that racial minorities likewise subscribe to it, few whites challenge it, and it "[extends] across white divisions of class, gender, and age." In fact, even if white Americans do not exhibit explicit racial prejudice, many still unconsciously inherit and disseminate pieces of the frame that reinforce white superiority, therefore advantaging whiteness. Thus, like an artwork's frame, the white racial frame also imposes structure, guides the gaze, and protects—though in this case, what is protected is racial hierarchy—and it does so in ways often unnoticed by the average person.

In both its artistic and ideological contexts, a frame also takes the otherwise incidental, a certain color, the curves of a costume as noted

---

[1] Feagin defines *systemic* as "the oppressive racist realities [that] have from the early decades been well institutionalized and manifested in all of this society's [America's] major parts" (x).

[2] When deploying *frame*, Feagin means "a perspectival frame that gets imbedded in individual minds (brains), as well as in collective memories and histories, and helps people make sense out of everyday situations" (9).

above, or a seemingly unremarkable narrative, and makes it central by drawing one's attention and helping guide one's interpretation, thereby conferring significance. This is precisely the case with the influence of the white racial frame upon a fleeting Shakespearean reference in the NPR podcast *Serial*.[3] As the first podcast to reach 5 million downloads on iTunes and over 90 million worldwide, cultural critics lauded the first season of *Serial* as a global phenomenon. As Ernesto Londoño observes, Season 1 is widely noted for being the most downloaded podcast on iTunes, "with roughly 5.7 million listeners per episode." He contextualizes this number: "By comparison, the average download rate for the next 20 most popular podcasts is 446,000 per episode, according to Mark McCrery, the head of Podtrac, which monitors podcast traffic." Lauren Davidson reports that "it has now been downloaded or streamed more than 68 m[illion] times." Debuting on October 3, 2014, the twelve-episode *This American Life* spin-off examines the 1999 case of Pakistani American Adnan Syed, a Baltimore teenager charged with murdering his Korean girlfriend, Hae Min Lee.[4] After two trials, he was found guilty and is currently serving a life sentence. The highly dramatic, weekly podcast was developed by journalist and host Sarah Koenig, its first season following Syed's case so that each week, Koenig delved into a different aspect of the murder case, thereby creating a serialized narrative (as the title suggests). Part of *Serial*'s popularity comes from its unique podcasting format. As Dan Fitchette explains, "Podcasts tend to be episodic, focused on thematic rather than a narrative exploration. Because it's structured as a multi-part narrative, 'Serial' is a real departure." Though *Serial*'s novelty has now faded, it is difficult to overstate Season 1's significance. It prompted changes in podcast production and consumption while also creating real-world implications for Syed's ongoing legal fight. And early on in the first episode of this landmark podcast, one finds an almost throwaway reference to Shakespeare in which claims about the racialized identities invite an interrogation of the white racial frame shaping the podcast. At the same time, however, this reference directs attention to

---

[3] As of July 2020, *Serial* is owned by the *New York Times*. Here, I only reference Season 1, which was released by NPR.

[4] During an interview with Josephine Yurcaba, Koenig explains how she came to follow the case of Hae Min Lee's murder: "I learned about Adnan's story well before we came up with the show. A friend of the Syed family, Rabia Chaudry, came to me because I had been at the *Baltimore Sun* and had written about this attorney who had been disbarred—the same lawyer who represented Adnan. The notion was that his defense had screwed up the case, and would I look into this?"

the way that same white racial frame shapes how people read, teach, understand, and reiterate the role of race in Shakespeare.

Othello Makes a Cameo

Just shy of six-and-a-half minutes into *Serial*'s first episode, titled "The Alibi," Koenig entices her listeners into following this obviously captivating yet unfamiliar narrative by employing a much more recognizable figure—Shakespeare—when describing the unfolding story as a "Shakespearean mashup." This "tune out and you'll miss it" moment alludes to *Romeo and Juliet* and *Othello* without naming the plays, their characters, or their lines, instead referencing key plot points and thematics from each tragedy, "evoking Shakespeare's aura without using any of his words" (Erickson, *Citing* 1). Koenig explains:

> And on paper, the case was like a Shakespearean mashup—young lovers from different worlds thwarting their families, secret assignations, jealousy, suspicion, and honor besmirched, the villain not a Moor exactly, but a Muslim all the same, and a final act of murderous revenge. And the main stage? A regular old high school across the street from a 7-Eleven. ("Episode 1")[5]

"Young lovers from different worlds thwarting their families" points to *Romeo and Juliet*. But "jealousy, suspicion, honor besmirched" and the "Moor" as the story's "villain" invoke *Othello*. The latter Shakespearean connection is made all the more compelling by the fact that *Othello* was found in Lee's backpack after her death. This citation functions, if only barely, as what Douglas M. Lanier terms a "cameo appearance": "passing references to recognizably Shakespearean lines, characters, scenes, or motifs separated from their source narratives" ("Introduction" 136). The moment's brevity invites the question, "What is Shakespeare doing here?" This Shakespearean cameo's concision and opacity suggest that what matters is "the transcendental signified that just might be Shakespeare"

---

[5] *Serial*'s producers do not provide transcripts for the podcast. The *Serial* website FAQ insists that *Serial* is meant to be heard, not read. I first transcribed episodes, then cross-referenced my transcription with those posted online. Ultimately, all quotations from *Serial* are based on my own transcription except for those from Episode One, for which *This American Life* provides an authorized transcript.

(Pittman, *Authorizing* 2). As L. Monique Pittman argues, "Adaptors proceed to claim an authority for their individual projects which depends upon the trans-historical authority of Shakespeare himself" (3, 4). Given the presumed privileged, educated NPR audience, one can assume Koenig uses Shakespeare for the same ends—authorization for her project. Thus, even if merely a passing reference, Shakespeare works to frame Koenig's story, both within the episode and across the podcast. In fact, this framing works in both of the most common senses of the word *frame*. Shakespeare provides narrative structure for the millions who know nothing about Syed and Lee but are likely familiar with Romeo, Juliet, Othello, and Desdemona thanks to high school English. Concurrently, Koenig deploys the benefit of Shakespeare's authorizing force.

For the average listener, this may be one of the least gripping moments in the gritty true-crime narrative. For a Shakespeare "nerd," or more professionally, the Shakespeare scholar,[6] Koenig's reference may be a pleasant reminder of the Swan of Avon's long-lasting cultural significance—an intellectual *bon mot* amid *Serial*'s more lurid elements.[7] Yet closer examination of a mere 30 seconds of dialogue reveals facile assertions that work at cross purposes to Koenig's ostensible aims and encapsulate problems with the podcast's construction of ethnic, religious, and racial Otherness. This presentation and treatment of Otherness result from a broader, less obvious ideological frame at work: Koenig's overarching white racial frame, evidenced through her privileging of her perspective, affective responses, and judgments.

As a digitally and therefore globally disseminated podcast, however, this white racial frame, its effects on Koenig's positioning of her narrative authority, and its ethical implications may become easily obscured. As Pittman argues, a text's dissemination into a "digitally flattened world" may "undermine the sociopolitical critique art so often provokes" by obscuring originary context ("Color-Conscious Casting," 177, 178). In the case of *Serial*, global citizens may not comprehend the racializing nature of *Othello* as deployed in the Shakespearean cameo; particularly, they may not grasp how it encapsulates *Serial*'s problems regarding racial characterization and narrative authority,

---

[6] I am indebted to Valerie M. Fazel for highlighting the connections between Shakespeare nerds and Shakespeare professionals.

[7] For a discussion of Shakespeare in/and podcasting, see Devori Kimbro, Michael Noschka, and Geoffrey Way, "Lend Us Your Earbuds: Shakespeare/Podcasting/Poesis," *Humanities* 8.2 (2019): n.p.

difficulties informed by America's pervasive white racial frame, which Feagin argues is unique.[8] He explains:

> This societal reality is significantly different from that of other leading industrialized countries in the west. Countries like Great Britain and France were central to centuries of European colonialism, including the Atlantic slave trade and slave plantations in the Americas, but their early and later growth as nations was not built directly on an internal labor force of enslaved Africans or local lands stolen by recent conquests of indigenous peoples. (Feagin ix)

Outside of an American context, then, listeners may comprehend race as playing a role in the podcast, but they may have trouble grasping the influence of the white racial frame and Shakespeare's usage within it. Thus, *Serial*'s Shakespearean citation reminds us that Shakespeare does not always work as a force of unmitigated social critique. Rather, as Shakespeare moves between contexts and mediums via global distribution, we must be wary about the invisibility of the ideological frames used to understand Shakespeare, and those frames that Shakespeare is used to reify, as Koenig does for the white racial frame in *Serial*.

Indeed, the *Othello* cameo highlights Koenig's careless engagement with immigrant and/or diasporic individuals and their experiences by exposing two methods that draw attention to the influence of the white racial frame upon issues of race and representation in *Serial*: first, Koenig's overt and surreptitious dependence on stereotypes to characterize the unfolding narrative's central figures; and second, her persistent privileging of her own perspective as normative and central instead of the perspectives of the first- and second-generation immigrants, as well as diasporic persons, at the heart of the unfolding narrative.

---

[8] David Theo Goldberg provides a helpful definition for "racialism": "Racial conception, or what some ... have called racialism, is the view that groups of people are marked by certain generalizable visible and heritable traits. These generalized traits may be physical or psychological, cultural or culturally inscribed on the body, and the physical and psychological, bodily and cultural traits are usually thought somehow indelibly connected" (*The Threat of Race* 4). Steve Martinot explains that *racialization* refers "not to the social status of people (of different colors) that produces itself culturally in this society ... but rather to what is done socially and culturally to people, for which personal derogation and alien status are part of the outcome" (10). As Kim F. Hall clarifies in her own use of the term, it proves "useful because it suggests a way of talking about notions of human difference that have political and social effects and that are different from more institutionalized forms of racism" (*Things of Darkness*, 4n).

The second method depends very much upon the first, for Koenig's use of Shakespeare as a narrative frame for *Serial* creates "a loose structural homology" between her story and *Othello*, with Koenig's narrative authority taking on Iago-like qualities that privilege whiteness at the expense of those positioned as Other (Desmet, Loper, and Casey 19). Here, it is helpful to consider Alexa Alice Joubin and Elizabeth Rivlin's call for an attention to ethics regarding Shakespeare and appropriation. Though "notoriously difficult to define," Joubin and Rivlin understand ethics most broadly as that which counts as "good action," especially "in terms of a responsibility to cultural otherness" (2). The cameo, then, becomes particularly useful for considering both Shakespeare and whiteness as important frames for *Serial*, especially their deployment in ways that could not be considered "good action" or what Christy Desmet calls "recognition" and "responsibility" to another ("Recognizing Shakespeare" 43), therefore proving unethical regarding racial representation.

At the same time, the cameo also draws attention to the ways that those within the podcast and those who analyze it in the media address the issue of race in *Serial*. Most notable in discussions of *Serial* and race are Jay Caspian Kang's and Julie Carrie Wong's respective critiques. In his essay for *The Awl*, Kang asks, "What happens when a white journalist stomps around in a cold case involving people from two distinctly separate immigrant communities? Does she get it right?" Kang responds with a resounding "no." He argues that Koenig's white reporter privilege manifests in the assumptions, logical leaps, and stereotypical characterizations she makes concerning Lee and Syed, even as she quickly dispenses with the difficulties concerning ethnicity, race, and religion that her topic raises. Essentially, Kang accuses Koenig of being "a flawed, unreliable narrator," as well as a "'cultural tourist,'" which results in "the difficult feat of both whitewashing and stereotyping Hae and Adnan." *Buzzfeed* contributor Wong criticizes Koenig for her fetishistic, stereotypical depiction of immigrant culture. More troubling to Wong, however, is Koenig's establishment of African American Jay Wilds as a "counterpoint to her portrayal of Adnan and Hae," so that Syed and Lee represent the model minorities in opposition to the more legally and socially troubled Wilds. The problem with this myth resides in the idea that "If Asians can succeed . . . that proves racism is over and black people are responsible for their own failure to thrive." Because of this dynamic, Wong reproves Koenig's "harmful" narrative, which she argues "[feeds] its listeners a steady dose of racist tropes." Kang's and Wong's arguments prove helpful not only for raising the issue of

Koenig's white privilege, but also for revealing the various terms and facets of identity related to Otherness in *Serial*: ethnicity, immigrant, race, religion, culture, stereotypes, minority, and racism, to name but a few. While it may be clear that the centrality of whiteness frames the podcast, what may be less easy to grasp is precisely how to frame the concept of *race* within it.

A careful analysis of the racial discourse in and about the podcast exposes the shifting nature of contemporary racial understandings. Even as academics attempt to use terms such as *culture*, *ethnicity*, and *race* as a means of imposing order and methodological specificity on the expansive, knotty subject of Otherness and identity, everyday discussions of race—such as those found in and about *Serial*—demonstrate the ways that *race* often becomes a catch-all term encompassing various forms of difference. This wide-ranging understanding and deployment of *race* thereby makes it a particularly fluid word *and* concept. For Shakespeare scholars intrigued by *Serial*'s framing, acknowledging this fluidity may seem familiar yet nevertheless disorienting: familiar because for many early modern scholars, fluidity has long been the marker of early modern constructions of race, but disorienting because stability has often functioned as the indicator of modern constructions of race. In other words, a key distinction between traditional scholarly conceptions of early modern and modern racial understandings depends on the binary of shifting vs. constant, ephemeral vs. biological. *Serial*'s racial discourse disrupts this familiar narrative.

Thus, though short, the Shakespearean cameo in *Serial* opens up two different strands of inquiry: race's role in Koenig's framing of the podcast and the shifting conception of race used to frame the central figures, predominantly persons of color, in *Serial*. Regarding the first strand, I want to focus on the way Koenig advances a white racial frame by centering her own perspective on the case in a way that silences the views and voices of the persons of color she interviews. Koenig does so through tactics reminiscent of Iago: crafting a racialized and chorus-like interpretive lens and stressing her reactions and interpretations, especially her affective ones, over those of her subjects. Admittedly, Iago focuses on other characters, Desdemona, Othello, Cassio, and Roderigo, while Koenig focuses on herself. Despite this difference, Koenig, like Iago, proves irresponsible, or to borrow Joubin and Rivlin's language, unethical, in her treatment of the persons of color at the heart of *Serial* by thinning out their voices and privileging hers, the representation of whiteness, in their stead. She therefore serves as a powerful reminder of the white racial frame's pervasiveness and, as she does so, raises questions about Shakespeare's function in authorizing that frame within popular culture.

Turning to the second strand, the varied considerations of race by individuals in the podcast and commentators writing about it point to the variable ways that we understand race in modern society. Despite being a post-racial work, *Serial* exemplifies how long-standing conceptions of race meet contemporary instantiations, suggesting that race's ideological legacy is not so much dismantled in modernity as it is utilized in whatever form necessary to reify hierarchies between the white self and varying marginalized identities. This recognition disrupts not only the post-racial narrative of racial progress, but also the characterization of racial stability founded in biology so frequently attributed to modernity. I argue that recognizing this continued fluidity of race should prompt early modern scholars to ultimately reject the stark distinction often made about constructions of race in the past and in the present, or put differently, prompt them to consider the way the white racial frame pervading *Serial* has likewise affected discussions of Shakespeare and race. Together, these strands encourage consumers of both Shakespeare and popular culture, and Shakespeare *in* popular culture, to account for not only the ways we frame race, but how we use Shakespeare to validate or invalidate particular racial framings pervading American society, both post-racial and contemporary.

Devaluing the Racial Other: Koenig and the White Racial Frame

Koenig's reference to *Othello* causes tension regarding the podcast's purported purpose, while also highlighting the subtle ways cultural and racial prejudice influence her characterizations of *Serial*'s protagonists. This misrepresentation is oddly apropos, for Othello becomes one of a number of first- and second-generation immigrants that Koenig mischaracterizes as she invokes the antiblack stereotype of the violent Black man, which in turn vexes her probing reconsideration of Syed. Koenig sought to investigate this compelling story in order to "get to the bottom of it all" (Syme). Part of that pursuit involves trying to affirm or deny Syed's guilt. As such, the choice to create a thematic and structural bridge between *Serial*'s story and *Othello* proves odd. Informed listeners know that Othello murders Desdemona. Curiously, if Koenig strives to reassess Syed's culpability, her early invocation of Othello, the character and play, muddles this aim. By aligning Syed with Othello, Koenig suggests Syed's guilt, even if inadvertently, thereby positioning him as the villain of her investigative endeavor. Koenig's shift from referencing *Romeo and Juliet* to *Othello* occurs as she addresses "jealousy, suspicion, and honor besmirched" ("Episode 1"). For the average listener, the joint characteristics of "jealousy, suspicion, and honor besmirched" apply more straightforwardly to Othello than they do to the play's central villain, Iago, especially given Koenig's explicit reference to the Moor. Furthermore, Othello calls himself "an honorable murderer," insisting, "For naught did I in hate, but all in honor" (V, ii, 303, 304). Thus, if these qualities signal villainy in Shakespeare's play, the logic of Koenig's comment, coupled with the emphasis on honor, positions Othello as villain despite assertions to the contrary. In doing so, Koenig suggests Syed's villainy as well.

The qualification for Syed's positioning within this Shakespearean cameo resides in its opening words—"On paper." As a suggestion of something hypothetical, an idea based in theory rather than fact, the idiom implies something too good to be true. But what does "On paper" modify in this instance? Is it the "Shakespearean mashup?" The qualities implicated as "Shakespearean" starting from "Young lovers" and through "suspicion" are all matters of fact in *Serial*'s narrative. In other words, while topics like "jealousy" and "suspicion" can be spun and interpreted differently depending on the listener, each Shakespearean attribute indeed comprises part of *Serial*'s story. Does "On paper" therefore refer to the more subjective assertions Koenig makes, namely the qualities of "honor besmirched, the villain not a Moor exactly, but a Muslim all the same, and a final act of murderous revenge"? Koenig's argument regarding Syed is unclear, more evocative than logical. Thus, for those who believe Syed murdered Lee, Koenig develops an effective frame for the first episode. For all others, Koenig troubles her quest to reconsider Syed's responsibility in Lee's death.

One might argue that Koenig intends this assignment of guilt, yet understanding the process of *Serial*'s construction undermines such a claim. Part of *Serial*'s widely noted popularity comes from its unique format as a serialized narrative rather than the thematic, episodic structure more common to podcasting in 2014. Despite public skepticism, Koenig insists that she did not craft an overarching story before creating *Serial*; rather, she developed one based on real-time investigation. In an interview with Rachel Syme, Koenig maintains, "I am not playing all of you . . . I'm not far ahead of you . . . I am pretty much creating this thing in real time now." Ostensibly, then, Koenig would not have desired to so strongly affirm Syed's guilt through her Shakespearean invocation given that she wanted to interrogate this very topic. Koenig thus operationalizes what this book demonstrates is in fact the common *Othello* narrative without truly thinking about its force, wielding Shakespearean authority without any regard as to the potentially subjugating purpose for which she is employing it.

The podcast's biweekly release would only have complicated this dynamic by making reconsideration and reevaluation of Koenig's opening more difficult. In transcript form, one can easily reread and fully grasp Koenig's meaning. But in its aural form, this quick shift in argumentation might be easily missed. In fact, the most common ways of listening to podcasting make distraction likely. Once podcasts moved to a "digital environment," it became "easier for listeners to ignore the pressures of 'appointment consumption' that meant they were limited to listening to a specific program at a specific time. Listeners with access to devices capable of storing downloaded versions of the programming could enjoy that programming at their leisure, multiple times, or in increments that best matched their own scheduling demands" (Kimbro, Noschka, and Way). Given this flexibility, podcast consumers tend to listen to them at home or in their cars, most often via their phones (Edison Research). Their appeal "is the capability for [them] to be used anytime-anywhere," which creates "another interesting advantage: users can do other tasks (e.g. cooking, taking notes, driving . . .) while they are listening to them" (Fernandez, Simo, and Sallan 386). In other words, "Podcasts aren't books, and can be easily consumed while engaging in another activity" (Porges). Consequently, people tend to listen to podcasts while distracted. Due to this multitasking, pinpointing that one has missed a particular claim, when in the podcast that claim was made, and therefore how to return to a specific moment proves more challenging with a podcast than with something in written form, thereby making *Serial* more difficult to review. Koenig's quick shift in argumentation might thus be overlooked, which makes the ethical imperative of thoughtful narration all the more significant. Thus, whether employed as an authorizing gesture, a devil's advocate characterization, or perhaps both, in thematic content and logical structure, Koenig's Shakespearean cameo undermines her podcast's purpose even as it introduces it, a biasing against Syed exacerbated by the racial stereotypes lurking within the cameo.

The issue here is one of association. By casting "the Moor" as villain, especially in relation to a murder, Koenig dredges up stereotypes of Black male violence. The specter of deviant Black masculinity looms over this case given the centrality of Jay Wilds. An African American young man known for selling marijuana, Wilds led the police to Lee's car and served as the prosecution's key witness after claiming that Syed confessed to him and forced him to participate in the disposal of Lee's body. As a result, here, Othello becomes associated with the "emotion-laden" and antiblack stereotype of the criminal Black man (Feagin 103). The stereotype may not be obvious, but as such, it helpfully exemplifies the white racial frame's logic, which associates those positioned as Other with negative behaviors—in this case, criminality, including homicide—even if only tacitly. Problematic in and of itself, through the *Othello* reference, the qualities of this stereotype extend to Syed, thereby further troubling Koenig's introduction of him, as well as her goal of reconsidering his involvement in Lee's murder. In this cameo, then, Shakespeare authorizes decidedly vexed characterizations of Black masculinity that more easily invoke rather than challenge common racial caricatures *and* that complicate Koenig's ostensible purpose.

In addition to deploying stereotypes associated with Black men, Koenig borrows from the prosecution's approach to the case by focusing on "honor besmirched," the motive asserted for the Muslim Syed's turn to murderous rage, in a way that also misrepresents Muslim masculinity. In doing so, she further reveals the prejudicial, racializing function of the white racial frame, and the way Shakespeare can be deployed to advance it. As early as Syed's bail hearing, prosecutor Vicki Wash characterizes him as a "young Pakistan [*sic*] . . . male who was jilted by his girlfriend" ("Episode 10"). Later, prosecutor Kevin Urick argues that Syed "became enraged, he felt betrayed, that his honor had been besmirched and he became very angry and he set out to kill Hae Min Lee." Knowledge of this prosecutorial focus informs Koenig's choice to employ the phrase "honor besmirched" in "Episode 1," as made clear when she tells listeners in "Episode 10," "you've heard this language before in an earlier episode, but it bears repeating." In "Episode 1," however, listeners do not yet know anything about the case, including the suggested motive or, according to some, the lack of evidence to support it. Koenig therefore joins the prosecution in disseminating the Islamophobic stereotype of Muslims as "irrational perpetrators of religion-inspired wickedness" (Morey and Yaqin 22). In doing so, she reinscribes the "rigid trace of an increasingly tendentious and narrow number of attributes" carried by Muslims (35). Moreover, by asserting such an emotionally evocative phrase in conjunction with a seemingly strong assertion of villainy on Syed's part *and* coupling it with a reference to a famous tragedy in which jealousy serves as the motive for murder, Koenig once again makes it difficult to attend to her qualifications. As such, even as this cameo invokes the violent Black man, it also draws upon the Orientalist vision of Muslim masculinity that positions it as a jealous, domineering force that can barely be controlled, even as it controls. Because Koenig expressly describes the villain as "Muslim," this stereotype appears much more clearly than the criminal Black man. In this introductory and therefore foundational moment, with one sweeping claim Koenig potentially recirculates the stereotypes of the violent Black man *and* the jealous Muslim male. Ultimately, both reside side by side in the logic of Koenig's Shakespearean cameo, where her use of Shakespeare and race can easily prompt a predisposition against Syed, especially when he is read through the white racial frame. The use of *Othello* in this citation thus highlights the podcast's laissez-faire attitude toward racial representation.

Just as troubling is the factual inaccuracy Koenig affirms in this *Othello* cameo. With the qualifier "not a Moor exactly," she cursorily acknowledges the distinction between Syed and Shakespeare's tragic general, though the listener may easily miss her qualification just as they may not fully digest the implications of "On paper." Yet even as she attempts to establish this important distinction, she simultaneously insists on a shared identity between Syed and Othello. She does so first by the "almost but not quite" nature of the qualifier, "not a Moor exactly." Her use of "exactly," instead of the more certain, "not a Moor" plants the suggestion that Syed *could almost be* a Moor, that he somehow falls just shy of that distinction. She then claims that both Syed and Othello are "Muslim all the same." The problem is that Othello is not, in fact, Muslim. Koenig, however, wants the listener to create, through Othello, an association between race and religion that transfers onto Syed in order to lend *gravitas* to her discussion. But her assertion is wrong.[9] This is not an issue of textual fidelity but rather one of accuracy. To return to Joubin and Rivlin's discussion of Shakespeare and ethics, such an incorrect collapse of different forms of Otherness—race and religion—cannot

---

[9] *Othello* also appeals to Koenig due to its focus on an interracial relationship. She and others repeatedly stress the cultural, ethnic, and perceived racial differences between Lee and Syed. In many ways, then, the framing of Syed and Lee in *Serial* works as an example of what Daileader terms "Othellophilia"—"the critical and cultural fixation on Shakespeare's tragedy of interracial marriage to the exclusion of broader definitions, and more positive visions, of inter-racial eroticism"— even though Syed and Lee are unmarried and differently raced than Othello and Desdemona (6).

be understood as "good action," especially from a reporter who enjoys white privilege discussing a story involving almost entirely persons of color. By mixing fact with interpretive imprecision and adding a dose of Shakespearean fiction for good measure, Koenig makes it hard to parse precisely what the listener should perceive as a mere rhetorical flourish.

Broadly, then, Shakespeare authorizes *Serial* as a whole. In this cameo, however, Shakespeare authorizes decidedly vexed characterizations of Othered identities that more easily invoke rather than challenge common racial stereotypes. This Shakespearean invocation thus directs attention to the stereotyping entrenched within the white racial frame that may not arise out of express prejudice—as I believe is the case with Koenig—but rather due to the ideological embeddedness of the belief in the inferiority of those considered Other. In other words, Koenig's approach instantiates the post-racial perspective of "racism without racists" (Bonilla-Silva 1). Furthermore, it demonstrates just how easily carelessness with Shakespearean appropriation can result in an irresponsible engagement with cultural Otherness. I stress the *cultural* here, for in a quintessential post-racial move, Koenig nowhere suggests a biological hierarchy between races, yet as demonstrated, her discourse nonetheless reifies a cultural distinction, even hierarchy, between them. Careful analysis of this brief yet ideologically potent Shakespearean citation thus exposes Koenig's incitement of prejudicial thinking, perpetuation of stereotypes, and unethical conflation of categories of difference *via* Shakespeare. Thus, as Shakespeare authorizes *Serial* as a project, he also authorizes the ideologies of the white racial frame.

Narrative Authority and the Centering of Whiteness: Koenig as *Serial*'s Iago

The podcast's white racial framing appears more widely than in just the Shakespearean cameo, however. In fact, the frame affects both the podcast's content and structure, particularly as Koenig's privileging of her own interpretations, impressions, and feelings functions to further promote the authority of whiteness. In some ways, then, Koenig's approach to *Serial*'s narrative directs us back to *Othello*. At the end of the tragedy, Othello poignantly requests that "When you shall these unlucky deeds relate," Venetians should, "Speak of me as I am; nothing extenuate,/Nor set down aught in malice" (V, ii, 350–53). Othello's final entreaty reveals his understanding of and concern with narrative authority and the way race colors retellings. The "When" of the letters from Cyprus back to the Venetian Senate indicates the inevitability of recounting, yet what Othello cannot trust is the nature of the tale told. "Speak of me as I am" (V, ii, 352), he insists, for he realizes that it is all too easy to leave pieces of the story out, to "extenuate" and shape him as the villain through "malice." Othello's request thus calls for complex narrative representation. Moments before his suicide, then, Othello recognizes the limits of his agency and tries to wrest whatever narrative authority he can from those whose racial perspectives he fears will taint their reiterations of his misfortune.[10] This fear derives from the fact that Iago has already crafted a version of himself he does not recognize; after all, "That's he that was Othello. Here I am" (V, ii, 292). In the process of fomenting this displaced sense of self within Othello, Iago famously deploys a racialized interpretive lens. In doing so, the frequent soliloquizer concomitantly performs a chorus-like function by offering up his epistemological interpretations as the means of "reading" a given moment or situation—such as Cassio's supposedly "guiltylike" departure in III, iii—to both the characters within the play and those without. By doing so, Iago positions himself as a "star" in the play he directs. Though familiar to Shakespeare scholars, Iago's strategies for endowing himself with narrative authority bear rehearsing because they likewise appear in *Serial* through Koenig.

Though without an invocation as direct as Othello's meditation on the afterlife of his narrative, the podcast raises similar questions about race and narrative authority, about the voice who fashions and controls ways of knowing within the unfolding chronicle, about who is able to "aestheticize real life, to wonder why all the details don't fit, to say what makes sense and what doesn't ... to explain to the world what these people were like" (Wallace-Wells). This grappling with narrative authority becomes more fraught in both *Othello* and *Serial* due to the marginalized status of those at the heart of each respective story. Imtiaz Habib reminds us that Othello's marginalization does not simply rest with his skin color but also with his "alien status, which positions him as the equivalent of a contemporary immigrant" given that both terms—*alien* and *immigrant*—function as "primary markers of the distinction between foreign/different and natural born/same" (138). As such, due to his vexed legal standing

---

[10] Ian Smith reminds us, "speaking 'of' Othello thus has multiple overlapping meanings, speaking for him or on his behalf; speaking about him; and because of Othello's blackness, speaking about race" ("We Are Othello" 112).

as a Black, formerly enslaved alien, "Othello's status is akin to that of an informal enslavement" (Habib 137). Skin color, personal history, and his social status as stranger all alienate Othello from Venice's hegemony. Similarly, *Serial*'s narrative is peopled by individuals who are likewise immigrants and/or diasporic, who are also judged by phenotypes designating Otherness, who also reside on society's margins due to their immigrant status, their social class, their racial/ethnic/religious background, their gender, or, most commonly, a combination of these factors, and who also must depend on white voices to tell their stories.

Just as first Iago and then other Venetians orchestrate Othello's story, and his status as Other within it, so too does Koenig orchestrate a story concerning individuals all considered Other in American society. She is the podcast's Iago figure who narrates, investigates, and produces the saga. She even inserts herself into the narrative, so much so that she becomes a "character" as significant to *Serial* as Syed, Lee, and Wilds. Admittedly, the comparison between Iago and Koenig can only be taken so far. Koenig's motives reside far from Iago's insidious plot of revenge. Koenig also inhabits a more advantaged space than Iago; an ensign, he serves under Othello while Koenig works for NPR reporting on a set of teenagers from 1999, none of whom share her socio-economically privileged position by 2014. Even so, like Iago, Koenig wields narrative authority and therefore responsibility over racial representation, and just as Iago's depiction of Othello has merited critical attention, so too should Koenig's depiction of the people of color whose stories she capitalizes upon, for attending to the way she deploys narrative authority further exposes the white racial frame at play in *Serial*.

While issues of racial representation and narrative authority pervade *Serial*, returning to "Episode 1: The Alibi" proves particularly important given that it establishes the series' foundation. Throughout the podcast, Koenig attempts to provide the appearance of authenticity, most notably by allowing the listener access to her thoughts and emotions, so that "The listener becomes more like a co-conspirator than a distant observer . . . [picking] up clues at the same time she does, [shifting] our view of the case in tandem with her" (Rosin). She takes pains to establish her *ethos* by stressing her good will toward the listener, such as when she warns that a tape she plays during the podcast "is a little upsetting to hear in parts." Such gestures suggest that Koenig provides listeners with the "real," unvarnished story. Part of this access comes through Koenig's "real time" divulging of her shifting perspectives and emotions. As Feagin notes, however, when one is white and those emotions relate to the racial or ethnic Other, they too are part of the white racial frame. As such, expectations about the racial Other predispose or even trigger particular emotions toward that Other. Koenig's emotions may thus be authentic, but they are not universally applicable in the way she attempts to position them throughout the podcast, for they cannot be divorced from her whiteness.

Indeed, careful analysis of Koenig's commentary demonstrates the subtle ways that she racializes her subjects while stressing her impressions and epistemological determinations. Take her discussion of her first meeting with Syed. She observes, "I was struck by two things. He was way bigger than I expected—barrel chested and tall ... He'd spent nearly half his life in prison, becoming larger and properly bearded" ("Episode 1"). Koenig's description of Syed carries potential racialization. It is a given that a thirty-two-year-old man would be larger than his seventeen-year-old self. But this attention to size takes on racial components when Koenig couples it with an emphasis on Syed's substantial, "proper" beard. Her description, in other words, pairs a reminder of his ethnic and religious difference with a stress on his size, which could easily seem menacing and thereby provoke negative emotional associations within her listeners. Specifically, Koenig invokes the same threatening Orientalized male that appears in the Shakespeare cameo. Even as she focuses on Syed, however, like Iago, Koenig shifts the spotlight to herself. She notes, "And the second thing, which you can't miss about Adnan, is that he has giant brown eyes like a dairy cow. That's what prompts my most idiotic lines of inquiry. Could someone who looks like that really strangle his girlfriend? Idiotic, I know." In this moment, Koenig presents an almost physiognomic approach toward judging Syed, wanting "Men [to be] what they seem" (III, iii, 139). By doing so, Koenig draws just as much focus on the person interpreting as the person interpreted, quickly moving from an examination of Syed to her "idiotic" inquiry. On its own, this moment may be read as a temporary lapse in thoughtfulness. But when taken together with numerous instances in the podcast, addressed further below, one instead finds a pattern of Koenig expressly stressing her subjectivity through her editorial and narrative choices as she "[leads] us through a re-enactment, not a discovery" (Rosin). Furthermore, she repeatedly makes universalizing gestures that assume that her experience and interpretations function as the "norm." Richard Dyer explains how, in Western society, being able to position oneself as the "norm" is expressly due to the privileging of whiteness: "As long as race is something only applied to non-white people, as long as white people are not racially seen and named, they/we function as a human norm. Other people are raced, we are just people. There is no more powerful position than that of being 'just' human" (1). This normalization and de-racialization of the white perspective is a tacit function of the white racial frame, for only those in the position of the "norm" have the license to make such universalizing claims (see also Chapter 6).

Even as Koenig crafts dubious, at times racialized chorus-like interpretations for her listeners, and even as she highlights her "role" in the podcast, she also deploys another of Iago's strategies: an emphasis on affective interpretive responses. Specifically, Koenig further centralizes herself within *Serial* by stressing her emotional reactions to the investigation rather than reserving space for and directing attention toward the people of color whose experiences and perspectives she tackles. This tactic differs somewhat from Iago's approach, for he rejects the signification of his emotions, asserting that his "outward action" is not in "compliment extern" to "The native act and figure of my heart" (I, i, 63–65). Koenig, on the other hand, claims to wear her heart on her sleeve as a means of signaling her truthfulness. Perhaps she may, but she does so while literally silencing the voice of social Others in order to advance her own perspective, as seen when she interviews African American Asia McClain, a potential alibi witness who was never contacted by the defense during the first two trials. During their exchange, McClain sighs after Koenig emphasizes that the time during which McClain claims she talked with Syed in the library is precisely the time frame the prosecution established for the murder. Rather than delving into McClain's sigh, however, Koenig posits, "That's how I feel a lot of the time. Because I talk to Adnan regularly, and he just doesn't seem like a murderer" ("Episode 1"). But is that why McClain in fact sighs? Listeners do not know, for Koenig highlights her own interactions with Syed and her interpretation of the sigh rather than McClain's explanation of it by never following up. McClain's race plays a role here only in that by accentuating her own thoughts and emotions, Koenig stresses the narrative and affective authority of whiteness rather than that of the Black woman she is interviewing, which could have been easily rectified if she had ceded space in the podcast to the people of color whose stories she was ostensibly committed to telling.

In fact, Koenig's singular focus regarding the significance of her emotions appears once again only moments later when she feels deflated because Syed seems "heartbroken" rather than excited over the fact that Koenig talked to McClain. Syed explains that he is happy that someone may be able to affirm that "I'm not making this up," but he expresses disappointment that McClain cannot help from "a legal perspective." Syed ultimately comforts Koenig, noting, "I'm sorry, I mean I, I definitely appreciate it. You know, and I definitely kind of hear the elation in your voice. But now I feel like I punctured your balloon." Koenig responds, "No, no, I mean I totally . . . I see what you're saying. I hadn't thought about it in that way." This interchange reveals that Koenig's previous move to assume a shared affective response between her and *Serial*'s investigative subjects proves fraught, for she has limited capacity to imagine their positions as subjects, positions informed by various facets of social difference, some as blatant as the demarcation between incarcerated and free. By stressing *her* voice, *her* reactions, *her* feelings, and *her* interpretations rather than letting them stand objectively or allowing the voices of her subjects to take priority, Koenig exposes the white racial frame that privileges and normalizes the feelings, analyses, and values of whiteness. This dynamic thus makes the narrative authority across the podcast a decidedly white one. To be clear, Koenig's decision to craft herself into one of the podcast's central characters is not a racialized move in and of itself. But because she undoubtedly becomes the most authoritative voice compared to those of the people of color who make up the narrative she interrogates, her podcast, even if inadvertently, reflects the dynamics of the white racial frame.

It also mirrors the dynamics in *Othello*, as Iago wrests narrative authority from Othello by employing disturbingly similar means. As such, while unethical, Koenig's Shakespearean cameo proves useful by revealing the overlaps between *Serial* and Shakespeare's famous Venetian tragedy in both themes and the racial dynamics that shape the unfolding tale.[11] Iago's and Koenig's intentions differ; nuances exist between the ways they assert narrative authority; and the questions each text raises about race, representation, and whiteness are not exactly the same, for both bear the imprints of their time. Yet noting the "cross-historical" approaches for establishing racialized narrative authority facilitates recognition of how white voices continue to extenuate the voice of marginalized racial identities (Erickson and Hall 7). Furthermore, considering the cameo's Shakespearean framing for the podcast redirects us to conversations about the ethics of Shakespearean appropriation, especially when those appropriations

---

[11] In a comparison of the respective racialization of Colin Powell and Othello, Kyle Grady likewise highlights "that discussing early modern interethnic relations finds important affinities with discussing today's racial concerns" (79).

continue to deploy Shakespeare as a way of undergirding the ideological supremacy of whiteness. During a time where Shakespeare studies questions whether "Shakespeare's work [can] adequately address current issues of racism and racial justice" (Erickson and Hall 10), we cannot ignore even brief Shakespearean references such as the one in *Serial*. It too becomes part of the ideological baggage of whiteness and its "exclusivity" that the signifier *Shakespeare* carries (Thompson, *Passing Strange* 37). Shakespearean scholars must therefore contend with the way the baggage of the white racial frame informs how they teach, receive, and recirculate Shakespeare.

The Stranger from "over there": Constructions of Race in *Serial*

Part of challenging this white Shakespearean exclusivity comes from revisiting, and, I argue, dismantling, the way that many Shakespearean purveyors have conceived of race today as compared to its presence, function, and construction in Shakespeare's time. As scholars of Renaissance literature agree, early modern people constructed alterity in inconsistent and varied ways. Shakespeare's dramas, for example, exemplify that early moderns established Otherness through skin color ("Aaron will have his soul black like his face" [*Titus Andronicus*, III, i, 204]); foreign locale ("This damned witch Sycorax [. . .] from Algiers,/Thou know'st, was banished" [*The Tempest*, I, ii, 263–66]); exoticism ("A lovely boy stolen from an Indian king./She never had so sweet a changeling" [*A Midsummer Night's Dream*, II, i, 22–23]); religion ("He tells me flatly there's no mercy for me in heaven because I am a Jew's daughter" [*The Merchant of Venice*, III, v, 28–29]); and associations with the subhuman ("an old black ram/Is tupping your white ewe" [*Othello*, I, i, 86–87]), to name just a few strategies.[12] Delineating and reifying alterity was a fluid process indeed.

This critical consensus regarding the fluidity of early modern constructions of Otherness has produced a dichotomy between "then" and "now" with which early modern race scholars have been forced to grapple. But it also challenges all scholars and teachers of Shakespeare who engage with race in the classroom—if it is conceded that

---

[12] All Shakespeare quotations aside from those found in *Othello* are taken from *The Norton Shakespeare*, gen. ed. Stephen Greenblatt, 3rd ed. (New York: W. W. Norton, 2016).

we can talk about *race* at all. The case for this dichotomy is well known. Some scholars view the use of the term *race* in relation to the Renaissance as anachronistic because *race* did not signify for early moderns as it does for us today. Race, they explain, was a term connected to family and lineage instead of to foreign otherness exclusively. Furthermore, the early modern definition of difference varied, in contrast to the more constant, scientific, and biological categorization with which we define race today. As such, in Renaissance England, people saw religion, familial ties, and bloodlines as more important signifiers of Othered identity than bodily markers such as skin color.[13] It was not until the mid to late seventeenth century, the argument goes, that scientific conceptions of racial difference

---

[13] As early as *Things of Darkness: Economies of Race and Gender in Early Modern England*, Hall addresses the "contemporary disagreement about the very existence of 'races' and therefore the viability of 'race' as a term in cultural or literary studies" (6). In *Shakespeare Jungle Fever: National-Imperial Re-Visions of Race, Rape, and Sacrifice*, Arthur L. Little Jr. observes, "It is worth noting from the outset that 'race' in the early modern era [. . .] works less as a stable identity category than as a semiotic field, one as infinitely varying as the cultural discourse constituting what we have come to identify as the early modern era or the Renaissance" (1). Sujata Iyengar's *Shades of Difference: Mythologies of Skin Color in Early Modern England* clarifies that her discussion about "'race,' embodiment and skin color" resists "the imposition of a straightforward historical trajectory 'toward' racialism or 'toward' color-prejudice" (1). Editors Ania Loomba and Jonathan Burton articulate the debate in the introduction to their sourcebook *Race and Early Modern England: A Documentary Companion*, explaining, "The place of the Renaissance (and particularly the English experience) in these histories [of race] is especially contentious. On the one hand, the question of race has in recent years become central to early modern studies [. . .] On the other hand, most theorists and historians of race still tend to exclude the sixteenth and seventeenth centuries from extended consideration. Often, they invoke premodern times only as a foil for later, more 'racialized' periods. Many early modernists concur, arguing that to speak of 'race' in the early modern period is to perpetuate an anachronism . . ." (1, 2). Lara Bovilsky more succinctly notes in *Barbarous Play: Race on the English Renaissance Stage*, "Most frequently, definitions root race and racism primarily in biology, in phenotype, and in the fixity of racial identity" (9). Ian Smith likewise engages with the debate in *Race and Rhetoric in the Renaissance: Barbarian Errors*, observing, "the broad consensus [. . .] has been that race, defined as the social and political outcome of an admittedly flawed biological enterprise and imperial self-interest, simply did not exist before the eighteenth century. To admit any other reading, especially in the English case, is, quite simply, to commit gross error" (11). And perhaps most succinctly, in *Passing Strange: Shakespeare, Race, and Contemporary America*, Ayanna Thompson notes, "there are still skeptics who argue that it is anachronistic to analyze depictions and constructions of race in Renaissance texts" (5).

emerged and, with them, a focus on phenotypes as markers of that difference.[14]

Yet scholars invested in PCRS vehemently counter these assertions and the historical division that underlies them. They claim that we can and should use the term *race* when discussing early modern conceptions of Otherness. Part of this response rests on the argument that even today understandings of race easily shift since we base them on factors such as language, phenotypes, filial ties, and religion. For example, Kim F. Hall contends, "Race was then (as it is now) a social construct that is fundamentally more about power and culture than about biological difference" (*Things of Darkness* 6). Arthur L. Little Jr. concurs, "We come up short, I would argue, when we fantasize that our contemporary constructions of race—through our well-honed technologies of racism—offer us proof of a real racial ontology more truly embedded in individual subjects than arbitrarily embodied in and across an infinite number of our cultural discourses" (*Shakespeare Jungle Fever* 1). And more recently, Ania Loomba and Jonathan Burton warn, "It is important to remember that even when racial ideologies and racist practices became more entrenched and pernicious, there was no singular approach to or agreement about human difference" (7). These early modern race scholars assert, moreover, that everyday conceptions of race are not necessarily grounded in scientific fact. At the same time, they push back against strict historical timelines, arguing that scientific understandings of race developed in the Renaissance.[15] Here, I join the PCRS scholars

---

[14] One counterargument to locating race in the Renaissance has been a caution against privileging phenotypes—especially Blackness—as markers of racial difference. Various scholars have pushed back against skepticism concerning the link between Black skin and otherness in Renaissance England. See especially Hall, *Things of Darkness*; Iyengar, *Shades of Difference*; and Virginia Mason Vaughan, *Performing Blackness on English Stages, 1500–1800* (Cambridge University Press, 2005).

[15] Other scholarly voices likewise challenge the dichotomy asserted between the early modern and the modern in regards to constructions of race. Smith, for example, insists, "'race' is less a unitary identity than a relationship predicated on difference in privilege, power, and perceived agency that reinforces a distinct status for an authorised subject; as such, terminological obsession obscures race's strategic, opportunistic, negotiating purpose" (*Race and Rhetoric* 12). Thompson also stresses, "Race likewise has multiple, and at times contradictory, uses in contemporary American discourse [. . .] there are times when race is also used to signify a set of cultural practices, such as specific ways of speaking, cooking, eating, and socializing and the historical narratives created that relate to these cultural practices. And there are also times when race is used to denote only nonwhite people, as if white Americans have no race" (*Passing Strange* 4).

who continue to point out the falsity of asserting that modern constructions of race are somehow more stable and emphatically biological than early modern ones.[16] Reiterating this assertion serves as a reminder of what I established in the Introduction: contemporary society's "racecraft," its use of imagination, discourse, and fantasy to create seeming racial truths (Fields and Fields 5).

It is vital to understand that even as skeptical scholars accuse PCRS scholars of imposing contemporary ideas on the Renaissance, by insisting that modern constructions of race are predominantly scientific, phenotypical and more stable than conceived of in the past, these critics enact a different methodological pitfall—imposing an assumed set of views about race upon modernity. One need only familiarize oneself with common approaches to race in post-racial America in order to recognize the term's shifting and varied significations (see Introduction). In short, any insistence on race's stability and purely biological basis in the modern world obfuscates how race functions in modernity, especially in the twentieth- and twenty-first centuries. While distinct, conceptualizations of race in these eras depend on and perpetuate an understanding of race no less fluid than the racial discourses of early modernity. Identifying this methodological problem returns to the issue of framing. Just as a painting's frame can emphasize or diminish certain visual details, so too does an incorrect theoretical or methodological frame stress or mute attention to a work's racial particulars. Embracing the fluidity of race in a modern epoch as a fundamental racial frame corrects such oversights. *Serial* thus helpfully demonstrates how myriad issues, such as language, religion, appearance, and descent, often play pivotal roles in modern constructions of race, even within a supposedly post-racial time. In other words, the racial constructions of the past are not easily discarded. Recognizing this racial legacy and multiplicity can help scholars reframe their work by more effectively

---

[16] One would expect that these contestations that emerged nearly twenty years ago would be resolved. Yet the 2013 SAA meeting (Toronto) demonstrated that the debate about race in the Renaissance continues. Across multiple sessions devoted to the topic, the same stances arose. Some scholars pointedly asserted that race did not exist in early modern England. Moreover, they stressed that the topic should not be discussed in the classroom for fear of confusing students. Others vehemently countered, arguing—most heatedly during a time for follow-up questions—that early modern conceptions of race were no more or less fluid than constructions of race today. Furthermore, these scholars stressed that we need to more forcefully consider the formation of race in early modern literature, both in our scholarship and pedagogy.

using the nuances of early modern writing on race to help uncover the complexities of twenty-first-century racial ideology, and just as significantly, by employing understandings of racial identity as a fresh way of reconsidering canonical Renaissance texts.

As Koenig herself and numerous online commentators assert, *Serial* unfolds like a "Shakespearean" tragedy—Syed hires a famous yet ultimately incompetent defense attorney; the state's star witness proves compromised due to his state-paid lawyer; a first trial favoring the defendant ends in a mistrial after a confrontation between the judge and the defense attorney taints a juror's perception. Of most interest here, however, is the way in which the voices of the podcast and the educated persons who analyze it online demonstrate that even today the term *race* often references much more than the biological. In the podcast as in *Othello*, Otherness becomes a matter of difference due to a complex set of issues including appearance, locale, and lineage. As such, *Serial* exemplifies the fallacy of affirming stable modern racial discourses and positioning them as fundamentally different in kind from those invoked by early moderns. Letting go of this false dichotomy encourages letting go of the impetus to whitewash the presence of racialization in great works of the Western literary canon, Shakespeare's among them.[17] Moreover, admitting the fluidity of modern constructions of race enables pedagogical discussions that make Shakespeare's works (and those of other early modern writers) especially pertinent and engaging to students who are increasingly multiracial, as well as increasingly skeptical about the value and pertinence of classic literature.

Rather than rejecting the protean nature of race, critical race theorists instead stress its unstable nature and its basis on factors other than biology. Richard Delgado and Jean Stefancic state, "A third theme of critical race theory, the 'social construction' thesis, holds that race and races are products of social thought and relations. Not objective, inherent, or fixed, they correspond to no biological or genetic reality; rather, races are categories that society invents, manipulates, or retires when convenient" (8). Similarly, David Theo Goldberg and John Solomos observe, "Race and ethnic groups, like nations, are now quite widely considered to be 'imagined communities' (Anderson, 1991), socially conceived and considered, manufactured and inflected

---

[17] In his discussion of Jews in England in *Shakespeare and the Jews*, James Shapiro explains that at stake in the debate about their presence in the Renaissance is "whether Jews should be recognized as belonging to England's past" (62–63). Here, what is at stake is whether race and racism are likewise part of England's past.

group formations ... They are discursively fashioned or ideologically produced, made and changed in relation to, and molded by, social conditions, relations, clashes, and struggles" (3). Michael Banton concurs when he asserts, "There is now general agreement that when in English-speaking countries reference is made to *race* ... the reference is to race as a *social construct* and not a biological category" (94). And explicitly invoking the language used to characterize the early modern, Steve Martinot argues that conceptions of race change over time by depending on various symbols that signal difference: "The important element of this racialization process is the *fluidity* of its symbolization. Indeed, that *fluidity* dispenses with the need to refer to anything real once it has served to socially and hierarchically categorize" (emphasis added, 19). These examples demonstrate that current understandings of race do not focus on biology as their singular or even predominant defining construct, and they are not any less protean than early modern racial conceptions.

The way scholars consider race in today's society not only affects conceptualizations of identity—whether our own or others'—but, it bears repeating, it also shapes how the field of Shakespeare studies frames the relationship between Shakespeare and race. As noted above, Koenig's opening Shakespearean reference indicates that in *Serial*, questions of descent, racial stereotypes, and the threat of religious difference collide in ways that appear more early modern than modern, varied and shifting rather than static and biological. As such, *Serial* works as a useful case study that helps us recognize the fluidity of race in twenty-first-century America, which in turn facilitates a rejection of the long-standing skeptical framing of race in early modern studies, as well as a more thoroughgoing grasp of how race functions today.

That Syed's Muslim, Pakistani American identity shapes the story exposes how, even in today's American culture, religion, skin color, community, and other facets of identity comprise understandings of race. These intertwined factors appear most clearly in Episode 10, titled "The Best Defense is a Good Defense." This episode examines how Syed's racial and religious identity may have influenced the case against him. Koenig explains that across the jury pool the judge "was on the lookout for prejudice, all kinds of prejudice. Against cops, against prosecutors, against Koreans, and against Muslims." Koenig's comment exposes the various identity politics at play in the case. Lee's identity opens up prejudice against Koreans, a potential racial prejudice. Yet Koenig does not choose to say that the judge looks for prejudice against Pakistanis. Rather, she notes a possible religious prejudice "against Muslims." By coupling race and religion, however, the potential for elision between ostensibly distinct categories of difference occurs.

In fact, as the segment continues, religious prejudice expressly becomes conflated with other issues, including race, as the shifting language employed by Koenig as well as by those involved in the case reveals. We learn that Koenig addresses questions of prejudice because Shamim Rahman, Syed's mother, inspired her to consider the problem. Rahman explains that Syed's family and their "whole [Muslim] community" believe Syed was arrested due to "discrimination," elaborating, "because he was a Muslim child that's why they took him. It was easy for them to take him, than the other people" ("Episode 10"). Rahman's comment clearly indicates that in her opinion, Syed's Islamic faith positioned him as Other. Her use of the term *discrimination* rather than *racism* suggests that she sees a difference between religion (Syed as Muslim) and race (Syed as South Asian), identifying the former as the underlying motivation in her son's arrest. In this way, Rahman's logic aligns with an alleged modern understanding of race; if discriminating against the Other is not biological, it is also not, strictly speaking, racial.

Yet the podcast quickly confuses any distinction between religion and race. Koenig clearly notes her skepticism concerning Rahman's claim, saying she has a hard time believing "the notion that the cops and prosecutors in this case were driven by anti-Muslim feeling, by racism, and by racism alone." Koenig's extreme reduction of Rahman's assertion (they are motivated "by racism alone") aside, the way she frames the issue bears attention. In her estimation, anti-Muslim feeling equals racism. Her language exposes semantic and ideological elision. "Anti-Muslim" clearly refers to religious discrimination. Even so, Koenig immediately invokes racism although she does not mention any anti-South Asian or even anti-Pakistani sentiment. Her unspoken assumption may be the difficulty in separating Pakistani identity from Islamic belief. If that is the case, issues of descent and religion shape each other so fundamentally that they invite Koenig's slippage. It seems, then, that, as in the Renaissance, everyday formulations of race do not solely depend on biology or phenotypes as their defining element, nor are they in any way stable.

The conflation between religion and various aspects of Syed's Otherness continues throughout the episode. Issues of dress and physical difference arise when one of Syed's first lawyers, Chris Flohr, describes how during the bail hearing the courtroom was full of people from Syed's religious and cultural community: "So, a lot of beards and a lot of traditional garb." The jury certainly took note of Syed's Otherness, as Koenig's interviews of various jury members reveal. The jury consisted of seven African Americans, and Koenig does not mention any Muslim jury members. As such, during this pre-9/11 but post-1993 first World Trade Center attack, one can safely surmise that for much of the jury, Syed truly was perceived as an Other, as their statements expose.[18] Juror William Owens comments, "I don't feel religion was why he did what he did. It may have been culture, but I don't think it was religion. I'm not sure how the culture is over there, how they treat their women." We can understand the capacious term "culture" here as roughly meaning, "The distinctive ideas, customs, social behaviour, products, or way of life of a particular nation, society, people, or period. Hence: a society or group characterized by such customs, etc."[19] Owens's comment indicates he sees religion and culture as distinct. In fact, Owens's statement about "how they treat their women" "over there" works as an Orientalizing gesture. Deepa Kumar explains how the "dominant narrative" crafted by Europeans about Muslims "was one that presented Muslim women as severely subjugated, oppressed, and little more than slaves. Just as Muslim despots tyrannized their subjects, it was argued, they also tyrannized their wives and daughters" (45). Even centuries later, Kumar observes, "the logic that Muslim women are oppressed and therefore need to be rescued by the west continues to hold ground" (46).[20] Owens's remark thus signals the stereotypical controlling, objectifying treatment of women by Muslim men as exemplified, somewhat paradoxically, by the Oriental image of the impenetrable harem.[21] For Owens, Syed is likely a racial Other from a different location when, in reality, the "over there" in which Syed resided would have been Owens's own Baltimore.

Juror Stella Armstrong likewise notes the significance Syed's difference played for the jury when she recalls, "They were trying to

---

[18] The podcast contains interviews with only two out of the twelve jurors, one likely Caucasian and the other of African American descent.

[19] OED, "Culture, n. 7a."

[20] Kumar argues that Western culture and its predominant religion, Christianity, are likewise oppressive to women. For arguments that counter the idea of Islam as a misogynistic religion, see Leila Ahmed, *Women and Gender in Islam* (Yale University Press, 1992) and Asma Barlas, *"Believing Women" in Islam: Unreading Patriarchal Interpretations of the Qur'an* (University of Texas Press, 2002).

[21] As Reina Lewis reminds us, "In alternative and proto-feminist strands of Orientalism, the plight of the harem inmate could be invoked as a metaphor for women's oppression" (96). Lewis attempts to provide alternative readings of this and other Orientalized images of women.

talk about in his culture, and uh [in] Arabic culture, men rule, not women. I remember hearing that" ("Episode 10"). Armstrong provides more specificity than Owens with the term "Arabic culture," and she illuminates the ways that stereotyping influenced jury thinking. Yet Armstrong's statement also exposes how definitions of race, ethnicity, and culture collapse into one another.[22] As a Pakistani American, Syed is not Arab. The jurors may have made the mistake due to Syed being Muslim, even though they said they were not taking religion into account. However, Arabs are not defined by religion but rather by culture, language, and genealogical descent. The jurors, however, did not take the time to carefully parse between religion (Muslim), ethnicity (Arab versus Pakistani), and race (potentially Caucasian versus Asian). Instead, they confused definitions because of prevalent stereotypes about Muslim men, all the while swearing that they did not consider religion. Thus, though none of them mentions race, their own persistence in disavowing religion as a factor suggests that, reflecting colonial Orientalist dynamics of positioning Muslims as a racial Other (Kumar 31-32), something *like* race informed their conceptions of Syed.

Koenig certainly suggests so: "The jurors we spoke to said Adnan's religion didn't affect their view of the case ... But when we pressed them a little more, it seems stereotypes about Adnan's culture were there, lurking in the background" ("Episode 10"). This parsing proves revealing. For the jurors, religion and culture supposedly worked distinctly. Yet because Syed was of Pakistani descent, they understood him as conforming to a "culture" they associated with "over there" even though Syed was, as Koenig pointedly reminds the listener, "American, with Pakistani heritage." In other words, he shared a culture with the jurors. Jury comments, however, indicate that some of them did not see Syed in this way. Moreover, positioning Syed's culture as predominantly Othered did not occur solely on an interpersonal level. During the police investigation, both when the case was considered a missing person case and later a homicide, a cultural specialist—who was initially hired by Lee's uncle—assisted the investigation. This specialist worked for the

---

[22] Though I am using *race* and *ethnicity* as distinct terms, the former based on an assumed association with biology and the latter with culture, the two cannot always be distinguished easily. For a helpful discussion of varying approaches toward these terms, see Werner Sollors, "Ethnicity and Race," in *A Companion to Racial and Ethnic Studies*, ed. Goldberg and Solomos (Wiley-Blackwell, 2002), 97–104.

Enehey Group. A report, entitled "Report on Islamic Thought and Culture with Emphasis on Pakistan. A Comparative Study Relevant to the Upcoming Trial of Adnan Syed," created by the director of the group, was given to the Baltimore City Police. In it the director asserts, "Several basic components exist within the Islamic culture, regardless of where the ethnic Pakistani Islamic actually resides" (The Enehey Group). As applied to Syed, this would indicate that his "Islamic culture" would supersede his American cultural identification. Later in the document, in a section entitled "Summary as It Relates to Mr. Syed," the director claims, "Given the social impact of growing up within the confines and rigid structure of Pakistani Islamic society based in the United States, attending a public school . . . where all students are entitled to an education, freedom of speech and co-ed activities must have presented major divisions in cultural and sociological allegiances." Yet as the report continues, it becomes clear that in the director's estimation being Muslim would have exerted the larger influence upon Syed: "Clearly Mr. Syed faced almost insurmountable odds to meet with this 'infidel or devil' in secret . . . For all intents and purpose [sic] he marked his territory by giving her a gift of great value within his culture [a scarf, which the report characterizes as a veil], and in doing so he sealed her fate with his . . . To have later been let down by her relationship with another man would certainly [sic] been an obvious violation of his culture, and a reason to destroy her." Interestingly, this report carries with it echoes of Koenig's early Shakespearean framing, the scarf functioning like the handkerchief Othello gives Desdemona, a gift signaling provisional affection and loyalty only if it remains valuable to the beloved recipient. But more important is the way that in this report, religion is culture, and the two categories cannot be separated from a Pakistani ethnicity, an ethnicity that trumps Syed's American nationality and culture. Such attitudes likely sparked Koenig's use of the term *racism* to describe the emphasis on and prejudice concerning Syed's alterity. Koenig's larger argument is that the confusion over Syed's religion, descent, and culture "shows how easy it is to stir stereotypes in with facts, all of which then gets baked into a story" ("Episode 10"). That is precisely the point. Jurors, Koenig, and the listener may try to distinguish between religion, culture, and race, but these elements inform one another. The complex and indistinguishable interrelationship between these various factors once again reveals that numerous facets of identity beyond biological descent constitute concepts of difference in a way that mirrors the fluid construction of race in early modern England.

Some scholars may argue that race did not factor into Syed's case but rather that culture or ethnicity informed the jurors' views. But we must remember that Syed looked different from the majority of jury members determining his fate, whether white or Black. The turbaned, bearded presence of his cultural community would only have heightened this distinction. Muslim lawyer Rabia Chaudry, Syed's family friend and advocate, explains, "You have an urban jury in Baltimore city, mostly African American, maybe people who identify with Jay [the prosecution's star witness against Syed] ... more than Adnan, who is represented by a community in headscarves and men in beards ... The visuals of the courtroom itself leaves an impression and there's no escaping the racial implications there" ("Episode 10"). Moreover, we must consider how the narrative constructed around Syed's guilt, specifically his motives, became tethered to concerns and stereotypes about both South Asian and Muslim masculinity and culture. For Koenig, and for many listeners, this narrative looks like an issue of race.

It may be easy to dismiss voices like the jurors' as representing a less informed perspective about distinctions between culture, religion, ethnicity, and race. Yet online discussions likewise exemplify how *race* becomes a term readily applied to the complex construction of difference found in *Serial* Season 1. Take an article entitled "*Serial* Episode 10: Did Racism Help Put Adnan in Prison?" in which four *Atlantic* staff members reflect on Episode 10. In the piece, the language moves between religion, culture, ethnicity, and race as much as it does in the podcast. Conor Friedersdorf notes that the episode takes on "anti-Muslim prejudice" as well as "stereotypes about Muslims," but the stereotypes addressed were actually against Pakistanis, not Muslims as a whole. This may seem like parsing, as Pakistanis are overwhelmingly Muslim. But the prosecutor made a point to group Pakistani men as a type, not Muslims in general. Friedersdorf's colleague Tanya Basu admits that for her, the most "thought provoking" part of the episode was the question of "what role, if any, did race play in Adnan's trial?" Yet nowhere does Basu mention biology or South Asian descent. Instead, she discusses Syed's Islamic faith and "Pakistani culture." She also notes, "That Cristina Gutierrez [Syed's defense attorney] must explain where Pakistan is, what an immigrant is, and how Adnan fits into that picture (he doesn't) shows how much progress has yet to be made to reduce racial stereotyping within the American criminal justice system." For Basu, prejudices about Syed's Islamic religion and Pakistani culture can be collapsed easily into the category of racial stereotyping even though, narrowly defined, these are not racial categories. In the most notable critique of race in *Serial*, Kang asserts that in Episode 10, "Koenig quickly dispenses with Syed's race and religion." Certainly, Koenig considers Syed's religion when she discusses anti-Muslim bias, admittedly in an all too cursory way. But Kang is incorrect. Koenig does not dismiss Syed's race because technically, she never acknowledges the implications of his South Asian racial identity. In other words, she examines Syed's religion but not race. Yet for Kang, the discussion of the former suggests the latter. One finds a similar slippage in Soraya Roberts's commentary in "Thoughts on Race, Journalism, and 'Serial.'" Roberts claims, "In the case of *Serial* in particular, it isn't even clear that this is a story about race . . . While the prosecutors in the case painted him [Syed] as a devout Muslim who was enraged by how his relationship with Lee had led him to lie to his family, in the second episode of *Serial*, Koenig says that 'Adnan claims he just wasn't that religious.' What to believe?" In the examples Roberts cites, she is correct; Syed's Muslim identity is not a matter of race. And yet, as I have demonstrated, conceptions of race and religion inextricably shape each other, both within the podcast and outside of it. As much as certain early modern scholars hold onto the idea of a neat, stable, scientific conceptualization of race today, these voices within and about *Serial*—including informed, educated voices—suggest that modern conceptualizations of race may have more in common with early modern ones than these scholars have admitted.

Shakespearean Implications: Reconsidering Premodern Critical Race Studies

But how can the depiction and discussion of race in *Serial* inform our engagement with Shakespeare? I contend that representations such as those in *Serial* prompt an ideological and methodological shift that further encourages existing efforts within the field to dislodge its own white racial framing. A post-racial work produced and discussed by some of the most privileged and educated voices in American society, *Serial* demonstrates that today's conceptions of race are no more stable or biologically based than those constructed in the early modern period. Acknowledging this correspondence allows those interested in PCRS to employ the contested term *race* without constant justification. Doing so mirrors the current methodological trends in race and ethnic studies, namely the recognition of race in the West's historical past as well as the presence of *racisms*—varying constructions of race and racial prejudice—in the present.[23]

This particular linkage between the early modern and the modern also allows scholars to grant that there may have been an ideology of race before a specific semantic articulation of it. Conceptions of alterity in the Renaissance do not *have* to be understood as race. But recognizing the varied, contradictory ways people consider and conceive of race opens up the possibility that these conceptions *can* be understood racially even if individual racial ideologies do not neatly align with strict definitions of the term. Doing so thereby identifies and acknowledges the cultural legacy of racialized art. Too often, it seems as if those hesitant to consider race in the Renaissance fear sullying great art. They are unnerved by the potential that works we love to teach and study, works on which we have built our careers, might be implicated in the prejudicial demarcation between "us" and "them."[24] Whether we like it or not, there is a political and ideological potency attached to the terms *race* and *racism* not carried by the terms *bigotry* or *ethnocentrism*.[25] *Race* and *racism* indicate a hierarchical distinction based not on religion, gender, sexuality (though these can be interrelated), or even on culture but on an aspect of identity often imagined as indelible even as it is ironically and paradoxically conceived of in fluid ways.[26]

---

[23] Goldberg explains in *The Anatomy of Racism* that across critical race studies, understandings of racism are also changing: "The presumption of a single monolithic racism is being displaced by a mapping of the multifarious historical formulations of *racisms*" (xiii). This displacement invites new questions, including two that apply directly to early modern race studies: "In what ways does the language used in expressing racist attitudes and in making accusations and denials of racism alter through historical time?" and "What are the factors . . . cultural, literary, and so on—that effect such alternations in language, expression, and attitude?" (xii).

[24] Smith reminds us, via Toni Morrison, that "we are subjected to and reproduce a dominant 'white' ideology that defines what we see and how we read" ("Othello's Black Handkerchief" 25). We can take Smith's claim even further by admitting that this white ideology likewise informs academic methodologies and the topics considered worthy of scholarly attention.

[25] The same can be said about using *ethnicity* rather than *race*. Peter Erickson notes that "*Ethnicity* is an appealing possibility" compared to "the highly charged term race," but he then cautions, "In the shift from race to a more inclusive ethnicity, the specificity of black-white power relations is in danger of disappearing" ("The Moment of Race" 30).

[26] As with most terms regarding difference, *racism* likewise has nuanced and divergent uses. Goldberg once again gives a useful definition: "Racism, in short, is about exclusion through depreciation, intrinsic or instrumental, timeless or time-bound . . . Racism concerns the maintenance of homogeneities' contours, militarizing their borders, patrolling their places of possible transgression" (*Threat of Race* 5).

Accepting both this contradiction and the ideological weight attached to the word *race* means understanding that considering race in Renaissance literature is not simply about semantic correctness. Rather, locating race in canonical texts prompts an identification of long-standing and potentially cross-historical practices used to discriminate against those considered as foreign Others, like Syed and Othello. More specifically, addressing early modern race pushes us to more fully understand great literature's role in disseminating the ideologies underpinning those discriminatory practices. By conceding race's presence even in the fluidity of early modern culture, we acknowledge that identifying race in great, foundational works of art—and in turn, combating racist ideology through our classrooms and research—is not as simple as pinpointing biologically based conceptions of Otherness.

Recognizing race in Shakespeare's works proves particularly crucial. BIPOCs can often feel as if Shakespeare's position as the apotheosis of elite, educated, white culture excludes them. As Alden T. Vaughan and Virginia Mason Vaughan point out, for African Americans this exclusion has come in the form of "the color bar" that "has often prevented African Americans who were born and raised in the United States from full participation in classical theater" (122). As a result, "many in the African American community remain ambivalent about Shakespeare and the cultural hierarchy he has come to represent." Vaughan and Vaughan likewise explain how this cultural alienation may be exacerbated for other persons of color: "The barriers seem even higher for America's newest immigrants—Latinos and Asian Americans—because Shakespeare is the premier poet of the English language and his vocabulary is more difficult to master than colloquial American speech ... As a result, for many Latino and Asian American artists Shakespeare has come to stand for Anglo-America's cultural hegemony."[27] Ruben Espinosa tackles this alienation head on when he addresses what he calls the "Shakespeare-Latinx divide," which encapsulates the idea "that either Shakespeare doesn't belong to Latinxs or Latinxs don't belong in Shakespeare" ("'Don't it make'" 49). And Mohegan theatremaker Madeline Sayet locates a similar displacement when

---

[27] Thompson provides an excellent example of the way language codes otherness in relation to Shakespeare when she discusses reviews of Peter Sellars's *Othello* in *Passing Strange*, esp. pp. 169–81. For further discussion of the ways English can be both hospitable and inhospitable to those considered strangers, see Kathryn Vomero Santos, "Hosting Language: Immigration and Translation in *The Merry Wives of Windsor*," *Shakespeare and Immigration*, ed. Ruben Espinosa and David Ruiter (Ashgate, 2014), 59–72.

she directs attention to the fact that the "immense amount of space [Shakespeare's] work currently takes up is an ongoing tool of colonization, just as his work has been used historically as a weapon to remove other people's cultures and teach them that one British playwright is superior to all other writers." There can be little doubt that even if Shakespeare may be for all time, frequently, he is not for all people.

If people Othered in and by American society already feel barred from engagement and identification with Shakespeare, refusing to consider race in relation to his texts may only exacerbate this alienation. For many BIPOCs, issues of race comprise daily life as they confront the realities of white privilege in America. Refusing to locate race in Shakespeare's work creates one more way that American culture marginalizes their experiences. The blinders of white privilege that direct attention to a universal Shakespeare unsullied by the potential presence of racial prejudice discourage identification by those who may locate their experiences of racial difference in Shakespeare's canonical works.[28] Furthermore, if early modern studies ignores the presence of race in Renaissance literature, it may also be inadvertently entrenching white privilege by deterring scholars of color and scholars invested in race and social justice from work in our field. Ayanna Thompson argues that "if the field were to support the inclusion of race studies more systematically and consistently, then our ranks may diversify more rapidly and thoroughly" (*Passing Strange* 180). It stands to reason that any continued resistance to the integration of race studies with Renaissance studies may alienate scholars deeply invested in matters of social justice who might feel as if there is little space for their interests and research among those who study Shakespeare.

On a specifically pedagogical level, allowing for a discussion of race in Shakespeare facilitates important textual approaches in the classroom. After *Serial*'s release, a California high school teacher, Michael Godsey, replaced *Hamlet* with *Serial* in his tenth- and eleventh-grade English classes. Godsey argues in favor of the substitution by asserting that *Serial* allows him to teach the Common Core's anchor standards in reading and writing more easily "than anything written by Shakespeare, Joyce, or anybody else. By far"

---

[28] Thompson argues that race plays a key role in disrupting the framing of Shakespeare as universal: "As my students do on the first day of class, most people will assume that an avowal of Shakespeare's universality is universally applicable, encompassing, timeless, and, well, good. The tensions arise, however, when race enters into Shakespeare's universe" (*Passing Strange* 41, 42).

("I'm Replacing Shakespeare"). In fact, on his blog Godsey addresses all nine reading standards and explicitly details how teaching *Serial* allows him to convey them to his students. More appealing, however, is the fact that, according to Godsey, students find *Serial* more engaging than Shakespeare: "They actually listen to the story" ("Standards Based 'Serial'"). In large part, this heightened attention comes from *Serial*'s apparent relevancy. Godsey explains, "Students find this [learning the standards] more exciting and relevant when using a contemporary story like 'Serial.'"

Godsey's experiment has garnered attention because his replacement of Shakespeare makes people uncomfortable. Matt Collette notes, "But Godsey's students are no longer reading and studying the iconic language and plots of Shakespeare, which is definitely not something the Common Core prescribes." The use of the term "iconic" stands in for the cultural evaluation of Shakespeare as great art, a status not achieved by *Serial*. In other words, part of the issue is that, achievement of Common Core standards notwithstanding, popular culture has displaced Shakespeare's great works. Collette cites Carol Jago, a member of the California Reading and Literature Project of UCLA and a participant of the "panel that oversaw" the instigation of the reading and writing Common Core standards: "'It's hard not to come off as the cranky old English teacher who just likes Shakespeare,' she admits. But Jago says there's a reason we still teach these classic texts: They carry deep lessons about our shared humanity that have lasted for decades, even centuries" (Colette). By invoking shared humanity, Jago appeals to the popular idea of humanistic Shakespeare. As Thompson reminds us, "Shakespeare is one of the few authors who is assumed to have written timeless and universal plays" ("The Blackfaced Bard" 451). Opening up space to discuss race in Shakespeare provides one more avenue to make Shakespeare all the more applicable for today's students by addressing distinctions and potential similarities across Western constructions of difference.[29]

Take, for example, the text invoked by Koenig herself—*Othello*. Asserting that race did not exist in the Renaissance means that race

---

[29] This chapter cannot do justice to existing scholarly work on race and pedagogy. For further discussions see Hall, "Beauty and the Beast of Whiteness: Teaching Race and Gender," *Shakespeare Quarterly* 47.4 (1996): 461–75; Ayanna Thompson and Laura Turchi, *Teaching Shakespeare with Purpose: A Student-Centred Approach* (Bloomsbury, 2016); *Teaching Social Justice through Shakespeare: Why Renaissance Literature Matters Now* (Edinburgh University Press, 2019); and the special collection *Teaching a Diverse and Inclusive Premodern World: Studies in Medieval and Renaissance Teaching*, edited by Sarah Davis-Secord, 27.2 (2020).

is not pertinent to this play. Students would likely (and rightly) find such an assertion absurd. By acknowledging rather than resisting the overlap between early modern and modern constructions of race, one would be able to more logically employ varying pedagogical strategies. For instance, teachers could request that students list the ways in which numerous characters racialize Othello. If not stymied by concerns about drawing false transhistorical connections due to strict definitions of race, they could then invite students to debate whether we construct race similarly today or not, and whether what we see in *Othello* is, in fact, a treatment of race. Thus, just as Godsey's students discuss Syed's guilt, students of Renaissance literature could contribute to the conversation about race and the Renaissance rather than simply being lectured on it.

By furthering a dialogue between the construction and depiction of race in the Renaissance and today, one could also more strategically and convincingly place *Othello* in conversation with contemporary racial issues, especially those that invite students to consider social justice. Francesca T. Royster asserts that "more than any other of Shakespeare's plays, *Othello* demands a method of teaching that bridges the past with the present" because "in our culture, the story of *Othello* is often retold as a story of the black experience in white culture" ("Rememorializing" 53). Creating such a bridge invites students to discuss *Othello* in relation to modern examples, from television shows to films to music to current events, such as the narrative of the criminal and/or violent Black male informing the Michael Brown and Eric Garner cases. Students could thus bring their interests in contemporary racial dynamics to bear on Shakespeare's canonical works, which would open up discussions about his universality and the politicization of his plays. Kim Newton, director of College Prep Programs for the American Shakespeare Center, suggests similar pedagogical strategies as a means for Shakespeare to "reach . . . students on a different level—a level that would engage them as much as *Serial* intrigued millions of attentive weekly listeners." For an in-class activity, Newton proposes the following discussion: "How do characters in *Othello* refer to Othello's otherness? What sets Othello apart from the Venetians? Do the same descriptions apply to Adnan? In what ways are Othello and Adnan similar to and different from one another?"

Newton's example, and my own, can certainly be used in the classroom even if one does not agree that too stark a distinction has been created between race as conceived in the Renaissance and race as conceived today. In fact, many scholars already approach *Othello* through the lens of race, while others take this connection a step further and frequently make links to contemporary culture as outlined above.[30] Yet if this is the case, there is a potential paradigmatic and methodological disconnect. The field's powerful institutions—conferences, editorial boards, library programming, etc.—cannot allow assertions that race does not exist in the Renaissance to remain uncontested on the one hand and then promote race as a context for exploring *Othello* and other early modern texts that consider difference on the other. In other words, without conceding the possibility that race in the Renaissance exists, these exercises and discussions carry little logical or methodological weight, for the worry will always be that students might be too careless; they might too easily conflate a fluid racial past with a stable racial present. By refusing a false delineation between race "then" and "now," activities such as those addressed above make more methodological sense. Stated differently, this refusal allows for more creativity as scholars consider how to craft approaches that breathe new life into the classroom and that allow for coupling Shakespeare with questions of social justice. In other words, teachers can more logically invite expressly relevant discussions and allow innovative pairings, like smartly and responsibly connecting "iconic" Shakespeare with "hip" *Serial*.

That is not to say that this approach means disregarding what proves distinctly early modern about Shakespeare's texts and modern about current narratives. Newton's remarks serve as an excellent example. As she explains of her pairing of *Serial* with *Othello*, "The story of Hae Min Lee's tragic death invokes the story of *Othello* more than any other [of Shakespeare's stories]. Hae Min, like Desdemona, was a well-liked young woman who found herself in a controversial relationship with a man whom society deemed to be an outsider. Adnan and Othello are the exotic 'other,' accomplished and admired by their communities, yet doomed to suffer through their own tragic endings." In some ways, Newton's comment invokes Koenig's opening to the podcast, a conflation of Syed with Othello as a murderous Other. Yet Newton carefully notes not an interracial but rather a "controversial relationship" between Lee and Syed. Moreover, she does not identify Adnan and Othello as fellow Muslims. Instead, she correctly observes that they are both "deemed . . . the exotic other." Newton's use of "deemed" here is key, for she points to Otherness as

---

[30] For a helpful resource that presents various pedagogical approaches to *Othello*, including specific ones engaging with race, see *Approaches to Teaching Shakespeare's Othello*, ed. Peter Erickson and Maurice Hunt (MLA 2005).

a construction, demonstrated just as potently by Iago as by the jurors of Syed's trial. In other words, unlike Koenig, Newton chooses her language carefully. She thereby demonstrates that one can discuss racial difference as present in the early modern and modern periods while still being thoughtful and accurate about ideological and semantic demarcations.

The examples provided above are in no way meant to be prescriptive. Rather, I include them to illustrate what we in the discipline gain if we carefully yet unhesitatingly consider race in the great works of early modernity, even if, especially if, doing so exposes discomfiting depictions of racial Otherness in early modern culture. As *Serial* exemplifies (and numerous other works, as well as lived experience, corroborate), even in the post-racial era and beyond, descent, foreignness, skin color, culture, and religion all shape ideological constructions of race. Accepting this premise entails likewise accepting that the concept of race existed in the Renaissance and its culturally significant literature, which addresses the seeming impasse plaguing discussions about race in early modern texts. It also opens up new yet still methodologically sound ways of helping Shakespeare matter to students whose increasingly mixed-race descent makes them a generation especially grappling with questions of identity, race, and Otherness. Considering the possibility of race in Renaissance texts can only provoke better, more thoughtful engagements with "iconic" literary works as well as potentially related pop-cultural texts. Moreover, tackling the difficult and shifting topic of race in the classroom refines our students' (and our own) understandings of how to define and deploy race across a range of eras. A reframing of how to methodologically and ideologically approach race thus breathes new life into the field's scholarly and pedagogical commitments.

Of the eight reasons Godsey provides for replacing *Hamlet* with *Serial*, his fourth reads, "My students' opinions might actually matter on social networking sites. Or in my class. Or in real life" ("Replacing Shakespeare"). He continues, "Nobody on the Internet really cares about their thoughts on Hamlet's suicidal tendencies." If we take his premise to be true, discussing race in the Renaissance does not necessarily solve this problem because maybe no one will care what students think about race in *Othello* either. Yet by affording the opportunity to pair a discussion of *Othello*, or any other applicable early modern text, with a relevant debate about post-racial or current American constructions of race and social justice, we make certain that our research on and pedagogy of Shakespeare does indeed matter in class and in "real life."

Essentially, discussing Renaissance race means dismantling the white racial frame that has long affected scholarly work on the era, and on Shakespeare more narrowly. In turn, it provides a way of challenging the white racial frame affecting those we reach through our scholarship, pedagogy, and activism. Similar to the almost invisible artistic frame, this white racial frame is designed precisely so that it remains difficult to identify and displace. As "texts" such as *Serial* disseminate globally via cyberspace or an iTunes download, this frame, and Shakespeare's problematic function within it, become that much harder to identify and combat. Thus, like the artists, museum curators, and art dealers who engage with the importance of a painting's frame, it remains crucial for purveyors of Shakespeare to use their expert gaze in order to dislodge *Shakespeare* from this racialized association. They must take Othello's request seriously, insisting that Shakespearean reanimations telling stories such as his, Syed's, Lee's, and Wild's manifest the complex racial interpretive prisms Othello so desperately desires.

Chapter 4

"No tools with which to hear": Adaptive Re-Vision, Audience Education, and *American Moor*

Whiteness and American Theatre

It is a truth (almost) universally acknowledged: the American theatre has a whiteness problem. In his discussion of whiteness and Broadway, for example, theatre scholar Warren Hoffman posits that "with few exceptions, [the musical] is written *by* white people, *for* white people, and is *about* white people" (5). Writing for *HowlRound* about race and the American theatre, producer, writer, and director Rebecca Stevens notes that "As a field, we are still struggling with this most rudimentary of challenges—giving people of colour enough seats at the table." And when comparing the ways that three 2019 New York City productions crafted by Black theatremakers engaged with white audiences, cultural critic Soraya Nadia McDonald places the presumption of whiteness in her title, "In theater, the white gaze takes center stage." These observations merely scratch the surface of the multifaceted difficulties presented by whiteness in American theatre. Even so, they direct attention to how widespread these issues run: from who gets to create artistic works to who is represented on stage to the themes and ideas explored in drama to who attends the theatre and in turn how the theatre caters to them. Whiteness, it would seem, pervades American theatre.

While such claims by theatre practitioners have long been supported predominantly by anecdotal evidence, in recent years, hard data shores up assertions of theatre's overwhelming whiteness. In 2017, Actors' Equity released a report in which it assessed numbers taken from contracts for performances that began between January

1, 2013 and December 31, 2015.[1] Actors' Equity found that "nationally over the course of 2013–2015, most principal contracts went to Caucasian members, accounting for 71 percent" (8). African Americans accounted for 7.56 percent, "those who identify as Hispanic or Latino" for 2.23 percent of the contracts, and Asian Americans only 1.57 percent (12). These numbers do not tell the whole story, however, for as the report notes, "16 percent of our membership have not identified their race/ethnic background. That means, for this research, there can be anywhere up to almost 20 percent of employment in any single analysis that we cannot quantify," a fact that gives an incomplete picture of the "problems we face." This lack of diversity extended to creative control as well. Actors' Equity reported that "The overwhelming majority (74 percent) of national stage management contracts went to Caucasians. In fact, stage management was the least ethnically diverse cohort in Equity's employment categories" (8), a homogeneity that contributes to the prevention of onstage patterns from changing. Both on and off stage, then, whiteness predominates in the American theatre industry.

Statistics from theatres in New York City add to these findings, reflecting the prevalence of Caucasian actors but also disclosing more about the racial and ethnic makeup of playwrights and directors. Through support provided by the American Theatre Wing, in March of 2019, the Asian American Performers Action Coalition (AAPAC) released information not just about performers, on whom they had been reporting for ten years, but also regarding "playwrights, composers, lyricists and directors," for "we realize that tracking statistics on all creatives employed may have a direct impact on the employment of actors of color, while also providing a more accurate picture of the inclusivity within our industry" (1). According to the AAPAC report, which took data for the 2016–17 season from all Broadway and nonprofit theatres, 66.8 percent of available roles went to Caucasian performers, making it "the only ethnicity to over-represent compared to their respective population size in New York" (2). The 33 percent of roles that went to minority actors break up accordingly: 18.6 percent for African American performers, 7.3 percent for Asian Americans, 5.1 percent Latinx performers, 1.7 percent Middle Eastern/North African (MENA) performers, and a dismal 0.1 percent for American Indian/Native/First Nation (AI/N/FN) performers. Moving offstage, "Caucasian playwrights wrote a whopping 86.8% of all shows

---

[1] These numbers excluded per-performance contracts as well as replacement contracts.

produced in the 2016–17 season and Caucasian directors were hired for 87.1% of all productions" (AAPAC 1). African American playwrights were 7.8 percent of the total, Latinx playwrights 2.5 percent, Asian Americans 1.5 percent, MENA 1.5 percent, and AI/N/FN playwrights made up 0 percent. The numbers for directing are similar: 6.1 percent African Americans, 2.3 percent Latinx, 3.0 percent Asian American, 1.5 percent MENA, and again, 0 percent AI/N/FN directors (2). I provide these numbers not to position New York theatre as more important or to suggest that somehow its statistics are representative of theatres across the nation, but rather to indicate that as the most famous and arguably successful theatre scene in the US located in one of the country's most diverse cities, one can safely presume that if *it* has a diversity problem on the stage, so too do many touring companies and regional theatres, perhaps even more so.

In fact, the meager representation of persons of color in American theatre extends beyond any specific region, and likewise affects those whose work makes it off the page. A report from the Dramatists' Guild entitled "The Count 2.0"—a 2018 follow-up of their 2015 study, "The Count"—asks a fundamental question that provides national context for the New York numbers: "Who's getting produced in the US?" (Jordan). The report articulates a clear answer: white writers, who account for 84.9 percent of the works that made it to the professional stage in the 2016–17 season. Conversely, only 15.1 percent came from writers of color, with the highest percentage of writers of color (23 percent) crafting new plays (vs. revivals, at only 8 percent). Whether in regard to who performs, directs, manages, or gets produced, in the words of the AAPAC report, "the numbers speak for themselves" (1). Acknowledged or not, American theatre indeed has a whiteness problem.

These figures invite the question: what relationship does the orientation toward whiteness *on* stage have toward the preponderance of whiteness *off* stage via the audience? For statistics make it clear that white audiences are also part of theatre's overwhelming similitude. The National Endowment for the Arts (NEA) released a report based on a 2017 survey of public participation in the arts, which gives a broad picture of who attends the arts and, more specifically, the theatre.[2] Generally, the report notes that "Regarding race and

---

[2] Compared to other artistic and cultural events, theatre falls third in popularity. While 54 percent of adults attended "at least one arts and cultural event in the course of a year," 24 percent attended a live play or musical (compared to 42 percent for live music performances and 40 percent for fairs or festivals featuring some form of art) (NEA 11).

ethnicity, a larger percentage of White adults attended any event in the past 12 months (61 percent), compared with Black adults (39 percent), Hispanic adults (41 percent), and Asian adults (45 percent)" and "Other" at 57 percent (NEA 22).[3] The predominance of white attendees was in fact a pattern across specific events, including "live music performances, fairs or festivals, live plays or musicals, and art exhibits" (22).[4] Regarding theatre specifically, the breakdown of race and ethnicity for those attending a live play or musical (which includes professional, community, or student performers) presents as follows: 28.1 percent White, 16.0 percent Black, 14.0 percent Hispanic, 20.7 percent Asian, and 21.1 percent Other (23). Separated by type of theatrical event, for musical stage plays the numbers are 20.2 percent White, 10.1 percent Black, 9.7 percent Hispanic, 9.4 percent Asian, and 11.5 percent Other, while for a non-musical stage play they are 11.6 percent White, 7.7 percent Black, 4.0 percent Hispanic, 4.8 percent Asian, and 7.0 percent Other (Appendix 7-A). Whiteness thus predominates on American theatre's boards (as well as the various spaces that help manifest what and who makes it onto those boards) and in its seats.

What does this prodigious presence of whiteness on and off the American stage mean for plays striving to tackle the topic of race via the theatre? How does the seeming givenness of whiteness in regard to both creators and audiences affect theatrical content, representation, and performance when staging dramas that tackle race? These are questions that Keith Hamilton Cobb's play *American Moor* (2011) puts front and center. *American Moor* follows a middle-aged African American actor auditioning for the role of *Othello* for a young, white

---

[3] Regarding how the questionnaire records race and ethnicity, the report explains in a footnote: "The basic CPS questionnaire records the race and ethnicity of each respondent. With respect to race, a respondent can be White, Black, Asian, American Indian and Alaskan Native (AIAN), Native Hawaiian and Other Pacific Islander (NHOPI), or combinations of two or more of the preceding. A respondent's ethnicity can be Hispanic or non-Hispanic, regardless of race. The categories presented throughout the report for White, Black, and Asian, refer to individuals who identified as non-Hispanic White, non-Hispanic Black, and non-Hispanic Asian, respectively. The category Hispanic refers to respondents who identified only as Hispanic, and not any other race. All other race and ethnicity compositions are included in the Other category" (NEA 16).

[4] When excluding elementary or high school performances, the numbers change, but the pattern remains for any artistic event: 59 percent White, 43 percent Black, 42 percent Hispanic, 50 percent Asian, and 46 percent Other. In regards to performing arts specifically, white attendance still predominates, with attendees 48 percent White, 35 percent Black, 35 percent Hispanic, 36 percent Asian, and 35 percent Other. (NEA 35)

director. This audition serves as a catalyst for the unnamed actor to dialogue not just with the director, but also with the audience—in fact, predominantly with the audience—with whom he shares intimate meditations not just on the audition process, but also regarding a wide range of topics including his love of and appreciation for Shakespeare, his education and training, what it is like being a Black man in America, his interpretation of Shakespeare's *Othello*, and his critique of American regional theatre. The play toggles between a linear structure that focuses on the actor as he awaits his audition until the audition's closing moments and a thematic one in which the actor interrupts the audition to share his reflections on past and present, a shift signaled by warm, yellow lighting when he articulates his most vulnerable self to spectators and cool, blue lighting when he speaks to the director much more guardedly.[5] This structural decision means that whatever the actor communicates to viewers in "private," stream-of-consciousness moments inflects their understandings and interpretations of the audition's dynamics. As such, questions about the interconnected and contentious relationships between race, whiteness, and theatrical interpretation—in Cobb's own words, questions such as, "Who gets to make art in America? Who gets to be seen? Who gets to be heard? Whose perspectives matter? What do we do when the answers to those questions suggest a very lopsided awareness of right and wrong?" (Cobb and Whitmore)—remain a constant, explicit, dynamic presence across *American Moor*'s 90 minutes.

Chapter 4 thus turns to *American Moor*, positioning it as an important counternarrative to the ones found in preceding chapters. Specifically, I engage most with *American Moor* in its earliest performed and scripted versions, ones that use drama as a powerful force for confronting race and racism on both individual and systemic levels. The 2012 script archived at the Folger Shakespeare Library in many ways creates a compelling though not obvious overlap with *Kill Shakespeare*, the work at the heart of the first chapter addressing antiblack post-racial *Othello*s. Just as *Kill Shakespeare* holds particular imaginative promise as a work of speculative fiction, so does this version of *American Moor*. The script is not thoroughly workshopped, and though workshopping can add polish, it also means taking into account more monetary concerns, like what content might appeal to or alienate an audience (see my discussion of

---

[5] This chapter focuses on the 2012 script of *American Moor* archived at the Folger Shakespeare Library. However, when I turn to subsequent versions of the play for comparative analysis, I indicate it clearly in the text.

Hamilton in Chapter 2). Thus, the Folger script offers up *American Moor* at its most imaginative, holding its most potential, perhaps even at its most daring. Indeed, before this chapter's close, I address the changes made to the script, and what is both gained and lost as a result. Thus, this chapter holds in tension how *American Moor* strives to reshape the perspectives and ideologies of theatre's predominantly white audiences with the ways the reality of that same audience might have reshaped, even if only slightly, *American Moor*.

Even as I claim that *American Moor* tackles particular questions about race and the American theatre that the prevalence of whiteness in theatre invites, I must also acknowledge from the outset that it does not offer up clear answers. Rather, *American Moor* effectively spotlights the important realizations and subsequent dialogues that must occur both within the theatre and across society more broadly in order to challenge the racialized misframings raised in Chapters 1 through 3: stereotypical cultural depictions of Black identities, color-blind approaches to art that invoke race without addressing racism, and the centering of white perspectives through racial frames that advance whiteness's cultural and social supremacy. *American Moor* tackles these misframings head on; in their stead, the play provides a narrative that depicts the importance of centering the voices of persons of color—in this case, particularly of Black masculinity—of acknowledging the complexity of Black subjectivities, and of identifying that giving a mere nod to race is not enough. Cobb's play explicitly encourages its audience to better recognize racism by: 1) identifying racism as a cross-historical force, as demonstrated through the overlaps between Othello's relationship to the Venetian Senate and the actor's to the white director; 2) acknowledging how important racial misrepresentation is to white supremacy's dominance, which the play explores through the actor's discussion of his acting journey and his view of Othello; and 3) understanding how racism functions not just on the individual but also on the systemic level, addressed in the play through the director's voice and in the actor's discussions of the interrelated systems of higher education and the American theatre. These are the fundamental recognitions, the play suggests, that open up true dialogue about race.

And in *American Moor*, this dialogue is key, for it provides the opportunity to decenter whiteness and therefore more holistically represent Black identities on the stage and in American culture more widely. This ultimately hopeful play thus calls for what I term an adaptive re-vision. I build on and bring together Margaret Jane Kidnie's argument that an "original" performance is always already intimately tied to and defined against adaptation and Peter Erickson's call for the necessity of moving beyond adaptation to "re-vision," meaning a perspective and attitude that breaks new ground and tradition's hold ("'Late'"). Through its critiques of regional American theatre and the educational system, *American Moor* lays bare how the relationship between original, adaptation, and authority Kidnie identifies is racialized, tied to the structures of whiteness in theatre *and* in society at large. Yet as Cobb states in interviews, the only answer should not be appropriations, works like *American Moor* that take the critical view Erickson champions but in ways decidedly far from the "original," as nebulous and shifting as it may be. For doing so does not change the problem of *who* is allowed access to performance's supposedly most authoritative forms. I thus assert that what *American Moor* calls for is another stop along the fluid spectrum between original, adaptation, re-vision, and appropriation; what I am calling adaptive re-vision. This term expands adaptation to include a performance that may approximate whatever is deemed "original" but that intentionally takes a critical point of view, embracing instead of rejecting adaptation as a mode for challenging the white-oriented viewpoints and therefore theatrical traditions and standards shaping Shakespearean theatre. It does so by inviting Erickson's re-vision, accepting adaptation at the level of perspective, namely, a perspective that does not need to conform to the right/white one that has so long shaped the authoritative standard for performance.

What becomes clear is that in *American Moor* this adaptive re-vision occurs through a frank yet generous conversation based on trust, one that sees the problem of white supremacy but lovingly invites audiences of color and white audiences alike on a journey to discourse about and collaborate on a vision forward. Importantly, Cobb models this journey through audience education. The term *audience education* encapsulates a range of public activities Cobb undertakes, activities that provide current and potential audiences with the tools to engage in this difficult discourse about not just *Othello* but also race and its role in America. These activities educate by offering terms, questions, and conversations. Reconciliatory interchange happens not just *within* the world of the play, then, but also, crucially, *without* it as well. This chapter thus begins this book's turn to the antiracist antidotes that can be found in post-racial reanimations of *Othello*, antidotes vital to challenging the antiblack strategies explored in the book thus far. Rather than offering pat answers to complex problems, *American Moor* instead stresses that one of the first steps toward antiracism is openness to a candid, uncomfortable exchange about race in America (and its theatre), yet in Cobb's own words, an exchange borne out of "love and an open heart" (1).

American Moor and Racism across (Crumpled) Time

Even as *American Moor* serves as a powerful example of a drama that starkly confronts racism in America both on and off the stage, not once does Cobb choose to include the term *racism* in the play. Cobb instead allows racism to unfold on stage, with the actor providing commentary on the various explicit and implicit methods of race making white supremacy uses in order to reify its power. By emphasizing the process rather than focusing on language, *American Moor* pushes back against the common conflation between the fantasy of *race* and the denigrating process of *racism*. This attention on racist actions exposes racism's cross-historical presence, thereby making evident the interrelatedness of its manifestation on a representational and systemic level. Through these emphases, *American Moor* eschews the facile language in American culture that focuses on substitutions for "racism," such as "race relations," instead crafting a narrative that places responsibility on the white oppressor rather than the oppressed person of color.

In order to recognize how effectively *American Moor* stages racism and its complexity, one must first comprehend racism and America's means for refusing to confront it. One way is the collapsing of racism into race. Karen E. Fields and Barbara J. Fields carefully lay out the discrepancy between these often interchanged terms. Race, they explain, "stands for the conception or the doctrine that nature produced humankind in distinct groups, each defined by inborn traits that its members share and that differentiate them from the members of other distinct groups of the same kind but of unequal rank" (16). Though "*race* is the principle unit and core concept of *racism*," the two are unique entities, a demarcation imperative to recognize (17). They elaborate:

> *Racism* refers to the theory and the practice of applying a social, civic, or legal double standard based on ancestry, and to the ideology surrounding such a double standard . . . *Racism* is not an emotion or state of mind, such as intolerance, bigotry, hatred, or malevolence . . . *Racism* is first and foremost a social practice, which means that it is an action and a rationale for that action, or both at once. *Racism* always takes for granted the objective reality of *race*, as just defined, so it is important to register their distinctness. The shorthand transforms

racism, something an aggressor *does*, into *race*, something the target *is*, in a sleight of hand that is easy to miss. (17)

What Fields and Fields stress here is that while race may be a social construct, one that belongs to the "same family as the evil eye," racism belongs to a different family, that of "murder and genocide," which is not an illusion but rather a "crime against humanity" (101). Eliding race and racism, they argue, alters accountability, making "immoral acts of discrimination disappear, and then reappear camouflaged as the victim's alleged difference" (96). Properly understanding and deploying these terms therefore facilitates the ability to focus on transforming the ideology and behavior of racist enactors rather than fixing the so-called problems supposedly embodied by the racialized persons enacted upon.

If racism *is* acknowledged, however, all too often it is characterized as the manifestation of a particular person's prejudiced thinking. Yet the term *racism* encapsulates not just the specific enactor's racial prejudice but also the systems that undergird and advance that prejudice. Richard Delgado and Jean Stefancic define racism as "Any program or practice of discrimination, segregation, persecution, or mistreatment based on membership in a race or ethnic group" (171). In their emphasis on both "program" and "practice," Delgado and Stefancic point out that racism manifests in the individual but is also tied to broader social structures. Ijeoma Oluo likewise notes competing definitions of racism, explaining that for most people, "(1) Racism is any prejudice against someone because of their race. Or (2) Racism is any prejudice against someone because of their race, when those views are reinforced by systems of power" (26). Despite their similarity, Oluo advocates for the second definition so as not to "reduce issues of race in America to a battle for the hearts and minds of individual racists—instead of seeing racists, racist behaviors, and racial oppression as part of a larger system" (27). To be clear, the individual still participates, but it is these systems and "not our hearts" that determine "Who we see as successful, who has access to that success, who we see as scary, what traits we value in society, who we see as 'smart' and 'beautiful'— these perceptions are determined by our proximity to the cultural values of the majority in power, the economic system of those in power, the education system of those in power, the media outlets of those in power" (29). Ibram X. Kendi streamlines these ideas, contending that "Racism is a marriage of racist policies and racist ideas that produces and normalizes racial inequities" (*How to Be* 18). Taking these definitions in mind, then, "to say something is inferior about a racial group is to say a racist idea" (7), Kendi explains, for this ideology not only expresses particular racial prejudice but also systemic ideals created for the purpose of racial oppression.

Yet despite these clear definitions, the problem with identifying racism and resisting its conflation with race is at least twofold: the breadth of the term *racism*, and the way society allows people to use it, or not. First, as Delgado and Stefancic assert, American society "has only one word . . . for a phenomenon that is much more complex than that. For example: biological racism; intentional racism; unconscious racism; microaggressions; nativism; institutional racism; racism tinged with homophobia or sexism; racism that takes the form of indifference or coldness; and white privilege . . ." (30). That all these different forms of racism get captured by a single term—*racism*—demonstrates how "our system, by reason of its structure and vocabulary, is ill equipped to redress certain types of wrong" (31). But precisely because of racism's wide-ranging manifestations, it becomes normalized, "ordinary, not aberrational . . . the usual way society does business" so that it is "difficult to address or cure because it is not acknowledged" (Delgado and Stefancic 7, 8). Moreover, using the terms *racism* or *racist* has become almost taboo. Euphemisms like "racially charged," "racial difference," and "racial discrimination" abound in place of *racism* and/or *racist*.[6] Kendi notes that "Denial is the heartbeat of racism," and that denial comes in the form of disavowing that racist ideas are, indeed, racist, but also in rejecting the ability to properly use the term and thereby identify racism (*How to Be* 9). Put differently, racism has become a pejorative term whereas, Kendi argues, it should function as a "descriptive [term], and the only way to undo racism is to consistently identify and describe it—and then dismantle it. The attempt to turn this usefully descriptive term into an almost unusable slur is, of course, designed to do the opposite: to freeze us into inaction" (9). Racism must therefore be understood as a complex, shifting, multifaceted process rather than a monolithic concept, and expressly named accordingly.

These conceptualizations of racism therefore dismantle common misconceptions regarding race and racism. As a concept, race is not merely biological; it takes different forms to serve the ideological needs of white supremacy. Race and racism are not the same; the former expresses identity while the latter articulates ideologies and actions

---

[6] For a discussion of racial euphemism and its interrelationship with Shakespeare studies, especially regarding Shakespearean adaptations and appropriations, see Vanessa I. Corredera, "When the Master's Tools Fail: Racial Euphemism in Shakespeare Appropriation, or, the Activist Value of Premodern Critical Race Studies," *Literature Compass* (2022).

that reinforce racial hierarchization and the systems that disseminate them. It does not, therefore, perpetuate racism to acknowledge race; doing so is actually antiracist, for it resists a colorblindness that turns away from social inequities created to preserve racial hierarchy. It is not immoral or even inappropriate to call something or someone *racist*; that term vitally identifies racial stratification that cannot be resisted unless called out.

American Moor undermines these common misconceptions by having the actor articulate three points about racism. First, by repeatedly comparing his audition with Othello's speech to the Venetian Senate, the actor creates clear through lines between racism in the past and racism in the present, thereby pushing back against racism as deriving merely from a belief in biological hierarchy and demonstrating its shape-shifting nature. Second, the actor compellingly critiques the director's vision for *Othello* while articulating his own struggles with identity, race, and performance. He thus communicates how racism depends on delimiting the subjectivity of persons of color through misrepresentations of that very subjectivity. Third, the actor exposes how racism manifests systemically rather than just individually. Specifically, by staging the director's racism and connecting it to the actor's past experiences, the play underscores the interrelatedness between a specific person's racist views and the systems that inform them, in this case, education and the theatre. Thus, even without using the obvious language of race and racism, *American Moor* deftly prepares its predominantly white audience for the dialogue about racial inequity in America that it hopes to facilitate.

American Moor is not subtle about racism's presence across history. The play's title announces this connection, juxtaposing the archaic-sounding, multidimensional yet nevertheless racialized term *Moor* with the more modern yet just as semiotically loaded term *American*. *American* and *Moor* therefore work together to signal the play's interest in issues of identity, insider and outsider status, and the construction of race across time. *American Moor* thereby mirrors what Jonathan Gil Harris identifies as *Othello*'s own refusal of "linear temporality," instead depicting time as "a dynamic field whose contours keep shifting, bringing into startling and anachronistic proximity supposedly distant and disparate moments" (169).[7]

---

[7] Harris elaborates that as a play in which the action most often takes place at night or in the dark yet that would have been performed at the Globe during daylight, "A preposterous double time, then, is the condition of [*Othello*] not only as read but also in its original conditions of performance" (183).

Building on the work of Michel Serres, Harris calls this approach to temporality "crumpled time" (170). Serres uses the image of a handkerchief to explain this concept, noting how when a handkerchief is crumpled and placed in a pocket, "Two distant points suddenly are close, even superimposed. If, further, you tear it in certain places, two points that were close can become very distant ... As we experience time—as much in our inner sense as externally in nature, as much as *le temps* of history as *le temps* of weather—it resembles this crumpled version much more than the flat, overly simplified one" (qtd. in Harris 170).[8] Particularly pertinent here is Harris's own emphasis on Serres's work—that "supposedly discrete points—different historical 'moments' but also temporally coded distinctions of religion, race, and sexuality—are repeatedly made to be 'suddenly ... close, even superimposed'" (170). *American Moor* superimposes supposed distinctions of race in past and present to suggest that, while not the same, they nevertheless resonate across place and (crumpled) time.

Cobb stresses these connections not only through the play's language but also through its structure, which ties race in early modernity to race in contemporary America via *Othello*. This connection comes to the fore as the actor and director contest the best way to perform Othello's speech to the Venetian Senate, thereby staging "a conversation with a man given the privilege of authority who speaks *for* Shakespeare to the Black man directed to ventriloquize that understanding" (Hall, "'Othello Was My Grandfather'" 11). While I will unpack the details further, here, it is sufficient to understand that after the actor performs the speech "with a self-assurance that never boils over into arrogance or bravado" (Cobb 9), the director, Michael Aaron Miller, asks for the actor to "do it again" with more "charm" and "obeisance."[9] In response to this request, the actor frankly connects the racist expectations in the

---

[8] Scholars would equally benefit from attending to Harris's point about the way crumpled time involves the critic. He observes, "Serres's crumpling of the past into the folds of the present is an act of strategic proximation—it requires the artful labor of the critic, a labor that goes beyond mere empirical description as they really are or were. Serres thus allows us to recognize how our critical activities *create* the past and the present, less in the sense of making them up than of persistently transforming the web of relations that tether the past to us—and us to it. We less obey the time, then, than make the time" (174).

[9] For those familiar with Shakespearean performance history, Miller's name may invoke director Jonathan Miller, who directed the famous *Othello* (1981) starring a blackface Anthony Hopkins as the lead.

past to racist expectations in the present by equating his audition with Othello's speech to the Senate, observing, "You think that he thinks that he needs to do . . . 'a number' for these guys" just as "in order to get this gig, ah wait! . . . in order to succeed in getting from *you* the thing that *you* think *I* want . . . you're implying that *I* need to do 'a number . . .' for you . . ." (11). In the repetition of doing "a number"—a phrase referencing minstrelsy, a topic which I will address further below—the actor stresses the performative nature not only of his audition but also of the actions Othello must undertake for the Venetians. Indeed, the actor's language exposes how easily Othello's status and performance as a Black man slips into his present situation when he asserts, "But meanwhile he stands here, in front of you, having to play this game of civility and field your stupid comments with a look of interest and a smile while wanting nothing so much as to slap you knowing, if he did, that the ages of ancestral animosity accumulated in that single stroke would probably kill you dead" (13). The "he" standing references Othello, but "you" invokes the director, a link that explains the "ancestral animosity." The play's discourse thus makes it seem, as Kim F. Hall notes, that "we [the audience] are also the Venetian Senate watching the actor make his case to the duke, who's also the director" ("'Othello Was My Grandfather'" 11). As such, *American Moor* does not allow audience members to shrug off Othello's "number" nor the actor's current one as individual, idiosyncratic instances. Rather, by emphasizing the "ancestral" nature of the antagonism framing this moment, the actor stresses that white society's demand for a circumscribed performance of Black identity for its pleasure is neither an early modern nor modern request but rather one stretching across history.

In the structure the actor establishes, then, the director serves a concomitant function as representative of the Senate at large for whom Othello performs, but also Brabantio specifically. Cobb avoids subtext, drawing this link from early on in the play to its closing moments in which the actor repeatedly characterizes the director as Brabantio, a link he initiates when he asserts, "You think *I* want to be *your* Othello . . . it's your first mistake. And you're not alone. It's Brabantio's too" (12). The actor then makes the links between Brabantio's white privilege and the director's clear in an inner monologue to which only the audience is privy, asserting, "*I* know that Brabantio invited Othello to his house again and again because it was a novelty for him to host the important Black general. I'm sure Colin Powell has had to deal with this sort'a dumb shit too . . .

I know that *Brabantio* liked the stories; that they amused *him* . . . *I* know it's embarrassing, and offensive, not unlike this distasteful scenario that presently engages us both . . ." (14). The reference to Colin Powell heightens the monologue's point: that the demands of white masculinity upon Black masculinity stretch across time from Brabantio's treatment of Othello to Miller's treatment of both Othello the character *and* toward the actor standing before him.[10] And just as Brabantio is ignorant about the reality of what is truly happening around him—his daughter falls in love right under his nose—the director likewise does not achieve true understanding, as indicated when he comments that "what fascinates us is not only the size of the man, but the size of his emotion, and I think we need to see it," to which the actor poignantly replies, "And you think you're not *in* this play . . ." (17). The director can simultaneously represent both the Venetian Senate and Brabantio because ultimately "[he] is a metaphor for that omniscient voice . . . that a great many African Americans hear in their daily lives—the voice of, here is what we will accept from you . . . these are the parameters" (Cobb, *Discussing American Moor*). In drawing an evident connection between Brabantio and the director, *American Moor* communicates two important ideas to the audience. First, it traces how racism appears for different purposes and in distinct forms but in service of the same aims across history— to uphold white domination, whether it be over the Black body and its behavior, as in the case of Othello, or over the representation of Blackness, as in the actor's audition. Second, in underlining how the director mistakenly interprets Othello yet insists on his own viewpoint, the play depicts the different shapes racism takes as revealed in the director and actor's dialogue, a point to which I will return.

If the director functions as representative of the ideologies held by the Venetian Senate and Brabantio, then the actor aligns with Othello.[11] *American Moor* thus further stresses racial formation across history, but it does so in a way that resists the privileging of

---

[10] For an incisive reading of the connections between Colin Powell and Othello, see Kyle Grady's "Othello, Colin Powell, and Post-Racial Anachronisms," *Shakespeare Quarterly* 67.1 (2016): 68–83.

[11] By turning to *American Moor*'s structure, Ambereen Dadabhoy identifies a different analog for the director: Iago. She argues that "The struggle between the director and actor mimics that between Iago and Othello over who will control Othello's narrative and the meanings of blackness" ("Wincing at Shakespeare" 87). Yet Cobb creates a director who "lacks the creative linguistic skill that gives Shakespeare's Iago his agency" (85), while also "[limiting] the director's speech, rendering him as a text that the actor can always already read" (87).

whiteness and its racist positions even as it critiques it.[12] The evidence provided above already makes the association between the actor and Othello unmistakable. But it merits unpacking in order to understand how recognizing racism's cross-historical presence is imperative to understanding its visceral effects and to discerning how to combat it in the future. As early as the first instance that the actor equates the director with Brabantio, he similarly connects himself to Othello, stating, "you wouldn't understand a single word of all that's *not* being said . . . if I said it . . . if Othello said it . . ." (12). The actor, however, does not deploy Othello to suggest that he and Othello undertake the same behavior in the way the director does Brabantio's. Rather, they have similar affective responses, as well as social struggles. For instance, in a moment that gestures toward the social pressures that extend beyond simply the actor and the misguided director, he claims, "My anger, Othello's anger, the guard dog, forever snarling at his chain's end, does not see you. He sees all the hovering forces in this room, in that senate chamber, in the world that have *made* you you, as they are all the same forces that have never allowed me to be me" (12). The language here exposes the cost of racism on Black subjectivity; it creates a justified "anger" that has lasted "forever." Crucially, this is not an interpersonal anger but rather one aimed at systems or "forces." In this way, even as the actor reveals the interpersonal cost caused by racist attitudes, he also rejects the favored argument of the post-racial (an emphasis on the personal or individual) by signaling how these attitudes manifest as a result of racist systems. What Cobb's elision of the actor and Othello stresses, however, is not just the systems at play, but also the fact that they are long-standing, "hovering" in both early modernity and modernity. The audience therefore has the opportunity to make the connection that while the specific systems may change—from Venetian courtroom to American audition

---

[12] Writing about her experience attending a workshop by the author of *White Fragility*, Robin DiAngelo, and her thoughts on the text itself for *Slate*, scholar and essayist Lauren Michele Jackson observes, "I couldn't help but notice the relative dearth of contemporary black studies scholarship cited in *White Fragility*." She elaborates, ". . . though scholars such as Frantz Fanon and Toni Morrison show up in *White Fragility* (the former relegated to a curious endnote), DiAngelo doesn't really consider black studies a disciplining force in the direction of her work. 'The voice that's missing for most white people is looking at what it means to be white,' she said. 'I see whiteness studies as white scholars responding to [scholars of color] saying "Stop looking at us, because, in fact, you are our problem."' But I am hard-pressed to imagine an accurate account of our world that doesn't include the rigor of those who analyze blackness as dutifully as DiAngelo attends to whiteness."

room, for example—across history, they serve the same racist function: to marginalize and limit Black subjectivity.

Black Masculinity and Misrepresentation

American Moor thus traces racism over periods in part to make it evident to predominantly white audiences that the actor and director do not function in a post-racial society but rather in a racial crucible existing across spaces, places, and time. In other words, it highlights the dire need for re-vision, for racism persists, unfolding right before viewers' eyes. But, as Kendi notes, in order to confront racism, one must identify it. *American Moor* undertakes this task for its audience, presenting the old vision that must be discarded by tracing the interconnectedness of a white perspective, stereotyping, and misrepresentation in *Othello* and still prevalent across post-racial twenty-first-century America. In *American Moor*, Othello therefore functions as a typological figure of misperceived and misunderstood Black masculinity by whiteness, or, put differently, of negrobilia. Actor Hugh Quarshie coined the term "negrobilia" to "describe the representations of black people commonly made by white people" (3). He turns to artifacts like "nigger-minstrel money boxes," *Tintin in the Congo*, the "African romances of Rider Haggard and Edgar Wallace," and even the characterization of the Moor in Mozart's *The Magic Flute* as examples of what elsewhere in this book I have addressed as caricatures and stereotypes, one-dimensional, even grotesque, representations of Black identity (3, 4). As an adaptation "endorsing a racist convention" and whose "performance conventions and conventional interpretations have reinforced racist views," *Othello*, he attests, belongs as part of this distorting collection.

Like Othello, Black men in post-racial America suffer from limited perceptions of both ability and character. This is why, for instance, the actor, like Quarshie in real life, has resisted the role for so long.[13] As he explains to the audience, he has always loved Shakespeare, whose characters "each had this depthless reservoir of emotion already roiling around within them," a depth which fostered a desire in him to play Titania or Hamlet or Romeo (4). His acting teacher, however, insisted on something "you might realistically play. Something befitting

---

[13] Quarshie eventually changed his stance, performing the role of Othello for the Royal Shakespeare Company's 2015 production of *Othello*, directed by Iqbal Khan and casting British Tanzanian actor Lucian Msamati as Iago.

your age, and experience," suggesting instead Aaron, Morocco, and of course, though he would be playing older, Othello (4). Interestingly, Quarshie decries these very characters, asserting, "I considered some of Shakespeare's characters for inclusion in this collection [of artifacts depicting negrobilia]: Aaron the Moor, the Prince of Morocco, and of course, Othello" (4). As I will address further below, long-standing theatrical tradition and conventions clearly make their way into the contemporary classroom, contracting both representational and educational possibilities for the Black actor. Othello, then, symbolizes the color line in Shakespeare, but also the delimiting of Black masculinity by American culture more broadly.

In addressing these restrictions imposed upon Black masculinity, the play emphasizes how subjective the (mis)characterization of Black masculinity proves to be by demonstrating that the racial caricatures crafted by the white imagination are in no way "something that the target *is*" (Fields and Fields 17). The play's stage directions in fact recognize yet resist negrobilia, noting that the actor "is a large man, powerfully built and handsome, but only imposing if *you* see him that way" (Cobb 1). These directions thereby insist that "Fear does not come from within the subject, nor does it reside in its object: we are not afraid of others because they are fearsome. Through the circulation of signs of fear, the black other 'becomes' fearsome" (Ahmed, "Affective Economies" 127). More precisely, by referencing that the actor *could* be imposing, the stage directions acknowledge what Kendi would categorize as the bodily racist specter of the violent Black man that so haunts Black masculinity, and that applies to any modern depiction of Othello (*How to Be* 71).[14] bell hooks explains how Western white supremacy created the stereotype of the "hypermasculine black male violent beast" (*We Real Cool* 50), a fabrication that "depicted black males as uncivilized brutes without the capacity to feel complex emotions or the ability to experience either fear or remorse" (48).[15] The goal of this characterization is to make it seem as if "black men embody a brutal patriarchal maleness that white men and women (and everyone else) must arm themselves to repress" (51). Unfortunately, "black

---

[14] Kendi defines a bodily racist as "one who is perceiving certain racialized bodies as more animal-like and violent than others" (*How to Be* 69).

[15] hooks elaborates on the logic of this stereotype, explaining, "According to racist ideology, white-supremacist subjugation of the black male was deemed necessary to contain the dehumanized beast. This perspective allowed racist folks to engage in extreme psychological denial when it came to assuming accountability for their ruthless and brutal dehumanization of black men" (*We Real Cool* 48).

males who reject racist sexist stereotypes must still cope with the imposition onto them of qualities that have no relation to their lived experience" (48).

Fundamental for *American Moor* is the way hooks highlights the "imposition" of this stereotype upon all Black men, a dynamic that *American Moor*'s stage directions stress by addressing how subjective this view of the actor proves to be. This is the "desiring and hostile white gaze" that Ambereen Dadabhoy explains the actor "excavates," a gaze "that seeks to circumscribe him in an episteme that determines the meaning and function of blackness within a white supremacist, patriarchal system" ("Wincing at Shakespeare" 87). For the Black actor, the circumscribing sign in the white supremacist episteme is his Black skin, and the very material, bodily nature of this sign is especially potent on the stage. Angel C. Pao observes, "More than any other single element, the actor's physical presence on stage controls the production of meaning as his or her body becomes the most arresting point of intersection for visual, auditory, sociocultural, and ideological codes" (27). *American Moor* displays a keen awareness of the "sociocultural and ideological codes" the audience may be ready to impose upon the Black actor as demonstrated by theatrical elements that work alongside his physical presence to help "[control] the production of meaning." For instance, Cobb dons a black, short-sleeved, collared shirt, khaki pants, and black Converse sneakers, an outfit that looks as if it came straight out of GAP's famous 1998 "Khakis Swing" commercial. This costume thus positions the actor as an "everyman," his nondescript apparel countering the notability of his Black skin in the white space that is the theatre in which Cobb performs and in the audition room seemingly filled by white spectators, such as the director, for whom the actor auditions. Furthermore, the limited "scenery," really more an amalgamation of props, situates the actor's audition within a long theatrical history. Though certain stage details have changed across performances, most consistent have been one classical column behind the actor which looks like the Lion of Venice sculpture residing in the Piazza San Marco, and another classical column down on its side in front of the first. The faux Lion of Venice invokes *Othello*'s setting and thus, subtly, *Othello*'s long stage history, while both classical columns could refer to the Grecian roots of traditional Western theatre. This staging thereby reminds viewers that regardless of his race, the actor is one in a long line of performers to tread the boards, even as the fallen column hints that perhaps he might challenge the stability of that very tradition. Cobb's stage directions therefore recognize the racialized perception of race as constructed into caricature, yet working alongside costuming and scenery, they resist its authenticity, making it clear that the white audience's racializing point of view is not reality.

What these stage directions and theatrical elements subtly gesture toward, then, is the presumed whiteness of most people who gaze at the actor *and* who influence *American Moor*. In fact, the emphasized *you* expressly presumes a distance between those reading the script and the actor. And who would be reading the script (at least before it was published)? Cobb's white director, Kim Weild, the white actor performing the voice and later the embodied role of the white director, Josh Tyson, and the white producers likewise shaping *American Moor* for largely white American theatregoing audiences. These stage directions therefore make it clear that the actor is always being viewed and constructed by a white gaze for which he must account, not just because he is an actor, but because he is a *Black* actor. Indeed, "A note on staging and stage directions," included in a 2018 version of the script, more expressly addresses how, from the beginning, Cobb imagined the play as a dialogue with others, but most especially the audience. In this note, Cobb explains that discerning what to do in a performance of *American Moor* can be challenging because the actor must address "at least three different amorphous entities, two or more that are not physically present, and an audience that very much is," so that at times those staging *American Moor* must turn to the text and at others to the stage directions (1). Most crucial for the play, however, is the audience, whom Cobb imagines as "fellow travelers." He observes, "It is not intended that this process leave them in comfort." But, the note continues, the audience has agreed to trust the actor by agreeing to watch *American Moor*; the actor is thus "responsible" for that trust and must therefore "return to them often with love" and "ingenuousness." Cobb never uses the term "white audience," but read in conjunction with each other, this note and the opening stage directions both indicate how *American Moor* negotiates largely white creators and audience members, ones who reside in a white supremacist society dependent upon projected misconstructions of Black selfhood. To return to the first stage directions, the "*you*" acknowledges these racist misjudgments by revealing that the imposing qualities of a Black man come not from nature but from the particular perception of the (most often) white gaze. Thus, from the outset, Cobb signals *American Moor*'s interest in exploring audience complicity in misconstruing Black masculinity, as well as in encouraging responsibility and growth regarding race, perception, and representation on the part of those engaging with the play through the journey they undertake with the performance.

Like the actor at the heart of *American Moor*, Othello also suffers from narrow representational parameters. As noted above, many of the actor's thoughtful meditations on race and identity arise as a result of the distinct visions he and Miller, the white director, have for depicting Othello. As the white director clarifies his approach toward the play for the Black actor, he explains, "I'm fascinated with this idea of irrational jealousy," stressing that he takes as his starting point the astronaut who drove across the country "in an adult diaper" in order to make his *Othello* one about the "utter abdication of self-control" (9). "Irrational jealousy," "utter abdication of self-control"—surely these terms apply to a wide range of people struggling with the human condition. The actor suggests as much when he observes how "Down underneath we're all getting our fragile human condition smacked around every gotdamn [sic] day, and nobody hears, sees, contemplates, gives a fuck, until it all comes out somewhere horrible . . ." (25). It would therefore be easy to overlook how race may play a role here, for the director points to a white, female astronaut as his reference. But the demands of white supremacy do not allow human feelings, good or bad ones, to apply neutrally. That is why when referenced in regard to Othello, irrationality and "abdication of self-control" echo the animalism identified with Black men throughout American history in the figure of "subhuman and feral" Black brute (Bogle 10). At the same time, the director slantly references early modernity in echoing pieces of *Othello*, for what is "one not easily jealous" who becomes "Perplexed in the extreme" but irrational jealousy (V, ii, 355, 356)? And what is "I'll tear her all to pieces" if not an abdication of self-control (III, iii, 447)? *Othello*'s past and present clash in what may seem a tautological reference loop in which the early modern and modern stereotypes elide, raising the question of which version of Othello informs the other. In other words, does Miller borrow from early modern tropes as found in Shakespeare's play in order to craft his vision or from modern American ones based on Black masculinity's supposed brutality?

Othello's performance history suggests that perhaps these two visions are ultimately indistinguishable. One cannot forget how minstrel *Othello*s flourished during the periods in American history where the violent Black brute stereotypes took clearest shape and strongest ideological hold. Ayanna Thompson notes how "these burlesques were an attempt to employ *Othello* to frame narratives about black masculinity as monstrous, laughable and yet potentially threatening if not properly controlled" ("Introduction" 105). Joyce Green MacDonald likewise explains that "audiences of minstrel shows or *Othello* 'burlettas' would be offered the more reassuring spectacle of whites acting black, of reasserting a relation between observer and object which affirmed white authority over, and authorship of, narratives of racial difference" ("Acting Black" 237). And Robert Hornback notes how the "rise of minstrelsy had much to do with expressing and disseminating racist responses to nineteenth-century African American actors' performance of Shakespeare" (*Racism* 211). As early appropriations, did these minstrel *Othello*s disseminate early modern racial thinking to Americans in the nineteenth century that reinforced their own prejudices? Or, did American racist thinking map onto and therefore inflect and transform the depiction of race in *Othello*? Such questions point to the difficulties in distinguishing between early modern and modern conceptualizations of race and racism that *American Moor* confronts. But just as significantly, they exemplify a legacy of negrobilia attached to *Othello*.

Subtext becomes explicit context as the play depicts how the director's narrow parameters for Othello's depiction are expressly tied to race. As such, *American Moor*'s audience watches as the imposition of a particular standard established upon skin color unfolds before their very eyes. Notably, even as the director's racist perceptions clarify, he uses Shakespeare as an authorizing tool for manifesting these ideas. After thanking the actor for his first attempt, the director wants him to run the lines again, but this time, he needs to keep in mind that "the stakes are really quite high" and consequences "rather dire," for lest the actor forget, Othello has "eloped with this white senator's daughter, yeah?" (11). The director's rhetoric both acknowledges yet sidelines race. It remains present in his reference to "this white senator's daughter," so that even if he refuses to recognize Desdemona's skin color explicitly, the audience becomes aware that the director registers it. It follows, then, that he must also recognize Othello's Blackness, though he sidesteps mentioning it outrightly with his shorthand reference to the white senator. Yet it is imperative to realize that the director sees race, for it informs his desire to have the actor play an Othello that "needs to charm this senate," one who must show "obeisance" in order to garner political and civic approval. In other words, the director masks his racist expectation of particular behavior by Black masculinity for white authority under the veil of interpreting Shakespeare; in the actor's words, he gives

Othello and the actor playing him a "bum rap into perpetuity and buy[s] it like gospel, sayin', 'Shakespeare said so'" (16). *American Moor* thus exposes how daily expectations regarding Black identity shape interpretive possibilities and re-presentations when it comes to Shakespeare, suggesting that the Shakespearean color line may have changed somewhat, BIPOC actors may now perform Shakespeare on stage after all, but it still exists in a different form.

This misrepresentation of Black masculinity extends beyond Shakespeare, however, to the American entertainment industry, as well as the actor's day-to-day life. The actor relates to the audience how, despite his "Visions of Hamlet, and prince Hal, and the tear-inducing poetry of Romeo," he knew that upon graduation, "the first role that I would be asked to play outside of school [would] be some version of a ghetto rat that said things like, 'Fuck you, punk-ass, bitch-ass nigga! I'll cut your shit, mothafucka!'" (18). For the actor, there was only "the Black sitcom buffoons, or the victim/scoundrel of America's preferred African American reality... Not a Hamlet in the lot" (19). Here, the actor meditates on what Ed Guerrero identifies as the limited representational opportunities for Black masculinity in Hollywood during the era of the 50-year-old actor's youth. Guerrero traces how the 1980s saw a turn to what he terms a "cinema of recuperation," in which films reinscribed the subordinations and inequalities fought so hard against in the sixties and seventies (*Framing Blackness* 113). This resulted not only in less African American filmmaking and fewer Black-focused narratives, but also in films dependent upon "neominstrelsy" (122), in which "blacks [are] positioned as funny, subordinate, and useful tools in the narrative" (126).[16] By the 1990s, Guerrero explains, "the commercial cinema system has continued to stock its productions with themes and formulas dealing with black issues and characters that are reassuring to the sensibilities and expectations of an uneasy white audience... images are polarized into celebrations of 'Buppie' success and consumer-driven individualism that are consonant with a sense of black political quietism, tokenism, and accommodation, or condemnations of violent ghetto criminals, gangsters, and drug lords" (162, 63). Thus, for even the most highbrow audience member, the gangster trope the actor invokes would be familiar, a reinvented, re-formed modern instantiation of the Black brute that hooks and Bogle identify. The actor therefore

---

[16] Guerrero explains that the other element of neominstrelsy was white actors dressed up as black characters, behaving in stereotypical ways.

not only has limited choices regarding Shakespeare, but he also has narrow possibilities in the American entertainment industry. And this restricted, one-dimensional version of Black masculinity depicted by the media simply reflects what it means to be a Black man in America, for being "Black here has only ever meant to be more misread, misrepresented, misinterpreted ... more misunderstood" (Cobb 29). *American Moor* thereby draws powerful connections between the imposed and "preferred" American reality backward in time to the actor's desire to perform Hamlet and then forward to the post-racial present and its continued misrepresentation of Blackness in America. Pao argues that "As a sociocultural institution, the theatre has always been closely linked to the political aspects of civic, state, and national life, and casting has been a visibly, even notoriously politicized process" (36). It is no wonder, then, that *American Moor* reveals how the color-line staged through the acting teacher's gatekeeping, which limited the actor to playing only Shakespeare's Moors, is in fact part and parcel of a larger white supremacist system that insists and depends upon mispresenting Black men, constructing their reality but making it seem innate by providing no alternative vision of Black masculine identity.

This threading of narrow roles across Shakespeare and American culture comes together as the actor confronts why, finally, he feels ready to tackle Othello. While he ultimately "envelops Othello in a familiar embrace of love and acceptance" (Dadabhoy, "Wincing at Shakespeare" 83), initially, the actor resisted the role, as revealed when he ripostes as he narrates to the audience, "What? I'll make a great emotionally unstable misogynist murderer? Why the fu--?" (19). Why, he queries, would he want to play a "self-loathing baboon?" (20). Poignantly, the actor reveals, "I was ashamed of him, ashamed that any reasonable person would look at me and see him, and I could no sooner portray him than I could show up for one of those Black urban dramas, or some fuckin' dancing monkey coon show sitcom that Tyler Perry made." Once again, the past and present overlap as the actor forces the audience to trace the powerful legacy of white supremacy that insists that Black men are not fully realized humans, whether in Shakespeare, Tyler Perry, or most other Western entertainment across periods, mediums, and statuses. *American Moor* therefore again and again stages moments emphasizing how the supposed superiority of white identity generates and relies upon racial caricatures, whether disseminated through high art such as *Othello*, low art such as American mass media, or non-fictional day-to-day life.

Even as *American Moor* stages racism through the director's caricaturing of Black masculinity, it also movingly stages resistance and resilience in the Black actor's refusal to acquiesce to the director's vision. His complex self-representation disrupts stereotypes of Black masculinity as he pleads for a re-vision, a new vision, of both Othello *and* contemporary American Black masculinity. A quick series of examples elucidate the actor's increasing defiance of the director's circumscribed limitations. When the director requests a charming, obsequious Othello, the actor initially attempts to run through the speech again, but as he does so, he falters, then stops entirely after the director asserts, "that's the correct attack on the text. That energy was right" (14). In invoking the text, the director attempts to access Shakespearean interpretive authority that seems to inhere in Shakespeare's words.[17] The actor challenges this perspective in a monologue heard only by the audience, inquiring, "Right for whom?" Yet the actor's resistance does not remain articulated solely to the audience. He later explicitly asks Miller, "I wonder, as an acting point of departure, is it perhaps too laughable of an arc to go 180 degrees from huge in one direction to huge in the opposite?" (16). The tension increases as the actor refuses to concede. The director questions whether extreme emotions are actually laughable; the actor insists, "Is it not the stuff of comedy" (17). The director stresses the "operatic pendulum swing of emotion" in *Othello*; the actor counters that perhaps Desdemona fell in love with Othello because of his "reluctance to put on a face." And most powerfully, the actor suggests that Othello "rallies a quiet strength to perform that belittling minstrel show yet one more time" without "bombast." By insisting on performing Othello with dignity and confidence, by perceiving him and in turn embodying him through a different perspective, the Black actor pushes back against all that Othello represents: the impositions on Black subjectivity that limit how Black men are perceived and in turn, what they can do.

Moreover, the director's facile imagining of Othello contrasts sharply with the emotional complexity exhibited, acknowledged, and embraced by the actor, a fully human subjectivity he extends to his interpretation of Othello. In other words, the actor himself and his description of how to thoughtfully re-present Othello upset the circumscribed vision of Black subjectivity established by white

---

[17] For instance, Kidnie explains how "Performance critics who invest in textual fidelity in effect posit the existence of a stable text which is then elevated . . . [in] status . . ." (21).

supremacy and echoed by the director. This distinction begins to signal the importance of re-vision, a new vision, championed by *American Moor*, for the director's is clearly the wrong one. But the director's perception is not the only problem. The issue lies with much broader cultural attitudes. The actor explains to the audience "that people in our American culture, who are not Black like me, do not respond in the same manner to Black men, like me, raising their voices, even slightly, as they do with one another . . . or changing tone. They do not respond well to my adamance" (3). Elaborating, the actor notes that when he longs to be "adamant," the "listener all too often has no place for it, no tools with which to hear it, because I have broken the fourth wall, and he does not recognize the overflown expression of my emotion as the same, simple, cathartic thing that it is for anyone, because he is not in the play. Or at least he thinks he is not. He thinks he's just a guy who lives by these American rules, and wants me to live by them too" (4). The impetus for this remark comes from the story the actor relates about his drama teacher limiting his performance options. But the comment could just as much apply to the director who cannot understand the actor's approach to Othello, and perhaps even to the audience, who likewise has no tools for hearing his anger. In observing that the "guy" listening to the actor "lives by these American rules" that must apply to the actor as well, Cobb exposes the different standards established for emotional expression created across a color divide, especially in regard to anger.

White supremacy frequently pathologizes a range of emotions in those it positions as Other, especially Black Americans. hooks notes, "In imperialist white-supremacist capitalist patriarchy black males are socialized to be rage-oholics" (*We Real Cool* 60), whereas white men "are perceived to be acting with reason" (57). The angry Black man relates to the violent Black man discussed above, for anger provides the motivation for his vicious behavior. As Bogle explains, the type known as the "black brute," perhaps most famously depicted in the 1915 film *The Birth of a Nation*, functions as "nameless characters setting out on a rampage full of black rage" (10). This association between Black anger and violence encapsulates Sara Ahmed's point about the sticky, metonymic affective terms that "restrict some bodies" while expanding others ("Affective Economies" 127). Ahmed contends that

> this containment is an effect of a movement between signs, as well as bodies. Such movement depends on past histories of association:

Negro, animal, bad, mean, ugly. In other words, it is the movement of fear between signs, which allows the object of fear to be generated in the present (the Negro is: an animal, bad, mean, ugly). The movement between signs is what allows others to be attributed with emotional value, in this case, as being fearsome, an attribution that depends on a history that "sticks," and which does not need to be declared. (127)

Thus, the "American rules" the actor references do not arise peculiarly from the mind of the white drama teacher or director. Rather, they come to them as the racial inheritance of a nation in which both the white "guy" and Black actor must live by American rules that are not the *same* rules, for they allow only the white man the subjectivity of conveying a range of emotions, including anger, while disallowing Black men the same form of emotional expression.

The actor, however, embraces anger, but disrupts the stereotype of Black rage by placing it as one on a continuum of feelings, emotions, and desires. When confronting the director in his mind, the actor declares, "I seem a little angry to you . . . You think any American Black man is gonna play Othello without being in touch with his anger . . . at you? If that's what you think, then you better go back to having white guys do it . . ." (16). This assertion of anger comes after the actor has already built a bond with the audience by sharing how his teacher barred him from performing the characters he wanted, by noting how the director's approach to him and Othello mirrors broader racist thinking, and by articulating his carefully, thoughtfully crafted vision of the character. In other words, the actor's anger here does not seem explosive but rather merited, deriving from injustice and exhaustion. But the actor is not only angry—he also admits to fear, for while the director is afraid of the actor, the actor is "afraid that nothing will ever change" (23). The problem, then, is not anger, but rather the circumscription of Black emotion in the service of white supremacy. In this white supremacist logic, most if not *all* emotions become suspect, for if allowed a range of feelings, Black individuals would have to be seen as fully human. The actor remarks, therefore, that "A black man burns a whole lotta calories trying to keep a rein on full *half* of himself just so people around him don't get nervous. I'm done. I don't mean to scare you, but I do it just standin' here, so how may I honestly express to you the joys, the hurts and the rages that would *realistically* compel this character's life without you piss yourself and call me crazy? You don't want a man, you want a cartoon . . ." (30). Joy, hurt, rage, fear. These varied emotions join together to insist on the actor's complexity, one that potently dismantles the "cartoon"-like misrepresentation of both Othello and Black masculinity more generally upon which the director and American culture insist.

American Moor thus knits together a complex network of ideas about race and identity, with Shakespeare's *Othello* as the framework for this exploration. Though my argument depends on linearity for clarity, in performance, these threads weave in and out, with some concepts highlighted in particular moments while muted in others. Nevertheless, Cobb's play persistently alerts white audiences to the fluid, cross-historical presence of antiblack racism, which depends on a mischaracterization of Black identity through stereotypes. These stereotypes, in turn, undergird interpersonal encounters that expose individual prejudice as well as resistance by Black subjectivity. In this thematic and logical interweaving created through the actor's meditations and confrontations, *American Moor* unapologetically stresses the need for adaptation through re-vision—changing perspective, changing attitudes, and changing theatrical approaches.

American Moor and Education

The play does so, however, by calling for change on the individual and systemic level. In other words, it reflects Oluo's definition of racism by placing responsibility on individuals *as well as* the systems reinforcing their racial prejudice as a means of signaling the "many structural disadvantages that black groups face in America" (Bhopal 101). What *American Moor* therefore powerfully communicates to predominantly white audiences is the fact that the contestations regarding race between the director and the actor cannot be excused as a mere interpersonal conflict, a dynamic which reinforces the belief "that racism exists as a result of the individual acts of a small number of people" (Bhopal 101). In other words, Cobb does not allow the audience to read the clash at the heart of *American Moor* as simply one about the director's particular racial bigotry. Rather, the play brings to the fore how systems foster the bias present in the director by turning to two institutions especially connected to those interested in Shakespeare: the educational system and Shakespearean theatre, situated within the structures of American regional theatre more broadly. By tackling both systems, Cobb illuminates their inherent interconnectedness. In other words, the respective ideologies of the university drama and English classrooms that the actor meditates upon bleed into each other as well as into the structures of American theatre in an interlocking web of systemically centered whiteness.

In addressing education across the play, Cobb makes it clear that institutions of higher learning "are the epitome of the legitimation and reproduction of institutional racism. They continue to play their part in the reproduction and reinforcement of racial and class inequalities" (Bhopal 103). In fact, Cobb opens the play noting, "I was an English major when I went to school," during which time the actor not only read Shakespeare, but also "saw Shakespeare . . . not in a book, but on the stage" (1). From the outset, then, *American Moor* highlights education, specifically college education. Importantly, the actor makes it clear that he first imagines it as a space and time imperative for shaping one's relationship to Shakespeare, but concurrently, for understanding oneself. For it is during this time that he realized "I wanted to be an actor . . . I *was* an actor . . . It *was* me," and ultimately, that "I learned that . . . I wanted to act Shakespeare." The two strands—Shakespeare and self-realization—come together as the actor explains, "At the place where I and his words intersected, I had been presumptuous enough to buy into the preposterous notion that I, my intellect, my instrument, and my crazy-ass African American emotionality could serve the canon well, *and* be served well by it." Tellingly, the actor imagines an exchange of service. Though he has yet to invoke *Othello* directly, the play is already in his hands as a prop, for he carries Hall's edited version of *Othello* from the production's outset, signaling what Brandi K. Adams argues are "larger issues raised in the play about reading and who controls the narrative of fundamental literacy about Shakespeare" ("Black '(un)bookishness'"3). Whereas Othello's service to Venice is unidirectional—Othello serves Venice while it uses and then discards him—the actor imagines more for himself as one serving yet *served by* the canon.

His use of words such as "presumptuous" and "preposterous," however, signposts what seems to be almost inevitable disillusionment with what his education ultimately provides him. The actor has already subtly stressed a distinction between what he has "learned," a term signifying knowledge he comes to on his own, and what he has been "taught," which represents knowledge derived from others. *American Moor* makes clear that the actor is taught his limited, decidedly unreciprocated place in the Shakespearean canon, a lesson that comes at the hands of his acting teacher. Education, which introduces him to Shakespeare and his future calling, at the same time robs him of the joy over and mutuality with the Shakespearean canon that he so seeks. As previously mentioned, this teacher rejects the actor's attempt to perform a monologue by a range of Shakespearean characters aside from Othello. But within this rejection reside microaggressions that remind those watching *American Moor* how pervasively and subtly exclusions within the educational system may appear (see also Chapter 6). For instance, as the actor suggests performing Titania, the teacher interrupts with the "'correct pronunciation . . . Titania,'" pronouncing the name to sound like *awful* rather than "canyon" (2). Perhaps this can be excused as typical pedagogical correction, but as the actor performs for the teacher, the teacher once again interrupts to comment, "The poetry trips up the best of'm," to which the actor responds, "The best? Who are they?" and the teacher replies, "*You* know . . . ?" (3). The emphasized *you* stresses the unstated reasoning here: *they* are white actors, white students, white people who have and will long continue to embody Shakespeare's roles.

A consideration of education's limits for the Black actor, and therefore perhaps for other Black individuals, in fact recurs throughout the play. For example, Cobb turns to the English (rather than drama) classroom when he recounts how he "admired the professor of the segment of Shakespeare *for English majors*," who did not seem to admire him back (21). He explains that "my attraction to his strength of ego [took] the form of an ever eagerness to engage him on the intricate points of textual analysis, [which] he received as a challenge, which made him irascible." As a result, the actor received a C; having held "a 'B' average on the written work, I could only assume that my professor rated his most engaged students' in-class contributions no worthier than a 'D.'" The actor poignantly concludes, "To me, the grade said 'Mind your place.'" If this narrative appeared at the play's start, one could suggest that perhaps this harsh grade came as a result of a teacher chafing against a particularly challenging student. By placing the story in the middle of *American Moor*, however, Cobb connects this retelling to prior moments in the play that meditate upon the ways white perceptions of racial identity inform education, teaching, and learning. Education, *American Moor* suggests, caters to whiteness, as noted when the actor discusses his parents taking courses at a community college and observes, "you're gonna find, which seniors have a hundred and fifty disposable bucks to spend on this kinda thing every so often that doesn't feed, shelter, or clothe them? Generally, most often? It's white ones" (31).[18] Placed in conversation with each other, these instances suggest that even if persons of color gain access to higher education, a difficulty in and of itself, there is no guarantee that the university will create ideological and intellectual space for them.

Kalwant Bhopal likewise identifies these two strands of argumentation regarding race and education—educational curriculum and access—as particularly significant in the role educational systems play in advancing racial exclusion. Bhopal explains that "Racism and racist practices dominate the experiences of black and minority students in higher education" (93), and this racism begins with "Inequalities in admissions processes," ones that function to ensure that "universities remain white middle-class spaces" (92). Once accepted into a university, students identify the prevalence of a "Eurocentric curriculum" as a key part of creating these white spaces, for, as Bhopal observes, this curriculum reinforces the "practices that define success in higher education: ways of writing, speaking, and the use of academic language." In *American Moor*, Cobb singles out precisely the "proper" academic approaches and language Bhopal identifies in order to articulate the actor's marginalization during his college experience, illustrating what Madeline Sayet calls the "Shakespeare system" at play in which an actor is deemed "good in Shakespeare class" by being "forced to hit the 'correct' posture and pronunciation and rhythm," with "correct" being the standard established by the "oppressor." As such, in the play, education as a system does not function as the conduit for social and ideological freedom that the actor first imagines. *American Moor* therefore exposes how a Eurocentric educational system circumscribes access to Shakespeare while frequently placing those in marginalized social positions in roles that serve and perpetuate another system, the "Shakespeare system," or, to quote Sayet, "the complex and oppressive role his work, legacy, and positionality hold in our contemporary society."

The actor connects this theme of race and educational barriers to Othello, wondering, "who answered the questions of a childish upstart Arab-Iberian soldier of fortune? And was *he* answered with encouragement, or allowed *his* learning only grudgingly. Either would

[18] Kalwant Bhopal elaborates, "Gaining access to a good college and a high-ranking university is understood to be part of a meritocratic society in which those who are competent, able and intelligent are rewarded for their efforts. However, such a system continues to privilege the few. Access to such privilege is related to the possession of cultural and social capital . . ." (99). The actor's commentary regarding the parts he is allowed to perform, or not, draws attention to financial capital as another resource education can grant or foreclose.

have been an education. Both make us who we become. We are never taught much. But we learn a great deal" (21). These musings tie the ideas together, indicating that the education imparted upon those forced into positions of social Otherness, like him as a Black youth in the largely white university or the Arab-Iberian Othello in the otherwise all-white Venice, cannot but be a limited one. He makes it clear—education makes the man. But because he must learn (on his own) rather than be taught (by others), the man of color fashions himself based on what he gleans from the exclusionary educational whiteness around him. In other words, he learns, but education nevertheless fails him as a result of racist assumptions that inform educational attitudes and practice, which prevent true teaching from occurring.

The wide-reaching significance of these racist teaching practices comes to the fore as the actor makes clear how they shape the parameters of another institution: the Shakespearean theatre. Cobb directs attention to the effects of a Eurocentric education on culture at large by tracing a direct line from the white educational system to an American regional theatre that is also white-run, and whose practices and points of view leave little to no room for alternative perspectives. Even before the actor begins the audition, he can envision how it might go, for though the director is "scared shitless of Shakespeare as most people," he comes from an educational genealogy where "he studied with somebody who studied with somebody who was British, so he's runnin' with it" (8). Here, Cobb directly addresses the issue of interpretive authority—who gets to shape and reshape Shakespeare. The depth of these lines comes from the fact that they expose just how intertwined Eurocentric educational practices and Eurocentric theatrical practices prove to be. In insisting on *his* viewpoint, one inherited from his studies, the director plays a role similar to the acting teacher who could not imagine the actor as anything other than one of Shakespeare's Moors; like him, Miller, the director, can only imagine "the Moor" one way. As Hall contends, "He [the actor] discovers that *Othello* is, in fact, on loan. Teachers and directors do *Othello*, give him *Othello*, only to make the Black actor their mouthpiece for how they understand blackness or difference" ("'Othello Was My Grandfather'" 11). The actor's first experience in the acting classroom thus takes on a deeper resonance as a lifelong template for grappling with the silencing of his voice and perspective as he attempts to perform Shakespeare.

In fact, Cobb makes the connections the play traces markedly clear when the actor critiques the fact that directors who want to be "would-be savior[s] of the American theatre perennially [pick] up this play like it needs you. Like it needs your theory, and your concept, and your venerated euro-centric scholarship" (15).[19] In his meditation, the systemic racism of the educational system and the theatre elide. Because it marginalizes Black voices, Black imaginations, and Black selves, teaching creates "euro-centric scholarship" that only advances identities like the director's "lily-white, MFA ass"; this privileging in turn results in Eurocentric Shakespearean performances that reject the experience of "sacrificing, shit-takin', strugglin' daily through the bullshit, bone thug thespian brothers." Stated differently, just as the acting and English teachers rejected the actor's contributions to their classrooms, so too does the director reject the actor's perspective on Othello, thinking instead—in further alignment of the theatrical and educational—that he is "gonna teach me something about Othello." Even though the actor's life provides him with a perspective on Othello that so "far surpasses your anemic awareness on the matter that I might as well be talkin' to a fuckin' monkey," neither the classroom nor the theatre allow space for his voice, a voice from which, if the director were to "Watch and listen . . . *YOU* might learn something" (15, 16). White privileging of voice and viewpoint therefore stretches across the classroom and the stage—in other words, across systems—in a trajectory in which acting teachers instruct future directors who then school actors during their auditions about the right/white way to interpret and perform Shakespeare.[20]

The actor, however, extends his critique of American regional theatre beyond what it inherits from a flawed educational system, noting how its very structures, those driven by economic concerns, limit how effective theatre can be as an agent for radical reinterpretation,

---

[19] Without stating it expressly, Cobb is engaging with the revered status of the auteur director. For a discussion of the relationship between adaptation, the concept of the auteur director, and Shakespeare, see Courtney Lehmann, *Shakespeare Remains: Theater to Film, Early Modern to Postmodern* (Cornell University Press, 2002).

[20] In an interview for *The Kojo Nnamdi Show*, Cobb in fact comments on this interrelatedness between education and theatre, asserting that "we don't talk about our failing educational system in the way that it needs to be discussed, and that includes education in theater arts. We are not training directors and actors to the same standard. I daresay we are not training journalists and critics in the same way. That very often, my experience has been over the past several years that critics are there to further augment what the production's already done. So, they'll say, that thing that they're doing over there, that may not be *Julius Caesar*, I know it's supposed to be, but isn't it a wonderful thing, you know. Isn't it a great thing? And [that] totally circumvents the purpose of criticism allowing us to be introspective, look at the work and transcend and go to another place, culturally."

and therefore for social change. Even as he traces how the director's "cookie cutter *Othello*" derives from the limited approach he learned in school, he also notes that even if the director wanted to strive for more in his production, he would be hard-pressed to do so (15). The actor explains to a likely unknowing audience that

> The period of time allotted for the rehearsal of a play in the American regional theater is, as a general rule, no more than three weeks. Matters of money will not allow for longer. And in many cases, owing to those same financial concerns, that period has been condensed even further to two weeks, thus more or less assuring us of an exercise in mediocrity that audiences will, nonetheless, applaud because we have lost our perspective on excellence thereby causing them to lose theirs too. (24)

While the emphasis on education and its influence on theatre focuses on the attendant univocality of theatrical perspectives, this charge against the theatre instead lays bare why its performances struggle with complexity, an ingredient crucial for grappling with issues of race. Indeed, if engaged with correctly, *Othello* confronts people's "deeply seated notions about sex and race and religion, and most important, self." The themes in this play cannot be taken up casually, the actor insists. Their intricacy demands a proper process, but "You ain't gonna confront those notions fully if you rehearse for a year, and you want to give it three weeks. Not to discover nothin' you ain't busy believin' already. How scary would that be?" In fact, the actor articulates how a narrow perspective and limited institutional parameters intersect, for all the actor can work with in a "three week hole" is "what you think you know . . . whether it fits or not" (25). Unmistakably, the short time given to grapple with thematic complexities in *any* play, especially one as difficult as *Othello*, means in fact no grappling at all but instead a retrenching of perspective, "what you think you know . . ." Put differently, the "white . . . imaginary . . . reproduces white modes of thought, behavior, and action" (Dadabhoy, "Wincing at Shakespeare" 88). Cobb's meditation on institutional practices via the actor returns the audience to the interpersonal conflict over race and interpretation shaping *American Moor*. Calling the two experiences "analogous," the actor admonishes that just as the director cannot grasp his complexity in "your five minutes looking at me in this room," a complexity which *American Moor* insists upon by providing the audience with 90 minutes to spend with the actor, the director likewise cannot comprehend *Othello*'s complexity in "Your two weeks and change in the rehearsal hall" because "you can't figure out shit in that time," nevertheless Shakespeare's *Othello* (24). Racism in the theatre, then, exists in a complicated relationship with other systems, economic forces, and personal bigotry, pieces that shape each other in ways difficult to unravel.

In *American Moor* the theatre therefore serves as a microcosm of what occurs in macrocosm across American culture: antiblack racism manifests at a number of levels across a number of systems for a number of reasons but nonetheless always depending on different forms of flattening out and marginalizing Black subjectivity. But *American Moor* does not rest there, potentially playing into the (often white) fantasy of Black patience in the face of injustice (Cahill and Hall 1–3). Instead, the play powerfully insists on the very subjectivity that the white voices within it—and those who they represent in the "real" world—try to deny. Cobb therefore uses Shakespeare "for resistance and pleasure" by insisting on the actor's perspective, complexity, and authority in the face of interpersonal and systemic racist oppression (Cahill and Hall 8).

Theatre and Adaptive Re-Vision

Grasping the profoundly interwoven nature of the multiple systems at play in shaping the representation of race in the American theatre elucidates just how hard it is to transform performance when it comes to matters of race. It means pushing back against ingrained Eurocentric, i.e. white, standards widely disseminated and thoroughly entrenched. What theatre needs, therefore, is a new vision, a re-vision. To revise, one must form a new "image" or "new concept"; one must essentially "reinterpret."[21] In *American Moor*, Cobb uses the voice of the actor to call for this reinterpretation or re-vision. This reconceptualization is twofold: it entails a new vision of *Othello* as the play suggests, but it also means, I contend, underscoring adaptation not as a movement from one medium or genre to another (Linda Hutcheon's adaptation as product), such as page to film, but rather what Hutcheon calls adaptation as process (16, 18). Specifically, it means emphasizing adaptation as offering what Julie Sanders characterizes as "a revised point of view from the 'original' . . . voicing what

---

[21] *OED*, "Revise" (v. 1 and 2).

the text silences or marginalizes" (23). In the world of performance, an adaptive re-vision is thus the process of taking on this new point of view to think not about just what the text silences, but also what the institution of the theatre silences, especially regarding the work race, power, and authority do across the "telling, showing, and interacting with stories" that occurs on the Shakespearean stage and in American culture at large (Hutcheon 27).

The relationship between authority and what people categorize as adapted or authentic Shakespeare poses a significant challenge for the reconceptualization championed by the actor and *American Moor* itself. Often, the stage serves as a site especially tied to authorization through "authentically Shakespearean meanings" (Worthen 3). W. B. Worthen explains that "Authenticity in performance is a function of the rhetoric of performance, the way in which a performance claims 'authority' by asserting 'proximity' to 'something we value'" (26). While the authentic may not have an ontological reality given its shifting nature—who counts as "we" and what designates "value" inevitably transforms over place and time—when it comes to Shakespeare, auteurs and audiences alike nevertheless desire "an authentic Shakespeare, to whom every generation's version of a classic drama may be ascribed" (Orgel 24). Therefore, as L. Monique Pittman asserts, Shakespearean "'authority' finds a close cousin in the term 'authenticity'" (*Authorizing Shakespeare* 2). Consequently, all too often, what becomes designated as "real" instead of adapted Shakespeare depends on whatever is perceived as an authentic theatrical representation, as nebulous as that authenticity might be. As Kidnie explains, genuine rather than adapted Shakespeare "is determined less by textual fidelity than by the extent to which an instance conforms to an insubstantial standard—the work—that seems to exist prior to, and untouched by, production" (64). In other words, adapted Shakespeare is perceived by those who receive it, including audiences, as touched, the authentic as untouched. Adaptation thus suggests a difference, a splitting off from Shakespeare, whether via media, mode, form, or content. Adaptation, in other words, is always already one step removed from (i.e. touched) what really "counts" as Shakespeare. Thus, because of its seemingly diluted authenticity, whatever becomes labeled an adaptation has the potential to limit the authority garnered through engaging with Shakespeare, with certain modes of adaptation more troubling than others. It is no wonder, then, that Nora J. Williams asserts, "Authenticity is, of course, a fraught concept for Shakespeareans . . . reviews of Shakespearean productions still measure success in terms of fidelity to Shakespeare's 'original.'" By this logic, in order to acquire the most cultural capital, whatever gets represented as *Shakespeare* needs to be as recognizably Shakespearean as possible, in other words, authentic Shakespeare.

American Moor exposes the role race plays in the quest for accessing authentic and therefore authoritative Shakespeare. Both the acting teacher and director exemplify the dependence on what does or does not get to count as proper, i.e. authentic, Shakespeare in order to shore up their respective power. The actor should not play Hamlet's or Titania's soliloquies because it would not be realistic since he is Black and, ostensibly, Hamlet and Titania are not (nor is Titania male). Authenticity in the guise of racial realism thus delimits acting opportunities. These famous characters could never be Black, thus, a Black man could never be them. For the director, race and authenticity inform not who performs a role, but rather how it is performed. The director never articulates his claims as starkly as the acting teacher, yet his description of Othello's position before the Senate—the "stakes are high"; he has committed a "crime"; the situation is "dire"; Othello must "ingratiate himself" (11)—indicates that he believes he has the authority to interpret the reality of Othello's situation in a way that contradicts the actor's confident interpretation. It is *his* reality of Othello as servile which must be performed for the actor to get the role. The director only further affirms that his way is the "right" way when the actor begins to perform the speech as the director requested and he remarks, "You were doing great" and "I think that's the correct attack on the text. That energy was right" (13, 14). Here, race hovers quietly over the interchange, not addressed by the director explicitly, but even so informing the interpretive possibilities he envisions for Othello. But the actor makes the implicit explicit when he movingly responds to the director's affirmations (speaking only to the audience), "Right for whom? Right for somebody who thinks he knows how Black guys behave and react? Right for somebody who thinks they know William Shakespeare like they were his therapist?" (14). As such, he reminds people of the way interpretations are not just inherently right nor neutral but rather ideological, even political, in ways that cause real pain.

What becomes evident, then, is that both the acting teacher and director want to offer audiences something they will recognize as true, not adapted Shakespeare, which entails reiterating what they deem to be authentic representations of both whiteness, however unstated, and Blackness. Margo Hendricks contends, "The desire for some authentic Shakespeare, dramatic representations that are 'real' to us . . . haunts spectators of Shakespeare's plays . . . The desire for authenticity in performing 'race' is even more profoundly framed by this sense of mourning" ("Visions of Color" 522). Kidnie's collectively imagined "insubstantial standard" therefore develops not just from how people conceive of Shakespeare, but also from the racialized ways people understand the narratives and characters within the plays, such as whether a Black man can indeed play Hamlet, or whether Othello's Blackness necessitates an obsequiousness in the face of the powerful Venetian Senate. For the authorizing emphasis on verisimilitude subtends both the racialized marginalization of the actor as well as the caricatured depiction of Othello the director envisions. This is the same rationale undergirding assertions of historical verisimilitude in long-standing debates about casting persons of color in Shakespearean performances on the stage and screen. Thus, concerns about genuine rather than adapted Shakespeare become smokescreens for white supremacist practices of marginalization.

Cobb's play makes it hard to deny how race affects what people perceive as touched or untouched, adapted or authentic, and in turn what they do and do not allow on the Shakespearean stage. Worthen asserts that "The only thing we can be sure of is that as audiences change, as a culture and its theatres change, Shakespeare will speak in different accents, in different forms of visibility, and embodiment that may (or may not) assert their own (in-)authentic claims to 'Shakespeare'" (15). What *American Moor* exposes, however, is that when the "insubstantial standard" Kidnie identifies that so shapes authenticity involves race, the resulting effect upon the American theatre is that the supposedly shifting accent, visibility, and embodiment Worthen stresses with such surety will not be different but rather homogeneously white. *American Moor*'s power is that in its very existence as well as narrative content, it embraces adaptation as a potent, *necessary* tool for race and Shakespeare. For, if unchallenged, both directors and audiences will be unlikely to re-view and therefore revise the racialized standard they apply to their interpretation of Shakespeare given that, as Carol Mejia LaPerle observes, "habits of spectatorship shape the spectacle, demand the respectability . . . that constitute" Shakespearean theatre ("Thou art"). Put differently, they will never re-view and therefore revise the racialized standard they apply to their interpretation of Shakespeare.

Importantly, adaptive re-vision requires two commitments: a reconsideration of the most frequent approach to adaptation and a comfort in embracing this view over "genuine" versions of Shakespeare. Thinking about adaptation not just in terms of fidelity or infidelity but even film versus stage is too limiting. It frequently cedes the space for the new vision Sanders identifies to appropriation. I wholeheartedly agree with Erickson that the re-vision afforded by appropriations is crucial. I also want to suggest, however, that discussions of Shakespearean performance lack a vocabulary that encourages transformation in/at the site of the "original" Shakespearean retellings that arguably still hold high-status cultural cache, in large part, we should admit, due to its exclusivity regarding what appears on stage and who attends offstage. What could be gained if adaptation simply signaled the necessary changes that must inform *any* Shakespearean performance? After all, even "original practice" productions are approximations, modern reimaginings of Renaissance performance, ones grounded in careful historical work, but approximations nevertheless. Adaptations, MacDonald contends, "imagine a way forward" from the "majoritarian political uses to which he [Shakespeare] has been put" (*Shakespearean Adaptation* 6, 7). Thus, if *all* performance is accepted and even stressed by theatrical practitioners and institutions as a form of adaptation, it both disrupts the seemingly monolithic power of authentic, genuine, "real" Shakespeare, and relatedly, it opens the door for more adaptive re-vision that contests white supremacist traditions on the Shakespearean stage. Letting go of the ties between whiteness and concepts of tradition, authenticity, and authority is vital. If adaptation and therefore an adaptive re-vision is by necessity always required, then the seemingly monolithic power of authentic, genuine, "real" Shakespeare no longer holds so much sway. And if that is the case, there is one less strategy for reinscribing white supremacy in the theatre. Put differently, the authentic would no longer be a compelling justification for upholding the theatre's white supremacist, exclusionary practices.

Despite criticizing theatre as a problematic institution, *American Moor* also expresses its potential to transform audiences by disseminating and in turn shaping the adaptive racial re-vision necessary not just for *Othello*, but also for American culture. The actor articulates this potential as he delineates what a newly conceptualized Othello would look like. Disrupting the structure of the play up to this moment, in which the actor shares his most intimate and challenging thoughts with the audience instead of with the director, here, the actor breaks free and speaks to Miller and the audience simultaneously. As he does so, he lays out his re-vision, and though he never uses the word, he clearly imagines adapting Othello as a character as a crucial tool in facilitating this re-vision. In contrast to the director's perception, the actor's Othello "is an arrogant, ill-mannered, precocious child in the body of an aging badass who would challenge you, because that's what boys do" (26). This Othello therefore balances between impulsiveness and strength, able to lift a Desdemona no matter her size "because Othello, *my* Othello, could do that. The full focus of his huge, boyish energy could, and would do that regardless of the size of his beloved. For me, such an image is essential. Because it says, 'How powerful this man is . . . How full of impetuosity[,] pathos and play. How joyous and intense to do such a thing . . .'" What the actor wants to emphasize is thus Othello the warrior, not to glorify violence, but rather as a means of emphasizing his fighting spirit and humanity. He asserts that a proper *Othello* should communicate "The warrior heart, manifesting in every last thing that this man does until the day he dies. Warrior as lover. Warrior as protector. Warrior as clown. Even warrior as wife murderer and abject disgrace to all that conspire to create him . . . But warrior. Putting it all on the line. In life and love . . . In death and despair . . ." (26, 27). Here, the actor's image of the warrior highlights both Othello's power and his limitations. This warrior Othello, with a "fire blazing in his guts," cuts a powerful figure in the play, powerful enough that "he shouts from the shore from the bottom of his voice to the tops of his mighty lungs . . . back through the ages of his people's glorious past, 'have I not done well? Am I not wonderful, just as you?' *This* is what stands before the Senate, his human being seeping out of every pore" (27). Cobb's language makes evident that a warrior Othello is a fully human Othello, powerful enough not only to lift up Desdemona, but also to confront the Senate in a way that Miller refuses to conceptualize.

Yet at the same time, the actor resists the impulse to idealize this humanity. He acknowledges, "But within where we fortress up our more fragile selves he knows he is old . . . He knows he is epileptic . . . He knows by now that no one is going to erect a statue in the Rialto to the memory of the great General Othello, the Moor" (28). In calling for a re-vision, the actor's goal is not to recuperate Othello, turning him into a perfect man, but rather to rehabilitate the one-dimensional view of him. He therefore insists for Othello the same complexity *American Moor* has asserted for him, acknowledging the tensions within Othello when he poignantly defends him against those who would criticize this attempt: "And he is lover, warrior, and fool all at once. Tragically flawed yes . . . Just like you, Brotherman, and like me. He is wholly human" (29). Recognizing this fully fleshed humanity means that one can therefore see Othello as struggling to "maintain one's sanity when so much of what one is has forever been held in such strict and unnecessary abeyance by other's fears and the rules that one never agreed" (28). It is this outside pressure, he suggests, that creates Othello's "mental fragility," the "tiny little breaks in Othello's armor that might make him finally snap completely and kill someone, even if that someone were the solitary love of his life." Granting Othello the humanity all too often prohibited Black men thus requires an adaptive re-vision—in this case, staged through adapting Othello as a character—that opens up space for the understanding, empathy, and multidimensionality denied him not just by the director, but also by the numerous racist cultural systems shaping all that the white director represents.

To be clear, it is not that the actor offers up a perfect Othello or the one right reading of either the character or the play. Rather, he stresses the value of authentic embodiment, an *Othello* borne out of his experience, which requires honoring Othello in all his humanity and complexity. There is no suggestion, however, that the actor merely wants to take the position of the director, somehow replacing one authoritative voice and perspective with another. *American Moor* instead suggests that a single-person mode toward interpreting the play is insufficient. This approach must give way to one that depends on ceding authority and engaging in a dialogue that invites multiple, diverse voices, voices committed not only to questioning what counts as an authentic *Othello* but also to challenging the concept of Shakespearean authenticity more generally. What does an *Othello* crafted out of a true adaptive re-vision look like? *American Moor* offers up not a firm conclusion but rather a start, a series of conversational threads that prepare listeners for the difficult dialogues hopefully to come.

The actor's re-vision of Othello thus brings *American Moor*'s attention full circle back to the audience and its perceptions, the very concern informing the play's first stage directions. Even as he recounts his new vision of Othello, the actor also recognizes the limitations pushing against this vision—the audience and their potential resistance to it. He admits:

> I can offer them the Moor from the inside out, and, standing before them, let what *I* feel be everything . . . Then, they will see whatever they see. And what they feel *about* me will be everything else. But I remain the intelligent, intuitive, indomitable, large Black American male. And perhaps the purpose is defeated, but it does not honor God not to act like *everything* that I am, hoping that they will say, "I see! I understand. Thank you!" but honoring God regardless. (29)

In this moment, the actor's language echoes the stage directions, which emphasize the *you* that so shapes the perception of the Black actor. In both the opening and closing moments of the play, then, the actor meditates on his lack of control over his artistic endeavor. He can offer "everything," all that he is, just as he has in *American Moor*, as well as in the audition it stages. Yet "what they feel *about* me will be everything else." Nevertheless, the actor exhibits the same resistance to the overpowering nature of the white gaze as he has throughout the play, insisting on his complex humanity (intelligence, intuitiveness, indomitability) as well as embracing his Blackness nonetheless. He will, he literally and metaphorically stresses and repeats, be "*everything* that I am." As *American Moor* closes, the actor thus meditates on theatre and whiteness as a way to consider American society and its limited racial perceptions. Within and without the theatre, whiteness is the view allowed to create and therefore catered to. And in his final moments of defiance, the actor refuses to concede, instead offering up an adaptive re-vision of *Othello* that stands in for the need to adapt and shift, to reconceive, the misrepresentation of Black masculinity in America.

The Hope of Audience Education

Cobb deploys another tool to assist in the project of adaptive re-vision: audience education. Through this education he crafts a means to take the endeavor begun in *American Moor* beyond the space created in the performance's 90 minutes. Before turning to what audience education is and how it functions, however, it is important to recognize how Cobb perceives the audience. Though the actor cannot be conflated entirely with Cobb, his understanding of the audience seems to mirror Cobb's own. On the one hand, he is cautious about audience perception, as argued above regarding what he says about their view of him as a Black man and how spectators might receive his reimagined Othello. On the other hand, he is also hopeful about the audience's ability to receive this new vision if, as he says in another part of the play, given the tools to hear. The actor exposes this hopeful yet vulnerable approach when he observes, "But *there's* our tragic flaw, Brotherman . . . It's these huge hearts, yours, Othello's, and mine, that need desperately to believe in the inherent goodness of men. Not wisely . . . But too, too well" (29). *American Moor*'s language therefore makes clear that Cobb does not take a naive approach toward the audience, yet neither does he succumb to cynicism.

Adaptive Re-Vision and Audience Education   197

   This tension regarding audience members' openness to reconsidering how they approach matters of race likewise manifests in one of the production's most interesting performance choices and revisions: how it stages Miller, the white director. Originally, Miller did not appear in the play. Rather, he came across as a disembodied voice projected from the back of the theatre. As a voice reverberating over the audience, Miller therefore seemed almost like a voice of God, his consuming volume emblematic of the overpowering nature of white supremacy and its cultural influence. Miller's presence as simply a voice also suggested, at least somewhat, audience complicity, for his dialogue flowed from the audience's direction toward the actor on stage. Such a choice might prompt audiences to question whether they are guilty of any of the racist perspectives articulated by Miller literally all around them. In other words, as Cobb describes this dynamic, the audience is somewhat "complicit in what he [the director] says" but also separate from him "because they have already made friends of the actor onstage" (Cobb interview with Stephen Greenblatt). By the time *American Moor* reached off-Broadway, a different artistic choice for depicting Miller had been made, one required by performance limitations. In the summer of 2018, *American Moor* served as part of the Globe Theatre's Shakespeare and Race Symposium. When planning the production's debut at the Blackfriars Theatre, *American Moor*'s creative team had to change the director's depiction because Blackfriars does not have an audio system that would allow for projecting the director's voice. This is how actor John Tyson became an embodied part of the play. Since that performance, Tyson has sat among the audience, only identified as the director through a spotlight and subsequent dialogue once the actor's audition begins. This staging therefore creates a conflation between the director and the audience, for he is literally one of them, taking the same visual perspective of the actor as audience members do.
   But does he take the same interpretative perspective? This is the fundamental question as *American Moor* closes, one which makes understanding the relationship between the director and the audience imperative. Whether a disembodied voice or an embodied presence, Miller represents the overpowering nature of whiteness in theatre and society. The actor hopes that dialogue can move him from his entrenched, racist vision of *Othello* to, if not a new vision, at least the possibility of one reached via exchanging ideas with the actor. He pleads:

> This play? I don't advise it. But, if you must, and if anything matters to you beyond what you think you know ... Please ... put down

your little brief authority, as you are certainly most ignorant of what you are most assured, and talk to me. Tell me what scares you, tell me what hurts you, tell me though you think it might be a huge mistake. Have the fearlessness to challenge me with your beliefs, but also the valor to have those beliefs challenged . . . Tell me what you hate, what you fear. Trust me. I'll protect you. I will not let anything hurt you. Talk *to* me. Show me you have something, anything more than simply Brabantio's privilege of place. Show me you have *half* of the courage of a Desdemona and I will lift you, in life and love, in death and despair. I don't give a fuck what English asshole you studied with, we will lift each other *and* this *American* form. Talk *to* me, and listen, really listen, when I talk to you. See me [. . .] If we're gonna do this, let's do this . . . (30)

I quote the closing speech at length to emphasize how important the actor perceives a conversation between him and the director to be. *Show* appears twice, *talk* and *tell* four times each, all of them pleas for discourse assisted by *challenge*, *trust*, and *lift*. The language here stresses the vital role of frank communication, as recognized when the actor admits the obstacles facing both him and the director. Yet this is an interchange based on trust and mutuality—what has so long been denied the actor—where, imperatively, the two can "lift each other *and* this American form." With clarity, these words articulate not just to the director but, just as importantly, to the audience the significance of communication for racial reconciliation. If the director is the audience, and vice versa, then the actor's plea to the director is a plea to the audience as well. *American Moor* thus leaves the audience with a final cliffhanger: How does the director respond? How do we? Only one of these two queries receives even a modicum of an answer. The director closes his role in the play by standing, staring at the actor, and replying to his entreaty with, "Thank you . . . thanks for coming in." What does this statement mean? Is it an expression of dismissal or gratitude? Cobb and Tyson have said they leave the ambiguity intentional. Audience members must determine for themselves how the director responds, and why. But their proximity to the director in all but the play's closing moments means that as they grapple with Miller's reaction, they must at the same time account for their own response to *American Moor*'s express call for a dialogue—a dialogue that develops a new vision not just for *Othello*, but also for how white and Black individuals might move forward in the face of historical oppression of the latter by the former.

It is in this accounting where audience education plays a crucial role. The actor makes it clear that he will assist the director, lift him up if needed. Cobb does the same for audiences through audience education. Thus, *American Moor* as a play offers itself up as an adaptive re-vision of *Othello*. At the same time, Cobb encourages adaptive re-vision to extend beyond the play's run by providing audience education as an important resource to make up for the interpretive tools the actor notes audiences are often missing. Put differently, Cobb instantiates the exchange we are not sure the director accepts through his dedication to audience education, an education spanning a variety of methods and forms.

One such appearance was Cobb's discussion with Stephen Greenblatt for the latter's free Harvard online course entitled "Shakespeare's Othello: The Moor." Cobb's discussion with Greenblatt came at the course's close in a unit called "Revisionist Othellos." In Part 12 of the interview, Greenblatt reveals a detail that I believe importantly frames the entire discussion. He notes that he does not always "get" the racial issues in the play; for him, "they come in and out of focus." In this way, Greenblatt plays a role similar to the director as one who does not quite see race in *Othello*, one whose position in life prevents clarity regarding both the play *and* on race and its functions. It is perhaps unsurprising then that in the interview, Cobb deploys strategies similar to the way the actor tackles the interrelationship between race, identity, America, theatre, Shakespeare, and *Othello*. He explains how he perceives Othello as "a man of color in a society that is not like him, generally. And that has rules and codes of behaviour specific to that culture and that society, so he is only allowed to play the game by those rules. And if he does not, there are consequences. I see that as no different than my pilgrimage through life as an African American." In this statement, Cobb communicates one of white supremacy's racist strategies—ascribing limited roles to persons of color and punishing them for stepping outside of those roles—as well as its cross-historical presence, for Othello's narrative journey and his own "pilgrimage" are "no different." That is not to say that Cobb naively or uneducatedly conflates the past and present. He notes how Shakespeare's characters are "not living the contemporary moment that you are living." Nevertheless, he pushes for a new perspective on *Othello*, provocatively asking, "Is that the equivalent of a lynch mob that has come for him?" Ultimately, Cobb stresses the importance of re-vision in the interview, explaining to Greenblatt that "You have to practice telling the truth . . . and if you pick up this play . . . that needs to be foremost in our thought. Why are we doing this? Why do it again if we're not going to find the truth, our truth, our twenty-first-century truth, in an age when it's so conspicuously missing?" Cobb thus establishes the terms for those who have seen or might eventually see his play, not shying away from racism, its limited representation of Black identity, nor the problems inherent in performing *Othello* without the adaptive re-vision so important to truly achieving any semblance of "truth," whatever it might end up being. In other words, Cobb educates audiences about how to approach not just *Othello*, but also *American Moor* and its calls for a new perspective.

One can see a similar educational approach in a recorded post-performance discussion between Cobb and Michael Witmore, the Folger Shakespeare Library's director. Rather than simply responding to questions by Witmore, who was functioning as the emcee, the recording shows Cobb serving as an interlocutor for Witmore, thus modeling the very dialogue the actor requests in *American Moor* between a Black actor providing his perspective and a white man in an authoritative position—in this case, the self-proclaimed "white guy from the Folger." Specifically, Cobb asks Witmore in regard to Witmore's claim about Shakespeare as an establishment author, "Is the establishment changing?" Here, Cobb subtly directs attention to systems (the establishment) that can be adapted and therefore transformed from racist to antiracist approaches. In this case, Cobb singles out both education and the American theatre just as he does in the play when he asks whether there will come a time when "People are sort of interchangeable in terms of casting a production of *Hamlet*," not in a facile "colorblind casting" way but rather one in which "having a black Hamlet" went side by side with "layering in characters, whether it is Gertrude, or whoever, that might make a brown baby . . .?" Cobb's point is not about *Hamlet* specifically but rather whether Witmore sees "people thinking that way? Or caring? Is Shakespeare for the scholars more about 'let's just continue looking at the plays' and not worry about what the American theatre is doing in presentation?" Cobb's questions thus invite the audience to reconsider the connections drawn in the play between education and American theatre, demonstrating that in the world outside of the play, the two work in tandem, even suggesting, if only tacitly, that the former—the Shakespeare scholars—can hold the latter accountable simply by caring. At the same time, Cobb continues his audience education by situating these institutions within American culture's racist structures, ones which, Cobb explains, require "cultiva[ting] all sorts of ways to navigate the structure just to get on," a structure so limiting that the options allowed for a Black man often feel as if "I'll keep doing this [coming back to attempt discourse] because there's nothing else for me to do except kill you. And that's not really an option." These moments demonstrate how Cobb strategically continues the conversation begun between the actor and the audience during the play once the lights come up. What the actor articulates within the world of the play, Cobb makes real in the world without it.

In *American Moor*, the actor makes it clear that the audience often does not have the "tools with which to hear" (4). In many ways, this may seem a discouraging statement, one indicating that white audiences may come to an antiracist play but leave unchanged. Such a result may be true, as suggested by the potential that the white director has likewise remained unchanged after his exchange with the actor. Yet Hall is right to call *American Moor* "exuberantly hopeful" for its "uncommon faith in us" ("Introduction" xi). It imagines that "we can stop the racism in theater and in our lives, if we can make the space and time for learning and listening. We don't have to passively play roles as others imagine them," she expounds. Cobb takes the average theatre experience a step further, participating in the process of "learning and listening" by creating the space and opportunity for that very audience education both before and after attending *American Moor*. It may be easy to disregard these instances of audience education as forms of promotion for *American Moor*, and to a degree, they certainly elevate the play's profile. But these opportunities for education are particularly important given the problems of whiteness and the theatre, whether it be who gets to create drama, who shapes it, or who attends it. Beverly Daniel Tatum advocates for the importance of education as a tool for fighting racism. She notes that "We have all been miseducated [when it comes to racism]. Educating ourselves and others is an essential step in the process of change . . . We can discover another way" (340). *American Moor* proves how powerfully theatre can participate in this re-education, not only in its content, but also through the extra-textual opportunities it provides for its audiences.

Conclusion: The Time for Theatre's Reckoning

One cannot underestimate the difficulty of this antiracist work. For even *American Moor* has felt the influence of whiteness at the hands of directors, producers, and dramaturgs. In the spring of 2020, Methuen Drama released the official published version of *American Moor*. This authoritative edition exposes the way Cobb has had to respond to requests for narrative streamlining, which have meant cuts to the play's script. Methuen decided to include these excisions in three appendices, for which Cobb provides the following explanation: "In writing *American Moor*, the attempt to create the best play from that density required inevitably that elements be removed, not because they were irrelevant, but because they were not helpful in achieving the most focused and impactful dramatic arc" (*American Moor* 43). In fact, he includes them "*because* of their relevance to the experience of at least one African American male actor, in the hope that they will be useful in the study and contemplation of this play and its themes as performance and as literature." Cobb graciously frames the excisions as ones related to focus. It is worth noting, however, that the director, dramaturg, and producers helping him determine that focus were all white. What do we make, then, of the fact that two of the most significant excisions are those related to the trenchant critiques of the two racist, antiblack systems Cobb most strenuously takes to task: the educational system and the American theatre? Ironically, in an edition that will likely be used in the classroom, gone are Cobb's discussion of being an English major whose inquisitiveness was not welcomed in the classroom (Appendix 1), as well as his meditation on the limited rehearsal time and attendant thematic and representational reinscription that shapes American theatre (Appendix 2). It is difficult to ignore the possibility that these cuts are not really about a matter of focus, but rather about catering to the white audiences who, Cobb admits, will already be discomfited by the play. At the opening of the edition published by Methuen Drama, "A note regarding staging and stage directions" recognizes that in "the discovery of the actor and director," the "audience should and will find itself playing many parts. It is not intended that this process leave them in comfort" (2). How much more uncomfortable would they be if the excised sections were included? Of course, such a query is difficult to answer because discomfort in an audience cannot accurately be measured. In its working script, educational components, and final edition, however, *American Moor* does allow one to comprehend the difficulty in creating antiracist theatre that challenges the centrality and supremacy of whiteness.

For some, calling theatre white supremacist might seem a step too far. Yes, it could stand to be more diverse, and yes, perhaps some of theatre's content may be insensitive, questionable, even, but surely not white supremacist. Doesn't the success of a multicultural and hybrid genre musical like *Hamilton* suggest a change? What about the non-musical *Slave Play*'s success? Pao cautions against such assertions, contending, "as far as the theater is concerned, there is no safe space—only safe times and safe places" (33). Indeed, I return attention to where this chapter began, to the cold, hard data indicating that despite particular successes (which in hindsight frequently seem less revolutionary than they first appeared), post-racial American theatre, and post-post-racial American theatre, has a whiteness problem. By centering the voices, experiences, thoughts, and artistic merit of white people over persons of color—a dynamic *American Moor* powerfully critiques—American theatre leaves little doubt about the ways that whiteness reigns supreme.

But it is a reign that may soon be coming to an end. On June 9, 2020, at the start of a third week full of worldwide protests against the systemic racial injustice epitomized by the murder of George Floyd by a white police officer, a group of BIPOC theatremakers calling themselves The Ground We Stand On, in an echo of August Wilson's "The Ground on Which I Stand," released an open letter to "White American Theater." Entitled, "We See You, White American Theater," the statement potently articulated the problem of white supremacy in American theatre while declaring a clarion call for change. Though I am not quoting this powerful statement in its entirety, I do quote it at length, particularly paragraphs that speak to the very issues highlighted by *American Moor*. The letter declares:

> We see you. We have always seen you. We have watched you pretend not to see us.
>
> We have watched you un-challenge your white privilege, inviting us to traffic in the very racism and patriarchy that festers in our bodies, while we protest against it on your stages. We see you.
>
> We have watched you program play after play, written, directed, cast, choreographed, designed, acted, dramaturged and produced by your rosters of white theatermakers for white audiences, while relegating a token, if any, slot for a BIPOC play. We see you.
>
> We have watched you inadequately compare us to each other, allowing the failure of entire productions to be attributed to decisions you forced upon us for the comfort of your theater's white patrons. Meanwhile, you continue to deprioritize the broadening of your audiences by building NO relationship with our communities. We see you.
>
> . . .
>
> We have watched you dangle opportunities like carrots before emerging BIPOC artists, using the power of development, production, and awards to quiet us into obedience at the expense of our art and integrity. We see you.
>
> . . .

We have watched you promote anti-Blackness again and again. We see you.

. . .

About theaters, executive leaders, critics, casting directors, agents, unions, commercial producers, universities and training programs. You are all a part of this house of cards built on white fragility and supremacy. And this is a house that will not stand.

This ends TODAY.

We are about to introduce you . . . to yourself.

Even as theatre can reiterate the racial status quo, it can also function as "a site, or more accurately as multiple sites, for the contestation of cultural power and as a potential location for restructuring the social and symbolic orders" (Pao 33). The Ground We Stand On's call demands this very restructuring, exemplifying what Patricia A. Cahill and Kim F. Hall identify as "a collective impatience with the monuments of white supremacy that masquerade as public art" (1). Fueled by this impatience, the collective lays the foundation for the work to be done. And I use *work* here very intentionally, for battling white supremacy entails emotional, psychological, physical, and ideological labor. This is precisely why Tatum describes the task of antiracism as hard, even overwhelming. In the face of such entrenched, wide-reaching systems, what can we do? How do we proceed? In a very practical way, Tatum suggests a "focus on my own sphere of influence" (340). How one does or does not influence one's sphere returns us to the letter, for it poignantly decries how white theatremakers have not done antiracist work in their sphere of influence—in fact, have done white supremacist work instead. The promise thus lies in the increased sphere of influence by BIPOC creatives and committed allies, an increase facilitated through the structural change suggested by both the end of the system as it has been and the self-recognition by white theatremakers of their complicity with that system.

Yet what does it mean to be introduced to oneself? To truly see oneself as a part of white supremacy and respond accordingly? As the letter indicates, that story is still being written for American theatre. What we do know, however, is that it will likely involve fear (Tatum 331–37). For true change to occur, "fear, whether of anger or isolation, must eventually give way to risk and trust. A leap of faith must be made" (337). It is precisely this leap of faith that *American*

Moor invites. As the play makes clear, self-discovery on the part of the white director entails confronting the misrepresentation of characters of color, the racist structures that value the artistic contributions of white actors, directors, and creators over those of artists of color, the complicity of the educational system in these processes, the emotional and psychological toll of these dynamics, and the deep-seated need to "loosen the grip of historical forces that haunt the Anglo-American stage" (Hall, "Introduction" ix). The fact that these same concerns appear in the letter indicates that the actor's call to the director so powerfully depicted by Cobb is not simply an interpersonal request but rather a new vision for American theatre, and American society more broadly. There can never be certainty regarding the director's response to the fear he faces over this self-discovery. All audiences can do is hold themselves accountable for their own reactions, for their receptiveness, or not, to the dialogue the actor and Cobb offer both on and off stage. As the play's call for adaptive re-vision and Cobb's commitment to audience education make clear, this is not a facile conversation meant to make everyone feel good about improved "race relations." Rather, this talk about race and racism in American theatre and culture "means meaningful, productive dialogue to raise consciousness and lead to effective action and social change" (Tatum 331). It is through this dialogue, and the education it enacts through the new vision that it provides, that the foundation for crafting an antiracist *Othello*, antiracist Shakespeare, antiracist theatre, and antiracist society begins.

Chapter 5

At the Intersection of Gender, Race, and White Privilege: A Case of Three Desdemona Plays

Othello's Desdemona Problem

"[I]nnocent, and sweet, and passive" (67). This is how lauded postcolonial Nigerian author Ben Okri describes Desdemona in his essay "Leaping Out of Shakespeare's Terror: Five Meditations on *Othello*" (1997).[1] As Okri meditates on the often evaded "terrors that are at the heart of the play" (59) after watching director Terry Hands's *Othello* starring Ben Kingsley and David Suchet at the Barbican, in the fourth and fifth sections he turns to the general's "general" and the way that the white, patriarchal powers shaping her worldview doom her and Othello's love from the outset. For Okri, Desdemona is a young woman loving but ignorant, devoted but sheltered. "She is," he explains, "the redemption and the victim of her history." What is this history? Okri never articulates it, and neither does Shakespeare's play. Yet even without its details, Okri understands that Desdemona is

> the type who likes romances and is seduced by exoticism. Today she might be an ardent lover of a glamorized Africa . . . She would have heard of slavery but never have thought about it. She would be shocked to hear that black people are treated badly because of their color . . . She would be shocked because she has never been allowed to confront reality, to face the Medusa-like truths of the world. (67)

---

[1] This essay appears in Okri's collection *A Way of Being Free*, but it was first published in 1989 in *West African Magazine*.

How can Okri make these assertions without access to the very history he says shapes Desdemona? He can articulate these claims because Desdemona's history is part of another history, one pervasive and well-known—that of white patriarchal control over the female body and mind. Okri never mentions patriarchal restrictions explicitly, but he implies them as he recognizes what Desdemona "has never been allowed." Whether applied to Shakespeare's Desdemona or the one Okri imagines for today, the protective sheltering of young white womanhood from the vagaries of the world depends upon a desire for silence, chastity, and obedience, for it is only through careful cultivation and protection by patriarchy that innocent, sweet, and passive femininity can endure.

According to Okri, such patriarchal circumscription serves to maintain a particular perspective, one that does not acknowledge or truly confront racial inequity. This ideological, perhaps even literal, cloistering of Desdemona is why "The source of her delusion is ignorance" (67). And this ignorance creates competing positions of marginality and disempowerment between constrained femininity and marginalized Black subjectivity. Okri once again implies rather than states his point starkly, but one grasps his meaning nevertheless when he explains that to be happy with Othello, Desdemona "would have to alter the way she sees her history, and that would alter almost everything else" (68). Thus, the patriarchal history that limits Desdemona does so in order to craft her into a woman "without scepticism, without knowledge." It is this lack, this blank space, that Desdemona fills with her daydreams about the exotic Othello. "The romantic reduces black people to a fantasy. And then they love the illusion they themselves have created," Okri observes. In Desdemona, then, one sees that the consequences of patriarchal control and the consequences of white supremacy are never too far from one another, in fact two draughts of the same paradigmatic poison that ensures the authority of white masculinity over all others.

Yet confronting even just two categories of oppression can be perceived as overwhelmingly difficult, even exhausting, especially when they challenge and subjugate each other. As such, if *Othello* has an Iago problem, which it undoubtedly does, then it also has a Desdemona problem, as Okri thoughtfully exposes. No one can deny that Desdemona is a product of a society that affords her limited agency and very prescribed roles. After all, if this were not true, Brabantio would not be able to use her up-until-then proper behavior as evidence of Othello's witchcraft. This is why Desdemona's speech to her father is so extraordinary. And one cannot sidestep that as comedic structure gives way to tragedy in the second half of the play, the tragedy is not just Othello's, but Desdemona's too. As Okri acknowledges, Othello "doesn't face her reality either" (68), meaning that fantasies about ideal femininity and a desire for her naiveté likewise threaten their romance, contributing to her untimely murder. Yet precisely because Othello's domestic violence is so morally wrong and based on factual error, and because Desdemona's agential decision to elope with Othello is used as the very thing that damns her, it can be easy to overlook how she participates in Othello's marginalization. Like the Venetians around her, even as she loves him, she Others him, exoticizing him and conceiving of him through difference, yet idealizing him at the same time (see Chapter 2). Desdemona thereby never understands Othello in his "own particular individuality" (Okri 68).

Indeed, the Desdemona problem extends beyond the potential to ignore her problematic treatment of Othello. Additionally, audiences may find it difficult to feel sympathy for Othello—to be open to seeing how racial oppression and abuse lead to his downfall—with Desdemona's white, female body on display given that for centuries, inculcated sympathy and paternalistic concern for white femininity has shaped antiblackness. As such, this dynamic shifts Othello from a tragic figure to a cautionary exemplum of Black masculine terror. Since, as numerous scholars have noted, Desdemona recedes into the traditional feminine role expected of her by the end of the play,[2] she hardly speaks (and her last declaration is a lie). Desdemona therefore functions as a blank, white canvas upon which the often predominantly white audience can project the twinned attitudes of pity for white womanhood and anger against Black masculinity.

The Desdemona problem makes it clear that crafting an antiracist *Othello* likely entails a radical reimagining of Desdemona, not just Othello. Yet, again, this dual attention is no easy task, which probably contributes to Desdemona's general absence across the engagements with *Othello* this book has addressed thus far. In *Kill Shakespeare*,

---

[2] The scholarship on Desdemona's role and eventual powerlessness in *Othello* is vast. For representative articles, see Eamon Grennan, "The Women's Voices in *Othello*: Speech, Song, Silence," *Shakespeare Quarterly* 38.3 (1987): 275–92; Peter Stallybrass, "Patriarchal Territories: The Body Enclosed," *Rewriting the Renaissance: The Discourses of Sexual Difference in Early Modern Europe*, edited by Margaret W. Ferguson, Maureen Quilligan, and Nancy J. Vickers (University of Chicago Press, 1986), 123–42; Emily C. Bartels, "Strategies of Submission: Desdemona, the Duchess, and the Assertion of Desire," *Studies in English Literature* 36 (1996): 417–33; and Martha Ronk, "Desdemona's Self-Presentation," *English Literary Renaissance* 35.1 (2005): 52–72.

Desdemona only "appears" as a disembodied voice, a decision likewise made by the Q Brothers in *Othello: The Remix*. *Serial* positions Adnan Sayed as the *Othello* of its story, so Hae Min Lee must be its Desdemona. But as a murder victim, her voice too is limited, reduced to Sarah Koenig reading from her diary. And while *American Moor* beautifully reimagines Othello as a character, at times mentioning his relationship with Desdemona, what understanding Othello anew means for understanding Desdemona anew is not Cobb's focus. It is no wonder, then, that Toni Morrison and Rokia Traoré identified Desdemona as suffering from "lacunae and poetic ambiguities in Shakespeare" (Sellars 10) that needed addressing. It was this lack, so difficult to negotiate, that led the famous African American author and prodigious Malian musician to collaborate on a text (Morrison) joined with music and lyrics (Traoré) to create the experimental operetta *Desdemona* (2011). In partnership with director Peter Sellers, Morrison and Traoré's play envisions a "new dimensionality" to Desdemona, for while Shakespeare crafted an "ideal creation" who nevertheless remains "mostly silent," in *Desdemona,* she "Finally . . . speaks," and in doing so "reveals secrets, hopes, dreams, but also her own imperfections" (Sellars 9). Morrison and Traoré therefore push back against the innocent, sweet, and passive Desdemona of Shakespeare's play. In the stead of Shakespeare's naive teenager, they offer up a thoughtful, articulate woman whose newly centered point of view fills in the gaps of Desdemona's history while indicting the toxic masculinity that shaped it.

Yet even as *Desdemona* undertakes this feminist re-vision, it refuses to gloss over the fact that Desdemona's white femininity is implicated in Othello's oppression. Whereas reanimations of *Othello* often take an "either/or" formulation when confronting the tangled web of gender and racial oppression in the play, Morrison provides a "both/and" approach. In other words, *Desdemona* rises to the challenge of the multifaceted attention one must pay in order to truly confront how different forms of oppression influence and constitute one another. The play thus articulates a clear antiracist approach, one that opposes the characters' misogyny in Shakespeare's tragedy while also pushing back against the antiblackness all too often present in both Shakespeare's "original" *and* in post-racial reinterpretations of the play.

Desdemona corrects this single-topic emphasis through its intersectional perspective by stressing relationality, or the "relationships across social divisions" (Collins and Bilge 27). As Patricia Hill Collins and Simone Bilge elucidate, "Relational thinking rejects *either/*

or binary thinking ... Instead, relationality embraces a *both/and* frame. The focus of relationality shifts from analyzing what distinguishes entities, for example, the differences between race and gender, to examining their interconnections" (27). I therefore use *intersectional* here both in its most familiar form as an exploration of overlapping forms of oppression in a single identity, and also in its relational form, as a matrix for understanding how power constitutes relationships across identity categories. One of the foundational aspects of a relational intersectional consideration is "conversation," "dialog," and "transaction," according to Collins and Bilge (28). This is precisely what Morrison's script adds to Desdemona's story. For *Desdemona* not only radically reimagines its central character, but also *Othello* itself by combining music with playtext (thereby changing performance conditions). Just as significantly, it includes new characters who dialogue with one another in a timeless, spaceless afterlife. The most notable of Morrison's additions are Soun, Othello's mother, and Barbary, now given her own name, Sar'an. For this reading, the latter becomes particularly significant because Sa'ran speaks back to her sidelining by Desdemona and the white privileged perspective she represents. *Desdemona* thus offers up a powerful riposte to post-racial America's favored colorblind perspective. It demonstrates instead that seeing "color," a.k.a. race, and gender alongside each other, whether embodied by one subjectivity or across more than one, is vital for beginning the process of reconciliation.

To fully grasp *Desdemona*'s contribution to reimagining *Othello*, especially the refreshing and underarticulated intersectional perspective this reanimation takes, it is helpful to place it in dialogue with and understand it as a corrective to two plays that likewise reimagine *Othello* by focusing on Desdemona—Ann-Marie MacDonald's *Goodnight Desdemona (Good Morning Juliet)* (1988) and Paula Vogel's *Desdemona: A Play about a Handkerchief* (1993).[3]

---

[3] For the sake of undertaking a comparison, both of these plays extend my timeframe, and MacDonald's play also expands my attention to place, for she is a Canadian playwright. For discussions of *Goodnight Desdemona (Good Morning Juliet)* contextualized through Canada's relationship with/to Shakespeare, see Louise Harrington, "'Excuse me while I turn this upside-down': Three Canadian Adaptations of Shakespeare," *British Journal of Canadian Studies* 20.1 (2007), 123–42; Michael Morrison, "Shakespeare in North America," in *The Cambridge Companion to Shakespeare on Stage*, edited by Stanley Wells and Sarah Stanton (Cambridge University Press, 2002), 230–58; and *Shakespeare in Canada: "A World Elsewhere?"*, edited by Diana Brydon and Irena R. Makaryk (University of Toronto Press, 2002).

While decidedly feminist, imaginative retellings, these plays encapsulate a long-held critique of mainstream feminism—a failure to consider the voices of people of color.[4] In this way, they illustrate Marianne Novy's assertion that "Desdemona has not been one of the most rewritten of Shakespeare's female characters, and her fictional and dramatic re-imaginers have usually paid attention to either race or gender but not both" (77). Specifically, in both plays, Othello is marginalized, even erased, for the sake of feminist revision. Conversely, *Desdemona* provides a more inclusive response. Through uneasy confrontations between Desdemona and Othello, the operetta demonstrates how a more nuanced, aware Desdemona emerges not at the expense of but rather due to, in part, a recognition of Othello's vexed status as a Black male in a predominantly white society. *Desdemona* thus stresses the value of intersectionality to feminist thought—and to antiracist Shakespearean reanimation.

Desdemona Plays and Feminism

To truly appreciate the feminist significance of MacDonald's, Vogel's, and Morrison's respective projects, it is helpful to review how Desdemona has appeared in performance over the centuries. Julie Hankey details *Othello*'s performance history from early modernity through the early 2000s, and her extensive overview makes evident that as much as performance tradition for *Othello* has varied, historically, very little attention has been paid to Desdemona. In the Restoration, as textual cuts became the norm, quite "obvious [was] the curtailment

---

[4] Much of this critique has focused on the silencing of women of color. Barbara Smith, for instance, criticizes white feminists "for making no serious effort to change older patterns of contempt. To look at how you still believe yourselves to be superior to Third World women and how you communicate these attitudes in blatant and subtle ways" (39). bell hooks traces how as the women's movement "attempted to take feminism beyond the realm of radical rhetoric and into the realm of American life, they revealed that they had not changed, had not undone the sexist and racist brainwashing that had taught them to regard women unlike themselves as Others." As a result, "the hierarchical pattern of race and sex relationship already established in American society merely took a different form under 'feminism' ... the myth that the social status of all women in America is the same" (*Ain't I a Woman* 121). And as Audre Lorde contends, "Ignoring the differences of race between women and the implications of those differences presents the most serious threat to the mobilization of women's joint power. As white women ignore their built-in privilege of whiteness and define *woman* in terms of their own experience alone, then the women of colour become 'other,' the outsider whose experience and tradition is too 'alien' to comprehend" (117).

of Desdemona's part," both in the Senate scene and her particularly affecting Willow song (19). Hankey asserts that the cuts "make way for the grand, majestic Othellos that succeeded each other from then on, up to the end of the eighteenth century," suggesting the long-standing divided attention between Othello and Desdemona.[5] Hankey explains that "not much" is subsequently heard about Desdemona until the late 1700s (26), when John Philip Kemble made further cuts involving her, including her "midnight entrance," a pattern which remained through the nineteenth century (32). This was also the same era during which Sarah Siddons "transformed" the character from a "shrinking girl" to a "warm and passionate woman" who represented "goodness and courage in a vicious world" (33, 34). For this version of Desdemona, a white satin gown became *de rigueur* (43). Tellingly, despite tracing a number of changes to depictions of both Othello and Iago across the European continent and the US, Hankey does not mention Desdemona again until remarking on her role in Orson Welles's 1951 film, for which "Welles hunted, not for a woman who could act the part, but for a collection of physical attributes that he could photograph, even if in the end, they belonged to different actresses" (78). Though by the 1960s onward Desdemona could not be separated "from the modern woman," she still struggled to come into focus, for choices such as Terry Hands's decision to stress a "homoerotic theme" for his 1987 Royal Shakespeare Company production worked to "deflect attention" from Desdemona (97). Hankey singles out Trevor Nunn's 1989 *Othello* for giving increased space to the women of the play (Imogen Stubbs as Desdemona and Zoë Wanamaker as Emilia) (99), an attention that would again recede with Oliver Parker's notable 1995 film which "diminishes" both Othello (Laurence Fishburn) and Desdemona (Irène Jacob) with its attention on Kenneth Branagh's Iago. I review this history to demonstrate the centuries-long inattention to Desdemona to which MacDonald, Vogel, and Morrison respond. For MacDonald and Vogel, it perhaps justifies why intersectional relationality is blunted in favor of highlighting the gender oppression that has so long been overlooked. For Morrison, however, it fuels a perspective that adds the complexity Desdemona has so long been lacking but that does so without idealizing her character's shortcomings regarding her privileged classed and racial stance.

---

[5] These cuts may be why in 1693, Thomas Rymer argues that "there is nothing in the noble Desdemona that is now below any country chambermaid with us" (qtd. in Hankey 20).

Indeed, with their articulate, interesting, and layered Desdemonas, one can see how MacDonald's and Vogel's reanimations sit alongside Nunn's traditional *Othello* as versions of the play intent on creating space for female voices. It is therefore unsurprising that scholars have jointly addressed MacDonald's *Good Night Desdemona (Good Morning Juliet)* and Vogel's *Desdemona: A Play about a Handkerchief* as feminist reworkings of Shakespeare reconceiving Desdemona in ways that push against traditional patriarchal conceptions of submissive, chaste femininity. Novy, for instance, considers how both MacDonald and Vogel "use Shakespeare to stress the limitations of his plays as well-known cultural myths about women's possibilities," namely, MacDonald's critique of "women in general as naturally or ideally passive" and Vogel's critique of "marital infidelity and of idealizations of this trait in women" (73, 74).[6] Sharon Friedman extends this analysis, situating the plays in conversation with Djanet Sears's *Harlem Duet* (1997) to demonstrate how all three "foreground the women's plight, depict female relationships, and refocus plot to reveal the 'high cost of patriarchal values' that several feminist scholars see embedded in Shakespeare's tragedies" (113). MacDonald's and Vogel's respective dramas are thus firmly established as "feminist theatrical appropriations and re-visions of *Othello*" (Thompson, "*Desdemona*" 495), what Sujata Iyengar has recently termed "woman-crafted Shakespeare" ("Woman-Crafted" 511).

I revisit the feminist underpinnings of MacDonald's and Vogel's familiar works in order to contrast the thoughtfulness with which they approach the issue of gender oppression with the less careful ways the plays address racial oppression (or not). Though staging distinct characterizations of Desdemona, both MacDonald and Vogel respond to common characteristics of male power, which Adrienne Rich, via Kathleen Gough, helpfully enumerates. For MacDonald, it means crafting a Desdemona who resists the physical confinement so often imposed upon women and who pushes back against attempts of what Rich identifies as the masculine desire to assimilate women (Rich 639). As such, in *Goodnight Desdemona*, Desdemona does not fit within the framework of a compliant wife. Rather, she is a warrior, just as ready to rush to the front lines as her general husband, in a depiction that, as Novy notes, challenges her Shakespearean characterization as ultimately both a submissive

---

[6] Harrington explains that rejecting Desdemona's victimhood not only speaks back to Shakespeare, but also "The 'typically Canadian' position of acknowledging your victimhood but accepting its inevitability" (129).

woman and victim (72, 74).⁷ Laurin R. Porter reads even further into this depiction of Desdemona, suggesting that MacDonald assigns her a number of Othello's lines because "she takes on his characteristics" (372), while Othello comes across as "a pompous windbag" (366). Desdemona's martial valor appears when she meets the play's protagonist, Constance Ledbelly, who has been transported into the world of Shakespeare's *Othello* and is now playing a key role in the story, even going so far as to show Othello that Desdemona did not lose her handkerchief. Due to her intercession, Othello and Desdemona mistake Constance for a virgin oracle. When Desdemona probes Constance about her identity, Desdemona's own subjectivity comes to the fore. Constance explains, "I'm from another world," a statement Desdemona interrupts with the telling exclamation, "Ay, Academe. And ruled by mighty Queens, a race of Amazons who brook no men" (29). Previously, Constance proclaimed, "I come from Queen's," a reference to the university where she works that Desdemona takes as an indication of the women Constance serves, thereby assuming the Amazonian context. This assumption on Desdemona's part functions as a shorthand to communicate to audiences more about the character. Up until Desdemona's reference, there has been no wordplay to introduce Amazons, nor has Constance demonstrated any martial skill. Audiences thus understand that Desdemona's fascination with the "nothing if not war-like" female community that "brook no men" and sing "songs of conquest . . . for sisters slain on honour's gory field" (29, 30) stems from her own desire, a projection upon Constance of the life she wishes she could lead. Notable in Desdemona's choice is the exclusionary nature of the Amazonian women, the way they create no space for men while celebrating female community and martial skill. For it is women lost in "gory" fighting which, according to Desdemona, merit communal mourning. From the outset, then, MacDonald's Desdemona aligns with traditional characterizations of feminist women: she is independent, speaks her mind, takes action, and seems to prefer the company of women over men.

Desdemona's feminist characterization appears once more when she learns that Constance is unmarried, and also that she refuses to "Learn to kill" (32). Desdemona admonishes Constance, asserting:

---

⁷ MacDonald's play was first written and performed in 1988 and subsequently revised, then published in 1990. Harrington calls it "probably the most famous, as well as the most mainstream, of Canadian adaptations of Shakespeare. It is certainly the most successful" (126).

That's a fault! Thy sole deficiency.
An errant woman that would live alone,
No husband there, her honour to defend,
Must study to be bloody and betimes. (32)

A tension between adherence to and subversion of traditional feminine expectations resides in these lines. On the one hand, Desdemona imagines a woman needing her husband in order to defend her honor. In fact, the idea of defending a woman's honor, a concept tied to virginity and chastity, is troubling, even antiquated. As such, MacDonald positions Desdemona as a woman "of her time" even as the play modernizes her. On the other hand, Constance's single status does not scandalize Desdemona in any way, and she responds to potential threats with a call to arms. This sounds more like a modern than early modern woman, a characterization stressed in a visually spectacular way when Desdemona runs without hesitation into an ensuing battle and returns with a severed head she "pluckéd off the beach!" (35). MacDonald crafts a decidedly valiant, courageous Desdemona, one whom we can imagine meant that she wished *she* could be a man when opining that "heaven had made her such a man" (I, iii, 165).

Furthering Desdemona's feminist characterization, the structure of the play reinforces the importance of the exclusive female community Desdemona imagines among the Amazons. Desdemona's significance to Constance is not signaled by her marriage to Othello but rather by the way she serves as one of Constance's two psychic avatars (the other being Juliet), figures who represent repressed parts of Constance's self and who thus help her "find herself" by the play's end. By the drama's conclusion, the three unite to create a gyno-trinity that allows Constance to realize she has unlocked Shakespeare's *urtext*, and through her translation and understanding of its "ancient hieroglyphs," is now the "Author" who can truly and accurately interpret the great literary master's works (89). While one may debate just how submissive or not, agential or not, Shakespeare's Desdemona may be, in MacDonald's play, one finds a pointedly independent, valiant, nontraditional woman who evokes twentieth-century feminist ideals of self-sufficiency, female community, and agential female subjectivity.

Despite a drastically different characterization of *Othello*'s female protagonist, Vogel's play likewise stages an independent Desdemona.[8] She can freely articulate this independence because she spends the entirety of the play in a decidedly female-centric space. Vogel places

[8] Vogel's play was first performed at Cornell University in 1987.

Desdemona and Emilia in a kitchen, and the two are only joined by Bianca, so that this domestic space allows them to escape Othello, Iago, and Cassio, who "collectively function as an absent presence that defines female behavior" (Gruber). Vogel's staging choices thus literalize the female-centric community, what Rich would call part of the lesbian continuum, that so appeals to the Desdemona of MacDonald's play, for these three women only ever interact with each other, so as to "focus the action on the women's intrigues and motivations" (Friedman 118). Even with its bickering, critique, and conflict, this unidealized female community creates a relatively safe space for Desdemona to explore and articulate the key facet of her feminist recharacterization in the play: her sexuality. As Elizabeth Gruber aptly points out, this Desdemona "appears to bear out the misogynistic arguments . . . that are discernible in *Othello*," so as to "[ensure] that readers must confront their own assumptions about the 'proper' behavior for female characters. An unfaithful heroine/victim requires a new calibration of empathy." In this way, she too rejects male power, specifically, the attempt to deny women their own sexuality (Rich 638). Desdemona in fact relishes her sexual expression, *especially* outside of the confines of marriage, as made clear by the fact that the Tuesday prior to the play's action, she worked as a substitute prostitute for Bianca, during which she saw "ten johns," thereby making "five bob, an' tuppence fer tips" (Scene 21, 32). As she points out to Emilia, she was so active that "I made more in twenty minutes than you do in a week of washing!" (32). As early as Scene 2, the play dispels any expectation of a virtuous Desdemona, for the audience learns that Desdemona and Emilia paid Bianca for the blood of an "old hen" that would "wash out clear as maidenhead or a baby's dropping" (8). Though not stated explicitly, it is clear that Desdemona had no such maidenhead to offer, thus the need for the facsimile. As Novy observes, here, Desdemona "is as wanton as Iago claims she is—with every man but Cassio" (72). Vogel's Desdemona is thus not only sexual, but capaciously so, invoking Shakespeare's Desdemona's devouring "greedy ear." What she consumes in Vogel's play, however, is not stories but men. According to Ryan M. Claycomb, such a representation forces the spectator to confront their "complicity in viewing textual constructions of women [they were] once forced to resist," thereby allowing Vogel to "[expose and refute] the sexist representations of women found in the source text" (87, 88). Vogel thus uses a clear focus on female voices alongside sexual independence, even prowess, as central to crafting her feminist reinterpretation of Desdemona. In doing so, she aims to have

Desdemona break free from patriarchal expectations of femininity that so plague her central character as well as the women in her twentieth-century audience.

Two key moments further stress the voracious capacity of Desdemona's sexuality, while also signaling its nonconformist nature. In Scene 3, Desdemona finds a hoof-pick, which the stage directions describe as *"a long, crooked bit of iron with a wicked point"* (9). Desdemona inquires about the instrument, upon which Emilia explains its use for picking stones out of a horse's foot. Desdemona responds, "if I could find a man with just such a hoof-pick—he could pluck out my stone—eh, Emilia?" The bawdy comradery between servant and mistress momentarily papers over the class divisions and contestations over female chastity the two women embody. Notably, in a reversal of *Othello*'s Willow scene, Desdemona initiates the sexual framework for the interchange. The audience thus begins to develop a sense of Desdemona's carnal nature. If the prop used is indeed long, crooked, and "wicked" in shape, the hoof-pick serves as a phallic symbol that concomitantly suggests Desdemona's pleasure in erotic danger, even pain. The stage directions enhance such an interpretation, for Scene 4 consists of total silence. Emilia scrubs Desdemona's stained sheets while Desdemona *"lies on her back on the table, feet propped up, absent-mindedly fondling the pick, and staring into space"* (10). Given the context of Scenes 2 and 3, Desdemona's supine position invokes sensuality, as does Vogel's use of *"fondling"* in the stage direction. As Desdemona stares into space, it would seem the audience watches her lost in sexual fantasy. A second key moment reinforces Desdemona's proclivity for sex that is more than "vanilla." In Scene 22, or *"the beating scene"* (35), Desdemona lies prone and *"spread-eagle"* on the table while Bianca takes a strap and brushes her with it, upon which Desdemona is to "move yer tail up . . ." Invoking the horse-pick, Desdemona likens the action to "rather like rising to the trot on a horse" (35, 36). Desdemona excels in this exercise, including faux-screams and moans, so that by its conclusion Bianca remarks, "Aw want you t'take this in th' right way, now; but if you weren't born a lady, you'd a been a bleedin'-good blowzabella. One o' the best" (36), reminding Desdemona and the audience that such unusual sexual play is not the provenance of well-born ladies. Vogel thus crafts a Desdemona whose "deviant" sexuality explicitly breaks societal expectations of both gender and class through her extensive couplings and facility with kink.

Desdemona's sexual proclivity may in fact be exacerbated by what Vogel represents as an unhappy union from the outset. *Desdemona* opens with her searching for the lost handkerchief, but this is no Desdemona worried about her husband's love. Rather, Vogel depicts an exasperated Desdemona frustrated by the mundane life she believes she leads. She explains her initial attraction to Othello, noting, "I thought—if I marry this strange dark man, I can leave this narrow little Venice with its whispering piazzas behind—I can escape and see other worlds" (Scene 11, 20). But Desdemona's fantasy does not turn into reality, for "under that exotic façade was a porcelain white Venetian." As a response to Othello's failure, she turns to sex as a relief for her ennui. The men she sleeps with provide her with a mental escape, she explains, for they "spill their seed into me, Emilia—seed from a thousand lands, passed down through generations of ancestors, with genealogies that cover the surface of the globe. And I simply lie still there in the darkness, taking them all into me; I close my eyes and in the dark of my mind—oh, how I travel!" (20). Though Desdemona does not mention Othello's stories of exotic adventures by name, her discussion of travel via sexual encounter indicates that Othello has not lived up to the promise proffered by the only witchcraft he used. Just as MacDonald's Desdemona positions Constance as an Amazonian proxy for her adventurous desires, so too does Vogel's Desdemona transform her "johns," or more precisely, their semen, into a proxy for the liberty she wishes she could enjoy. In other words, sexual freedom appears to be her only escape from the confining conditions and patriarchal expectations placed upon her, first by Venetian society, and then by her disappointment of a husband. Vogel's Desdemona therefore articulates her feminist subjectivity through ownership and use of her body, turning forbidden sexual expression into an articulation of feminine resistance and true selfhood. Thus, despite starkly distinct characterizations, MacDonald and Vogel write back to Shakespeare's Desdemona, creating protagonists that reject various forms of male power in order to distinguish their versions from the Desdemona who succumbs to precisely this power—a denial of her sexuality, an enforcement of male sexual ideals upon her, a confinement of her movement, a use of her as an object in male transactions, and a constraint of her "creativeness" (Rich 638, 639)—as she meets her passive, tragic end in *Othello*.[9]

---

[9] Novy interestingly notes how "These two plays have had radically different fates," with MacDonald's a success and Vogel's "closed after very short runs at the Bay Street Theatre," a distinction she ascribes to the "difference in tone between the plays ... MacDonald's is much more affectionate, and thus more likely to appeal to an audience drawn by the Shakespearean names in the title" (71).

Intersectionality and Feminist Racial Erasure

I trace the well-established feminist elements of MacDonald's and Vogel's respective Desdemona plays in order to reveal the tension between ideological presence and absence: the centered feminist characterizations that at the same time erase the racism and prejudice in *Othello*. Put differently, while remarkable in their pointedly feminist (and at times even unflattering) re-creations of Desdemona, both these plays enact a pitfall of white feminist praxis—a lack of intersectionality. Intersectionality began as a corrective to oversights in both feminist and antiracist practices. Credited with popularizing the term, Kimberlé Williams Crenshaw notes in her landmark 1991 article "Mapping the Margins: Intersectionality, Identity, Politics, and Violence Against Women of Color," "Although racism and sexism readily intersect in the lives of real people, they seldom do in feminist and antiracist practices" (1242).[10] Getting lost among these perspectives and approaches, critics argued, were the voices of women of color, for by ignoring intersection, feminist and antiracist practices "relegate the identity of women of color to a location that resists telling." Crenshaw elaborates, "Because of their intersectional identity as both women *and* of color within discourses shaped to respond to one *or* the other, women of color are marginalized within both" (1244). Understood in this way, the term *intersectionality* thus "refers to actual intersecting oppressions as they manifest in the empirical universe" (Grzanka xviii).

Initially most present in the works of Black feminist scholars, intersectionality proved so influential that it broadened into a methodology for studying multifaceted, interlocking forms of oppression. The term has now expanded to also encompass "a kind of theory, method, or mode of analysis that incorporates the tenets of the field, broadly construed" (Grzanka xviii). As Margaret L. Andersen explains, the work of women of color, especially Black feminist thought, initiated a shift in academic approaches toward both gender and race, so that in the 1990s and especially by the new millennium, "The new race/gen-

---

[10] Patrick R. Grzanka likewise notes Crenshaw's contributions to intersectionality, but he also explains that the concept has multiple origin narratives, such as those who locate it "even further back [than Crenshaw], with the Combahee River Collective Statement of 1977" (xiv). Nevertheless, most scholars agree that whatever its precise origins, intersectionality is grounded "in US Black women's community activism and intellectual labor, but also include[s] contributions from other women of color feminists from within and outside the United States whose work has influenced how we understand the key concepts and concerns of the field" (xiv).

der/class paradigm is specifically framed around the *social structural intersections* of race, class, and gender" (167). Key to understanding the intersectional aspect of this new paradigm is acknowledging that race, gender, and class are "*interlocking systems* of inequalities, subordination and domination" that people experience "*simultaneously*" (Andersen 169). Thus, as Collins and Bilge explain, intersectionality is now often used as a "*heuristic*, a problem-solving analytical tool" (4). Patrick R. Grzanka cautions, however, that intersectionality should not be "reduce[d] . . . to a theory about identity. Intersectionality is a structural analysis and critique . . . [that is] foremost about studying multiple dimensions of inequality and developing ways to resist and challenge these various forms of oppression" (xv). But what is analyzed in addition to the social divisions of "Race, class, gender, sexuality, dis/ability, ethnicity, nation, religion, and age" (Collins and Bilge 7)? Collins and Bilge identify "six core ideas that appear and reappear when people use intersectionality as an analytical tool: inequality, relationality, power, social context, complexity, and social justice" (25). Intersectionality thus functions as a methodological approach that takes into account the Gordian knot of race, gender, class, and even sexuality, their respective influences upon both individuals and relationships, and actively strives for the transformation of the various systems of oppression it identifies.

Often, however, it can seem as if intersectionality only examines interlocking systems of oppression as applied to one multifaceted identity. Leslie McCall identifies this approach as "intracategorical complexity," which focuses on "the single group represented by the individual" so that "The intersection of identities takes place through the articulation of a single dimension of each category. That is, the 'multiple' in these intersectional analyses refers not to dimensions within categories but to dimensions across categories" (1781). While this may be the most common intersectional method, McCall proposes the importance of "intercategorical complexity" or a "categorical approach" which examines "relationships of inequality among already constituted social groups, as imperfect and ever changing as they are, and takes those relationships as the center of analysis" (1784, 1785). She elaborates, "The categorical approach formally compares—say, in terms of income or education—each of the groups constituting a category: men and women, blacks and whites, working and middle classes, and so on. Moreover, the categorical approach takes as its point of departure that these categories form more detailed social groups: white women and black women, working- and middle-class men, and so on" (1787). McCall's distinction is helpful here, for it takes the relational consideration Collins and Bilge identify and positions it as a distinct method interrogating how multiple systems of oppression work across identities and are often encouraged to compete with and therefore subjugate one another for access to power.

The competition for power informing Vogel's and MacDonald's plays is the one white patriarchy fosters between white women and all persons of color, including men. Such a contestation may be easy to overlook, for neither of these plays includes embodiments of either women or men of color.[11] But even if he just serves as a specter over the dramatic action, perhaps only ever spoken of, both plays do include Othello. Their respective depictions of Othello, however, demonstrate dichotomous thinking, wherein a feminist approach discounts the social subordination of a Black man. In other words, they ignore "how some groups of men can feel and be powerless (or at least less powerful) because of their class, race or even sexual status, even when there is a rigid patriarchal system operating at the structural level" (Andersen 172). Put bluntly, both plays challenge patriarchal conventions and speak back to the male-centric literary canon, but they do so in a way that marginalizes Othello; they thereby promote feminist versions of Desdemona and female-focused responses to Shakespeare by subordinating Black masculinity in order to advance the aims of white feminist ideology. In other words, these two plays highlight the power and travails of white femininity at the expense of Black masculinity by enacting the erasure of Othello, and with him, of the question of racism and white supremacy's inequity raised by Shakespeare's tragedy.

Much scholarship about these two plays—either when analyzed separately or together—also eschews an intersectional methodology, either entirely ignoring their elision of race or mentioning the fact without tackling the ramifications of this choice. Louise Harrington focuses on the colonial context embedded in MacDonald's play due

---

[11] I grant, however, that persons of color could be cast in these plays. The possibilities in *Goodnight Desdemona (Good Morning Juliet)* are in fact quite viable for color-conscious casting. Assuming a desire to keep Desdemona white (which if Othello is white, is entirely unnecessary), there is no reason, for instance, that Juliet could not be played by a person of color. Vogel's play poses a greater challenge. Again, if the desire is to keep Desdemona white, that means a woman of color would play either Emilia or Bianca. With the former, it would continue the long tradition of casting actors of color in ancillary or servant roles. If the latter, it would risk reifying the stereotype of profligate "foreign" female sexuality, such as that embodied by the antiblack stereotype of the Jezebel or the Orientalist conceptualization of the exotic harem.

to Constance's Canadian identity in distinction with Dr. Night's English one, but she does not address race as part of this discussion, while Beverley Curran only comments that "Instead of interracial love, *Desdemona* turns on the desire of one woman for another" (214). And, despite noting a reviewer critiquing MacDonald for not engaging with race and subsequently suggesting that "Perhaps in a still more subversive feminist comedy she [Constance] would marry a woman of colour," Shannon Hengen likewise does not consider the omission of race in MacDonald's play. Others, like Porter, do not even come close to mentioning race at all, likely because, as Melanie A. Stevenson makes clear, *Goodnight Desdemona* itself "avoids any discussion of race, racism, or societal attitudes towards miscegenation," an intentional decision on MacDonald's part (36). Vogel's play directly mentions Othello's Blackness, yet even so, scholars like Claycomb still sidestep how race functions in *Desdemona*, as does Friedman, who analyzes both MacDonald's and Vogel's plays yet does not mention race in relationship to either. Some scholars address race only briefly, such as Gruber, who notes how *Desdemona* "has been faulted" for its "neglect" of race as it appears "to evade treating race as a specific source of tension between Desdemona, Emilia, and Bianca." Gruber does not mention Othello, however, and ultimately concludes that "If this stance fails adequately to address matters of race or ethnicity, it does shed light on a past and current objective of feminism, namely achieving an equitable balance between celebrating differences between women and working on behalf of all of them." Only Novy acknowledges both gender and race, recognizing that "Performed in an often self-consciously multicultural Canada and United States, MacDonald's and Vogel's plays remain in the tradition of pre-Gordimer women's rewritings of *Othello* mostly concerned with women's gender issues—deliberately decentering the play to de-emphasize Othello himself—but racial issues emerge in both" (78). Her discussion of these racial issues is nevertheless limited. She goes on to note that Vogel's Desdemona explicitly remarks on Othello's Blackness, while race in MacDonald's play depends on casting that might "flirt with racism in its contemporary plot," but she demurs that "a white spectator, at least, is likely to find flirtation with racism dissolved in the kaleidoscope reshuffling of many different kinds of stereotypes of race, gender, and sexuality, which alludes to and goes beyond the ambiguous eroticism of Shakespeare's cross-dressing plays" (78, 79). Novy is likely right. White spectators may very easily sideline considering the racial issues in these plays. But these issues nevertheless remain and deserve much more attention than given to them thus far. For ignoring race in both Desdemona plays not only ignores whiteness as raced, but it also overlooks the ways that both dramas reify negative ideologies associated with Black masculinity.

MacDonald's *Goodnight Desdemona* makes the surprising choice to return to a by now almost antiquated performance tradition: having a white actor play Othello. The official text of the play includes a cast page which indicates that Derek Boyes performed the role in both the first production at Toronto's Annex Theatre and again during the 1990 Canadian national tour. Unlike historical performances of *Othello* featuring white actors, Boyes did not perform in blackface.[12] Instead, in this version of *Othello*, Othello is transformed into a white man, not just on stage, but also in the text. After intervening in Iago's scheming, Constance converses with both him and Othello, observing in an aside, "He's [Othello] not a Moor." (27). This observation accounts for the whitewashing of the character. Not much more is made of Othello's whiteness in the play; it is mentioned and then dismissed. Gone, then, are discussions of exoticism, marginalization, and racialization raised by Othello's Blackness and Desdemona's attraction to him. And MacDonald includes no academic musings on Constance's part over the significance of Othello's newfound whiteness in their place. Indeed, it is the white Constance who gets blackened by her ghostwriting work for Professor Claude Night, Othello's double, for Desdemona describes her as "an inky slave in paper chains" (36). I will address the implications of casting Night further below, but here it is enough to observe that if a white actor plays Night, then MacDonald uses racialized language not to explore Othello's plight but rather the struggles of white womanhood within academia. If Night is performed by a Black actor, then this language suggests that associating with the Black Night in turn blackens Constance too, just as Desdemona is understood as blackened by her association with Othello in Shakespeare's play. This original performance decision thus suggests that there is only enough space to discuss one marginalized societal figure—women—and one social issue, constructions of femininity. But it also demonstrates what happens when dramatists do not center race as a consideration from the outset: ethical racial representation likely becomes unrecoverable.

Admittedly, as I have gestured to, just because MacDonald made the performance choice to cast Night with a white actor does not mean that the role cannot be played by a Black actor. The published

---

[12] For a discussion of blackface's history, continued presence across cultures, and significance, see Thompson's *Blackface* (Bloomsbury, 2021).

edition of the play would suggest as much, for the main text is prefaced by a section of "Production Notes," which lists optional cuts that include Constance's line about Othello's whiteness and Iago's response to it. This excision would open up the possibility for any actor to play Othello. Yet a Black actor cannot step unproblematically into the role. MacDonald's Othello is not charismatic but rather the butt of jokes, untrustworthy about his reputation, and never depicted as the martial hero of Shakespeare's Venice. For instance, when meeting Constance, Othello declares:

> In Egypt, kicked I sand into the eyes
> of infidels who thought I made a truce.
> When I did give to them a pyramid
> On wheels they pulled into the garrison.
> But I had packed it full with Christian men,
> who slit the savage throat of every Turk. (26)

Constance is the first to cast doubt upon this assertion, responding, "That sounds like Troy." Iago follows in an aside, "Not Troy, but false." While one should be cautious about Iago's characterizations, Constance's qualified reaction to Othello, coupled with qualms about Othello's character created by the doubling, suggests that Iago may in fact be right in calling Othello's claim a falsehood. This characterization of Othello is not fully developed, however, for once Desdemona appears, he receives little attention. Yet by creating even this modicum of doubt, MacDonald positions Othello as a more pleasant but still potentially dishonest male figure. As such, a Black actor playing this role would need to embody an Othello stripped of all honor and nobility, reducing the status of this already psychically harmful role that, as Ayanna Thompson notes, often results in "the actor of color . . . who's been trained his whole life to strive for this role . . . having . . . [a] mental breakdown" ("All that Glisters"). Granted, this Othello does not murder Desdemona, thereby avoiding the stereotype of the Black brute. Nevertheless, MacDonald's depiction of Othello does nothing to elevate the often one-dimensional depiction of Black masculinity, making this just one more of a number of reanimated Othellos, like the one in *Kill Shakespeare* (Chapter 1), who remain on the margins as other, often white characters, move toward a more fully developed subjectivity.

The play's use of doubling only further complicates a Black actor taking on the role, for any actor playing Othello must also play Professor Night. The latter role causes different, even more vexed representational problems regarding race. Just as Constance finds versions of herself in Desdemona and Juliet, so too do the people in Constance's "reality" have proxies in the Shakespearean universe Constance visits, including her caddish love interest. Night embodies the worst stereotypes of academia, patronizing Constance ("relax, my little titmouse" (15); "Oh Connie. You have such an interesting little mind" (17)), building his reputation by critiquing others' arguments rather than his own ("I hope I've destroyed Professor Hollowfern's book to your satisfaction" (18)), wooing and proposing to an undergraduate (Ramona), and thoughtlessly building his career at the expense of others ("I've decided to take that lecturing post at Oxford myself. Even if it does fall somewhat short of a challenge" (19)). It is no wonder that Harrington claims, "If there is a villain in this piece, it is not Iago or Tybalt, but Claude Night, a symbol not only of sexual and academic inequality, but also of colonial repression" (127) given his position of power afforded him due to his gender, his elevated status in academia, his class, and his "English nationality" (128). By doubling the part, MacDonald stresses that Othello is the Jungian, Shakespearean counterpart to Night, in some ways, reinscribing Othello's Blackness discursively and metaphorically in a move that Porter calls "symbolically appropriate" (369). To have a Black actor take on Professor Night moves from the symbolic to the politics of embodiment, however. The implication would be that a Black professor would only reach a position of academic stature through deceit and, if Constance's role remained performed by a white woman as it has long been, at the expense of a white female academic. Such a depiction would not align with a reality in which data released in 2019 shows that, in 2017, only 6 percent of faculty in US postsecondary education were Black (Davis and Fry), a bump of only 1 percent since 1997. A study undertaken by the *Hispanic Journal of Law and Policy* collected data from 2013–17 and revealed that if only looking at tenured faculty, the number of Black faculty is only 4 percent (Hazelrigg). While the numbers do not speak for the play's original Canadian context, they nonetheless point to just how false it would be to suggest that a Black male professor would somehow be undeserving of his status when Black professors are already so underrepresented. Thus, rather than serving as a critique of the worst parts of academia, the part of Professor Night would instead reinforce doubts about a Black man's ability to achieve meaningful intellectual and professional success. MacDonald thereby creates a representational conundrum, for, conversely, if Othello remains whitewashed, the ability to interrogate the way white supremacy delimits Black identity present in Shakespeare's *Othello*—as demonstrated, for example, in *American Moor* (see Chapter 4)—recedes to make room for her feminist reconsideration of Desdemona. MacDonald's play thus exemplifies white feminism's tendency to sideline race in order to center questions of gender, a perspective that ignores intersectional approaches that more powerfully combat how white supremacist, capitalist, patriarchal societies depend on the strategy of setting various identity categories in contention with each other in a competition for hegemonic power.

Vogel's *Desdemona* likewise erases Othello by excising his role in the story altogether. In other words, the women discuss him, but there is no Othello present in this play. Yet even though he only appears discursively, this Othello too becomes whitewashed. Careful attention to Desdemona's language reveals that she imagines Othello as both white *and* Black, crafting his identity in such a way that he moves between a figure representing the stereotype of the ineffectual, almost barbaric Black man and the traditional, white, patriarchal Venetian. In scene 13, Emilia gestures toward Othello as jealous and violent, warning Desdemona that "your sin's goin' to catch m'lord's whiffin' about, and he's as jealous as he's black. If m'lord Othello had a mind to it, he could have that little lollin' tongue of yours cut clean out of your head, with none of the citizens of Cyprus to say him nay" (25). Though Emilia does not posit Blackness as a cause of jealousy, her comment crafts an inextricable link between the two, for the degree of Othello's jealousy matches the degree of his darkness. He is very Black, her comment indicates, just as he is very jealous. Her admonition thereby establishes two defining characteristics of Othello's identity, and by linking the two, blackness takes on negative connotations in a way that mirrors the racialized moral associations with blackness found in the Renaissance. At the same time, Emilia's comment taps into more than Shakespeare's Othello's military prowess. Notably, in transforming Cinthio's tale, Shakespeare omitted the graphic violence executed upon Desdemona's body in favor of the more intimate method of strangling. Emilia's Ovidian imagery of Othello cutting out Desdemona's tongue seems to echo the former story rather than the latter adaptation, or if it does invoke Shakespeare's text, it evokes *Titus Andronicus* mixed with Othello's worst imaginings of tearing Desdemona "all to pieces" (III, iii, 147). Thus, though he remains unseen, the play's discourse imagines Othello as a Black, jealous brute (see Chapters 1 and 4), thereby marginalizing him from the outset and positioning him as the embodiment of white racist fantasies regarding Black masculinity and white femininity.

Indeed, all the women in the play participate in this discursive ostracism, thereby entrenching this racist view of Othello's identity. In the following scene, for example, Desdemona further undercuts Othello's identity by calling into question the "services which I have done the seigniory" (I, ii, 18) when she asserts that "Othello's out in the night somewhere playing Roman Orator to his troops" (27). Her use of "playing" points to the performative rather than inherent nature of Othello's speech while invoking not the brave, active Othello whose assistance the Venetian state so desires but rather Iago's description of Cassio, "mere prattle without practice,/Is all his soldiership" (I, i, 17, 18). In Scene 15, she characterizes Othello as "stingy" (28), and by Scene 16 she taps into stereotypes about Black male sexuality, noting, "My husband refuses to buy new linen for his drawers, so Emilia must constantly mend the old. (*Confidentially.*) He's constantly tearing his crotch-hole somehow" (29). When Bianca asks amusedly, "And how does that happen?", Desdemona demurely responds, "I have no idea." Clearly, this interchange suggests that Othello's torn pants result from the erection of his stereotypically large penis. In addition to objectifying Othello, the moment heightens the significance of the women's previous maligning of him. Desdemona's sly response implies that she is the reason Othello needs new linens due to his sexual desire for her. Desdemona's depiction—the very facet so central to Vogel's feminist reinterpretation of her—would suggest that succumbing to one's erotic drive is not considered negatively in this play. But the underlying insinuation of this comment about Othello's sexuality must be understood in light of the fact that the women have articulated Othello's identity only in negative terms up to this point. Rather than celebrating sexual appetite, it seems more likely that Desdemona is giving a nod to the racist stereotypical sexual rapacity associated with Black masculinity.

When coupled with concerns about Othello's uncontrollable jealousy, this characterization leads to one of the most foreboding, racist images in Vogel's play. After explaining to Desdemona that she has seen Othello watching her in the garden and outside of her room while she is "unawares" and "asleep," Emilia shares that she also saw him "in your chamber room—and he gathered up the sheets from your bed, like a body, and . . . and he held it to his face, like, like a bouquet, all breathin' it in—" (Scene 27, 45). This moment prefigures Desdemona's death upon her wedding sheets, for Othello treats the sheets like a body, holding them as he will soon hold her own form in his murderous clasp. The overall effect is of an almost animal-like Othello who treats Desdemona as prey, hunting and stalking her until he finds an opportune moment. Emilia's previous linkage of jealousy with Othello's Blackness therefore opens up the possibility for the audience to likewise connect this jealousy to his race rather than his masculinity. This is not just a jealous man, but a jealous *Black* man who then destroys white femininity in a way that embodies the white supremacist nightmares of Black/white interracial unions.[13] As such, Vogel heightens the long-standing racialized depiction of Othello's nature as "barbaric" in order to recuperate her potentially alienating Desdemona. In other words, even as Vogel highlights the price women pay in a patriarchal culture for their sexual expression, she does so in a way that reinscribes the stereotypes about Black masculinity so long used to justify Black men's subjugation by white supremacy. This stereotyping of Othello becomes particularly notable in distinction with the way Vogel eschews stereotyping the women in her play. As Friedman argues, "Vogel produces multiple and shifting identities as she dramatizes a whoring Desdemona, a spiritually monogamous Bianca devoted to Cassio, and a sassy Emilia who does not understand or always support the lady she serves. The subtext of this subversion of stereotype and depiction of difference is that women do not constitute a monolithic body or a unified stance" (121). Unfortunately, the multifaceted nature of these women comes through to the audience even as they, and the play itself, caricature Black masculinity. Through this stereotyping, Desdemona not only becomes more sympathetic, but if audiences interpolate Shakespeare's ending onto the conclusion of Vogel's play as they likely do, then by the logic of the racist caricatures upon which Vogel depends, they may believe that the murderous, jealous, Black Othello gets what he deserves.

These characterizations of Othello that stress his Blackness contradict Vogel's Desdemona, however, for in a revelatory moment, she also positions Othello as a man who is indeed "far more fair than black" (I, iii, 292). Even so, her characterization only further portrays Othello as a failure on all accounts. This crucial representation occurs in a moment discussed above, when she describes meeting and falling for Othello. She recalls, "I remember the first time I saw my husband and I caught a glimpse of his skin, and oh,

---

[13] Werner Sollors traces how interracial marriage, particularly bans against it, have long been "important building blocks in the construction of 'race'" (4). For racial purity to be upheld, interracial marriage must be prohibited not only legally, but also ideologically, which is why Werner characterizes *Othello* as a "permanent provocation" (6).

how I thrilled. I thought—aha—a man of a different color. From another world and planet. I thought—if I marry this strange dark man, I can leave this narrow little Venice with its whispering piazzas behind—I can escape and see other worlds. (*Pause.*) But under that exotic façade was a porcelain white Venetian" (Scene 11, 20). By focusing on "skin" and "color" as well as the travel that Othello may provide, Desdemona objectifies Othello by ignoring his subjectivity and fetishizing his Blackness, for it is his skin, not Othello as a person, that entices her. In a significant change from Shakespeare's play, his stories of travel play no role. Thus, the weight of Desdemona's attraction resides entirely upon his skin color, which works as the "spice, seasoning that can liven up the dull dish that is mainstream white culture" (hooks, *Black Looks* 21). Read through bell hooks's conceptualization of consuming the Other, Desdemona consumes Othello, seeking a sexual experience that supposedly offers "the seductive promise . . . that it will counter the terrorizing force of the status quo that makes identity fixed, static, a condition of containment and death" (22). This stress upon Othello's Blackness sets up Desdemona's deflated desire, for her language makes clear that Othello is not what he seems. Discursively whitewashing him, she characterizes him as "a porcelain white Venetian." Furthermore, her reference to Othello's "exotic façade" suggests duplicity on Othello's part concerning his true selfhood. Instead of being exotic, he has instead achieved his "one destiny" as Frantz Fanon articulates it: being white (xii, xiv). Yet Desdemona does not make it clear precisely *why* Othello should be considered a white Venetian. While he may not have provided Desdemona with travel across the world, they are in fact in Cyprus, thereby suggesting that she has escaped Venice, if only modestly. What, then, is the issue? His jealousy? His patriarchal tendencies? Neither Desdemona nor the play provide answers. Moreover, as discussed above, she goes on to claim that the semen of the men with whom she sleeps affords her the escape she so desires. Why does sex with Othello not offer her the same release? The matter remains unresolved. What the audience is left with, then, is an Othello both barbaric and not exotic enough, a sexually rapacious yet stingy husband, a decidedly uncomplex character whose subjectivity is erased not just by his lack of presence but also by the discourses used to describe him. In both Desdemona plays, then, one finds that feminist reinterpretations of Desdemona are understood as necessitating a marginalization of Othello, a dynamic which enacts the intersectional blinders often attributed to predominantly white feminist perspectives.

Desdemona's Imperfection: Confronting Class and White Privilege

In many ways, Morrison's *Desdemona* seems to follow in the footsteps of previous Desdemona plays. It too centers Desdemona, focusing on her perspective. It too emphasizes women and community through Desdemona's interactions with Emilia and Sa'ran, as well as through both the collaboration between Traoré and Morrison and Traoré performing her music on stage surrounded by female Malian backing singers. And it too minimizes Othello's presence, for in *Desdemona*, the white actress performing the titular role (Tina Benko) also performs Othello's lines. The fundamental difference, however, is the way that Morrison takes an intersectional approach, committing to interrogating racial subjugation alongside gendered oppression not as an afterthought but rather as a fundamental aspect of the performance. Thus, even as Desdemona powerfully fills in the history of patriarchal control that Okri can only assume and therefore hint at, she must also come to terms with her complicity in asserting supremacy over the already marginalized people within her sphere. Desdemona's poignant journey leads scholars such as Peter Erickson and Jo Eldridge Carney to emphasize that a significant shift between Shakespeare's tragedy and the operetta is Desdemona's increased self-awareness, which develops from the epistemological nuance she gains during the uneasy posthumous encounters she undertakes with Emilia, Sa'ran, and Othello. To press this assertion even further, I suggest that Desdemona must confront, though she may not fully address, the social privileges that sit alongside her constrained femininity—specifically, the privileges afforded her by her class and whiteness—as dual forces shaping her subjectivity. Though *Desdemona* concludes only with the possibility of reconciliation rather than its realization, the operetta nevertheless makes clear the necessary steps on the journey toward understanding. It rejects the one-topic approach taken by both MacDonald and Vogel, instead stressing the importance of honest self-reflection paired with authentic interpersonal dialogues. In turn, this pairing speaks to the multifaceted oppressive forces alienating individuals from one another.

By taking this intersectional approach, however, Morrison in no way mutes an interrogation and critique of patriarchal domination. Desdemona's first words quickly direct the audience's attention to the patriarchal circumscription that has plagued her since birth. It may be appropriate that her name means "misery ... ill fated ... doomed ...," she meditates, for "Perhaps my parents believed or imagined or knew my fortune at the moment of my birth. Perhaps being born a girl gave them all they needed to know of what my life would be like. That it would be subject to the whims of my elders and the control of men" (13). In a swift eight lines, Morrison makes the prevailing structures stifling Desdemona evident, as well as their cost. The audience knows that she will indeed end in misery and doom, and Morrison exposes how patriarchal authority, the "whims of my elders and the control of men," cannot be divorced from this fated end. It is, in fact, the very power that fates it. But Desdemona resists the passivity that becomes her hallmark in the second half of Shakespeare's play. She insists not only that "they [her parents] did not know me," but also affirms a status other than victim when she declares, "I am not the meaning of a name I did not choose." As such, from the outset, Desdemona articulates her resistance to Venice's patriarchal expectations while at the same time underscoring the importance of her agency.

Significantly, Morrison enhances her feminist representation of Desdemona by attending to a dynamic that MacDonald and Vogel do not: the personal and emotional cost of resisting patriarchal norms from her childhood onward. *Desdemona* conveys this facet of the protagonist's experience by exploring precisely who and what Desdemona must defy, the pressures that perhaps make her speech to the senators radical. Namely, from her youth, both of Desdemona's parents encourage her to acquiesce to Venetian expectations. They are "keenly aware and approving of the system" (14), and to emphasize the point, Desdemona reflects on one instance in which each of her parents made their attitudes toward her prescribed agency and future explicit. For her mother, only ever given the name M. Brabantio, it is when Desdemona splashed in a puddle, getting her slippers and dress wet, playing with "unleashed laughter [that] was long and loud" (17). "Unleashed" signals precisely the problem. Desdemona is not abiding by the rules her mother establishes for her, ones in which "Constraint was the theme of behavior. Duty was its plot." Because of this "unseemliness," M. Brabantio takes away Desdemona's slippers, leaving her barefoot for ten days. Desdemona divulges to the audience the lesson she learns here: "It meant my desires, my imagination must remain hidden." For Brabantio, Desdemona reflects on a moment after her mother's death as suitors visit her. She recalls, "They came into my father's house with empty ornate boxes designed to hold coins of dowry gold, or deeds of property" (21). Her entire contemplation in fact stresses this emphasis on material wealth, for "Each one, whether a stuttering boy or an aged widower, was eager for a chatelaine weighted with riches ... Those already wealthy ranked me with other virgins on their menu. Those in desperate straits needed no evaluation" (21). Desdemona's language lays bare the reality of the marriage market, exemplifying what Gayle Rubin has famously noted as the exchange of women between men. Indeed, Morrison's language reveals how, to the suitors, Desdemona is a usable good, the coins or deeds of property a metonym for her being, and her body a consumable on their "menu."

Morrison's attention to Desdemona's childhood and youth not only fills in gaps, it also provides two important correctives for the audience. First, it dismantles any romanticized notions they may bring to bear on the production regarding the way patriarchal marital circumscriptions function. Perhaps they might make connections to the other Shakespearean play that the suitors' "ornate boxes" bring to mind—Portia and the casket test. Like Desdemona, Portia too must contend with unwanted suitors, but in that case, the casket test allows her to wed a man of her choosing—in many interpretations, with help from Portia herself—however problematic Bassanio might be. For Desdemona, no potential love awaits. Or perhaps even more cynically, the language makes clear she can see through the Bassanios in her midst, men seeking her fortune rather than her person. And unlike other heroines of literature who have at least one parent advocating for them, such as Jane Austen's spunky Elizabeth Bennet, aided by her father, Desdemona stands alone knowing that even if her mother had lived, she would have offered no help. My point is that audiences understand the tropes of female restriction confronted in *Desdemona* but typically as presented in ways where "everything works out all right in the end." In fact, an audience particularly unsympathetic toward Othello might wish Desdemona had married one of these suitors instead. But Desdemona's recollection of the suitors' calls upon her home indicates that she would have suffered marrying them as well. That is not to say that *Desdemona* is entirely radical in its depiction of Desdemona's travails. But by providing the audience with a young woman not sheltered by the affections of a loving parent but rather cared for only by a father whose "sole interest in me as I grew into womanhood was making certain I was transferred, profitably and securely, into the hands of another man" (20), Morrison challenges a romanticized view of feminine resistance in which women only exert agency in covert ways that do not disrupt patriarchal power structures.

Second, the language in Desdemona's scene with her mother provides a reason for Desdemona's subservience and silence in

Shakespeare's play. Often, her move from a woman bold enough to speak out in the Senate to meek wife who falsely takes blame for her murder troubles theatre practitioners, scholars, and audiences alike. Morrison indicates, however, that this is her learned behavior, inculcated in her for decades. In Morrison's interpretation of Desdemona, what audiences see in Shakespeare is her character "unleashed" at the play's start. The version of Desdemona who jumps into puddles is the same woman who marries Venice's famous general. But just as she does with her mother, once Othello likewise insists on Desdemona making herself smaller, more obsequious for his sake, she once again hides. In other words, whereas some performances explain Emilia's silence in the first half of the play by depicting her as an abused woman, Morrison offers up the same explanation for Desdemona, a woman first abused not by her husband, but by her family even before she turns 10, barefoot for a week, all in the service of patriarchal ideals. Thus, just as she does for Othello (a point to which I will return below), Morrison makes the inexplicable in Shakespeare's text understandable. For Desdemona, it entails critiquing patriarchal control, not only by exposing its central role in Desdemona's life, but also by expressly and poignantly communicating its personal and interpersonal cost for her subjectivity.

Yet even as Morrison recuperates Desdemona from Shakespeare's limited vision of "divine perfection" (Sellars 9), she does not do so in an idealized way, for she critiques Desdemona's assumption that agency can only be expressed in masculinist ways. As Desdemona articulates her embracement of female authority, Traoré's first interweaved song, titled "Desdemona," complicates the titular character by critiquing her limited and incorrect perspective.[14] The lyrics reproach her for being "envious of manhood," then declare, "You are unworthy of the femininity/that you haven't recognized in yourself" (Morrison 14). Traoré's song thereby indicates that the most valorized form of feminist expression need not be one that rejects the feminine so as to subscribe to patriarchy's values, if not its mandates. Thus, when juxtaposed with Desdemona's subsequent lines that she can now "speak, at last, words that in earth life were sealed or twisted into the language of obedience," one must question whether this speaking is sufficient given her still limited point of view (14).

---

[14] While in the published version of the play the lyrics appear in English, in performance, as Thompson explains, Traoré sings the words in Bambara, and the words are projected on screen in the predominant language of the performance's current location (i.e. French in France) ("*Desdemona*" 499).

The song returns after this speech, correcting her by asserting that "Manhood in itself is not a plus" (15). It closes with the admonition:

> How can you confuse
> finesse with obedience,
> discretion with ignorance,
> tenderness with submission,
> seductiveness with prostitution,
> woman with weakness? (16)

Even as Desdemona has made clear her desire for self-assertion and personal freedom, this opening song implicates her in the acceptance of the very patriarchal values she attempts to challenge. She may have a strong sense of herself, as indicated by her riposte to the audience that disabuses those who might interpret her as passive—"Is it your final summation of me that I was a foolish naïf who surrendered to her husband's brutality because she had no choice? Nothing could be more false . . . my life was shaped by my own choices and it was mine" (16). However, Traoré's song suggests that Desdemona still lacks a full understanding of her complicity in systems of oppression.

This facet of Desdemona—her need for personal and ideological growth—is in fact one of the most significant features of her depiction in the operetta. In their readings of the play, both Carney and Erickson argue that a key feature of Desdemona's reimagining is her newly gained knowledge. Carney, for example, notes that by encountering other characters and hearing their voices, "Desdemona fully internalizes their experiences, signifying her developing empathy and understanding," and regarding Othello, their discussions are "marked by a tentative progression towards revelation and acceptance." Erickson makes similar claims, observing that in this timeless afterlife, Desdemona "can not only resume speaking but also begin rethinking" ("'Late'"). I build upon Carney's and Erickson's analyses by adding specificity to their more general assertions about Desdemona's trajectory. Indeed, her confrontations with Emilia, Sa'ran, and Othello indicate that part of Desdemona's personal growth entails that she acknowledge her various social privileges and the harm they allow her to enact on others. Specifically, her dialogue with Emilia reveals Desdemona's need to confront privileges afforded to her by her class, while her respective conversations with Sa'ran and Othello expose Desdemona's white privilege.

There are numerous forms of social privilege, for as Allan Johnson explains, privilege "exists when one group has something of value that is denied to others simply because of the groups they belong to, rather than because of anything they've done or failed to do" (21). He adds that privilege is not just about advantage but also about "the lopsided distribution of power" that maintains privilege (Johnson 12). As such, "privilege simply *confers dominance*" as a result of various factors associated with one's identity (McIntosh 2). Significantly, a key feature of all forms of privilege is the way maintaining it depends on denial, for as Peggy McIntosh famously observes, privileges are "an invisible package of unearned assets that I can count on cashing in each day, but about which I was 'meant' to remain oblivious" (1). Part of the reason for privilege's invisibility is a desire to ignore its darker side. Johnson contends, "For every social category that is privileged, one or more others are oppressed in relation to it" (32). This oppression is decidedly not the "negative side effects of privilege," no matter how guilty one may feel, for any costs "are far outweighed by the benefits" (33). Rather, oppression results from being placed in a social category over which another has the power to oppress (33). As Johnson notes, if privilege opens doors, then "oppression tends to hold them shut" (32). It is no wonder, then, that in a supposedly post-racial society, privileges, especially race-based ones, are effaced by pathologizing the racialized Others facing oppression (see Introduction). If oppression is *their* fault due to bad choices, poor work ethic, or problematic cultural values, privilege thereby does not need to be confronted.

Regarding the specific privileges Desdemona holds, it is very difficult to disentangle the interrelatedness of class and white privilege, for the effects of oppression based on the power derived from these respective categories often overlap. The reasons undergirding that oppression differ, however. In regard to social class, a general attitude of classism or denigration of those positioned below a culture's equivalent of "middle-class" means that those with class privilege enjoy the privileges of "housing and neighborhood," "economic liberty," "sociostructural support," "power," "familiarity with middle-class behavioral norms," "self-satisfaction," "leaving a heritage," and "leisure" (Liu, Pickett Jr., and Ivey 199). White privilege, or what Paula S. Rothenberg describes in her book's subtitle as "the other side of racism," is "the systemic advantages of being White" (Tatum 88). In many ways, it can be difficult to pin down because it is so all-encompassing. White privilege means being established as the racial norm, against which every other race is measured and categorized. This entails wide-ranging power across spectrums, from access to economic success to elevated workplace status to educational admittance to enacting social authority to establishing behavioral standards and more (McIntosh 2–3). Understood through the lens of privilege, then, Desdemona's newfound knowledge involves recognizing her imbrication in a system of classed and racialized dominance that encourages a steadfast ignorance to this very domination. Thus, in many ways, Desdemona's attitude overlaps with the dynamics of the colorblind. She does not need to see her race, nor others'. And alongside that refusal, she does not see a need to recognize the social benefits afforded to her by her class either. Morrison's intersectional approach therefore comes into view here, for Desdemona's trajectory means changing her limited perspective so that she can recognize not just her subjugation, but also the ways in which she subjugates others.

Just as Vogel uses distinct class differences to contextualize the relationship between Desdemona and Emilia, so too does Morrison turn to class in order to explore the conflict between these women, and throughout their exchange, both Desdemona's class privilege and Emilia's classed (and gendered) oppression come to the fore. The interchange between Emilia and Desdemona is full of friction, antagonistic from the outset as Emilia greets Desdemona with a sarcastic, "Well, well. If it isn't the martyr of Venice" (42). Any comradery existing between the two women in Shakespeare's play remains absent here, for Emilia even asks, "Remember me?" That Desdemona's privilege as a high-status woman of Venice causes the division between the women crystallizes when their conversation exposes the different levels of agency each woman can attempt. Emilia bluntly asserts that "we failed," a claim Desdemona roundly rejects when she questions, "Failed? As women?" What becomes evident is that the women define success and failure very differently due to their distinct social positions. For Emilia, "Women try to survive, since we cannot flourish." As an orphan who married out of lust but ended up with "no progeny; no future," survival is all, her death thereby indicating failure. The language of survival suggests that no support exists for Emilia, and, as a childless orphan, neither can she cling to heredity nor progeny as markers of identity. Desdemona, on the other hand, never articulates a specific vision about what success as women could mean. As previously addressed, she may not have had sufficient parental support, but she can imagine more than simply surviving. In other words, Desdemona has the ability to elope for love when other women, like Emilia, simply seek to endure. She also understands herself as having the capacity to grasp and uphold moral norms, for her defense depends on recriminating Emilia. As soon as their conflict arises, she blames Emilia for desiring to "acquiesce to all of Iago's demands," thereby being willing to betray her mistress, and she subsequently resists Emilia's articulation of failure by declaring, "I wonder if collapse of virtue is not survival at all but cowardice" (42). Though the language of class here is not stark, it resides in the final accusation Desdemona launches at Emilia: "I relied on your help and mistook it for benevolence. I was deceived" (43). On the one hand, Desdemona strips the language of service from her allegation, rendering it "help" or assistance. On the other hand, she also rejects the language of friendship and human kindness by disavowing Emilia's "benevolence." Desdemona thereby makes it clear that she was "deceived" in thinking that they were equals, that she could receive "benevolence" from Emilia, but she does so in a way that never marks her own social superiority and therefore position of power. Desdemona's elevated status thus gives her the confidence to try and define the terms of the women's relationships as well as the behavioral standard that Emilia should meet to achieve a nebulous "success" as a woman.

The play does more than simply highlight privilege, however. It also exposes its effects, namely, the way privilege for a few results in the repression of those excluded. Moreover, *Desdemona* stresses how reconciliation depends upon confronting this dynamic. Emilia becomes the more compelling of the two women precisely because she stridently expresses how Desdemona's framing of their relationship has been based on ignorance of her suppression. She reminds Desdemona that Desdemona too "had no defense against lies or her husband's strangling fingers" (42) and confronts Desdemona's ignorance when she notes that all she ever performed for Desdemona was service at her request. "That is not how you treat a friend," she chides, "that's how you treat a servant. Someone beneath you, beneath your class which takes devotion for granted" (43). Emilia's words could not be starker. Desdemona mistakes necessary service for friendship because she is the one in a position of power, thereby preventing Emilia from pursuing the relational intimacy she so desires. However, Emilia does not allow her subjugated status to recede from either Desdemona's or the audience's view. Rather, she resists Desdemona's appeals to a shared experience when Desdemona says she wishes Emilia had told her about being an orphan for "You had no mother. I had no mother's love" (44). Emilia tersely responds, "It's not the same. An orphan knows how quickly love can be withdrawn; knows that complete safety is a child's hopeless dream." Once again, the discussion of class here is subtle, but Emilia clarifies how

Desdemona's lack of motherly love, an issue of quality of life, does not threaten her being to the same degree that Emilia's complete solitude and self-sufficiency or "safety" as an orphan does, for Emilia's threat is not one merely of quality, but rather of her very existence.

Through the discussion between Desdemona and Emilia, then, it becomes evident that understanding occurs by recognizing abuses of power. Emilia prompts this recognition by preventing Desdemona from imposing upon her established moral norms and by rejecting Desdemona's facile support. Rather, because she insists on their distinctive experiences and therefore stresses their divergent points of view, Emilia initiates change in Desdemona, who replies, "You are right to correct me. Instead of judging, I should have been understanding" (44).[15] This challenging exchange does not indicate that Emilia and Desdemona achieve a resolution. In fact, the scene's close leaves the audience in an uneasy space as Emilia recounts her life of "servility" in which she rushed "to hide from lascivious men—including your husband." As a result, she had to become like a lizard who transformed into new skin while always dragging her old skin with her as "camouflage [that] would still be needed to disguise her true dazzle." Desdemona and the audience alike must grapple with what this stunning yet disturbing closing image means. But the dialogue between the two women, particularly Desdemona's deferral to Emilia's perspective, indicates that Desdemona finds the space for contemplation—the possibility of inching toward an expanded point of view—by accepting that her privileged position as a high-status woman in Venice may create more difference between her and Emilia than shared femininity can afford them.

If Desdemona must confront her class privilege with Emilia, in the scene that follows, when she meets the woman she knew as Barbary, she must address the ways her whiteness likewise forecloses her recognition of the power differentials informing her relationships. The imbalance in power between Desdemona and Barbary is evident from the scene's first lines, when Desdemona opens with the command, "Barbary! Barbary. Come closer" (45). For Desdemona, this is a call of friendship, a reunion of women who "ate sweets," with Barbary saving "the honey for me eating none yourself. We shared so much." This recollection clarifies two dynamics of the relationship for the audience. First, Barbary

---

[15] Emilia's race is never specified in Morrison's playtext. One can presume her whiteness, however, for when Benko performs the roles of Black characters, such as Soun and Othello, she does so with an accent. Emilia is not given an accent.

provided the maternal affection Desdemona otherwise lacked. This is why she fixates on Barbary's generosity, her willingness to forgo pleasures for Desdemona's sake. But the second point challenges the first. Desdemona's language betrays her. Even as she asserts that they "shared so much," the example she retells in fact involves no sharing of any kind, for "Barbary *must* give to Desdemona, and thus it is true that nothing is shared" (Espinosa, *Shakespeare on the Shades* 25). Urvashi Chakravarty addresses how in early modernity, the relationship between "service family" and "blood family" blur in *Othello*, so that "Barbary evokes not only the 'wheeling stranger' at the heart of the play but also those 'strange' servants who were racially and legally distinct in English society yet quite literally members of 'English' families—both alien and intimate, strange and proximate, un-'kind' and alike" (26). In this moment, Desdemona's language tries to position Barbary similarly, at once evoking her blood family by characterizing Barbary as a surrogate mother but also distinctly as a member of her service family, a domestic servant expected to give without question. Thus, just as with Emilia (and in a mirroring of the self-focus undertaken by Sarah Koenig in *Serial*), Desdemona believes that her perspective alone defines the women's relationship, thereby centering herself and her subjectivity as the norm.

Yet just as before, the interchange between women exposes the fault lines in Desdemona's thinking and attitudes. Barbary denies Desdemona's overture with the matter-of-fact reply, "We shared nothing" (45). As Desdemona attempts to counter Barbary's rejection, the distinction between Desdemona as a noble white woman and Barbary as a Black African servant comes to the fore. Notably, after Desdemona asks, "What do you mean?", the line designations in the playtext change from Barbary to Sa'ran as she replies, "I mean you don't even know my name." Echoing the Desdemona imagined by Okri, Sa'ran addresses how Desdemona embodies a white-oriented perspective that erases her identity: "Barbary? Barbary is what you call Africa. Barbary is the geography of the foreigner, the savage ... Barbary is the name of those without whom you could neither live nor prosper." If Desdemona's memory of Sa'ran carries with it vestiges of the Mammy, the Black woman happy to care for her white ward even at her own expense, Sa'ran demolishes such a vision. Her riposte makes it clear that she served Desdemona, but not uncritically. She understands that Desdemona's need for life and prosperity depends on her erasure. But just as in her interaction with Emilia, Desdemona initially persists in her approach, responding, "Well, Sa'ran, whatever your name, you were my best friend," thereby diminishing Sa'ran by refusing to say her name in acknowledgment of her identity (45). What these competing views on the women's past reveal is precisely how much privilege Desdemona's whiteness affords her. She may reject the connotations of the name her parents gave her, yet she is able to embrace it and redefine it without others rejecting her as baldly as she does Sa'ran. She once again continues crafting the parameters of her relationship, insisting that her perspective is accurate despite evidence to the contrary. As much as Sa'ran attempts to resist, Desdemona persists in imposing her authority over Sa'ran, thereby both exposing and allowing her to flex her white privilege.

As with class privilege, this white privilege also brings with it forms of oppression, as Sa'ran uncovers. With the simple yet profound line, Sa'ran counters, "I was your slave" (45). If audiences have, until this point, been somehow unclear about where the play aligns its sympathies, the use of *slave* leaves no doubt. Even for a global audience, *slave* carries with it the history of colonial imperialism and domination. It is a powerful indictment of Desdemona, whose flippant reply—"What does that matter? I have known and loved you all my life"—only positions her in an even more unsympathetic light. Her whiteness allows such a callous, silencing response, one that has her mirror the silencing and constraining patriarchal dynamics against which she so chafed. Yet here, she thoughtlessly employs them in service of maintaining the romanticized view of a relationship with Sa'ran enabled by her whiteness. For Morrison makes clear that Desdemona's white privilege allows her not only to frame their relationship, but also to insist that her desire and understanding supersedes Sa'ran's. Sa'ran, however, makes this white privilege evident to Desdemona: "I am black-skinned. You are white-skinned" (46). For Sa'ran, that means that "you [Desdemona] don't know me. Have never known me." The oppression Sa'ran experiences, then, is of not being known—her history, her locale, the dynamics of her service, even her very name, all erased.

Though Emilia receives an acknowledgment from Desdemona, ultimately, Sa'ran gets none, only Desdemona's universalizing insistence that "We are women" (48). Morrison therefore suggests a lingering unease in this interchange, for "Mutual recognition of racism, its impact both on those who are dominated and those who dominate, is the only standpoint that makes possible an encounter between races that is not based on denial and fantasy," and such mutual recognition does not exist here (hooks, *Black Looks* 28). Heightening Desdemona's defensiveness, she even forces Sa'ran to answer the question, "Was I ever cruel to you? Ever?" (48). While Sa'ran admits, "No. You never hurt or abused me," that is cold comfort for a woman who, like Desdemona, in fact even more than Desdemona, had to "do what I am told" (48). Indeed, when Sa'ran notes that Desdemona never abused her, Desdemona replies with, "Who did?" Sa'ran remarks, "You know who did." Desdemona's refusal to fully recognize Sa'ran is therefore passed on to the audience, for as Joyce Green MacDonald asserts, "We in the audience can only guess. Was it Othello himself, who tells us that he and Iago were bound by the rapes and depredations they committed while soldiering together? Was it Signora Brabantio, whose 'maid' (IV, iii, 25) Othello tells us 'Barbary' was? Or was it Brabantio, who failed to control his daughter, but would have had much less trouble holding down a slave for his own pleasure? We cannot be sure" (*Shakespearean Adaptation* 5, 6). The scene ends with a new song by Sa'ran, which replaces the Willow Song, suggesting that somehow Sa'ran has found peace in the afterlife. But there is no resolution between the two women. Thus, even as Morrison captures the challenges of Desdemona's position as a white noblewoman, she also stresses its advantages. And she takes the point a step further by suggesting that only when Desdemona can likewise hold that duality in mind—to use theoretical language, when she can take an intersectional approach—is a move toward interpersonal rather than only individual healing possible.

Desdemona and Othello: Competing Forms of Oppression

Desdemona's interactions with both Emilia and Sa'ran expose the need for her to complicate her perspective by rejecting universalizing gestures toward shared womanhood in favor of considering the multiple and conflicting forms of oppression uniquely experienced by different women. Such a need may likely be easy for the audience to accept because Desdemona serves as an oppressor to both Emilia and Sa'ran, treating the former not as a friend but as a servant, and the latter not as a friend nor servant, but as a slave. Yet audience sympathy is much more difficult to negotiate when it comes to Desdemona's confrontations with Othello. Theirs is an especially challenging dynamic to navigate, for in their relationship, Desdemona is both oppressor and oppressed. And it is likely because of this very dichotomy that Morrison equally stresses the need for Desdemona to open her eyes to her complicity in Othello's marginalization as she does for Othello to grapple with his toxic masculinity. What these final dialogues therefore demonstrate is that an ethical feminist paradigm must reject an "either/or" approach in favor of the more challenging "both/and" intersectional perspective.

Unlike Desdemona's discussions with other characters, which are limited to one scene, her extensive interactions with Othello weave in and out of other dialogues. As such, audiences receive a broader, more detailed picture of the lovers, one that balances compassion for their respective plights with an exposure of their flaws. For instance, Morrison does not sidestep the Desdemona problem; rather, she tackles Desdemona's naiveté and exoticization of Othello head on. In a narrative change, Morrison has Desdemona fall in love with Othello when she is "Not yet recovered from Barbary's death" (23). Desdemona is thus grieving and vulnerable when she meets Othello. But this addition likewise suggests a projection onto Othello of Desdemona's love for Barbary. She sees in him not who he is, but rather the potential he represents. The conflation between Othello and Barbary sharpens when Desdemona shares, "I saw a glint of brass in his eyes identical to the light in Barbary's eyes" (23). Here, Blackness functions as a monolith for Desdemona, one identity easily collapsible with another. Furthermore, Desdemona's description of Othello reveals that even though she has previously criticized suitors for their materialistic romantic pursuits, she too objectifies Othello. She describes him as a "mass of a man . . . glittering in metal and red wool" (23). The language of the material—mass, glittering metal, red wool—stands out here, signaling that her desire for Othello is in many ways about what he can offer her, to a degree mirroring what she could offer the Venetian suitors. And part of what he can afford her is the exotic, as indicated by her observation that "In accented language his voice underscored the kiss." To return to Okri's observation, Desdemona's first encounter with Othello communicates how she does not really see him but rather the potential for affection, adventure, and difference that he can provide her.

At the same time, however, other moments offer a dialectic for this superficial exchange, signaling that Desdemona develops a deeper understanding of Othello's identity. She asks, "Who could have thought a military commander, trained to let blood, would be more, could be more, than a brutal arm educated solely to kill? I knew. How did I know? We sat on a stone bench under an arch. I remember the well of softness in his eyes" (30). In Morrison's version of their love story, Desdemona must no longer locate Othello's true self "in his mind" (I, iii, 254). She uncovers it through conversations with him instead. Indeed, Desdemona emphasizes to the audience that she understands Othello better than others as a result of their discussions and time spent together. Significantly, the play's text makes clear that their conversations were not idealized, for Othello eventually confesses a deep secret—his and Iago's rape of two elderly women during their military service, a point to which I will return. When Othello asks Desdemona's forgiveness, Desdemona demurs, saying she cannot forgive, "But I can love you and remain committed to you" (39). Love, she explains, is not about "choosing the ripe and discarding the rot." What we find, then, is that a feminist understanding of Desdemona does not inherently necessitate marginalization of Othello. Rather, by highlighting the intricacies driving Desdemona's relationship with Othello—both positive and those less so—the play adeptly undercuts the view of Desdemona as "naïf" without glossing over her imperfections, including the ones that ultimately harm Othello.

Similarly, *Desdemona* offers audiences a complex portrait of Othello. With the story in Morrison's hands, it becomes evident that this Othello's downfall is not gullibility, but rather a toxic tendency toward anger and violence inculcated through the very thing that has provided him with a sense of identity: his martial prowess. Before Othello ever speaks, Traoré's song, "Othello," warns him:

> Great Othello
> handsome Othello
> only your anger
> can make you lose
> yourself.
> Othello, a great man
> Does not give in to anger.
> Contain your rage. (24)

Traoré's lyrics carefully balance Othello's positive qualities—he is great and handsome—with a recognition of his volatility. "Othello" thus intervenes in the view of Othello audiences bring to the play, providing a corrective to a holistically negative, frequently antiblack conception of him by offering up a more balanced characterization. Also significant is the way that *Desdemona* rejects the post-racial and antiblack dynamic of placing blame for Othello's downfall on the personal by instead emphasizing the systemic. Put differently, the operetta stresses that culpability for Othello's rage falls not on his race, on some innate bestiality, but rather is instilled in him by his history as a warrior. Setting *Othello* in a contemporary militaristic context is now a familiar performance decision, as demonstrated by Nicholas Hytner's 2013 production for the National Theatre,

Iqbal Khan's 2018 *Othello* for the Royal Shakespeare Company, and countless other performances. What Morrison adds, however, is not a milieu or a vision of war's aftereffects, but instead a detailed explanation of the ways that Othello's history as a soldier poisons his relationship with Desdemona. In Scene 6, we learn that Othello, like Emilia, was an orphan, adopted by a "root woman" who cared for him until he was subsequently "captured by Syrians" (31). With nothing to eat or drink, he describes it as "a happy day for me to be sold into an army where food was regular and clothes respectable" (31). In detailing his past, the very one Okri notes audiences are typically missing, Othello forces both Desdemona and audiences to check their presuppositions. Yes, involuntary conscription is unethical, but for him, it provides vital sustenance. Yet it does more than that. He further explains that "Only as a soldier could I excel and turn the loneliness inside into exhilaration." Another lonely orphan, one always on the precipice of unsafety, Othello develops a sense of self from war, however problematic that might be. It provides companionship, even comradery. In a particularly evocative moment he recounts:

> Part, perhaps, most of the joy, the pleasure, of battle I took as a child soldier came from having comrades who were like me and who loved the fresh green leaves we were given to eat. Chewing them infused us with more than courage: we were potent and indifferent to blood, cries of pain, debasement—to life, even our own. Rape was perfunctory. Death our brother. It took capture, imprisonment for months to be rid of the craving for the leaves and to absorb what we had become. (36)

This scene's poignancy comes from the fact that this trauma is communal, experienced by "comrades" who according to Othello were "like me." The army has indeed quelled his loneliness by providing him with the company that his enslavement stripped from him. And all these boys suffer as they feed on the fruits or "leaves" of war, both the metaphorical and the drug-like "green leaves" they were fed. Importantly, Othello's recollection places responsibility on these leaves that debased the boys, transforming them into heartless, violent monsters. This emphasis makes it clear that Othello and his companions' violent behaviors derive not from their inherent natures but rather from a powerful substance that transforms them into men of war. In fact, "It took capture, imprisonment for months to be rid of the craving of the leaves and to absorb what we had become," he expounds (36). It is a literalization of toxic masculinity, imbued into the boys' blood but perhaps never really gone, for while the cravings leave, it is only through "the glint of honor and an honorable army provided" that Othello can be rid of "self loathing." Like the titular character, *Desdemona*'s Othello likewise comes across as multifaceted, traumatized, and regretful yet unwilling to let go of the very structures that harmed him.

The play's feminist perspective comes to the fore as Desdemona confronts the ramifications of Othello's history. So attentive to the effects of patriarchal domination in her life, Desdemona functions as the teacher who wisely interprets for the audience the toxicity of Othello's past, the way that toxicity lingered into his present during his marriage with her, and how that toxicity is intricately tied up in masculinity. This realization occurs when Othello exposes his most nefarious deed, what Desdemona recalls as his "last confession"— the rape of two women by him and Iago (37). He details not only how he and Iago "took turns slaking the thirst of our loins" as the women softly cried, but also how they "turned to see a child, a boy, staring wild-eyed at a scene that must have seemed to him a grotesque dream" (37, 38). Othello further admits that in addition to shame, he felt "mutual pleasure. Pleasure in the degradation we had caused; more pleasure in leaving a witness to it" (38). This revelation illuminates the actions the audience knows Othello will take by the end of Shakespeare's play, the ones that haunt Desdemona. It establishes a bond, however grotesque, between Othello and Iago that explains Othello's insistence on Iago's honesty. These men know each other's worst selves. The confession also provides the twisted logic for Desdemona's murder. Othello's martial context means that degradation brings pleasure, and that pleasure intensifies if there are witnesses. Thus, in strangling Desdemona, Othello reenacts his patterns of masculine domination, as well as his desire to expose that form of violent masculine control. Desdemona draws these connections for the audience, astutely articulating the poisonous potential not of the chewed leaves but of male homosocial bonding when she observes in response to the question of why Othello believed Iago when he "knew Iago was lying":

> Brotherhood. The quiet approval beamed from one male eye to another. Bright, tight, camaraderie. Like-mindedness born of the exchange of musk; the buck's regard of the doe; the mild contempt following her capture. The wide, wild celebrity men find with each other cannot compete with the narrow comfort of a wife. (37)

Desdemona's speech lays out plainly what scholars have identified as the struggle in the play between the marital and the martial. What Desdemona adds here is a more express articulation for the audience of the way that the martial, the hunt, maps onto a misogynistic view of women in romance. They are the doe, captured and devalued precisely because they have not been strong or capable enough to further resist. If, as Francis Bacon notably argues in "On Friendship," like draws to like, Desdemona's speech here reveals the way that the toxicity of masculine martial ideology only makes women even more inferior, so that the "narrow" circumscribed "comfort of a wife" can never dislodge the intoxicating brotherhood created by shared subordination of women. The patriarchal domination that Desdemona fled from thus reappears, and more intensely, demonstrating how pervasive and powerful it proves to be as it moves between mothers, fathers, brothers in war, and even beloved husbands.

Yet even as Desdemona stresses the plight of women, indicting Othello's participation in, indeed relishing of, toxic masculine culture, her own complicity in systems of oppression arises, namely, the ignorance of racial inequity afforded to her by her whiteness. For even though gendered expectations have driven Othello's toxic masculinity, so has racial marginalization. In their final discussion, Othello declares:

> It's clear now. You never loved me. You fancied the idea of me, the exotic foreigner who kills for the State, who will die for the State . . . How comforting it must have been—protected by a loyal black warrior . . . And you thought that was all there was to me—a useful myth, a fairy's tale cut to suit a princess' hunger for real life, not the dull existence of her home. (51)

In this moment, Othello articulates the most problematic aspects of Desdemona's desires, found in Shakespeare's text and amplified in reanimations like Vogel's. Rather than left as a disquieting facet of Desdemona, Othello directly conveys the way he believes race and military identity combined to incite Desdemona's love. Put differently, though he may be mistaken, Othello forces Desdemona to confront the potentially discomfiting racial motivations underlying her attraction to him. Thus, even as *Desdemona* lays bare the plight of women in a patriarchal culture, it refuses to turn away from the culpability of (white) women in enacting racial oppression. Rather, just as the operetta manifests Othello's shortcomings, it displays Desdemona's as well. In a response typifying white fragility, Desdemona rejects

Othello's assertions, immediately refuting, "You are wrong!" (51). Once again, as in her discussion with Emilia, her lack of specific logic or clear explanation diminishes her rebuttal. And just as she did with Emilia, she begins casting blame. In an Adam-and-Eve-like rejoinder, she reminds Othello that he believed a lie, thereby turning focus away from her potential misconceptions to his faults. Notably, however, Othello refuses capitulation to white women's tears. He once again presses the issue, making certain that Desdemona faces his identity as a Black man in ways she has previously not done. "More than infidelity," he explains, "my rage was toward your delusion. Your requirements for a bleached, ultra-civilized soul framed in blood, for court manners honed by violence." Othello's language here positions him as a subject acted upon, for he is bleached by others, placed in a position of accepted comportment no less stifling than what was expected of Desdemona, but perhaps less clear in its parameters given the necessary balancing act between noble gentleman and savage warrior. Othello thus indicates that Desdemona longs for a figure similar to what Vogel's Desdemona claims he is: white on the inside while Black on the outside. Yet in this case, this is not a pejorative claim against Othello's identity but rather a criticism against Desdemona's paradoxical construction of him.

Significantly, however, Othello does not frame his critique as simply an interpersonal one. Instead, he reveals how the issue extends beyond Desdemona, locating her within a systemic Venetian resistance to integrating him as a result of his racial difference. He notes, "Have you any idea what it took to get to the position I held? Who sabotaged me, delayed promotions, took credit for my victories . . . Even with the gore of their enemies, the smell of it, the drips of it on my sword, their contempt over-powered what should have been glistening gratitude" (51). While Othello previously asserted he found belonging as a soldier, his own façade begins to crack here. This cracking suggests that even as his turn to violence was a piece of maintaining his self-image, it was also part of performing above and beyond expectations—the infamous expectation of people of color, particularly Black people, that they work twice as hard for half as much—in order to establish himself among the Venetians. His tendency to rage and viciousness could not be subdued entirely, for even as Venetians demanded of him a Black man contained in their presence, they likewise desired a Black man unleashed in their service. Othello later elaborates, "Fidelity is a necessity in the military. Lives depend on it, but I could not. I was doubted and deceived at every turn. Why? Because I am African? Because I was sold into slavery?

Or because I was better than they? Whatever the reason, I had to prove myself over and over again" (53). Othello's comments reveal the enmeshed nature of identity—neither race nor status nor jealousy nor personal history can fully account for his alienation. All play a role, as does Desdemona, who like the other Venetians wanted the exotic soldier as well as the civilized Venetian all at once without recognizing the conflicting natures of these identities, nor the way Othello's race influenced his difficulties negotiating the clash. Desdemona refused to confront her white privilege with Sa'ran; she once again attempts to deny it here. But for the audience, Othello affectingly expresses the interleaved nature of his toxic masculinity with the oppression he faces as a result of his Blackness. No one can nor should deny his culpability in murdering his wife. Yet in expressly placing issues of race alongside issues of gender, *Desdemona* tackles the Desdemona problem by demonstrating Othello's alienation from his wife in part due to her inability to truly comprehend his identity as a Black man.

Initially, it appears as if Desdemona and Othello will experience the same pitfall present in MacDonald's and Vogel's plays: the inability to recognize that oppression of white femininity and Black masculinity exist alongside, and in this case constitute, one another. However, the white patriarchal voice represented by Cassio disrupts this ideological and emotional stalemate. Only ever a projected voice, Cassio interrupts Othello and Desdemona and exemplifies to the audience how the patriarchal voice seeks to control both women and other men, especially men of color who threaten the ascendancy of white mediocrity. Cassio decries Desdemona's pure reputation, declaring, "I have touched her and she neither screamed nor slapped my hands away" (52). The interrelated challenges to Cassio's white male identity posed by Desdemona's agency and Othello's excellence are made quickly apparent as he notes how Othello appeared, "swanning about above his station and way above his geography and his history. A dangerous, godless mix, unable to govern, to know with certainty what is best for the State" (52). The surface meaning of Cassio's remarks appears to be that the "godless mix" is Othello's overreaching "above his geography and his history." But his comment likewise suggests that the interracial love between Othello and Desdemona is also "godless," the very thing that challenges what "is best for the State," in that their romance threatens and therefore destabilizes Venice's racial purity. Yet Cassio reveals that the threat is also of a more personal nature. He admits that "Othello was competent, even intelligent. I understand he had vision," but he makes a case instead for his white male mediocrity by insisting, "Who needs vision to declare war and win it at all costs? The needs of the State are mundane, and therein safety lies" (52). In Cassio's white supremacist, patriarchal paradigm, there is no space for upstart women or ambitious Black men. There is only space for those like him. As he illuminates in language echoing ideals of manifest destiny, "Power is more than responsibility; it is destiny. Destiny few men are able to handle . . . Me alone. I am its servant and it is mine" (53). Thus, even as Othello and Desdemona blame each other, doing more than asking for accountability on the other's part, perhaps even desiring abjection from each other, a voice representing all that has oppressed them both intrudes, reminding them and the audience of the true enemy.

This is not to say that somehow Othello and Desdemona achieve the mutual understanding hooks stresses as so important to racial reconciliation. Compounding and competing forms of oppression are neither easily confronted nor rectified. But *Desdemona* holds out the possibility of moving forward through honest dialogue, as slippery as such encounters may be. After Cassio disturbs their conversation, Desdemona finally admits some culpability, which notably, she could not with Sa'ran, when she asserts, "To think I tried to save him. I was wrong, so wrong" (53). It is here where Othello recounts the lack of fidelity experienced from Venice as a whole, discussed above, to which Desdemona replies, "I apologize for a profound error in judgement" (54). This admission seems to respond directly to Othello's perception of Desdemona as misunderstanding him and shaping him inaccurately in her mind. As such, it can be read as her acknowledging her white privilege, admitting that she glossed over the implications of his racial status in a way he could not afford to do. Yet the scene is complex in that it is not clear precisely what her error in judgment has been. For perhaps the error in judgment is only what she has already conceded, her defense of Cassio. Morrison's text thus provides no easy answer.

Othello's reply to Desdemona suggests a move toward reconciliation, however. He poignantly admits, "Apology is a pale word for what I am called upon to recognize. I am beyond sorry; it is shame that strafes me" (54). Key here is Othello's use of "recognize." He sees that he must change his perspective, a transformation which may in fact be unfolding in the moment as the shame he articulates here appears to be without the pleasure his previous shame carried, for this shame "strafes," the language and pain of military endeavors turned against himself instead of others. Mutual blame abounds as Desdemona responds, "Your doubt and my righteousness mangled our love," and further comments, "My mistake was believing that you hated war as much as I did. You believed I loved Othello the warrior. I did not" (54). While Desdemona never directly returns to the racial issues Othello raises, her second assertion opens up the possibility that his revelations have likewise prompted new thinking in her regarding her whiteness and his Blackness. Because the play establishes that Othello's martial nature and his racial marginalization are so intertwined, by acknowledging her mistake regarding Othello's penchant for war, Desdemona also moves toward a recognition of his marginalized status within white-dominated Venetian society. In this way, Morrison's Desdemona and Othello mirror the dynamic Emily Shortslef identifies in Shakespeare's plays, wherein one's conscience "is the site and sign . . . of a specifically ethical relationality, a responsiveness oriented toward the voices of others in the arena of the social" (123). Because they speak and at least endeavor to hear each other, Desdemona and Othello thereby attempt to see each other in the very ways Okri notes they are denied in Shakespeare's play.

That said, this recognition concerning race is never made explicit, foreclosing any uncomplicated answer to the issues both Othello and Desdemona face. The point thus seems to be not answers, but the journey, the very attempt to dialogue even if no firm resolution is reached. "We should have had such honest talk, not fantasy, the evening we wed," Othello laments (54). *Desdemona*'s concluding song conveys a similar sentiment. "Kélé Mandi" shares:

> When two beings meet,
> each brings to the other a bit of themselves.
> So we learn, we construct our selves, we evolve.
> I bring what makes me different from you.
> Give me a bit of what you are . . .
> In accepting what you have to give,
> I open to you what I have to offer. (55)

This final song highlights the importance of self and Other—as the song reminds the audience, the identities are "different," after all—and the way they can be mutually constitutive. As Achille Mbembe observes, "Short of its total extermination, the Other is no longer external to us. It is within us, in the double figure of the alter ego and the altered ego (*l'autre Moi et du Moi autré*), each mortally exposed to the other and to itself" (47). Yet Morrison's depiction of the afterlife is not completely idealistic about the complexities of this mutually constitutive process, indeed admitting to this mortal exposure, for the song likewise cautions, "But do it with gentleness and tolerance,/since all that you impose upon me with force,/will only leave the imprint/of your violence and your arrogance" (55). When it comes to dialoguing about the interpersonal and ideological harm inflicted by both gendered and racial oppression, the play does not sentimentalize the process. It can be traumatic, even violent if not done correctly, for as Traoré's lyrics convey, "all that you impose upon me with force will only leave the imprint of your violence and your arrogance" (55). What *Desdemona* does value, however, is what the eponymous heroine stresses in her final speech: "the *possibility* of wisdom" (emphasis added, 55). Coupled with the closing song, this statement highlights the intersectional nature of the operetta. Identity is best shaped when difference is confronted but done so with grace and honesty. Given the way *Desdemona* highlights both issues of gender *and* race, there can be no question that such a confrontation is imagined as intersectional. What *Desdemona* demonstrates, then, is that featuring Desdemona's subjectivity does not have to come at the expense of Othello. The answer to the Desdemona problem, whether in a straightforward performance or a reanimation, does not mean ignoring her subjugation. But it does not mean ignoring Othello's either. Rather, *Desdemona* suggests that it entails holding them in uneasy, authentic tension with each other, stressing their interrelatedness. Certainly, *Desdemona* does not directly respond either to *Goodnight Desdemona (Good Morning Juliet)* nor *Desdemona: A Play about a Handkerchief*. But read together, one can see that the "possibility of wisdom" truly comes with an intersectional focus, which more fully and responsibly reveals what shapes self and Other, both in Shakespearean adaptation and in day-to-day encounters.

Epilogue: The Accessibility Problem

Lest this conclusion appear overly idealistic, however, I cannot gloss over a particular challenge posed by *Desdemona*: the problem of accessibility. Thompson observes about the operetta, "the performance mode seems to forestall the generative nature of the reimagined futurities" ("*Desdemona*" 503). At issue is how much the performance depends on Traoré, whose "singularity as an artist and collaborator," Thompson contends, "seems to contract instead of expand the potentialities for *Desdemona*." Her voice, her performance, her presence makes it so that *Desdemona* "is not reproducible without her," hence its very limited run. There is also the issue of the skill needed to perform the central role. Granted, as Thompson notes, two actresses have played Desdemona (Benko and Elizabeth Marvel), making any particular actress seem more replaceable than Traoré. Yet the actress playing Desdemona must be able to embody every character except Sa'ran (performed by Traoré) and Cassio. At particular stake here is her ability to use accents in order to aurally shift between the white Desdemona and the African Soun and Othello. How does a performer do so without slipping into stereotype and minstrelsy? Because of the seeming insurmountable nature of these challenges, *Desdemona* as a performance has reached limited audiences, including me. The readings here all rely on the text alone, even as I know that they could change significantly depending on staged delivery.

Unfortunately, such limitations invite a very different comparison with MacDonald's and Vogel's plays. A simple YouTube search reveals that MacDonald's play has been frequently performed by local theatre companies, college drama groups, and high schoolers alike. Vogel's play is likewise staged, most often by local companies and college/university drama groups. *Desdemona*, however, remains staunchly associated with Benko and Traoré. This means that the antiblack, anti-Othello views in *Goodnight Desdemona (Good Morning Juliet)* and *Desdemona: A Play about a Handkerchief* continue to circulate both in and out of the classroom, while those in *Desdemona* are much more likely to be limited to the page and therefore only considered in a pedagogical and scholarly context. Together, Morrison, Traoré, and Sellars collaborated to create a Desdemona that may newly speak, but unfortunately, she does not get to speak often enough.

Recognizing the way access shapes audiences is thus a helpful framework for those wishing to decenter Shakespeare to consider from the outset. Theatre is already ephemeral in nature, its very status as an "event" making it much more expensive, and therefore already inaccessible to a degree. If these constraints leave theatre with a well-established whiteness problem (see Chapter 4), how does creating a piece of art dependent on even more elusive factors (a particular musician, an actress with particular skill), however ethical its point, even further whittle down its audience? As artists continue to think about how to create antiracist art, it is essential to begin from a place that considers who can and cannot receive this vital message. Hopefully, the imperative should not be just to reinterpret Shakespeare nor recenter marginalized fictional voices, nor even to establish a recuperative social message. Rather, the imperative should be to craft powerful feminist, antiracist, intersectional art that allows, invites, and can be accessed by not only the Desdemonas and Cassios, but just as importantly the Emilias, Souns, Sa'rans, and Othellos of the world.

Chapter 6

Resisting Lobotomized Shakespeare: Whiteness and Universality in *Key & Peele* and *Get Out*

> A criticism that needs to insist that literature is not only "universal" but also "race-free" risks lobotomizing that literature, and diminishes both the art and the artist.
> —Toni Morrison, *Playing in the Dark* (12)

The Allure of Universal Shakespeare

On April 27, 2016, actor David Tennant appeared on *The Late Show with Stephen Colbert* for an interview during which Colbert inquired, "Why do you think Shakespeare is still so resonant to us today?" Tennant observed that Shakespeare speaks to a "universal human condition." Similar language characterized a range of 2016 promotional materials for celebrations of the 400th anniversary of the Bard's death, with words and phrases like "lasting legacy," "relevance," "timeless," and "international appeal" recurring. Shakespeare Lives, sponsored by the British Council, was a series of events and activities marketed as "exploring Shakespeare as a living writer who still speaks for all people and nations." The Shakespeare Theatre Association "chronicl[ed] celebrations of Shakespeare's life, work and universal appeal" through performances and readings. And in an article on the quatercentenary celebrations in *The Independent*, Clarisse Loughrey similarly asserts, "his influence pervades so much in our lives, because his work has become so timeless in its ability to touch upon human nature." These are, essentially, claims for a universal Shakespeare.

Appeals to Shakespeare's universality are not solely the provenance of late-night repartee or celebratory promotions. Harold Bloom famously credits Shakespeare with inventing personality and claims that Shakespeare is "a more adequate representer of the universe of fact than anyone else" (16). Kiernan Ryan has more recently considered Shakespeare's universal appeal. He argues that problems with claims to universality lie with "the *conservative construction*" (7), which fails to account for Shakespeare's use "to make class society, patriarchy, racial divisions and colonial domination vanish behind the smokescreen of the eternal human predicament his drama allegedly reflects" (4). Instead, Ryan calls for attention to what he terms Shakespeare's "*universal human potential*" (9). Shakespeare's plays, Ryan asserts, communicate "the potential of human beings, then and now, to base their lives together on values that possess universal validity, because they are founded on the simple, irrefutable fact that we belong to the same species" (10).

Other scholars remind us to be wary about such claims. In Chapter 2 of *Passing Strange*, Ayanna Thompson turns to the films *Suture* and *Bringing Down the House*, which she argues depict differing visions of Shakespearean universality. The former presents a "colorblind" universality that "is not only blind to the important cultural differences between races but also blind to the important cultural specificity and cannibalistic tendencies of whiteness" (42). The latter film instead "reveals another popular understanding of universal as an exclusive and excluding white culture, one that promotes unity solely through the elimination of other cultural productions." Both versions are "not only suspect but also dangerous" (43). Peter Erickson and Kim F. Hall similarly contend that "one of the major challenges is considering the vulnerabilities and limitations that universality glosses over. Part of the discussion concerns the prospect that Shakespeare's work cannot always adequately address current issues of racism and racial justice" (9). Indeed, as Patricia A. Cahill and Kim F. Hall note, "Terms like 'genius' and 'universality' are too often codes for white dominance" (7). And Brandi K. Adams argues that when approaching Shakespeare, "More often than not, the lens through which we are asked to consider these plays is that of a white, cisgender, able-bodied man who often vociferously insists that he embodies the universal interpretive mode for all conversations about Shakespeare" ("The King").[1]

---

[1] Adams further argues that this positionality challenges the idea of a "neutral" Shakespeare, for as she poignantly articulates: "There is no neutral Shakespeare. There never was" ("The King").

Assertions of universality thus ignore Shakespeare's potential to function as an alienating entity—a shibboleth for approved "high culture" often tacitly imagined as white.

This elision between universality and whiteness is precisely what challenges Ryan's call to focus on a universal human *potential*, for the ideal may be that people will recognize each other's "universal validity," but, at least in the West, the term *universal* undoubtedly carries with it the weight of racial distinction not easily shaken off. Achille Mbembe explains that "monocolored" Europe, or the West, reserves for itself the status of "the decisive site of being. That is what makes it universal, its meanings being valid unconditionally, beyond all geographical specificity, that is to say, in all places, in all times, independently of all language, all history, indeed of any condition whatsoever" (64). In Mbembe's comment, one finds echoes of attributes commonly associated with Shakespeare's universality: applicability across spaces and times, or put differently, a lack of specificity. Yet Mbembe reminds us that universality is very much specific, for "universal here [in sociopolitical context] is the name given to the violence of the victors of wars that are, of course, conflicts of predation" (64). Though Mbembe does not explicitly mention whiteness, the postcolonial context he addresses makes it clear precisely *who* enacts this predatory conquest.

In *White*, Richard Dyer more explicitly traces the connections between whiteness as a racial identity and the dependence on its being the measuring stick for universality. Making whites universal, Dyer explains, rests on the ability to concomitantly make whiteness the "human norm" so that "Other people are raced, we are just people" (1). By positioning themselves as the "norm," whites can therefore "claim to speak for the commonality of humanity" in a way that raced people cannot, for whites have the privilege of not representing any particular interests (2). It is for this reason that Dyer asserts, "There is no more powerful position than that of being 'just' human." Maintaining this "position of power" depends on hiding its constructed nature by achieving invisibility through a control of perspective (45). "Perspective places the individual spectator as the addressee of an image and yet keeps him or her out of the image—we are the spatially privileged observer who is none the less not 'in' the picture," he elaborates. According to Dyer, it is the white male gaze that most often shapes the dominant perspective, both within the world of film and without it (45). By positioning themselves in "the realm of the unseen," whites create an image in which the non-white Other is excluded while whites are "unmarked, unspecific, universal." Put differently, whites position themselves as normal, human, and therefore universal in opposition to the Othered, raced, particular non-white individual. As such, claiming that Shakespeare is universal more often than not carries the presumption of universality as whiteness.

The idea of Shakespeare as a marker of whiteness appeared in an unexpected place shortly after Tennant and Colbert's conversation, reminding us once again that for every claim of Shakespearean universality, a competing voice can assert otherwise, and usually, that voice belongs to those excluded from the white, cisgender, male identity Shakespeare so often represents. During the 2016 White House Correspondents' Dinner (April 30, 2016), President Barack Obama likewise commented on Shakespeare's universality, or, more accurately, lack thereof. Recently returned from a trip to London, Obama remarked, "I did have lunch with Her Majesty, the Queen, took in a performance of Shakespeare, hit the links with David Cameron . . ." He concluded with the punchline, "Just in case anybody is still debating whether I'm black enough, I think that settles the debate." Here, we find Shakespeare couched amid signifiers of the unstated signified—these activities suggest that Obama is indeed *not* Black enough. Rather than speaking to Shakespeare's universality, Obama's joke indicates that Shakespeare functions not as a symbol of a universal human condition, but rather a decidedly white one.

Of course, Shakespeare was not President Obama's focus. As such, the reference functioned as a joke at Obama's expense rather than as a provocative comment about the Swan of Avon. Biracial comedy duo Keegan-Michael Key and Jordan Peele, however, likewise tackled Shakespeare's whiteness, with much more pointed results. A sketch entitled "Othello 'Tis My Shite" appeared in Season 3 of their Comedy Central sketch show *Key & Peele*, which often explored, critiqued, and upended issues of race and identity.[2] A close reading reveals how Key and Peele imagine Shakespeare and race, specifically, Shakespeare's representation of Blackness. Like Obama's remarks, Key and Peele invoke Shakespeare to explore the racialized boundaries of the dramatist and his iconic work. According to this sketch, Shakespeare's universality finds its limits when confronted by its inauthentic depiction of and therefore potential irrelevance to Black experience. The characters' commentary on *Othello* depends on an understanding of a recognizable Black experience that can be authentically represented (or not), a project at which Shakespeare fails.

---

[2] Nick Marx characterizes the show as one whose sketches "repeatedly point beyond the program to how racial identities circulate as industrial constructions" (281).

As such, Key and Peele's satire challenges the narrative of universal Shakespeare. The sketch instead calls for a dislodging of the white point of view that crafts narratives misrepresenting Black masculinity. Thus, Shakespeare becomes a stand-in for culture at large, one that must be forced to recognize and make visible its whiteness—often at the insistence of those marginalized by this very whiteness—so as to reorient its vision. This reorientation in turn creates space to tell stories that properly encapsulate the complexities of persons of color.

The interrogation of white narrative control begun in Key and Peele's critique of *Othello*, I argue, extends to Peele's 2017 film *Get Out*, which exemplifies a more extensive writing back against the white situatedness challenged in the sketch. The *Get Out* plot carries significant echoes of *Othello*, thereby likewise prompting a reconsideration of Black representation in the play. In fact, its monetary success and wide-ranging cultural impact provide a potent corrective to assertions that audiences only desire universal, i.e. white, stories. In other words, through its emphasis on the coagula, this *Othello*-like story dislodges whiteness from the heart of the narrative, making Black identity the focus in a way that lays bare whiteness's continued antiblack oppression in a supposedly post-racial America. I contend that this retelling of *Othello*'s story of racial subjugation provides a powerful framework for how appropriators, adaptors, teachers, and scholars can ethically reconceive of the play and Othello's role within it by recognizing the strategies for and effects of antiblackness. Beyond Shakespeare, however, both "Othello 'Tis My Shite" and *Get Out* potently demonstrate the importance of challenging the white universal perspective by awakening audiences to its presence and the way it shapes the stories American culture tells and we receive. To expose the whiteness of seemingly universal perspectives, these works demonstrate, is to insist on a space for the particular, diverse storytelling so long silenced across mediums.

Whiteness, Narratives, and the Universal "We"

Before addressing either *Key & Peele* or *Get Out*, I want to continue putting pressure on the ties between universality, whiteness, and representation in order to expose the pernicious assumptions undergirding claims to Shakespearean universality. Dyer's analysis of whiteness as the norm in fact corresponds with long-standing concerns over how the invisible universality of whiteness shapes the narratives culture does and does not tell. Toni Morrison observes that literary scholars have long seen American literature as "the preserve of white male views, genius, and power" (5), one which becomes the standard for universal literature (12). It is similarly well known that the white male gaze predominates in the narratives presented on both the small and big screen. In an essay for *The Guardian,* Lili Loofbourow identifies the overarching perspective prioritized in television and film as "white cis masculinity," arguing that this positionality is the one with the authority to shape the universal "we," a "we" by which culture sets the standard for what counts as both widely applicable and aesthetically valuable storytelling. In other words, by privileging the white male gaze, storytelling across mediums narrows the types of narratives deemed acceptable for wide (or universal) audience appeal. As a result, stories by and focusing on women as well as by and about persons of color, regardless of gender, are relegated to the margins, if told at all.

Perhaps nothing encapsulates long-standing concerns about entertainment's white male dominance as clearly as the 2015 #OscarsSoWhite controversy, where

> In snubbing individual films and performances from 2015, and in recognizing a plurality of movies dominated by one ethnicity and gender, the message of the Academy of Motion Picture Arts and Sciences was clear: When it comes to narratives we accept as universal—as representing the world we all supposedly live in—the organization's comfort zone, like its membership, is overwhelmingly white and male. (Hornaday)

Ann Hornaday explains how as a result, "everyone has been invited to adopt a critically engaged vision of what audiences heretofore accepted as 'neutral' entertainment, whether that means questioning a movie whose hero is yet another Man on a Mission, raising a skeptical eyebrow when a filmmaker confuses 'universal' with 'white,' or wondering why all female roles in a movie are merely decorative rather than substantive, dynamic, and fully realized." Thus, the overarching emphasis on the cis white male gaze bears repeating, for as Hornaday's analysis emphasizes, recognizing and shifting it from a neutral, universal position to a particular one both dismantles the false claims to universality that Dyer stresses as particularly powerful and invites creators and audiences alike to seek out and pursue expansive, diverse narrative possibilities.

This shift, however, is not one easily enacted, in large part due to the power of whiteness, especially white masculinity. Hornaday's framing of the response to #OscarsSoWhite as an invitation matters, for an invitation rather than a mandate indicates that recipients may or may not choose to respond. The cold, hard, discouraging facts indicate that at least in Hollywood, the reaction to calls for increased diversity concerning entertainment content and creative control have occurred, but only minimally. In an article for the *New York Times*, Maya Salam reports that a recent study from the University of Southern California's Annenberg School for Communication and Journalism found that "of the top 100 films each year from 2007 to 2017 (that's 1,100 films in total), representation of women, people of color, LGBTQ people and the disabled has remained overwhelmingly stagnant." Concerning gender, "Women have never accounted for more than 33 percent of speaking roles in a given year." The numbers concerning racial and ethnic diversity are likewise abysmal, with white characters making up 70.7 percent of the characters pictured. These numbers only tell the story in front of the camera. Salam explains that a mere forty-three women directed films during this period. An article by USC Annenberg provides more details, noting that "Women of color were almost absent from these ranks, with just 3 Black or African American females and 1 Asian female in the director's chair. Overall, directors from underrepresented racial groups fared poorly. Only 5.5% of the 886 directors examined were black or African American and 2.8% were Asian or Asian American." In an article for the *Washington Post*, academy member, film producer, and former executive at Colombia Pictures Stephanie Allain explains the ideological assumptions shaping these numbers. She points out, as Drew Harwell reports, that "High-quality films with diverse ideas and characters are out there . . . But in today's monochromatic Hollywood, executives tend to overlook such movies—or undercut them altogether." Allain directly comments on moneymaking stories about women or persons of color, stating, "If it's a hit, it's an anomaly. It's not a trend, it's a one-off." This narrowing of narrative possibility matters, she claims, because "we set the tone for what the whole world sees" (Harwell). Hollywood therefore serves as a useful microcosm that exemplifies how easy it can be to recognize white supremacy's grip on cultural objects and the stories they tell, but that this recognition demands repeating, for this grip proves difficult to dislodge.

 This nearly totalizing dominance over cultural entertainment creates impactful consequences concerning *whose* stories get told and *in what ways* they get told across culture, all in the name of a desire for a supposedly unraced, yet truly white, universal narrative. In an opinion piece for NPR, Black author LJ Alonge addresses "the assumption that the reader is white and the resulting self-consciousness in your thinking and writing. Stories you know to be true and interesting somehow become distorted and unfamiliar." This pressure stymied Alonge's writing because every time he sat down to write, he worried about the broader implications of representing his characters in certain ways. Alonge recounts, "Respectable. I wanted my characters to be *respectable*. I wanted them to somehow escape the judgment they'd get for just being, the same kind of judgement I've gotten for just being: stupid, angry, criminal." He continues, "I couldn't make them unkind or silly or petty or in any way complicated. Which is to say that I couldn't make them human." Alonge's description demonstrates the cost of the white control Dyer addresses. As the sole neutral, universal individuals, only white people get to be *just human*. All others carry the weight of group representation and therefore feel the pressure to limit their complexity. Alonge also draws a direct line to the way that overarching white universality affects *how* stories get told, sometimes consciously, at other times not.[3]

Chef and author Eddie Huang has even more famously recounted the effects the desire for universality had on the narrative he created when discussing what happened as his memoir, *Fresh Off the Boat*, became a sitcom for the television network ABC (2015–20). According to Huang, his executive producer, Melvin Mar, explained that he would have to accept changes to his original vision for the show because audiences needed a television version of "Panda Express" rather than the sophisticated Baohaus, Huang's flagship restaurant. Huang recalls how, despite *Fresh Off the Boat* being a "very specific narrative about SPECIFIC moments in my life," the network wanted "to tell a universal, ambiguous, cornstarch story about Asian Americans resembling moo goo gai pan . . ." This desire

---

[3] An emphasis on *how* could also be extended to the technologies used to communicate televisual narratives. Dyer, for example, extensively discusses how the history of photography and film demonstrates that "as media of light, [photography and cinema] at the very least lend themselves to privileging white people" (83). In an article for *The Washington Post*, Hornaday explains that by privileging white people, lighting technologies and traditions in film have at the same time limited the "varied, nuanced spectrum of black faces" depicted on screen. She notes how "For the first hundred years of cinema, when images were captured on celluloid and processed photochemically, disregard for black skin and its subtle shadings was inscribed in the technology itself, from how film-stock emulsions and light meters were calibrated, to the models used as standards for adjusting color and tone," so that "the technology and grammar of cinema and photography have been centered on the unspoken assumption that their rightful subjects would be white." This exclusivity, she explains, is now shifting with more diverse storytelling and with changes in the technologies used to film.

meant transforming what Huang believed to be important details, such as having a Black kid and Chinese kid "breaking bread" at a Beastie Boys concert instead of a "Gravediggaz show" or a scene about macaroni and cheese becoming about on-screen Eddie's distaste for a particular *type* of macaroni and cheese rather than dislike for the dish altogether. According to Huang:

> The only way they could even mention some of the stories in the book was by building a Trojan horse and feeding the pathogenic stereotypes that still define us [Chinese and Chinese Americans] to a lot of American cyclope [a sea snail]. Randall [the father] was neutered, Constance [the mother] was exoticized, and Young Eddie was urbanized so that the viewers got their mise-en-place. People watching these channels have never seen us, and the network's approach to pacifying them is to say we're all the same.

Huang's account once again demonstrates the pitfalls of obsessions with universality, for universality functions as a stand-in for homogeneity and whiteness. The on-screen Huang family becomes, paradoxically, at once both more foreign *and* more American, i.e. more Orientalized and more white, all in order to be deemed suitable for the highly sought after "universal demographic" (Huang). Put simply, this serves as just one more example of the ways that white universality demands a certain perspective—one particular and subservient to whiteness—in order to be accepted.

This tracing of *universal* as a cover for whiteness and the perspectival commitments this dynamic insists upon helps contextualize the weight the term holds when applied to Shakespeare. While *universal* carries ideological burdens even within the narrow world of Shakespeare studies, it bears even more when considered in light of what that word symbolizes in American culture at large. Saying blithely that Shakespeare is universal, despite best intentions, conveys that Shakespeare is really representative of a white perspective, that he is white property just as the narratives addressed above have become or struggle against.[4]

---

[4] For PCRS scholarship on Shakespeare as white property, see Arthur Little Jr., "Re-Historicizing Race, White Melancholia, and the Shakespearean Property," *Shakespeare Quarterly* 67.1 (2016): 84–103; Ian Smith, "We Are Othello: Speaking of Race in Early Modern Studies," *Shakespeare Quarterly* 67.1 (2016): 104–24; Kim F. Hall, "Can You Be White and Hear This? The Racial Art of Listening in *American Moor* and *Desdemona*," in *White People in Shakespeare: Essays on Race, Culture, and the Elite*, ed. Arthur Little Jr. (The Arden Shakespeare, forthcoming); and Ayanna Thompson, "On Protean Acting in Shakespeare: Race and Virtuosity," Centre for Renaissance and Reformation Studies, March 9, 2021, University of Toronto.

Key and Peele's "Othello 'Tis My Shite" directly contests the fantasy of Shakespearean universality. In its stead, it foregrounds Shakespearean reanimation founded on collaboration as a more ethical response to a Shakespeare that misunderstands and misrepresents Black experience. *Get Out* continues the challenge begun by the sketch, serving as Peele's long-form meditation on destabilizing white supremacy. Together, these works contest the white perspectival dominance undergirding assertions of universal storytelling, including the narratives produced by Shakespeare.

"How dey goin to kill Othello?!": Questioning Shakespearean Universality

Set in seventeenth-century England, Key and Peele's sketch finds two Black men, Martinzion and Lashawnio, attending *Othello*.[5] According to Key and Peele, they serve as the "spiritual ancestors" of the recurring "Liam Neesons" action movie lovers, also known as the Valets (Martin).[6] While an exploration of Black identity functions as a hallmark of *Key & Peele*, this sketch deviates from most others on the show in that it depends on the idea of an "authentic" Black identity, a concept which other sketches explicitly eschew. Increasingly, scholars and cultural critics alike have scrutinized the idea of a homogeneous and/or authentic Black identity. Cultural critic Touré, for example, convincingly argues that "we are in a post-Black era, which means simply that the definition and boundaries of Blackness are expanding

---

[5] A compelling element of the sketch is its chronological pastiche. The music and costumes signal seventeenth-century England, but Martinzion and Lashawnio's hybrid language ("Elizabethan" English mixed with contemporary slang), the presence of *Shafte*, and the ideological concerns voiced—the representation of Black masculinity, the Shakespearean authorship controversy, Shakespeare's relationship to Blackness—point toward modernity. Indeed, this mishmash of time (and, loosely, place) complicates the sketch's exploration of Blackness. The men could be referencing Afro-Anglo Blackness, for they are "Moors" in seventeenth-century England. Yet their accents, speech, and references more directly point to a contemporary American construction of Blackness, one which would be more familiar to their American audience.

[6] In a typical Valet sketch, the two men discuss a traditional action hero whom they love, such as Liam Neeson, change the actor's name slightly by pluralizing it, "Liam Neesons," and effusively articulate their adoration for the actor and his oeuvre, escalating their praise as they go (in one sketch, one of their heads explodes). A "twist" in this recurring sketch is when the men discuss their favorite female actors, such as "Anne Hathaways."

in forty million directions—or really, into infinity" (12). As such, "There is no dogmatically narrow, authentic Blackness because the possibilities for Black identity are infinite" (5). In a foreword to Touré's book, scholar Michael Eric Dyson concurs, calling for a "move from exhaustive Blackness to expansive Blackness" (xix). In fact, it is precisely this dynamic that leads David Gillota, who borrows from Touré's discussion of post-Blackness, to position Key and Peele as post-soul comics: "These humorists approach the idea of blackness in a playful and ironic manner; they . . . allude to yet parody other black texts; and their comic personae suggest little concern with ideas about 'authentic' visions of black culture" (19). Yet the sketch's internal logic invites this totalizing framing so that "Othello 'Tis My Shite" seems to be an exception to Gillota's rule. This is how important Key and Peele perceive challenging the overwhelming dominance of the white narrative perspective to be—they imagine and articulate something close to an overarching Black experience that, while not universal, nevertheless depends on broadly accepted commonalities.

As a result, more so than in other sketches featuring these characters (or, more accurately, their modern-day counterparts), "Othello 'Tis My Shite" emphasizes the men's Blackness, not just through their skin color amid an all-white Globe audience, but also through various signifiers of Black identity. These signifiers show Key and Peele walking the line between characterization and stereotyping. Take, for example, the men's names, which if stripped of their Renaissance affectations become Martin and Lashawn. The latter functions as the "unusual Black name" sent up by Key and Peele in several of their recurring sketches while the former, though not exclusively a Black name, invokes Black identity in its echo of Martin Luther King Jr.[7]

---

[7] A comedic exploration of "Black" names appears in several of Key and Peele's recurring sketches. In one, Mr. Garvey, a former inner-city teacher, now substitute teaches in the suburbs. When he visits a predominantly white classroom, he calls roll, pronouncing common "white" names as if they were Black, so that Aaron becomes "A-A-Ron" and Blake "B-lack-ay." When corrected, he becomes increasingly distressed and threatens the students with discipline. As the sketch closes, he calls on "Tim-O-Thee," and a young Black man responds, "pray-sent." Also in this vein, the popular East/West Bowl sketches have football players— each played by Key or Peele—introducing themselves and stressing their highly unusual names (Hingle McCringleberry and Ozamataz Buckshank, for example), to the point where one man simply makes sounds that echo a velociraptor's (His name is Eeeeee Eeeee). While these sketches may seem to focus on football, the punchline of the very first East/West Bowl sketch stresses the racialized nature of these names, for the final player, the only white one, introduces himself as "Dan Smith, BYU" (the role is in fact played by Dan Smith of BYU).

Though the men speak in a mixture of modern and "Shakespearean" English, their speech is likewise signaled as "Black" with words such as "brother," "dope," and "pimpin" peppering their exchange. Martinzion and Lashawnio's behavior also registers stereotypical Blackness. During intermission, Martinzion turns down the offer to "borrow two ducats for a capon." He responds, "Moor, please," as he pulls out a "concealed" Cornish game hen from his doublet, the side eye he gives suggesting that he snuck it in because he was too cheap to pay for the Globe's concessions. Thus, Martinzion and Lashawnio snack on the early modern version of fried chicken. Yet even as their depiction threatens to devolve into stereotype, as Shanelle E. Kim observes, they are "consumers, not commodities, in the early modern English market" (171). Indeed, their elevated status is signaled by the fact that these richly dressed "Moors" attend a Shakespeare play, analyze it, even enjoy it, which places them firmly as connoisseurs of high culture, thus fleshing out their depiction.

Touré helps account for why this sketch can initially seem almost stereotypical in its depiction of Martinzion and Lashawnio, and why it trades on an understanding of authentic Blackness when most other sketches crafted by Key and Peele expressly do not. Touré theorizes "three primary dimensions of Blackness": introverted, where Blackness is private; ambiverted, where Blackness is embraced but does not wholly define the individual; and extroverted, where Blackness informs one's entire identity. Different situations require shifts between these modes. Specifically, "The ability to maneuver within white society . . . is often tied to your ability to modulate" (10, 11). As Touré notes, "there's times you need to throw up Black signifiers like they're gang signs and be extroverted" (10). These are precisely the signs used to characterize Martinzion and Lashawnio in order to stress their Blackness amid the whiteness signified by the Globe *and* Shakespeare. These signs are also the measures by which the men evaluate Othello's representation. These nearly stereotypical signs in fact work to highlight the sketch's central idea. The point is that men that can and do fit stereotypes often associated with assumptions about low socioeconomic and marginalized racial status can and do find a connection with and pleasure in the decidedly high-status and overwhelmingly white-oriented works of Shakespeare.

What Martinzion and Lashawnio value in *Othello* stresses Black masculinity while communicating what they perceive as authentic Black entertainment. As precursors to the Valet action movie lovers—who in contemporary sketches declare their favorite actors to be "Liam Neesons" and "Mels Gibsons"—it is unsurprising that the potential violence in Shakespeare's drama excites them. For example, though Othello does not kill any "white person" until the last act, at intermission, the two "Moors" bound out of the Globe squealing in delight about Othello's violent potential: "If I know Shakespeare, Othello about to kill everybody up in this bitch." What makes the Valet's progenitors so excited is that this time, a Black man participates in the action. Furthermore, they find the first half of the play enticing because Othello "doth the beast with two backs with that comely white maiden, and didst not anyone speaketh against him! He straight pimpin!" This exclamation praises the seeming equality achieved by Othello. At the same time, however, these celebratory exclamations invoke racist caricatures of Black masculinity. The image of Othello killing everybody, a community identified expressly as white, invokes the "brute," criminal Black man even as it brings to mind the modern-day action star (see Chapters 1 and 4). Moreover, by equating Othello with a pimp, these men also associate him with negative characterizations of Black male sexuality. Thus, even as the sketch unfolds in Renaissance England, it also plays with modernization, invoking current and often distinctly American conceptions of Black masculinity.[8] The sketch thus communicates competing frameworks relevant to Black masculinity and raises the question of *Othello*'s relationship to them. Stated differently, Key and Peele repeatedly stress a joy in Black identity even as they gesture toward the complications associated with that very identity, complications resulting from racial inequity.

Ultimately, exploring this duality associated with Black masculinity underpins the sketch's interrogation of Shakespeare's intersection with Black identity. Initially, the sketch appears to present the often-revered universal Shakespeare by suggesting that through *Othello*, he may finally speak to Black people. Especially thrilled with Othello as a Black hero, the men mimic sword play, declaring, "You dead white person!" and "This play doth seem dope to me!" Martinzion and Lashawnio take pleasure in seeing someone that looks like them represented on Shakespeare's stage. In this imaginary world, Shakespeare's reputation as a great dramatist seems established. Thus,

---

[8] It is difficult to say definitively whether Key and Peele are familiar with common cultural and academic debates about *Othello*—simply put, is the play racist, or, rather, does it explore and critique racism—but there is little question that they understand the way that Othello, the character and the eponymous play, can resonate with contemporary American stereotypes about Black men, even if, according to them, he and the play do not live up to their original, seemingly progressive promise.

focusing on a Black man in one of Shakespeare's dramas invokes the idea of the great Shakespeare ahead of his time who depicts the racial Other in an empowering way. They happily declare, "And 'tis about time Shakespeare doth scriven the play that placeth a brother amongst the firmament!" This comment simultaneously notes the lack of diversity in Shakespeare's canon while praising Shakespeare's new, Black, inspiring protagonist. This sketch thus aligns with the observation that "One of *Key & Peele*'s preferred tactics is to explore the tension of racial signifiers in genre parodies where they might not be expected—black characters in putatively white genres such as science fiction and fantasy, for instance" (Marx 281, 282). Here, the two men's comments make clear that they see Shakespeare as crafting a "putatively white genre." *Othello* is therefore Shakespeare's saving grace. In fact, Martinzion affirms Othello's depiction, noting, "Me thinks things are looking up for people of the darker hue." He thus subtly suggests that this play's representation may have social implications. These enthusiastic responses depict a progressive Shakespeare who represents Black experience in high-status ways. According to the sketch, even in his own age, Shakespeare speaks to and therefore influences all people, including those often marginalized in seventeenth-century England, post-racial America (when the sketch was created), and today.

Yet the sketch takes an ideological turn. As it appears to reify Shakespeare's progressive genius, it complicates the idea of universal Shakespeare, for "the intermission between the first and second halves of *Othello* reveals the gap between the depiction of the black individual as a brother in the 'vast human family of human beings' and his literal and ontological death" (Kim 168). By the end of the play, Martinzion and Lashawnio lament, "How they going to kill Othello?" Their disappointment stems from the fact that "A black man got it going on and you [Shakespeare] shuffle off his mortal coil?" The men thus critique Shakespeare's participation in the problematic representation of Black masculinity. This observation makes it clear that the quasi-stereotypical characterization of Martinzion and Lashawnio is a self-aware one. Key and Peele clearly understand expectations about the depiction of Black men, and the message of the sketch is that, at least in *Othello*, Shakespeare decidedly does not know these expectations, or worse, he *does* know and falls into the expected tropes anyway. Furthermore, Shakespeare does not appear to understand Black experience.[9] They declare the play's ending

---

[9] It should not escape attention that while the sketch explores Black experience, it is a decidedly masculine one.

unbelievable because no reasonable Black man would commit suicide after breaking up with a "white bitch" or "this world would be bereft of brothers." Invoking *Hamlet*, Lashawnio replies, "And you'd be talking to a skull right now," whereupon Martinzion responds with a knowing, emphatic, "Oooh-kay!" These remarks suggest a commonality between the men and by extension between a community of Black men united by their interracial relationships. They have not killed themselves, and thus their very existence points to the inaccuracy and inauthenticity of Shakespeare's representation of Black male experience. Therefore, through these critiques of *Othello*, the men, and therefore the sketch, suggest that Shakespeare's engagement with and depiction of Blackness fails both then and now, for this play is largely understood as Shakespeare's racial legacy, and it is clearly insufficient.[10]

As a way of further questioning the concept of Shakespearean universality, the sketch disrupts the narrative of Shakespearean authority. Central to this polemic is Shakespeare's representation. Played by actor James Callis, best known for embodying the duplicitous Dr. Gaius Baltar on the sci-fi drama *Battlestar Galactica* (2004–9), this Shakespeare does not resemble Ben Jonson's "Beloved Author." Rather, the representational choices made in Shakespeare's depiction—including Callis's casting and performance—reveals an irreverent approach to Shakespeare the literary genius. Martinzion and Lashawnio confront the Bard after the performance, menacingly pushing Shakespeare against the wall. A cowering, sniveling Shakespeare consequently foists authorial responsibility upon Christopher Marlowe, asserting, "'tis not I that penned this dreadful play. 'Twas Christopher Marlowe." In this moment, Callis's past performance as Dr. Baltar ghosts this depiction of Shakespeare, for Baltar, a selfish, neurotic character, spent much of *Battlestar Galactica*'s four seasons lying for personal gain. While for some Comedy Central viewers the

---

[10] Noting the way *Othello* allows one to make global Shakespearean connections, Peter Erickson calls Othello "Shakespeare's state servant ... whose wide-ranging 'traveler's history' seems to promise convenient world wide access" (*Citing* x). Speaking more narrowly about the play in an American context, Francesca T. Royster argues, "Many students know about *Othello* even if they haven't read it. Perhaps this is because in our culture the story of *Othello* is often retold as a story of the black experience in white culture" ("Rememorializing" 53). In fact, Michael Neill argues that *Othello* has replaced *Hamlet* as the most commonly considered text "as critics and directors alike began to trace in the cultural, religious, and ethnic animosities of its Mediterranean setting, the genealogy of the racial conflicts that fractured their own societies" ("Introduction" 1). As such, "it is as a foundational document in the history of 'race' that much recent criticism has treated the play."

reference may remain inaccessible, for others, especially those more connected to sci-fi nerd culture, casting Callis as Shakespeare provides a way of reading the duplicitous, often weak nature of Baltar onto Shakespeare, thereby stripping Shakespeare's identity of authority. Martinzion and Lashawnio likewise position Shakespeare as a liar by refusing to believe "slick Willy," the common "Willy" signaling the deterioration of Shakespeare's awe-inspiring effect upon them.[11] As they loom over Shakespeare, they reply to his authorial renunciation—which slyly invokes the authorship debate—with an emphatic, "Nay! Nay!" In fact, their response to Shakespeare's claim that Marlowe wrote the play elicits perhaps the most pointed critique of Shakespeare and his representation of people considered racial (and religious) Others, for Martinzion and Lashawnio remind him, "Thou already tried to use that line of argument when the Jews wanted to kick your ass after *The Merchant of Venice*." This quick but potent rebuttal suggests that rather than being an anomaly, Shakespeare's problematic characterization and representation of those positioned as Others, as Martinzion and Lashawnio believe him to have done in *Othello*, indicates a pattern in his work as a whole. The sketch thus suggests a fairly radical reimagining of not only the progressive nature of Shakespeare's oeuvre, but also of how one imagines the author himself. Quashing Bardolatry, the sketch deauthorizes Shakespeare in both literal and figurative ways that challenge his universal appeal to audiences broadly, and more narrowly, to the racialized Others he has misrepresented in plays.

Even as Martinzion and Lashawnio challenge Shakespearean universality, however, they cannot ignore the siren song of Shakespeare and his cultural authority. Shakespeare attempts to placate them, stating, "'Twill not be long before another black hero graceth the stage." But the men take this as another of Shakespeare's deflections. The time for a Black hero is not the future; instead, they insist, "You goin to write that hero ... now." The scene immediately cuts to a sign promoting *Shafte: A Play in Five Acts*. By choosing *Shafte* as Shakespeare's new drama, the men force Shakespeare to shift the genre from one associated with whiteness to one decisively associated with Blackness. *Shaft* is one of the foundational Blaxploitation films, a genre that "focused on black narratives [and] featured black casts in action-adventures in an urban setting" (Bausch 258). Blaxploitation films not only created Black narratives but also "exploded what

---

[11] "Willy" may be a further deauthorizing nickname as it was employed as an insulting term for Bill Clinton, which viewers of Key and Peele's age might recognize.

they saw as the old fantasies of black masculinity" by pushing back against white America's stereotypical assumptions (259). Closely tied to Black Power rhetoric and ideology, Blaxploitation films depicted sexuality under Black rather than white control and staged violence as a form of freedom (259). In *Shaft*, this violence serves the Black community. The eponymous protagonist functions as "a paladin-warrior, more concerned with protecting a particular community, in this case a Black one, than in preserving the state" (Bates and Garner 140). In contrast, while Othello may experience sexual freedom with Desdemona, their mutual desire soon sours. And though his martial violence may be celebrated initially, ultimately, it threatens the white, Venetian community. *Shafte* thus serves as what Martinzion and Lashawnio perceive as the necessary corrective for Shakespeare's inadequate representation of Black masculinity. Diana E. Henderson explains how the concept of "collaboration focuses attention on the connections among individuals, allowing artists credit and responsibility, but at the same time refusing to separate them from their social location and the work of others" (8). Ultimately, then, the sketch advocates for this type of collaboration, one drawing stronger connections between Shakespeare and people of color by inviting all that the signifier *Shakespeare* represents to work alongside the artistic contributions of people of color, even as the collaboration holds him responsible for the social dominance of whiteness in his canon. The sketch thereby indicates that the answer to the tension between accurate racial representation and Shakespeare is an investment in Shakespearean authority and product, but one that divests Shakespeare of literary genius by instead advocating for a multiracial, collaborative approach.

Yet *Shaft* does not provide an unquestionably admirable version of Black masculinity that completely rectifies the pitfalls in Shakespeare's tragedy. Shaft's sexual prowess, for example, comes alongside a treatment of women as disposable, one lover easily and eagerly traded for another with only his desires taken into account. Furthermore, it remains unclear precisely which *Shaft* Key and Peele hope the audience references, the 1971 original or the 2000 remake. The reference point matters, for as Matthew Henry explains, the 2000 film trades sexuality for heightened violence, which is used to reinforce the state by threatening men of color. These complications raise the question, "why reference *Shaft*?" This choice stresses the limited Black entertainment produced by Hollywood. Where should the action movie lovers turn for inspiration? Slave narratives that immerse the viewer in racial oppression? The minstrel world of Tyler Perry's Madea films?

Superhero films, action movies, and thrillers alike—the types of films ostensibly enjoyed by the Valets—may feature a Black character and appeal to Black audiences, but they are not considered specialized entertainment. By that very fact, they are de facto white entertainment. This problem of representational limitation is not only due to race, but also to gender, according to Ed Guerrero. Black masculinity, he argues, exists in "a vast, empty space in representation" ("The Black Man" 397). He elaborates:

> What is missing from Hollywood's flat, binary construction of black manhood is the intellectual, cultural, and political depth and humanity of black men, as well as their very significant contribution to the culture and progress of this nation ... Hollywood has given us enough "noble Negroes," de-sexed comedian buddies, and upwardly mobile, black "exceptions" to fuel several film waves to come.

Thus, both Hollywood and Shakespeare create a similar problem; they provide these men limited options within which they can find themselves represented.

This sketch's uneasy conclusion holds in balance its competing ideologies. On the one hand, Shakespeare inaccurately and ineffectively represents Black experience. On the other hand, *Shafte* trades on Shakespeare's authority. This sketch thus acknowledges the limits of Shakespeare regarding Black representation, but for all its critique, its ending indicates the desire to reclaim Shakespeare instead of completely disregarding Shakespeare in relationship to Blackness. His authority can be redirected, not altogether eliminated. It is perhaps unsurprising that the *Othello* sketch remains invested in Shakespeare even as it troubles his reification. The fact that *Key & Peele* addresses anything Shakespearean speaks to Shakespeare's enduring cultural capital. And yet, even that may be waning. In an interview with *Vulture*, Key and Peele's comments suggest that Shakespearean influence may not be limited simply due to race; rather, there may be a larger lack of cultural relevance. Interviewer Denise Martin explains, "Comedy Central was initially concerned about giving the go-ahead to a sketch that presumed its audience knew the basic story of Shakespeare's *Othello*." According to Key and Peele, "I think the problem was, for the 26-year-old watching the show, smoking weed, do they know who Othello is?" (Martin). Just as the sketch demonstrates that Shakespeare may not speak for all people, network concerns indicate that Shakespeare may not speak for all time. Indeed, no Shakespearean version of *Shafte* exists. As such, the sketch ends with the idea that perhaps Shakespeare never can and never will speak to all people, including Black ones. Universal Shakespeare may be appealing, but, like *Shafte*, it is just a fantasy.

Yet the sketch's creation and content offers one possible means of recuperating Shakespeare and his works. Rather than overinvesting in the idea of Shakespeare's universality, both the sketch and *Shafte* within it appropriate and reimagine Shakespeare to speak to the very audiences to which he may be irrelevant. Following 2016, a year which celebrated Shakespeare because he "lives on," this sketch helpfully reminds us that Shakespeare may not speak to all people. But it also reminds us that we can imaginatively transform Shakespeare in ways that may extend his relevancy and authenticity for those often excluded from thoughtful representation on his page and stage. Though Shakespeare is not always antithetical to Black identity, when filtered through the universal white perspective, he very likely proves to be so, as the sketch suggests. It is crucial, then, that in transforming Shakespeare, adaptors and appropriators not only prove imaginative but also invested in dislodging the centrality of the white universal perspective to make way for competing narrative voices and foci. Peele's *Get Out* provides an exemplary model of just this type of narrative reconsideration, crafting a story that accomplishes the decentering of the universal white point of view only gestured toward by the end of "Othello 'Tis My Shite."

"I told you not to go in . . .": Horror and the Framing of Blackness in *Get Out* and *Othello*

A Black protagonist lives in an overwhelmingly white community and embodies a valuable skill coveted by white counterparts. He journeys to a threatening locale and over the course of roughly twenty-four hours develops a paranoia fostered by white antagonism, a threat he puts to rest by choking his young, white female lover. For those in tune with popular American culture, these plot details probably invoke writer and director Jordan Peele's 2017 breakout horror-thriller *Get Out*. Made on a 4.5-million-dollar budget, the film achieved commercial and critical success, making $254.3 million and garnering four Academy Award nominations and one win for best adapted screenplay (Ramos).

In the process, the film challenged traditional horror film tropes, particularly the marginalization of Black individuals in the genre. For instance, *Get Out* notably includes a Black protagonist who survives the film, thereby rewriting another famous horror movie with a Black central figure, George A. Romero's *Night of the Living Dead* (1968), whose Black main character, Ben (Duane Jones), fends off zombies for the film's totality only to be shot at its conclusion. *Get Out* thus subverts the traditional ways that the horror genre "speaks" difference. That is, it still marks "Black people and culture as Other—apart from dominant (White) populations and cultures in the US" (Means Coleman 2)—but it transforms the narrative trajectory into one of Black survival rather than eradication. As such, "*Get Out* redresses decades of erasure, abuse, clichés, and damaging tropes that have stained horror cinema, Hollywood, and American history" (Due 8).

In its multifaceted focus on protagonist Chris Washington (Daniel Kaluuya), the movie also counteracts the dearth of film roles for Black leading men. In response to what he identifies as limited possibilities for Hollywood representations of Black masculinity, Guerrero asserts:

> What is now needed is an expanded, heterogeneous range of complex portrayals of black men that transcends the one-dimensional, positive-negative characters contained within Hollywood's formulaic narratives and its most common strategy for representing *blackness*, that is, channeling most black talent and film production into the genres of comedy or the ghetto-action-adventure. ("The Black Man" 397)

Chris is multidimensional in the way Guerrero calls for: a successful photographer who appears to focus on Black communities but is also in an interracial relationship; a sexy, confident man with a small dog for a pet; a loyal friend and good boyfriend who has a smoking problem. Particularly important is that this complex character not only features in the film, but he survives it. Indeed, *Get Out*'s title invokes the joke used to "explain the virtual absence of Blacks in horror movies before the 1970s," which Steven Torriano Berry relates as, "QUESTION: Why are there no Black people in horror movies? ANSWER: Because when the ominous voice says, 'Get Out!', we do!" (Means Coleman xi). Furthermore, Chris's role as the Black man in an interracial relationship who functions as a horror film's hero rather than villain also upends traditional horror movie expectations. As Steven Jay Schneider observes, the expectation in a horror film is that in an interracial relationship, the Black man will play the monstrous "seductive villain" while the woman plays the often passive victim, a dynamic Schneider argues is much more complex, with these binaries "open to multiple, even contradictory interpretations" (74). Nevertheless, the framework Schneider argues against is instructive in that it exposes the traditional scholarly readings of Black men in interracial relationships within the "race horror movie" genre, an expectation that Chris challenges in being neither seductive nor a villain. Peele therefore both upends the typical representation of Black masculinity in Hollywood movies *and* creates a more dynamic space for Black masculinity within the horror film tradition.

In fact, reconciling these shifts in the horror genre, and in the Black male's characterization within it, created some controversy concerning the film, particularly regarding its generic classification. There is no doubt that *Get Out* fits readily within the horror genre. I will address the film's plot more below, but here I include details to clarify how clearly *Get Out* is a horror film. Though "Today, especially in the age of multimedia and new media technologies, purist generic boundaries are extraordinarily difficult to define," the horror genre does have some foundational characteristics, even if the finer details continue to be debated (Means Coleman 3). Kinitra D. Brooks traces especially useful scholarly definitions, such as Isabel Cristina Piñedo's, whereby she identifies three characteristics of postmodern horror: "The first characteristic presents a violent disruption with the everyday world; the second characteristic portrays a horror that transgresses and violates boundaries; and the final characteristic questions the validity of rationalism" (Brooks, *Searching* 2). Even with the broadest strokes through which I have described *Get Out* above, one can identify that Chris experiences a violent disruption as a result of the physical threats the Armitage family, whom he visits, place upon him; their machinations, as I will discuss further below, transgress Chris's physical and psychological boundaries; and the twist ending certainly calls into question all forms of rationality. Brooks also addresses Noël Carroll's definition of horror, which depends on "an emotion of fear instigated by the simultaneity of threat and disgust" (*Searching* 4, 5). Once again, in *Get Out* audiences experience the threat posed to Chris and perhaps physical disgust as people are run over, gored by a mounted buck's antlers, and as mentioned, choked. Or, take the definition of horror that Brooks privileges, that of Robin Wood, who defines it as "when Normality is threatened by The Monster . . . [or The Other]" (quoted in Brooks, *Searching* 5). Chris's normality is certainly threatened by the Other, the white Armitage family. Thus, in spite of the various formulations for determining the horror designation, *Get Out* clearly fits within any of these frameworks, lending gravitas to its antiracist agenda.

Yet despite the evident overlaps between *Get Out* and a number of generic definitions, there has been debate about how to categorize the film. Notably, and at least in part due to Peele's reputation as one half of *Key & Peele*, "The classification of *Get Out* has become a hot topic amid news that the film has been submitted as a comedy for the upcoming [2018] Golden Globe Awards" (Lawrence). While there is debate about whether this decision rested with production company Blumhouse or with the Hollywood Foreign Press Association, the decision is notable in that it attempts to move *Get Out* into one of the genres that Guerrero explicitly identifies as acceptable for representing Blackness—comedy. In response to this (mis)categorization, actor Lil Rel Howery, who plays Chris's best friend Rod, expressed confusion, tweeting that the classification was "weird" and that "Their [sic] is nothing funny about racism" (Kohn). Peele too responded via tweet, asserting, "*Get Out* is a documentary" (Kohn). Peele elaborated on his stance concerning the film's genre, claiming that it defied any "genre box," and despite calling it a "social thriller" he reiterated, "the movie subverts the idea of all genres" (Kohn). Whatever genre one applies, with its exploration of the horrors enacted by white supremacy against Black individuals in modern America, *Get Out* is clearly not a comedy, as the artists associated with crafting and developing the movie make clear.

This issue with the film's miscategorization is not merely a result of determining the correct genre in order to ensure proper awards competition, but rather one of recognizing the gravitas of the movie's thematic focus. Peele explains, "I've had many black people come up to me and say, 'man, this is the movie we've been talking about for a while and you did it.' That's a very powerful thing. For that to be put in a smaller box than it deserves is where the controversy comes from" (Kohn). The subtext of Peele's identification of Black people's enthusiasm for the film, and the focus of Howery's tweet, is that the film deserves proper consideration because it tackles racism in gripping, previously unexplored ways. Peele's film began as a rebuttal against claims of a post-racial America following Barack Obama's historical 2008 election, only later morphing into a horror movie that functions as a pointed commentary on the oppressive experience of Black Americans. He explains, "What originally started as a movie to combat the lie that America had become post-racial became a movie where the cat is out of the bag . . . It became less about trying to create wokeness and more about trying to offer us a hero out of this turmoil, to offer escape and joy" (Zinoman). Thus, perhaps most significantly, this film has been transformative, for this reimagining of the horror genre produced a racially polemic film that has substantially affected the way we think about and approach race in media and in culture at large.

For the Shakespeare scholar, the same narrative particulars that make up *Get Out*'s central story likely outline, if only loosely, *Othello*. And just as with *Get Out*, *Othello* faces critical neutering, not in regard to genre but instead in regard to its thematic emphasis. For despite sharing much narrative DNA with *Get Out*, it is still positioned as "not about race." Take actor Chiwetel Ejiofor's remarks in a 2016 *Financial Times* interview: "to me, *Othello*'s not talking about race, other than incidentally" (Harrod). Less directly, in a 2016 interview with *The Stage*, director Iqbal Khan asserts that by casting a Black Iago, he "made the play less about the black-and-white race issue" and thereby "liberated, I hope, the more complex powers within that play" (Wicker). Even if unintentionally, Khan's remark suggests that the "race issue" is less "complex" than the unnamed other "powers" at work in *Othello*. More recently, reviews of the Public Theater's Shakespeare in the Park staging of *Othello* (2018) repeatedly note the way the production de-emphasized anything that could be perceived as "political," including race. Perhaps this choice is explained by the fact that, as Isaac Butler reports, director Ruben Santiago-Hudson "has said in interviews that he thinks of *Othello* primarily as a play about love, and he has crafted a tragedy of intimacy, a powerful examination of the loss of boundaries that can be a part of love's power, and how this can lead swiftly to a kind of madness" (Butler). Once again, there seems to be little space for more than one theme to serve as a motivating factor for productions of *Othello*; if jealousy, love, or other matters drive the play, then the logic seems to be that race must not.

Despite this muting of race's role in *Othello*, reading it as an analog to *Get Out* suggests that sidelining race in *Othello* may restrict its narrative potency and thematic resonance just as attempts to classify *Get Out* as a comedy did for the film. Indeed, putting these two "texts" in conversation with each other proves useful, for even though both stories end with a white woman strangled by the hands of a Black man, *Othello* remains a play mired in questions about if and how it can be presented in ways that shake off its legacy of vexed racial dynamics. *Get Out*, however, does not suffer from such questioning; instead, it achieves the difficult feat of spurring multicultural audiences to root for the Black Chris as he murders the Armitages, an upper-middle-class, politically liberal, white family.[12] *Get Out*'s

---

[12] Due to its being a Black film "in which killing white people is gloriously cathartic," Peele did not believe *Get Out* would be produced (Anthony).

unexpected success indicates that there may be efficacious ways to consider race in *Othello* in the twenty-first century. In fact, I propose that *Get Out* proves an important tool for reorienting how scholars, teachers, and a wide range of adaptors conceive of *Othello*'s racial dynamics. In turn, this reorientation allows for the possibility of re-mediating the tragedy by tapping into a more thoughtful racial narrative than the "noble Moor to savage" trope that haunts even modern instantiations of the play.

As a canonical tragedy and a contemporary horror film, *Othello* and *Get Out* may seem odd intertexts. Yet as Douglas M. Lanier argues, Shakespearean connections between artifacts need not be tidy in order to be effective. Instead, he proposes the rhizome, a capacious network of Shakespearean intertextuality that invites wide-ranging artifacts to "count" as part of that network ("Shakespearean Rhizomatics," 27–30). In many ways, *Get Out* functions as an artifact rhizomatically related to Shakespeare, though Celia Daileader's discussion of *Othellophilia* makes the pairing a tidier match; her theorization suggests that *Get Out* can be placed alongside a series of slant-*Othello*s, texts centering on negative depictions of a Black/white interracial relationship (6). For numerous online commentators, the dénouement of *Get Out*'s interracial romance explicitly invokes *Othello*. Scholar Sydnee Wagner observes how "[Chris] proceeds to choke her [Rose]—an image that bears a striking resemblance to Othello's murder of Desdemona"; Aisha Harris argues that in choking Rose, Chris "[conjures] up images of Othello strangling Desdemona"; Princess Weekes notes, "If you don't think that scene from *Get Out* with Chris choking Rose is a reference to *Othello* then you need to look closer"; Ina Diane Archer comments on the similarities between Chris and Othello, the latter "who is plainly referenced by Peele"; and Marvin C. Pittman declares, "*Get Out* showed me Othello strangling Desdemona, and had me cheer for Othello." Though interviews make it clear that Peele had the horror film tradition most centrally in mind when crafting *Get Out*, his previous consideration of *Othello* in "Othello 'Tis My Shite" suggests that the reference to *Othello* may be plain indeed.

But *Get Out* does more than reference *Othello*; it also provides a counterpoint that allows one to consider the *Othello* narrative in a way that privileges Black experience over a more frequently represented white one. Specifically, through its central concepts of the "coagula" and "the sunken place"—concepts that explain the social threats to and psychology of Black individuals amid a predominant and predatory white culture—the film articulates a racial framework that illuminates how and why Othello experiences the plot of the play differently than those around him. *Get Out* literalizes the horror of Othello's racial experience by stressing the physical and psychological violence against Black bodies, the attendant dominance of whiteness, and the strategies—such as microaggressions—that weaken the Black self in order to make it susceptible to white bodily and mental appropriation. Thus, if we use *Get Out* as a framework for reconsidering *Othello*, just as Peele re-mediated the horror genre in order to reorient its focus on white narratives and bodies onto Black ones, we can re-mediate *Othello*'s narrative representation into one that no longer raises questions about a Black man's humanity but rather directs attention to the racist inhumanity directed against him through the shifting, potent tools of white supremacy.

Get Out and the Necropolitics of White Supremacy

Before analyzing how *Get Out* can reorient how we view *Othello*, an overview of its plot proves helpful. Successful African American photographer Chris joins his white girlfriend, Rose (Allison Williams), for a weekend in the suburbs to visit her family for the first time—a family, he learns, unaware that he is Black. Rose assures Chris of her family's liberal, antiracist bonafides, a characterization their warm welcome validates. Yet Chris feels unease, even paranoia, as he meets Walter (Marcus Henderson) and Georgina (Betty Gabriel), the friendly, if odd, Black help. His apprehension increases after Missy Armitage (Catherine Keener), a psychologist, hypnotizes him in order to help him quit smoking. During the hypnotism, the audience sees Missy send Chris's mind to the "sunken place." Thinking he experienced a dream—or at least forgetting his visit to the sunken place—Chris's anxiety intensifies as small, disturbing incidents accrue, such as Walter charging him then dodging at the last second or his phone mysteriously and repeatedly becoming unplugged. At a party hosted by the Armitages, the fabrication unravels as unbeknownst to Chris, the white attendees bid on him. Chris only realizes the danger when a missing Black man, André, now going by Logan (Lakeith Stanfield), appears with no recollection of his identity and subsequently develops a nosebleed, screaming "Get out!" after Chris takes his photo. We learn that the Armitages have created a process and product called the coagula, a white brain surgically implanted into a Black body so that an aging or physically disadvantaged white person can live on. However, a piece of the Black psyche, and thus Black self, remains, which necessitates the sunken place—the psychological corner reserved for the hypnotized, appropriated Black self, where the person can see what occurs but cannot respond. Chris miraculously escapes before neurosurgeon Dean Armitage (Bradley Whitford) can perform the procedure, murdering the family in the process and culminating in a confrontation with Rose, an enthusiastic participant in the façade whom he almost strangles to death minutes before his friend, TSA agent Rod Williams, rescues him.

Through the coagula, *Get Out* viscerally confronts modern society's violent appropriation of Black bodies in a way that can help us reconsider Othello's service to the Venetian state and his tragic end.[13] Ta-Nehisi Coates addresses precisely this violence, arguing that the "elevation" of whiteness comes not from benign activities like "ice cream socials, but rather through the pillaging of life, liberty, labor, and land; through the flaying of backs; the chaining of limbs; the strangling of dissidents; the destruction of families; the rape of mothers; the sale of children; and various other acts meant, first and foremost, to deny you and me the right to secure and govern our own bodies" (*Between* 8). This violence, however, cannot be relegated to America's racial history. Even today, "racism is a visceral experience … it dislodges brains, blocks airways, rips muscle, extracts organs, cracks bones, breaks teeth. You must never look away from this. You must always remember that the sociology, the history, the economics, the graphs, the charts, the regressions all land, with great violence, upon the body" (10). Mbembe provides a philosophical framing for this social and state-sanctioned violence. Building on Michel Foucault's concept of biopolitics—with particular attention to Foucault's consideration of race—Mbembe establishes the concept of *necropolitics*, or "contemporary forms of subjugating life to the power of death" (92). According to Mbembe, the relationship between "resistance, sacrifice, and terror" have transformed too significantly to be explained by biopolitics. Thus, Mbembe elaborates upon Foucault's concept that "The ultimate expression of sovereignty largely resides in the power and capacity to dictate who is able to live and who must die," paying particular attention to modern terror and the specific technologies used to enact it (66). Necropolitics, then, is precisely the type of violent power and subjugation Coates

---

[13] In many conversations about *Get Out*, the term *sunken place* has come to represent what I am treating here as the coagula and the sunken place distinctly. In other words, *sunken place* is often used to explore all forms of marginalization explored in the film. I have separated the terms for clarity and precision.

articulates. In necropolitics, sovereignty comes from being able to "define who matters and who does not, who is *disposable* and who is not" (Mbembe 80), which is precisely the dynamic Coates articulates in regard to the way whiteness treats Black Americans. Thus, Mbembe's discussion of necropolitics exposes how, even though not technically enslaved, Black Americans are nevertheless placed in a position of "unfreedom" (91).

It is perhaps unsurprising, then, that to account for modern terror, Mbembe argues that one must address slavery and its plantation system. Mbembe's discussion of slavery creates an especially helpful conceptualization for understanding how the horror genre functions as a vehicle for Peele to explore race in post-racial America, and even more so, for the dynamics he highlights through his conceptualization of the coagula. Mbembe explains that "the slave condition results from a triple loss: loss of a 'home,' loss of rights over one's body, and loss of political status. This triple loss is identical with absolute domination, natal alienation, and social death (expulsion from humanity altogether)" (75). It is no wonder, then, that Tananarive Due asserts, "Black history *is* Black horror," thereby making the genre "an excellent mechanism to visualize, confront, and try to overcome racial trauma" because it "can serve as a coping mechanism by helping us visualize allegorical monsters, as well as offering release and lessons on survival and rebellion against seemingly overwhelming forces" (7). Mbembe's discussion of slavery as modern terror also provides a framing for Peele's conceptualization of the coagula. In the necropolitics of the plantation, because enslaved people are needed for labor, they are "kept alive, but in a *state of injury*, in a phantom-like world of horrors and intense cruelty and profanity . . . Slave life, in many ways, is a form of death-in-life" because "a person's humanity is dissolved to the point that the slave's life can be said to be possessed by the master" (75). Similarly, the coagula and its dependence on the sunken place positions Black Americans permanently in a state of psychic, emotional injury, so that they wander around the Armitage estate and beyond in precisely the state of necropolitical death-in-life Mbembe describes. *Get Out* thus tacitly acknowledges the legacy of America's racial past while at the same time viscerally demonstrating how it lingers into its supposedly post-racial present, thereby making the film "a cautionary tale about the monsters hidden in plain sight" (Due 11). It is no wonder, then, that *Get Out* refuses to allow one to look away from either violence or its attendant trauma, for this violence functions as the Armitages' modus operandi as they seek to create more coagula, demonstrated most notably through André, Walter, and Georgina, who suffer under the monstrous Armitages.

The film's first horror moment begins with André walking at night in what we learn is an all-white suburb in a scene that signals the film's insistence on stressing the violence enacted on Black bodies. In a fairly close medium shot, the camera starts by focusing on André's head then circles around to his face, covered in darkness except for the small light cast from the streetlight he passes. The viewer likely feels as disoriented and lost as he does. While he tries to find an address, a car makes a u-turn, pulling up beside him. Suspense mounts as the lyrics "Run rabbit, run rabbit, run, run, run, run" emanate from the car. These lyrics come from the 1939 song "Run Rabbbit Run" (Peele 27), performed by Flanagan and Allen, that centers on a farmer hunting a rabbit "every Friday" for "rabbit pie day." Viewers may largely be unfamiliar with this creepy-sounding tune; even so, its presence positions André as the hunted rabbit. André responds to the car parking beside him with a confused "Okay."[14] The racial dynamics of the moment slyly suggested by the scene's musical cues—a Black man as prey—clarify as he talks to himself, coaching, "All right, just keep on walking, brah. Don't do nothing stupid. Just keep on . . ." André makes the "them" versus "us" threat already established by his being in an all-white neighborhood explicit when he tells himself, "Not today. Not me. You know how *they* like to do motherfuckers out here, man. I'm gone" (emphasis added). This refusal to engage with the increasingly odd situation points to the dangers experienced by Black bodies in all-white spaces, as well as the ways that Black individuals must constantly negotiate this threat even at the most unexpected times. As André turns around to stare at the illuminated bright white car, doors open, red lights shining on the left of the screen in a stark contrast to André shrouded in darkness on the right. A person wearing a medieval-style iron mask exits the car, jumps out of the shadows, chokes him out until his body collapses, and stuffs him in the trunk as the refrains from "Run Rabbit Run" play louder. We later learn this is Jeremy Armitage (Caleb Landry Jones), Rose's brother, who is responsible for the family's more violent methods of accruing Black subjects. As we watch André's body crumple, unsure whether he survived the attack, we cannot escape the film's emphasis on the violence against Black bodies enacted by the hands of whiteness.

---

[14] All dialogue from *Get Out* is my transcription from the film. I referenced the authorized script, but the film dialogue and the script at times deviate. As such, all quotations, unless otherwise designated, come from the film, not the script.

The film reiterates this emphasis once again when André later reappears as Logan. Chris takes his picture in an act of recognition, for he identifies André and attempts to send photo evidence to Rod, the process momentarily liberating André from the sunken place. The camera briefly closes in on André's face, where his smiling eyes suddenly open wide in shock, as if abruptly awoken and startled. Peele's script in fact describes it as a shift from a "peaceful expression" to "maddened horror" (111). Whereas music drives André's first appearance in the film, immediately after Chris takes the photo, the film's score disappears so that all attention shifts toward André's awakening, during which his smile falls and lips tremble. As he momentarily transforms, he warns Chris, "Get out," first softly, then again loudly, yelling at Chris while charging toward him. He repeats his plea with urgency (which at this point seems like a menacing confrontation over an unwanted photo), screaming and pushing Chris as he does so. André must be dragged away, kicking and screaming. This moment likewise traumatizes the Black body, as signaled by the nosebleed that accompanies the look of recognition on his face and by the fact that as he screams, Jeremy, his captor, drags him off with his arms firmly encircling and therefore entrapping André's body. This pivotal scene, from which the film derives its title, suggests that once devastated by white hands, the Black body continuously struggles against further wounding, even as the Black self strives for recognition. This is Mbembe's death-in-life writ small, made achingly personal in André's devastated warning to Chris, and his heartbreaking return to Logan.

As André disappears from the film's narrative, Peele moves attention to Walter and Georgina, who likewise stress the seizure of and harm to Black bodies. Walter the gardener is actually Rose's grandfather, Roman Armitage, and his form bears the scars of the surgery as exposed when he removes his hat near the film's end. As the film's closing scenes speed toward *Get Out*'s climactic conclusion, Walter tackles Chris to the ground upon Rose declaring, "Get him, Grandpa." While Walter and Chris wrestle in the darkness of the forest-lined driveway, the low-angle close-up shot of Walter's face emphasizes the physical scar left by the coagula process. In desperation, Chris takes his picture. Once again, as happened with Logan/André, after the "click" of the camera phone, the soundtrack disappears so that total silence fills the moment as Walter's eyes similarly widen in a brief window of self-recognition. The real Walter emerges for a moment, though to viewers his identity is unclear initially when he asks Rose for the shotgun, stating, "Let me do it." Even as she hands the gun to him, the viewer cannot help but see the scar, evocative of Frankenstein's monster, which stretches across his forehead. Surprisingly, Walter turns the gun on Rose, shooting her in the abdomen. He then reloads and appears ready to shoot Chris, who is still in shock on the ground. Yet in a poignant moment, as the two men stare at each other face to face, Walter turns the shotgun he has only moments before fixed on Chris upon himself, shooting himself in the head. He destroys Roman's brain, which controls his body, but he must annihilate the only vestige of who he was in the process. Certainly, this moment can serve as a form of agency via suicide, a "preference for death over continued servitude," which "is a commentary on the nature of freedom itself (or lack thereof)" (Mbembe 91). I would argue, however, that Walter's suicide stresses his lack of freedom. In the world of *Get Out*, racialized violence begets a desperate personal violence, creating a circle of harm from which, the film suggests, the Black individual may be unable to escape.

Georgina, actually Rose's grandmother Marianne, also reminds the viewer of the physical devastation enacted on Black bodies. Her scar, her pressed, formal hair, and her elderly woman's attire all contrast with a photo Chris finds of the young woman, pre-surgery, posing with Rose; the selfie shows her with a Millennial pout, luscious natural curls, and contemporary clothes. All facets of her previous self have been stripped away, the hidden scar the only tell-tale sign. But perhaps most notable is the narrative insistence on her destruction. As Chris flees the Armitage's house, he crashes his car into her. Chris glances at her body on the ground, which triggers remembrances of his mother, who died alone, on the side of the road after being hit by a car when Chris was a boy. Viewers know this because there is a brief flashback to a scene of him watching television as a boy during a rainstorm, a scene that previously appeared in the movie when Chris discussed his mother's death. A second quick flashback follows the first, this one of the close-up of Georgina's tearful face when talking to Chris earlier in the film, which I will address further below. The juxtaposition of these two moments points to Chris's personal struggles, so that Georgina "symbolizes his mother and his mother's tears" (Peele n. 47, 176). Thus, for Chris, Georgina is not the white brain inside but rather the Black woman signaled by her physical appearance. Chris therefore sees hope for Black subjectivity despite its appropriation by whiteness.[15] As a result, he attempts to save

---

[15] I use "Black subjectivity" here to indicate that Chris holds out hope for the recovery of Georgina's Black inner self, that this woman can be more than simply the bodily object Marianne Armitage has appropriated.

her. His recognition of her potential Black selfhood juxtaposes with Rose, who exits the house declaring, "Grandma," indicating that for her, the white interior supersedes the woman's Black exterior. The camera returns to the car, where Georgina's wig slides off, thereby emphasizing the surgical scar marring her forehead. She revives, grabbing Chris and screaming, "You ruined my house!" Clearly, despite Chris's attempts, the eradication of the Black self who once inhabited the body next to him is complete. Peele suggests the futility of Chris's attempt through his musical choice, for after Chris hits Georgina and ponders whether to try and save her, "Run Rabbit Run" once again emanates from the car's radio. Through Georgina, then, the film comments on the ramifications of white domination over Black bodies. Once part of the coagula, the Black self becomes inaccessible and unrecoverable. As demonstrated through both Walter and Georgina, the only way to disrupt the Armitage's necropolitics is to destroy the Black body that houses the white self; the destruction of Blackness must be totalizing. This is the logical extreme of the violence Coates argues permeates the treatment of Black bodies and Black selves in America. As a broader framework, then, the coagula makes all viewers—those already cognizant and those woefully not so—hyperaware of the constant physical and metaphysical threat whiteness poses to Blackness.

In addition to stressing the corporeal and mental ramifications of the white appropriation of Black bodies, the coagula also demonstrates the white brain's overpowering nature, a literalization of the way that a white view of the world strives to govern Black experience. As discussed at length in Chapter 3, sociologist Joe R. Feagin calls this the "white racial frame": the "white worldview" dominant "throughout the country and, indeed, in much of the Western world" that through wide-ranging methods crafts "a strong positive orientation to whites and whiteness . . . and a strong negative orientation to racial 'others' who are exploited and oppressed" (3, 10).[16] Sociologist Eduardo Bonilla-Silva notes how "the frameworks of the dominant race tend to become the master frameworks upon which *all* racial actors

---

[16] Feagin's assertion about the white racial frame's prevalence opens up the possibility that one could apply the racial framing that *Get Out* provides for *Othello* to productions that do not directly use a US racial milieu. The wide reach of white supremacy also informed *Get Out*. Peele remarks, "I didn't want to go with a British actor ... because this movie was so much about representation of the African American experience. Early on, Daniel and I had a Skype session where we talked about this and I was made to understand how universal this issue is" (Anthony).

ground (for or against) their ideological positions," and in the US, this framework is white supremacy (9, 11). A confrontation between Chris and Georgina particularly communicates this white domination in a scene that Peele calls "one of the most dynamic scenes in the movie" (n. 47, 175). During the party, Chris tells Georgina: "All I know is sometimes, if there's too many white people, I get nervous, you know?" The camera turns to Georgina, framing her in a close-up shot just short of extreme with her eyes and smile wide. In this moment, Georgina's true self struggles to emerge. The shot's proximity to her face makes its appearance the focus so that the viewer clearly sees her smile fall slowly as her eyes well up with tears "as if there is a pain behind her otherwise vacant smile" (Peele 108). Georgina begins trembling and crying, never taking her eyes off Chris. It is a moment of pure silence, significant by association given that silence likewise accompanies André's and Walter's respective awakenings. She opens her mouth as if to speak, yet can only gasp in response. But the white Marianne's brain overcomes this temporary lapse, as signaled by the return of the oversized grin and the reintroduction of the film's score. Georgina responds, "No . . . no . . . no, no, no no no [10 times] . . . That's not my experience. Not at all." Upon first viewing, the repeated "nos" seem meant for Chris, but considered in light of the film's big reveal as well as the use of silence in this scene, these "nos" may be a message not just for Chris but also for the young woman whose body hosts Marianne's white mind. As Peele clarifies, "Grandma Armitage is pushing Georgina back down . . . So the 'Nos' mean two things: to Chris, to say 'there's nothing to worry about' and to the real Georgina to say 'get back in your Sunken Place.' The tear is Georgina's, but the words are Grandma Armitage's" (n. 48, 176). White control over the Black self may lapse for a moment, as suggested by the gasp that never fully actualizes into speech, but the dynamic here makes it clear that in the coagula, the white brain demands totalizing authority, thus embodying white supremacy's sociological dynamics.

A New Perspective: Reconsidering *Othello* via *Get Out*

As an indicator of the physical, mental, and sociological effects of white supremacy upon the Black self, the coagula provides a lens for reconsidering Othello's role as a Black man navigating the white-dominated Venetian society. For individuals creating modernized performances or other contemporary adaptations, this lens can help them more thoughtfully integrate issues of race by contemplating how "universal" themes such as jealousy and love have meanings contingent upon race. For those engaging with the play in more traditional forms, professors in the classroom or undertaking historically focused research for instance, making connections between *Get Out*'s coagula and *Othello* may seem more of a stretch given the very contemporary dynamics informing Peele's film. This distinction, however, can provide an interrogative opportunity rather than a methodological barrier. This is not to say that race and whiteness function in exactly the same ways during early modernity as they do in the movie. Yet as Peter Erickson and Kim F. Hall note, the early modern and the modern "are not two completely separate compartments to keep strictly disconnected" (6). Thus, placing *Othello* and *Get Out* in conversation with each other, or at least having the racial dynamics of the latter inform one's reading of the former, invites "cross-historical" tracing that might foster reflection upon what strategies for racial Othering may have been successful in the early modern period, and in *Othello* more specifically, even if there was not a precise vocabulary to define them.[17]

Despite differences in historical context, form, and narrative structure, one productive similarity between the film and the play is the way that, like Walter and Georgina, Othello too is deployed in the service of whiteness. Ambereen Dadabhoy stresses the dominating nature of this service, arguing, "His narrative enslavement 'by the insolent foe' and subsequent 'redemption' supposes his free-alien status in Venice, yet his commitment to Venice's imperial wars signals an obligation to the state that exceeds volunteer, or even paid, mercenary service. Venice, it seems, can (and does) deploy him with impunity" (Dadabhoy, "Two Faced" 13). Not only does Othello work for a coterie of all-white Venetians who order him at will, but as a Christianized Moor opposing the Turks, he also champions Christianity and its function as a force at once civilizing (for the converted) yet exclusionary (against the unconverted). In other words, because the play portrays a contest for power between Venetian Christians and Muslim Turks, landing on the side of the Christians, *Othello* concomitantly stresses the supremacy of whiteness through entrenched associations with Christianity. Janet Adelman's discussion of race and religion in *The Merchant of Venice* proves helpful here. She notes that as concerns

---

[17] One can make these cross-historical connections while keeping an eye toward "distinct ideas of race" (Erickson and Hall 6) such as, for example, the way race and religion function as significant contexts for *Othello* while that intersection does not appear in *Get Out*.

about Jessica's conversion come to the fore, the play "does so only by simultaneously reinstating the discourse of race" (13). Adelman comments on the way Salerio associates Shylock with "jet" and Jessica with "ivory" in order to "secure the difference between them," which is to say, the difference between Jew and potential Christian. While according to Adelman Salerio's religious and racial logic falls apart, her reading helpfully demonstrates that whether imagined as Christian versus Jew or Christian versus Turk, these religious distinctions function—even if only ideologically—across racialized lines: white versus not white. As Dennis Britton explains, Ethiopians, Moors, Turks, and Jews were "dually recognized in the early modern period as figures of alterity, which [were] made to stand for modes of experience and being that [were] foreign to normative white Christianity" (3). In his role as a soldier, then, Othello defends not just Venice, but along with it, whiteness as well. Moments of a more circumscribed significance likewise reveal the way Venetians perceive Othello as functioning for their purposes, perhaps most notably Brabantio, who welcomes Othello into his home to share tales of the foreign and exotic. Yet this welcome finds its limits when the threat of miscegenation looms. Thus, in civil and interpersonal contexts, Othello—like *Get Out*'s André, Walter, and Georgina—serves whiteness in both a literal and ideological sense.

While the terms of "service" may differ for Othello and the bodily proxies in *Get Out*, the resistance to it remains similar. Like Walter, Othello sees suicide as the only way to free himself from his entrapment by a white antagonist, in this case, Iago, but perhaps the Venetian state as well. Erickson, for example, reads Othello's closing speech as a denunciation of his service, his suicide an "[implicit rejection of] the entire racial formulation on which his career was based" so that, like Walter in *Get Out*, "At the cost of death, he takes back the power to define his own identity" (Erickson, "Images" 144). Re-reading the play's ending through the dynamics stressed by the coagula strengthens this interpretation. Suicide no longer functions as a generic feature of tragedy nor as a means for Othello to reclaim his honor. Rather, Othello's suicide becomes his confrontation of his racial marginalization by Iago and his strategic use by the white Venetian state.

In fact, such an understanding of Othello opens up the possibility of interpreting him as a Black man whose brain figuratively undergoes the coagula process of whitening his identity, only to grapple with the ramifications of that process in his final moments. Dadabhoy interprets Othello in precisely this way, arguing that "the duality of Othello's visage points to a psychological fairness belied by his somatic one" ("Two Faced" 122). Britton too stresses how "Venetian imperial interests necessitate an Othello who is 'more fair than black (1.3.291)'" (128). This progression of Othello's view of his selfhood often serves as the play's racial "saving grace," suggesting that the tragedy comments on the creation of racial self and Other in Othello's mind rather than working as a piece of racist propaganda. My claim here is not that this reading is new but rather that the concept of the coagula helps us see that this process is not necessarily sudden nor simply due to Iago. Admittedly, Iago serves as the predominant influence upon Othello at his most vulnerable point. As Dadabhoy posits, "'the Moor' that Othello becomes is Iago's creation" ("Two Faced" 140). However, the coagula indicates that Othello's perception of himself as Other has already been primed by the white-dominated society in which he lives and by, as Erickson notes, the discourse this society deploys, which stresses his Blackness amid their whiteness. In relation to *Get Out*, a distinction exists. Chris begins the film with racial self-awareness—as exemplified by his dubiousness that Rose's parents will accept his Blackness—while Othello expresses confidence at the outset that "My parts, my title, and my perfect soul/Shall manifest me rightly" (I, ii, 31, 32). But as the film makes clear, the coagula process privileges a white view of the world, which entails a marginalization of Black selfhood. This is precisely Othello's journey in the play, so much so that he disavows his own name—"That's he that was Othello. Here I am" (V, ii, 292)—becoming, like Walter, an unnamed entity traumatized by whiteness.

Get Out stresses the violence inflicted upon Black bodies as part of this process much more so than *Othello*. The concept of the coagula as presented in *Get Out* therefore reminds one that in a predominantly white society, the Black individual, though not technically a slave, is not truly free but rather constantly under potential threat. If applied to Othello, this dynamic can inform, to some degree, *why* Othello might believe Iago's assertions about Desdemona, despite the lack of firm evidence. Certainly, gender dynamics play a role here.[18] But so do racial ones. If, for example, a production can help audiences perceive Othello as living within a culture where white individuals consistently use Black bodies without discretion, and at

---

[18] Britton, for instance, argues that "The play seems to shift from racial to misogynist discourse in the gradual undoing of Othello" (135), and Arthur Little Jr. observes, "Othello is finally driven not only by his thievery but by his misogyny as he gives into those suspicions that a woman once raped, once stolen, will be eager to be again so violated" (*Shakespeare Jungle Fever* 88, 89).

the expense of Black selfhood, then his belief of Iago becomes more understandable. It is not that Iago is particularly trustworthy or convincing per se; rather, he confirms a truth Othello already knows not about Desdemona specifically but about the white world in which he resides: if one is not sufficiently white, then one cannot be integrated and is therefore expendable.

Microaggressions and Black Paranoia

In addition to providing a way of understanding Othello's relationship with the white society around him, *Get Out* can also help audiences garner insight into Othello's state of mind and his attendant vulnerability by directing attention to the persistent microaggressions that place stress upon Black identity, therefore priming it for white appropriation. Particularly important to *Get Out*'s effectiveness is its depiction of less obvious forms of racial exclusion, those which more likely mirror the day-to-day, and significantly, which implicate liberal white America—"the kind of people who pride themselves on their post-racial sensibilities"—in the oppression and Othering of Blackness (Anthony). In the film, a litany of seemingly small occurrences predominantly with white suburbanites remind Chris of his status as a Black man in a white society: a policeman asks for his license after an accident even though he was not driving; Dean, Rose's father, refers to Chris's romance with Rose as a "thang" and continuously calls him "my man"; Jeremy comments on his physical strength over dinner; at the party, the Greens discuss Tiger Woods with him, while later, Lisa squeezes his arm and pecs, asking, "Is it true . . . Is it [sex with a Black man] better?", and another guest references the fact that "Black [skin color] is in fashion." These occurrences exemplify the concept of microaggressions.

Derald Wing Sue explains that "Microaggressions are the everyday verbal, nonverbal, and environmental slights, snubs, or insults, whether intentional or unintentional, that communicate hostile, derogatory, or negative messages to target persons based solely upon their marginalized group membership" (3). In more philosophical terms, Mbembe names these "seemingly anodyne everyday gestures" *nanoracism* (58), a term encompassing "daily racist injuries" enacted by

> an institution, a voice, or a public or private authority, that asks them [the racial Other] to justify who they are, why they are here, where

they have come from, where they are going, why they do not go back to where they come from, that is, a voice or authority that deliberately seeks to occasion in them a large or small jolt, to irritate them, to upset them, to insult them, to get them to lose their cool precisely so as to have a pretext to violate them, to unceremoniously undermine that which is most private, most intimate, and vulnerable in them. (58, 59)

Both Mbembe and Sue note how these behaviors are perpetual and often subtle, though they differ in the degree of intentionality they ascribe, for Mbembe sees nanoracism as a deliberate strategy for exclusion while Sue notes that microaggressions are more often than not enacted subconsciously. According to Sue, microaggressions become difficult to identify and confront due to "their invisibility to perpetrators and oftentimes the recipients" (6). Microaggressions can take three forms: those that articulate conscious bias (microassaults), those that unconsciously insult a person's identity (microinsults), and those that invalidate a person's thoughts, feelings, and beliefs (microinvalidations) (8–9). With this context in mind, one can see that Chris experiences all three forms of microaggressions. Whether coming from the Armitages or their friends, these microaggressions marginalize Chris, reminding him of his Blackness while fetishizing it.

Moreover, regardless of the particular form they take, these microaggressions frequently appear in the guise of compliments, precisely the articulation Sue identifies as most common for microaggressions (9). This complimentary articulation draws attention to the individuals enacting these microaggressions—wealthy, elite whites who populate the Armitages' party. According to Rose, her family, at the very least, is liberal; her father would have voted for Obama three times, she explains in order to quell Chris's fears about her parents' potential racial prejudice. But even as the Armitages attempt to keep up their liberal façade, they cannot help but enact microaggressions against Chris, thereby revealing the divisive racial thinking that ideologically allows them to take their appropriative use of Black bodies to the extreme. Peele articulates his interest in shining a spotlight on precisely this population. "The liberal elite who communicates that we're not racist in any way is as much of the problem as anything else. This movie is about the lack of acknowledgment that racism exists," he notes (Zinoman). These occurrences therefore serve two purposes. They point to liberal white America's complicity in reenacting and further entrenching racial hierarchies that they supposedly abhor yet that maintain the racial status quo of white supremacy.

At the same time, they exemplify how microaggressions work *and* their constant presence, a presence with psychological and physiological implications.

Analyzing how *Get Out* deploys microaggressions reveals Peele's attention to their overwhelming effect upon the marginalized person. Peele has Chris move from one racial conversation to the next during the fete, so that while he can smile away the initial reference to Tiger Woods, by the time the guest references Black skin, his stony face signals that he has had enough. For Chris, these microaggressions coupled with the moment where Logan warns "Get out" push him to ask Rose that they leave her parents' house. Microaggressions "can signal a hostile or invalidating climate that threatens the physical and emotional safety of the devalued group" (Sue 15, 16), which is precisely what happens to Chris. Even within the party's short time frame, the film vividly expresses the mental toll microaggressions take upon their recipients, thereby creating "the thesis of the movie . . . connecting the dots between the subtlest forms of microaggression to the most violent, unimaginable racial violence" (Peele n. 35, 174). Sue notes how microaggressions create four different kinds of stressful effects: biological and physical (e.g. increased stress and heart problems), emotional (e.g. depression and mental health issues), cognitive (e.g. stereotype threat or disrupted cognition), and behavioral (e.g. aggression and hypervigilance) (15, 16). Of all the effects Peele stresses, the most obvious for Chris is what Sue characterizes as "suspiciousness toward the majority group," or stated differently, paranoia, in Chris's case, toward whiteness (16). The film in fact invites reflection on the justifiable nature of Black paranoia through Rod, whose admonitions that Chris has been kidnapped by a white family appear paranoid to the cops he attempts to report to but instead come across as prescient to the viewer. Thus, the paranoia fostered in Chris by the party proves to be an intense instantiation of the mistrust Black individuals must grapple with daily amid the dominance of whiteness, a suspicion, the film suggests, that is not only understandable but also crucial for protecting the physical and mental Black self continuously under threat.

The way racial microaggressions contextualize Black paranoia provides a means of better comprehending Othello's mental state. Indeed, Erickson's discussion of the racialized language in *Othello* noted above echoes the dynamics of microaggressions. But before reconsidering the implications of the Duke's and Desdemona's respective racial assertions, it bears revisiting some of the more explicitly racist language in the play in order to consider its contribution toward

Othello's state of mind as the tragedy advances. While audiences or readers experience Iago's and Roderigo's racist diatribes first, Othello does not face racialized language directly until confronted by Brabantio. Iago has already primed Othello by emphasizing the "scurvy and provoking terms/Against your honor" that Brabantio has supposedly deployed (I, ii, 7, 8). Even as these lines stress Iago's perfidy, they also signal how Othello must negotiate his racial difference from his introduction. Almost immediately, Othello experiences a direct microinsult from Brabantio as the seething father denigrates Othello for his marriage to Desdemona. Brabantio's invective against Othello begins with terms not racial in and of themselves as he castigates Othello by declaring him a "foul thief" and "Damned as thou art" (I, ii, 63, 64). By the time Brabantio notes that Desdemona rejected "wealthy curled darlings of our nation" for Othello's "sooty bosom," his argument turns into a microassault, for his speech exposes his bias *against* Othello precisely because Brabantio devalues Othello's social positionality due to his racial Otherness (I, ii, 69, 71). Carol Mejia LaPerle observes how this moment "articulates the expected emotional response to darkened skin," one of a number of instances on the early modern stage "grounded in a powerful cultural memory that associated scorn and suspicion with begrimed, pigmented characters. Thus, conventional curses turn into something else: instruction for how physical difference is to be perceived, especially in a genre [tragedy] of fraught, grim encounters" ("Race" 79). In response to this racialized curse, Othello expresses confidence in his "services which I have done the seigniory," and in doing so, suggests his integration in Venetian society via his role as one of its foremost martial protectors (I, ii, 18). Yet Brabantio attempts to dismantle this integration by contrasting Othello with the men of "our nation." It is the language of nationhood before nationhood fully flourished, the "our" implying an excluded "you," an unsurprising tactic given that, as Arthur Little Jr. explains, "In the self-preserving instinct of Shakespeare's Venice or Shakespeare's England, a white woman's marrying a black man . . . amounts to nothing less than a violation of national proportions" (*Shakespeare Jungle Fever* 87). As the logic of Brabantio's berating of Othello makes clear, the "our" here encompasses him and Desdemona, and perhaps even the officers of the state called to bring Othello to the Duke; it does not, however, include Othello. Brabantio's speech in fact prefigures what will become a prominent colonizing dynamic in which those with political power objectify the racial Other in order to reify that very power. As Aimé Césaire famously theorizes: "colonization = 'thingification'" (42). This explains the objectifying nature of Brabantio's speech, where in comparison to the "darlings" of Venice, Othello only merits the status of "a *thing* as thou" (emphasis added). By using the familiar "thou" following "thing," Brabantio is clearly not signaling intimacy but rather attempting to discursively solidify his superiority in relation to Othello. Though Othello depends on his rank within Venice for status, Brabantio deploys language to reassert the social hierarchy he believes Othello has challenged. Brabantio's microassault reveals that his bias against Othello marrying his daughter derives not from the potentially dishonorable act of elopement itself but instead because of Othello's secondary status as a "sooty . . . thing." As a result, Brabantio must reassert that marginalization through his demeaning, objectifying discourse.

In addition to revealing that Othello experiences a microassault directly, this moment also indicates that as much as Othello may *seem* integrated into Venetian society, this integration always rests on uneasy ground, one easily disrupted by any misstep that challenges the white-dominated status quo. Just as importantly, this interchange also ties Desdemona's affections to Othello's positionality within Venetian society, both of which Brabantio characterizes as shifting and easily changeable. Thus, it is not difficult to suggest that in this moment we see the genesis of Othello's paranoia, for this is the very argumentation, even some of the very lines, Iago uses in III, iii that cause Othello to shift from a man unbothered by other men's praise of his wife to a man consumed by the "green-eyed monster" (III, iii, 180). Put differently, Brabantio's microassault not only places Othello in a mental and social position of stress as he publicly rails against the elopement, but it also creates the suspicion and racial self-doubt upon which Iago will so insidiously capitalize.

Brabantio's microassault serves as the most extreme version of the comments that appear in the Duke's presence as the Venetians confront the Turkish threat and Othello's marriage. In other words, the binaries that Brabantio's speech establishes for Othello between Black and white, Other and Venetian, unworthy thing and person worthy of affection, unnatural and natural, become mirrored in less virulent ways during I, iii. As such, microinsults pair with this microassault to create a series of contiguous moments, where, like Chris, Othello must grapple with microaggressions. Erickson helpfully reminds us that because the play opens with Iago's and Roderigo's virulent racist language, "we are in danger of seeing this vicious rhetoric as the whole story of race in the play" (Erickson, "Images" 137). Yet even the discourse of "'positive'" characters such as Desdemona and the Duke demonstrates "subtle versions of prejudice along a spectrum of prejudicial white views" (137), or to use Sue's framing, microinsults that expose an unconscious bias, in this case, against Blackness.

Paying careful attention to the Duke's and Desdemona's respective comments mirrors *Get Out*'s aforementioned focus on the racial formulations articulated by those that, at least on the surface, seem progressive about racial difference, such as the Armitages. The Duke and Desdemona are by no means the Armitages. Even so, their articulations of racial difference also bear scrutiny, for as Sue explains, microaggressions arise even more commonly from unconscious bias, a dynamic present in both the Duke's and Desdemona's comments about Othello, which follow Brabantio's very public microassault against him.

In his well-known declaration that Othello is "far more fair than black," for example, the Duke leaves ambiguity about how to interpret his meaning, for even as he praises Othello, the logic of his rhetoric makes it so that "acceptance is contingent on overlooking or sidestepping the outer blackness" (Erickson, "Images" 139). Similarly, Erickson explains, Desdemona's claim that she saw Othello's "visage in his mind" makes his Blackness "an awkward problem" (140). Desdemona speaks these lines when addressing how she would like to respond to Othello's call to Cyprus. She means her speech to communicate her sincere love for Othello, and thus her desire to "Let me go with him" (I, iii, 261). To make her case, she enumerates that her heart belongs to Othello due to his honor, qualities, and personal virtues. But for whatever reason, these qualities do not appear on his literal visage. In this moment, Desdemona subtly invokes the occult practice of physiognomy, which involved "reading" bodily features—particularly the face—in order to discern a person's character (Corredera, "Faces"). Desdemona suggests that Othello's face does not function physiognomically; it does not appropriately communicate his innermost qualities, which is why she had to turn to the "visage in his mind." A discrepancy between character and physical appearance was a common point of contention in physiognomic treatises, with many physiognomic tracts discussing famous philosophers, such as Socrates, whose visages likewise seemed to express their inner selves inadequately. As these arguments go, Socrates responded that physiognomy *did* work, for his wretched visage communicated who he *would be* without extreme self-control. With Othello, however, the issue is not how ugly he is; rather, what makes his visage fail him is his Blackness, which is why Desdemona must turn to his mind to see his true character reflected. Thus, both the Duke's and Desdemona's seeming moments of praise for Othello depend on a denigration of his Blackness, a denigration that echoes what Brabantio articulated when confronting Othello at the Saggitary.[19] These are, then, insults passed off as compliments, microinsults reflecting similar yet less obvious biases as those embedded in Brabantio's more blatant racist claims.

If read in this way, these moments help disrupt the version of *Othello* where the "savage" overtakes the "noble Moor's" better nature. Or, to use the language of physiognomy, it is not that Othello loses self-control so that the savage "true self" indicated by his Black visage ultimately appears. Instead, these microaggressions point to the real, repeated, racial stress imposed upon Othello, stress known to disrupt cognition, create paranoia, and foster anger and aggression. Little Jr. argues that "the presence of Othello's self depends (in the play and in criticism) on the success of culture to render invisible itself and its 'racialist ideology.' It depends, finally, on the ability to accuse Othello the man rather than the culture than damns him from the start" (Little Jr., *Shakespeare Jungle Fever* 75). Reading, discussing, and reinterpreting *Othello* through the context of microaggressions makes visible this hidden role of racist culture, for it suggests that the fault does not reside with the supposedly animalistic racial self lurking just under the "noble Moor's" surface; instead, the fault lies with, at least in significant part, a white society that enacts various forms of microaggressions upon Othello, actions that in turn place the one Black man in its midst under constant strain through its conscious and unconscious marginalization of him.

Conclusion: *Othello* and the Sunken Place

Thus, from highlighting the violent appropriation of Black bodies by whiteness to emphasizing the white racial frame to stressing the insidiousness of microaggressions, rereading *Othello* through the racial dynamics emphasized in *Get Out* reorients how audiences—scholars, educators, students, directors, actors, myriad future adaptors—might perceive of race's role in Othello's tragic downfall. With a beautiful, often petite, blonde, young white woman lying suffocated on the bed, it can be difficult to remember that this play is not only Desdemona's tragedy, for "In drama's fixation on emotional pitch, the dead white woman as 'monumental alabaster' is the pinnacle of pathos" (LaPerle, "Race" 85). In fact, the public sympathy for white femininity is so

---

[19] For a discussion of race and early modern physiognomy, see Vanessa Corredera, "Complex Complexions: The Facial Signification of the Black Other in *Lust's Dominion*," in *Shakespeare and the Power of the Face*, ed. James A. Knapp (Ashgate, 2015), 93–114.

strong that it even shapes responses to *Get Out*, in which Rose directly abuses Chris. Numerous moments in the film make clear Rose's full participation in the Armitage family's scheme, including a scene that particularly exposes her nefarious character. As Chris attempts to flee the house, Rose sits cross-legged on her bed listening to the 1987 song made famous by the film *Dirty Dancing*, "(I've Had) The Time of My Life." The low-angle shot reveals that behind her, she has placed a series of photos from victims she previously lured to her home. Dressed in a white shirt and khakis in front of her trophy wall, Rose is a pith helmet shy of depicting the quintessential colonizer of Africa. She eats fruit loops out of a bowl while drinking milk from a glass as she surfs the internet to find her next victim, as indicated when she types in "Top NCAA Prospects." The details of this scene work together to stress Rose's complicity in the racial abuse of her home. Her clothes signal her affinity for whiteness and white purity, as does the fact that she refuses to mix the "white" milk with "colored" fruit loops so as not to adulterate it. The song choice communicates that no one has forced Rose; she is not hypnotized; rather, she has been having the time of her life entrapping a series of Black victims. Actress Allison Williams explains that during the film's promotional tour, despite scenes such as this, people repeatedly tried to justify Rose's actions, and that those justifications were divided along racial lines:

> They'd say "she was hypnotized, right?" And I'm like, no! She's just evil! How hard is that to accept? She's bad! We gave you so many ways to know that she's bad! She has photos of people whose lives she ended behind her! [. . .] And they're still like, "but maybe she's also a victim?" And I'm like, NO! No! And I will say, that is one hundred percent white people who say that to me. (*Late Night with Seth Meyers*)

Audiences' potential desire to sympathize with Rose and wish for her to meet a fate different from her family's inheres in the film itself, for Chris begins strangling her but as Brooks observes, "he is unable to put an end to his white temptress" ("What Becky").[20] If Chris

---

[20] This raises the question for Brooks, "Why not?" She argues that Peele's editorial decisions "show that white women are still valued as fragile and occupy a unique cultural privilege . . . even in the blackest horror film of this decade" ("What Becky"). A less critical reading might be that Peele attempts to avoid having Chris fall into the stereotype of the Black buck that threatens white femininity, a stereotype the film in fact references, according to John Jennings, when Chris kills Dean Armitage by skewering him with a stuffed and mounted buck's head. For more on the Black buck stereotype and Othello, see Vanessa Corredera, "Far More Black than Black: Stereotypes, Black Masculinity, and Americanization in Tim Blake Nelson's O," *Literature/Film Quarterly* 45.3 (2017): n.p.

somewhat pardons Rose, then audiences may want to as well. And if white audiences strive to excuse Rose's behavior despite her participation in the Armitages' house of horrors, then one can see why Desdemona's plight would be even more affecting. *Get Out*'s reception thus reveals the challenges inherent in any narrative undertaking a visceral exploration of white supremacy.

Yet the film's overwhelming financial and critical success, as well as its indelible contributions to current discussions of race, indicates that just as people can recognize Chris's tragedy, they may also be able to identify Othello's. The struggle, however, is to position the tragedy as something other than Othello's "savage" fall from white grace. Through its representation of the coagula, *Get Out* provides an alternative narrative that can be incorporated into interpretations of Othello, both the protagonist and the play. This narrative opens up the possibility for those in charge of wide-reaching spaces like the classroom, the stage, or televisual media to deploy *Othello* as a tool for ethical racial representation. For, interpreted through the racial dynamics highlighted by *Get Out*, *Othello*'s racial tragedy is the annihilation of Black selfhood at the hands of a white society that destroys Black subjectivity, both knowingly and unknowingly. This reading prompts white individuals to question their complicity in similar systems, while Black individuals can see their struggles against domination and appropriation recognized by the authorizing force of Shakespeare. This attention to Othello's personal tragedy does not take away from the dreadfulness of Desdemona's murder. She is not Rose Armitage, after all. But it does raise one's awareness of the cost of white supremacy for and its effects upon Othello. Responsibility can thereby land not just on Othello and perhaps Iago, but more broadly on the culture that produces the very conditions that allow Iago to successfully foster the racialized thinking and attendant paranoia that eventually overtake Othello.

This discussion of *Othello* reconsidered via the coagula, that is to say, through the trappings of horror films themselves newly imagined in order to comment on race, prompts the question: even if one were to reconceive of *Othello* through the framing of the coagula, what would that mean for the process of reanimating the play? This leads to another of *Get Out*'s central concepts: the sunken place. When Chris falls into the sunken place, viewers see him floating in a black space, as if having an out-of-body experience, staring up at a square the shape of a television screen, looking at the white face hypnotizing him. According to Peele, the sunken place represents "the system that silences the voice of women, minorities, and of other people"

(Ramos 2018), as well as "the lack of representation of black people in film, in genre" (Sharf 2017). How might *Othello* suffer from the sunken place, from systems of silencing and limited representation? More pointedly, how have the dominance of white producers, directors, and audiences that influence and craft the play's representation on stage and film, as well as the white-dominated professoriate who does not "speak" for Othello, as Ian Smith so movingly argues ("We Are Othello" 107–09), limited the interpretation and depiction of race's role in the play? Peele created a transformative artwork because as a Black director and screenwriter, he "[asked] a white person to see the world through the eyes of a black person for an hour and a half" (Zinoman 2017). Here, we once again see the importance of perspective. This is not simply about telling a "Black" story but rather about telling one in a way that privileges a point of view other than the white male cisgendered one so prominent across American culture and its media. In other words, Peele rejected the universal in favor of the particular. Perhaps, then, understanding *Othello* anew means rejecting the idea of universal Shakespeare so critiqued by Key and Peele's sketch, for as they suggest, a universal Shakespeare is actually often a white Shakespeare simply and falsely positioned as raceless. But who are the forces reanimating *Othello*, and are these forces perceiving the play through "the eyes of a black person," through Othello's eyes? The framework provided by *Get Out* demonstrates the power of a very similar story understood through a very different racial point of view; at the same time, it spotlights the importance of a voice willing to advance that retelling.

Those of us who study, write on, and teach Shakespeare can collectively work to be part of that voice. As we continue to consider not just *Othello* but also the ways that Shakespeare can more broadly speak to issues of race and social justice, it behooves us to reject Shakespearean universality. We must instead evaluate the perspectives used to both discuss and represent this well-known play, and to ponder how we can dislodge *Othello* from the sunken place in which it has resided for so long. But this call does not stop with *Othello*. Those of us who study and teach stories understand particularly well their affective power and wide reach. As such, we must challenge ourselves to resist complacency. As the Morrison epigraph opening this chapter makes clear, whether found in a television show, film, play, or novel, a universal, raceless narrative is lobotomized literature: an incomplete, simplified product, one not all that dissimilar from the creations crafted through the Armitages' coagula process. Returning to questions posed at the start of this chapter, how much longer are we willing to allow a limited yet supposedly universal point of view hold sway—one gendered and racialized but expressly made not to seem so? When and how do we start demanding different stories or allowing stories from a unique perspective? I want to revisit the series of questions Hornaday posed in response to #OscarsSoWhite. She notes, "everyone has been invited to adopt a critically engaged vision of what audiences heretofore accepted as 'neutral' entertainment, whether that means questioning a movie whose hero is yet another Man on a Mission, raising a skeptical eyebrow when a filmmaker confuses 'universal' with 'white,' or wondering why all female roles in a movie are merely decorative rather than substantive, dynamic, and fully realized." Are scholars of literature and culture making the same invitation? We sit in a position where we influence future storytellers just like Peele, as Keith Hamilton Cobb so movingly stages in *American Moor* (Chapter 4). What foundations have we provided these storytellers as they create narrative perspectives? The claim to universality is appealing because it becomes an easy shorthand to explain the purpose and significance of humanities scholarship, especially literary studies. But instead, in a nation (indeed nations) struggling with the racial divisions caused when the universal dominance of whiteness and its centrality are seen and therefore challenged, we are called to the much more difficult work of asking our various audiences—students, administrators, colleagues, institutions—to see through and relate to the perspective of unique, different, and distinctly specific eyes. What we have to offer, then, is not universality but rather the tools to negotiate plurality, not perfectly but productively, so as to transform old narratives—such as *Othello* into *Shafte* or *Get Out*—into new, diverse, more ethical ones.

Epilogue

"Come Desdemona, Othello and tragedies/Shakespearean sorrows, where do I begin/(Where do we begin?)"
—"Child's Play," SZA

While this book takes up some of the most prominent *Othello*s in post-racial America, other *Othello*-esque works remain to be considered both within and outside of the post-racial American context through which I frame my analysis. Given that the white/black moral binary extends into the post-racial world, often in association with gender, what resonances exist when Frank Ocean raps in his 2016 song "Nikes," "Said she need a ring like Carmelo/Must be on that white like Othello/All you want is Nikes"? Might *Othello* be as equally compelling an intertext for the 2016 FX series *The People v. OJ Simpson: An American Crime Story* as the media made it for the original 1995 trial? How might the consideration in *Reanimating Shakespeare's Othello in Post-Racial America* of stereotypes, Black masculinity, and *Othello* inform an analysis of the BBC series *Luther*'s (2010) first season, where Idris Elba plays a brilliant Afro-British detective with a volatile personality accused of murdering his not-white-yet-still-lighter-skinned wife, Zoe (Indira Varma)? Can the relationship between *Othello*, prestige, authority, whiteness, and American theatre help one make meaning of the otherwise nonsensical 2013 indie film *OJ: The Musical*, where the white artist Eugene Olivier (Jordan Kenneth Kamp) leaves NYC and his Broadway success to return to his hometown in Ohio to stage an OJ Simpson musical based on *Othello*? What to make of British band Bastille's single "Send Them Off!" (2016), which white lead singer Dan Smith tweeted "is *Othello* meets the *Exorcist*" (Topham) and has him lamenting, "Desdemona, won't you liberate me/When I'm haunted by your ancient history"? And what might we learn from cultural artifacts that, following Kristin N. Denslow's theorization, meme-ify *Othello*, "not—for whatever reason—mak[ing] explicit (or perhaps recogniz[ing] at all) the associations" with the play by "refrain[ing], nearly studiously, from citing the play itself" (98)? I raise these questions because they gesture toward the way *Othello*'s presence lingers across Western culture with a ubiquity that dramas like *King John* or *A Comedy of Errors* do not. In other words, these questions signal how *Othello* persists, in spite of its toxicity, in spite of the mental and emotional harm it causes actors who must embody the "Moor of Venice" (even in modernized contexts), in spite of how easy it is for reanimations of this play to circulate caricatures of Black identity that are most often left to artists of color, particularly Black artists, to contest.

In fact, novels such as Nicole Galland's *I, Iago* (2012), David Snodin's *Iago: A Novel* (2012), or Christopher Moore's *The Serpent of Venice* (2014) indicate that rather than challenging Othello's historically atavistic depictions on page and stage, reanimations instead frequently signal their distance from Shakespeare's "original" text by speaking for Iago rather than the play's maligned protagonist. They make this choice despite the fact that Othello already speaks less in the early modern tragedy and has been less spoken for in both the scholarly and cultural afterlife of this (in)famous Shakespearean race play. Douglas M. Lanier observes the tendency for contemporary authors to make up for the literariness supposedly lost in their eschewing of Shakespeare's language by "flesh[ing] out the protagonists' psychologies, providing them with extensive backstories and explicit chains of motivation that make their behavior plausible (and suitably complicated) for the reader well-versed in contemporary psychoanalysis" ("The Hogarth" 238). This is precisely the approach taken in these Iago-focused reanimations, with artistic authority derived from turning to a point of view already stressed in Shakespeare, rewriting it so as to garner audience sympathy or provide otherwise absent motivation. Still missing from most reanimations of *Othello* is thus a perspective willing to center Othello and the role race plays in shaping his downfall. In other words, still missing is a preponderance of voices ready, willing, and able to speak for Othello.

To bring together the various pressures that prevent speaking for Othello, but also to offer up potential solutions, this Epilogue takes various turns. First, I briefly address one final example that demonstrates just how easily *Othello* can be utilized to advance a supposedly universal yet distinctly white perspective instead of a Black one that at times manifests—as Keith Hamilton Cobb's, Toni

Morrison's, and Keegan-Michael Key's and Jordan Peele's respective works illustrate—but more often than not remains absent from *Othello*'s retellings: Tracy Chevalier's novel *New Boy* (2017). I then situate Chevalier's colorblind narrative approach within the broader cultural desire for racial innocence, which I explore by placing the January 6, 2021 insurrection in conversation with *Othello*'s surprising absence in post-post-racial America. Finally, I conclude with five suggestions crafted to rectify the antiblack and reify the antiracist frames my six chapters explore. I intend these propositions as a starting point for contemplating various strategies that can assist those seeking to speak through and for Othello.

New Boy was commissioned as part of the Hogarth Shakespeare series, which was announced in 2014 and timed to be released with celebrations honoring the 400th anniversary of Shakespeare's death in 2016, "even though its publication schedule extends well beyond that time" (Lanier, "The Hogarth" 230). In his analysis of the first four novels comprising the series, Lanier argues that the updated milieus of the Hogarth Shakespearean "retellings" allow scholars to "reflect on the nature of Shakespearean transpositions, the affordances and pleasures it provides, the varied motives it serves, the aesthetic challenges it raises, and the ideological possibilities it fulfills and occludes" ("The Hogarth" 234). I want to shine a light on Chevalier's own comments about her engagement with *Othello* to illuminate the last of the reflections Lanier catalogs, the ideological possibilities Chevalier's novel fulfills and occludes through its reanimation of *Othello*. In short, her comments reveal just how easy it is for those who tackle the play *not* to speak for the titular character.

In many ways, the concerns articulated by the first half of this book reappear and coalesce in Chevalier's novel, thereby signaling the deeply entrenched facets of America's racial habitus that inform very different types of works—novels, comics, performances, visual media—but nevertheless result in a similar outcome: white-centered and therefore antiblack reanimations of *Othello*. Take, for instance, Chevalier's invocation of Shakespearean universality as a frame for undertaking *New Boy*. In an addendum to the novel entitled "A Conversation with Tracy Chevalier," she observes that "*Othello*'s themes of jealousy and discrimination are universal and tantalizing" (214). Granted, her comment is not the same as claiming that Shakespeare's oeuvre is universal. However, it is telling that she singles out "jealousy" and "discrimination" broadly understood as the universal themes. Why not mention race as universal? Perhaps because she is ignoring whiteness as raced. Indeed, Chevalier's comments suggest a desire to "have it both ways," at times seeing race while at other times preferring a post-racial colorblind approach. For example, when Chevalier discusses "what it is like to be different from those around you," she mentions "skin color, religion, age, accent, size, shape, gender, or whatever . . ." (218). Her reference to "skin color" here stands in for race, allowing her to avoid the actual term. Moreover, the concept, if not the word, gets lumped together in a list of other forms of difference, important ones, yes, but perhaps not all as essential to *Othello* as the former. On the surface, such a rhetorical and ideological move may not seem antiblack, especially when compared with other examples of Othello's misrepresentations I have examined here. I contend, however, that any version of *Othello* refusing to engage with the power dynamics shaping Othello's status as the only Black person in an otherwise all-white society is antiblack in its diminishment of how racial prejudice marginalizes Othello within Venice.

In contrast, there are instances when Chevalier does address *race* directly; however, like *Serial*'s Sarah Koenig (Chapter 3), she approaches the topic by focusing on herself rather than on racial injustice. For example, despite setting the book in 1970s Washington, DC, she does not mention any racial unrest in the US capital during that time. Rather, she divulges that "in thinking about the themes of *Othello*—namely the idea of the outsider—I was reminded of my own childhood. I had an unusual experience, in that I lived in an integrated neighborhood and went to a school that was mostly black. I often felt different, though it was not always about race" (217). The story of a Black general racially abused by his seemingly closest friend becomes, for Chevalier, analogous to her experience as a white girl in an integrated neighborhood. Chevalier provides another biographical anecdote to explain her interest in this particular story. Like Othello, she knows what it feels like to be an "outsider" because "I am a bit of an outsider myself—I grew up in the United States and moved to Britain when I was twenty-two. Over thirty years later, I still have an American accent and am still treated like a foreigner" (214). I press on Chevalier's revelations not to diminish her past but rather to expose how, in an epistemic verification similar to Koenig's in *Serial*, she stresses the primacy of her personal, affective experiences, making them equivalent to Othello's. Through *Othello*, she thus speaks for herself and her history, which she imagines in some ways as universal given that "we have all felt out of it, and sensed people treating us as different" (218), instead of trying to speak for Othello's particular pain, history, and story. It might therefore be unsurprising to learn that the novel begins and ends not with the Ghanaian Osei's (the Othello character) voice and perspective, but rather with the character most reflective of Chevalier, the eleven-year-old American and white Dee, the novel's Desdemona. This decision thereby makes a novel which should be stressing Osei's voice align with the series' overall structure in which "By and large the protagonists . . . are white and straight" (Lanier, "The Hogarth" 234).[1]

Perhaps without realizing it, Chevalier reveals just how little effort went into trying to speak for Othello. While "Normally I do months of research before I start writing," for *New Boy*, she visited the British Library and "After two days I was done and thought: Now what should I research? And I realized there was nothing to research; I just had to start" (215). One wonders why *Othello*'s performance history, understandings of race in premodernity, or even an immersion into race and racial inequity in her chosen era and setting did not merit the same two-month investigative commitment as her other works. Moreover, when discussing how she crafted *New Boy*'s characters, Chevalier recounts, "With the differences between the characters—race, age, gender—I try not to think too much about those obvious differences, but focus more on the differences of personality, of character" (217). Chevalier thereby mentions *race* only to disavow it. In doing so, she once again raises a perplexing question that she does not answer: how is it that social positionings based on race, age, and gender do not shape personality? By evading any attempt to provide answers to these queries, Chevalier makes it appear as if Othello's story does not merit the same effort as her previous projects. And as a result, she suggests, even if unintentionally, that understanding the particularity of Othello's Black perspective is likewise not worth undertaking.

Ian Smith's sage point is therefore well taken. People may not speak for Othello because they do not see themselves in him ("We Are Othello" 106–09). But Chevalier's engagement with *Othello*

---

[1] Lanier further remarks of this narrow artistic focus, "Most notably the protagonists of the Hogarth series so far hail from roughly the same social stratum; they are from the middle to upper middle class, college-educated professionals, engaged in intellectual labor. Since this appears to be the target readership of the series, the project seems open to criticism that the series remakes Shakespeare in the image of its audience or, more trenchantly, that it recuperates a particular version of Shakespeare (spiced up with certain elements of ethnic and sexual diversity) at a moment when global adaptation has offered us a more capacious notion of what Shakespeare might mean and how his tales might be relevant to different cultural contexts" ("The Hogarth" 234).

suggests that identification is not enough. I am not trying to launch an ad hominem attack on Chevalier. Rather, I critique her to illustrate that seeing oneself in Othello is simply a first yet insufficient step. If one brings a white-focused racial habitus to bear upon the play, as so often happens, and if one is unwilling to put labor into reimagining *Othello*, as Chevalier did not, then even works with the latitude for radically reimagining Shakespeare produce just one more antiblack version of both Othello and the play itself. This depiction of Othello stretches back to premodernity, up and through post-racial America, and without broadly undertaken change, likely endures in the post-post-racial present.

Chevalier's silence on race, so typical of the *Othello* "canon," triggers a broader question: what does *Othello* in America look like in the wake of Donald J. Trump's white supremacist presidency and the culture wars it restoked? Interestingly, *Othello* seems to have receded in artistic attention, at least for the moment. While some reanimations of *Othello* remain, such as Debra Ann Byrd's *Becoming Othello: A Black Girl's Journey*, by and large, despite its long-standing omnipresence, *Othello* is, perhaps surprisingly, not the text to which theatres nor television and filmmakers are turning to currently. And the play's absence in this precise historical moment says as much about race today as its presence in other epochs speaks to conceptualizations of race and racial inequities in those eras. In the summer of 2020, as I watched my television and computer screens in awe as antiracist protests broke out across the world in the wake of George Floyd's tragic murder, I felt a spark of hope that these protests would help usher in a time of true, revolutionary antiracist transformation. Following these moments, some ill-advised Shakespeareans swiftly wrote op-eds exploring how Shakespeare could speak to such antiracist efforts. I was working on this book, and I wondered whether *Othello* would be trotted out as the Shakespearean response to the given racial moment. The global COVID-19 pandemic, which closed theatres across the world, thwarted the potential for such wholesale endeavors. A year later, as theatres hopefully announce their 2021–22 seasons, there is nary an *Othello* in sight. In many ways, I am glad because, despite my longing to see *Becoming Othello*, overall, my research makes me wary, even cynical, about most of the artistic outcomes that would result from reanimating this play once more. At the same time, however, I question whether the structures upholding the Shakespeare system (Sayet) are eager to simply ignore the antiracist reverberations of summer 2020 by eschewing the potential divisiveness of *Othello*, especially as culture wars about race ignite both tacitly and expressly in debates about "cancel culture," Critical Race Theory, and "wokeness." Might institutions cracking under the financial pressures created by a year of lockdowns instead desire to turn audience attention to an uncomplicated celebration of America's grand, (supposedly) post-COVID reopening, a time seemingly far removed from the trauma that recognizing persistent antiblackness would bring to the fore?

It may seem that I want it both ways—*Othello* not to be deployed as a Shakespearean response to global antiblackness yet ready with a critique when *Othello* does not appear. Let me thus be very clear about what I *do* want: I desire the time, space, courage, support, and overall artistic and cultural investment in making certain that the future of this play, what will eventually become its cultural history, is an imaginative, daring, courageous, antiracist one where those who engage with it bravely leave all that is dreadful about *Othello* behind. What I want to know, then, is where are the post-post-racial *American Moors*, *Desdemonas*, and *Get Outs* in American culture, and from other international places and spaces, works willing to undertake this play for expressly antiracist purposes? And, if we are not going to stop returning to this play entirely (which does not seem likely), how can we help make more of these types of antiracist reanimations of *Othello*, like Byrd's, manifest and accessible? The absence of such reanimations raises concerns for me about the versions of Shakespeare, and *Othello* specifically, widely disseminated when experiments in theatre, television, and film are no longer needed as people long to return to what many, tongue in cheek, refer to as the "before times." Are they antiracist ones or ones that hearken back to the post-racial dynamics of "before"? Time will tell, but I fear the answer.

The responses to my questions matter, for as this monograph demonstrates, *Othello*'s sustained presence in American culture (and beyond) is not the entire problem. Rather, the play's reanimations are symptomatic of a continued desire to avoid true racial reckoning. In the wake of the January 6, 2021 insurrection on the US Capitol, President Joseph R. Biden swiftly denounced the domestic terrorists, declaring in a nationally televised speech, "The scenes of chaos at the Capitol do not reflect the true America, do not represent who we are" (Bloomberg). These "scenes of chaos" included people illegally swarming into the building, violence, broken glass, blood, destruction, and ultimately, the tragic loss of life. But most pertinent here is how these "scenes" also included details that signaled white supremacist motivations for the "chaos": "Kekistan" flags, which were "humorously" derived from a Nazi-era flag; "America First" flags, a slogan which the Anti-Defamation League critiques for echoing the antisemitic sentiments articulated for keeping America out of World War Two; a "Camp Auschwitz" sweatshirt declaring that "Work brings freedom"; stickers for the Nationalist Social Club, a neo-Nazi group; and of course, in a particularly haunting image, the Confederate flag, a symbol of slavery that never made it to the Capitol during America's Civil War, yet was flown proudly on January 6th (Simon and Sidner). These signs and symbols expose how white supremacy fueled many who stormed the Capitol that day. Whether Americans desire to face US society's racist underpinnings or not, the confrontation has been forced upon them. Yet President Biden's response exposes just how eager many people are to sidestep it with seemingly comforting yet ultimately meaningless, and incorrect, platitudes.

To articulate a version of "this is not who we are" is a post-racial move, one perhaps unsurprisingly utilized by the man who served as vice president during America's supposed post-racial era. Ruben Espinosa explains why such claims ring hollow—"When US citizens say in regard to the injustices that Black and brown people in the United States face, 'we are better than that,' what they don't understand is that we dark of skin have no reason to believe that. When, exactly, has this nation been better than that? When have Black and brown people not been at a disadvantage in this country?" (*Shakespeare on the Shades* 140). Espinosa poses such rhetorical questions because assertions like President Biden's literally ignore the very US history the terrorists' signs and symbols expressly invoked, the broader expanse of the nation's white supremacist past, and the reality of America's racial "present," as signaled by the fact that the insurrectionists were there in support of a president whose early racist dog whistles became, over four years, explicit racist invectives. As cultural critic Soraya Nadia McDonald attests:

> if one is honest about the history of the United States, it prominently features white violence, terrorism and revanchism, particularly toward Black people, Indigenous people and women. Such attitudes have been codified within our laws and institutions, and it has taken enormous, multigenerational work to chip away at the bigotry that metastasizes within our nation. Even now, we witness the defanging of the Voting Rights Act or the Violence Against Women Act, attacks on Black churches, synagogues and mosques, and the daily deployment of police officers on calls that originate with racist grievance. In so many ways, great and small, we are not honest about who "we" are. Instead, too often, Americans traffic in mythology and denial . . . ("The dangerous magical thinking")

This denial of the need to address and rectify racial injustice is inculcated. And that is why the answers to my questions about Shakespeare, race, and re-presentation matter. For approaches to re-creating, disseminating, and studying Shakespeare's dramas, including *Othello*, can both reflect and reify this ideological conditioning by continuing to appeal to the universal, the historical, the apolitical in order to advance colorblind negations of race.

What, then, can scholars, teachers, and artists who value Shakespeare's works yet seek to push back against the pervasiveness of colorblind racial denial do? If I may be allowed to assume the existence of such a collective, how can we especially recognize, analyze, and confront the racial formation Shakespeare undertakes in day-to-day life, whether through performances, song lyrics, or commercials? And how can we facilitate antiracist Shakespeare so that it becomes equally as quotidian? To use the words of musical artist SZA, "where do I begin? Where do we begin?" These questions dovetail with the one I am most often asked when presenting my research on *Othello*—a version of "what would a better *Othello* look like?" I do not want to provide a singular answer, as if it would solve all the issues with reanimating the play. Nor do I want to simply focus on how to "fix" *Othello*. Rather, I want to conclude by reviewing the commitments this book calls for when thinking about how to approach ethically the intersections of Shakespeare and race in contemporary culture, American and otherwise, especially providing suggestions about what changes in the field of Shakespeare studies, what Beverly Daniel Tatum would call my "sphere of influence," advance these aims.

1. *Framing*: We must eschew colorblind approaches in the creative endeavors, scholarship, and teaching that shape how Shakespeare lives on today. Colorblind perspectives most frequently function to reanimate age-old racial and ethnic stereotypes—such as the Black brute or the white woman in distress—some stretching as far back as the premodern world. One need only look at the 1990s feminist reanimations of *Othello* discussed in Chapter 5 that consider gender but not race to identify the pitfalls of this perspective. The idea that not seeing and talking about race draws people together is misguided, for instead, this dynamic silences the voices of people of color while allowing others to remain comfortable in their supposed racial innocence.

Attacks in both the US and UK against Critical Race Theory signal just how threatening a true historical account of the racial animus undergirding some of the most powerful nations in the world proves to be. In other words, to deny the critique of historical, systemic racism Critical Race Theory puts forth is just another manifestation of the ideological hydra that is colorblind racism. And it wields its ugly head not just in response to Critical Race Theory, but also Shakespeare. In May 2021, I participated in a discussion with scholar Farah Karim-Cooper and scholar and theatre practitioner Aldo Billingslea for Shakespeare's Globe entitled "Anti-racist Shakespeare: *A Midsummer Night's Dream*" (Shakespeare's Globe). Even before anyone heard what we had to say, the Twitterverse was alight with concerns that we were demeaning or bastardizing Shakespeare by considering his great comedy alongside issues of race, or alternately, that we were actively trying to cancel Shakespeare (an odd claim about people whose professional lives depend on Shakespeare at a talk hosted by an institution wanting people to pay to see his plays). These were not good faith arguments and ideally deserve no recognition. But I point to them because they indicate just how swiftly and viscerally people respond to the idea of "sullying" Shakespeare with discussions of race. They prefer colorblind approaches that do not see race, for that means they too do not have to confront race and racism.

It is very easy to give audiences what they want in this regard. After all, that is what has long been offered them, and doing so does not involve grappling with hate speech, even threats. But, as the reanimations undertaken by Cobb, Morrison, Key, and Peele that make up the second half of this monograph demonstrate, antiracist commitments take labor, labor that should not be shouldered entirely by BIPOC individuals, often at great cost. The scholarship of PCRS voices makes clear the challenges inherent in disentangling Shakespeare's plays from the racial ideologies propping up early modern England's burgeoning national identity and nascent imperial endeavors, ideologies which infuse the Bard's canon in ways both great and small. Debapriya Sarkar, for example, observes how "Often, it is impossible to untangle imaginative projections from fantasies of power," meaning that the fantastic worlds populating early modern literature "instead of furthering ethical practices, harbor seeds of injustice" (180). Ceasing the eras-long reiteration of these ideologies occurs when the frames shaping Shakespearean reanimations are informed by commitments to racial justice and equity. Employing new, different, antiracist frames entails an expansive imagination willing to forgo the familiar (and comfortable). Yet it also necessitates particular grit to withstand the closed doors, the repeated "no"s, the wide-ranging challenges to one's antiracist vision. Both institutions and individuals in positions of power who benefit from Shakespeare's enduring cultural capital thus have an ethical obligation to invest in antiracist Shakespeare, to speak for his Othellos, Aarons, Shylocks, Calibans, Barbarys, and the unnamed female "Moors." If they deny this responsibility, whether they want to acknowledge it or not, they prop up white supremacist structures and ideologies that prefer the days not of racial equity (they have never really existed), but rather of white superiority hidden behind the polite veneer of racial neutrality.

2. *Speaking*: Clearly, dismantling the white racial frame carries with it numerous challenges. As several chapters in this book make clear, the frame begins to splinter when new voices, and therefore perspectives, can present ideas that abandon the allegedly universal but actually white point of view. At all levels, then, the Shakespeare system needs more diverse voices whose unique, particular outlooks can challenge the system's norms. Such multiplicity must occur at the creative level, certainly. As Chapter 4 reveals, American theatre is frequently white theatre, not just regarding the audience, but also when it comes to those both in front of and behind the curtain. The same holds true of television and film, as Chapter 6 exposes. Diversifying the respective industries' various structures would help expand what stories are told and how, including reanimations of Shakespeare within them.

But increasing the voices speaking on and to Shakespeare and race also needs to happen within the field of Shakespeare studies. Particularly, the field can amplify its antiracist efforts not just through the important work of diversifying its makeup, but also by more intentionally embracing interdisciplinarity. Grasping the scope and significance of the intersections between Shakespeare and race in everyday culture benefits from bringing as many resources as possible to the investigative table. In other words, just as "The global awareness that is made possible by internet connectivity is an asset in the Shakespeare classroom because it emphasizes that there are always multiple and varied interpretive viewpoints," so too can increased connectivity be an asset to Shakespeare scholarship by emphasizing the multiple and varied viewpoints from unique fields (Thompson and Turchi 5). It behooves us to remember that Shakespearean works as they appear "right now" will become the future's historical artifacts. We have the opportunity to turn to Shakespearean reanimations of the recent past and the present in order to historicize them with immediacy, thereby providing a record of how they signified in their given moment. After all, as Stuart Hall contends, "The meaning of a cultural symbol is given in part by the social field into which it is incorporated, the practices with which it articulates and is made to resonate" ("Notes on Deconstructing" 356). Shakespeare is precisely such a cultural symbol, one whose meaning we most fully understand when we take into account a premodern *and* contemporary social field. As an early modern scholar trained in historicist methodology, including debates about its application, I understand the care that must be taken when treading on another field's ground. Doing so responsibly, however, does not reduce disciplinary rigor but rather stretches our methodological capacities. The same holds true for non-historicist methodologies. Of course, reticence develops from the fact that "To contemplate a temporal reframing potentially provokes feelings of great inadequacy" because scholars can no longer "use time as a boundary" for expertise (Grier 235). Yet as Miles P. Grier (via Hortense Spillers) contends, this disciplinary undoing can "stir . . . productive intellectual trouble" (233). Indeed, as I hope this book demonstrates, placing the analytical work of Shakespeare studies in conversation with other disciplines such as sociology, American cultural studies, and media studies, as well as the incisive questions and concepts offered up by non-academic cultural critics, provides a richer, broader understanding of the way Shakespeare props up or challenges America's racecraft—the racial narratives and fantasies American culture advances as reality.

Shakespeare studies itself is not immune to the allure of America's racecraft, and opening up to new voices might help with that realization. Take McDonald's concept of TROT: "Those Racists Over There." She elaborates, "The TROT, fundamentally, is a figment of white imagination and absolution, a tool to avoid reckoning in any meaningful way with The Problem We All Live With" ("The dangerous magical thinking"). TROT props up white innocence by making racism appear to be the purview of a select, easily identifiable few, such as attributing the racist motivations for the insurrection to "a hillbilly malignancy when, in fact, this was a mob spanning lines of class, religion, education and athletic ability" (McDonald, "The dangerous magical thinking"). For me, TROT, particularly its perseveration of racial innocence, resonates with the insistence by certain corners of Shakespeare studies that work on Shakespeare and race is and should be a distinctly American phenomenon, or that exploring antiblackness in Shakespeare is only applicable to a US milieu. In short, for certain subfields or international locales, the US becomes TROT, providing an "out" for disengaging with PCRS and global antiblackness. One need only examine a conversation between Farah

Karim-Cooper and Eoin Price to understand the dynamics of this line of thought, with Price asserting that while institutions in the US have increasingly "sought to ensure that Shakespeare and race is a regular topic of high profile plenaries," in the UK, "The situation is different ... but it is vitally important that scholars based on this side of the Atlantic engage seriously and sustainedly, with critical race studies" (3). Clearly, TROT applies in Shakespeare studies as it does in culture at large. Such resonances exemplify how interdisciplinary antiracist work affords new and important avenues of inquiry by knitting together the race work undertaken within distinct social and cultural avenues that nonetheless function across domains.

Socio-politics, popular culture, racial ideologies, and Shakespeare interweave with one another in the daily lives of scholars, students, artists, adaptors, and appropriators, whether they realize it or not. It is the work of Shakespeare studies to assist with this vital awareness. We therefore require rigorous methods, robust frameworks, and creative theoretical vocabularies that speak to these particular interrelationships in their particular historical moments. As such, just as is needed from the theatre and entertainment industries, we should be open to locating these methods, frameworks, and vocabularies in new, exciting, and varied antiracist people and places.

3. *Engaging (or, Speaking Part 2)*: If my previous suggestion focuses on who gets to speak, this one amplifies such concerns by taking Shakespeare's predominantly white audience into further account. Articulated differently, what needs to happen in order to advance what in Chapter 4 I call audience education regarding Shakespeare and race? There is no ignoring the blossoming of public humanities work over the last decade. This type of writing and speaking allows PCRS scholarship to reach wider audiences than ever before. As such, public humanities work could and should be part and parcel of the audience education I champion in Chapter 4, which helps produce increased antiracist engagement with Shakespeare. The more we can help those outside of academia learn to see Shakespeare anew by locating race and its ideological function across his canon (if they do not know how to do so already), the more tools they carry with them as they attend the theatre or view a Shakespearean film adaptation or even consider a brief Shakespearean reference in a comedy sketch, music video, or television advertisement.

But, if we are honest, the scholarship of the most prominent public Shakespeareans does not focus on race, whether as conceptualized in the premodern world or as represented in contemporary culture.

Who is most likely to be invited to speak about Shakespeare to wider audiences? Even with increasing interest in PCRS, the answer is still scholars like Stephen Greenblatt and James Shapiro. While both men have thoughtfully addressed the way their Jewish identity informs them as Shakespeareans, and while each has engaged with the concept of race (to varying degrees) in their earlier criticism, neither has chosen to center the topic in their respective academic work. It therefore stands to reason that as eloquently as they may each speak about Shakespeare, there are other scholars better equipped to educate public audiences regarding Shakespeare and race. What might a PCRS scholar bring to the table instead, for instance? What connections could an expert in performance studies or adaptation and appropriation studies make regarding Shakespeare and race that a historicist scholar may not as readily see? How might professors who teach less privileged, often more diverse students be differently able to speak to wider audiences about Shakespeare and race? How could a contingent scholar teaching across institutions with distinct resources and student bodies even more pointedly address the intersections between Shakespeare, race, and (in)equity?

I would be remiss if I did not acknowledge that Ayanna Thompson has made inroads into the predominantly male, Ivy League company. But one additional voice is insufficient for pushing back against the racial cultural conditioning undertaken daily. As Grier trenchantly reminds us, "a scholarly community is not functioning when one source is assigned as arbiter of that which is true or ethical" (232). If the most prominent public Shakespeareans do not tend to address race as scholars, then they are more likely than not to keep the conversation about Shakespeare race neutral. That approach, however, upholds rather than challenges the colorblind status quo. Just as creating avenues for Jordan Peele to craft *Get Out* allowed him to articulate his particularly Black, distinct perspective to the masses, so too should artistic directors, media specialists, colloquium organizers, continuing education coordinators, and even established scholars who are frequently asked to speak make the effort to cede space to new viewpoints (a.k.a. pass the mic) by intentionally reaching out to scholars representing a variety of voices, racial and ethnic identities, teaching experiences, and expertise so as to offer new "tools with which to hear" (Cobb, *American Moor* 4). Ultimately, then, if Shakespeare is truly to function as a vehicle for advancing public understandings of race and power, we cannot and should not depend on a limited number of creators, methods, or scholarly voices to reach out to a (frequently white) public commonly hungry for more Shakespeare but often much more uncertain about using the Bard to tackle questions of race and injustice, even as Shakespearean references undertake race work in their daily lives.

4. *(Re)Training*: In 2018, *Variety.com* announced that white actress and writer Lena Dunham had been tapped to write the script for a film adaptation of *A Hope More Powerful than the Sea: One Refugee's Incredible Story of Love, Loss, and Survival,* which traces the journey of Syrian refugee Doaa al-Zamel (Donnelly). Online backlash came swiftly. I remember seeing a tweet to the effect of "Has Lena Dunham ever even taken an ethnic studies class? Her work would suggest not." The tweet—which references debates about the whiteness of Dunham's HBO series *Girls* (2012–17) as well as controversies caused by Dunham's racist public comments—stayed with me because it suggested that education holds out the possibility of ideological transformation, including of one's racial habitus. Of course, Cobb's engagement with the educational system in Chapter 4 cautions that such a transformation is never guaranteed. Even so, I resonate with the promise held out by the tweet because I agree with bell hooks that "The classroom remains the most radical space of possibility in the academy" (*Teaching* 12).

The realization of this possibility, however, depends on training, and the same holds true for the potential to expand those who can astutely analyze the relationship between Shakespeare and race across all forms of culture, high or low, rarefied or popular. Yet training in Shakespeare studies has not taken this expansive approach, choosing instead to focus overwhelmingly on historical methodologies and a focus on the archives rather than on Shakespearean performance and/or adaptation and appropriation. The average person, however, has much more access to Shakespearean performances, and even more so, to Shakespearean appearances across popular culture, than to the historical archives so hallowed by the field. And, like the archives, these especially accessible Shakespearean reanimations are never ideologically neutral regarding race. All Shakespeare studies scholars should therefore be trained in the basics of both performance studies and adaptation and appropriation studies, and as I have written elsewhere, this training must come with careful attention to the race work performances and popular culture undertake. As this book exemplifies, the details that comprise a Shakespearean performance or Shakespearean pop culture citation all do race work—casting, lighting, music, mise en scène, shading, characterization, intertextual referencing, camera angles, narration and more (nor are these details or the genres to which they apply mutually exclusive). Thus, just as scholars become better practitioners from learning how to approach and navigate a historical archive, so too would they grow from learning how to discern between colorblind and color-conscious casting or the ways lighting has long been racialized in televisual mediums, in other words, from learning how to approach and navigate a performance or pop culture archive. The skills and methods employed by both Shakespeare performance studies and Shakespeare adaptation and appropriation studies should become the norm for undergraduate and graduate instruction. If students graduate understanding recto and verso or the difference between a quarto and a folio, they should likewise understand the intimacy and disorientation created by a close-up shot in a Shakespearean film or know that most Restoration Shakespeare was actually deeply adapted, even appropriated Shakespeare, for example.

It is crucial to realize that the capaciousness of undergraduate and graduate training informs the possible versions of Shakespeare that reach wider audiences, including their radicalness or lack thereof. Future reanimators of Shakespeare (theatremakers, actors, novelists, comic book artists, and more) frequently learn to see the relationship between Shakespeare and race, or not, in the undergraduate classroom (though this training is increasingly occurring at the secondary level). Education should, in hooks's words, be "about the practice of freedom" (*Teaching* 4). Ayanna Thompson and Laura Turchi advocate for that freedom when they conceptualize "the *teaching* of Shakespeare as a vehicle rather than a destination," including Shakespeare as a vehicle for understanding "complex texts" that include "moments of maddeningly mundane expressions of racism, sexism, anti-Semitism, etc." (7). Understanding how this relationship between Shakespeare and mundane expressions of racism functions in the modern world, not just the premodern one, hopefully provides students with the foundational resources and therefore the freedom vital for closing the imagination gap (Chapter 1) plaguing Shakespeare and race in American theatre and popular culture.

Regarding graduate training, "more than ever before in the recent history of this nation, educators are compelled ... to create new ways of knowing, different strategies for the sharing of knowledge" (hooks, *Teaching* 12). These "new ways of knowing" include what I am calling for here, "Expanding beyond boundaries," including those that focus traditional training on only one kind of archive. hooks argues that this type of intellectual expansion (she mentions "anticolonial, critical, and feminist pedagogies" specifically) allowed her to "engage directly both the concern for interrogating biases in curricula that reinscribe systems of domination (such as racism and sexism) while simultaneously providing new ways to teach diverse groups of students" (*Teaching* 10). Similarly expanding the boundaries of typical early modern graduate training could help achieve the same ends. For example, robust preparation in PCRS, performance studies, and adaptation and appropriation studies would assist those who inevitably teach a Shakespeare and Film or Global Shakespeare class to do so with a keener attention to race and the elements that communicate a given piece's racecraft or antiracist message than they would otherwise have, or help a potential library program director develop events focusing on Shakespeare and race across historical eras.

Wendy Beth Hyman and Hillary Eklund recognize that "Shakespeare, perhaps more than any other literary figure, has been trotted out as a symbol of white cultural supremacy" (2). Students are best able to understand the purpose and trajectory of that symbolism when they can effectively place the past and present in dialogue with one another. Paulo Freire speaks to the relationship between history and dialogue when he contends that "true dialogue cannot exist unless the dialoguers engage in critical thinking . . . thinking which perceives reality as process, as transformation, rather than as a static entity—thinking which . . . immerses itself in temporality without fear of the risks involved" (92). While naive thinkers believe "the present should emerge normalized and 'well-behaved,'" he argues that critical thinkers invest in the "continuing transformation of reality" (92). Building on Freire, Hyman and Eklund identify the "liberatory potential" in "there being multiple Shakespeares, existing across a wide range of temporalities, locations, and idioms. Comparing these instantiations affords us critical distance from our own troubling era" (7). More expansive educational training at both the undergraduate and graduate levels would provide the other side of what Hyman and Eklund identify, the means to critically engage with and, in Freire's words, transform, our own troubling era, including the racecraft Shakespeare is used to authorize in day-to-day life.

5. *Re-presenting*: Diverse voices can be invited to speak. Unfamiliar methods may be employed. Fresh frames might even appear. But antiracist success is *still* not guaranteed. Koenig utilized diverse voices in *Serial* (Chapter 3), yet her podcast nevertheless recirculated the trope of the violent Black male, the controlling Muslim man, and the model minority myth. The Q Brothers wrote and staged a version of *Othello* creatively combining hip hop, comedy,

and Shakespeare that nonetheless resulted in a colorblind, antiblack production of *Othello* (Chapter 2). Cobb's *American Moor* rectifies the white-centeredness of *Serial* and the colorblindness of *Othello: The Remix* (Chapter 4), but it has not been fully embraced by the American theatre community as indicated by the fact that, as of this time, it has yet to reach Broadway in spite of its off-Broadway run. All three works thus expose the trials plaguing racial re-presentation, meaning the aim of not just depicting racial difference but of depicting racial difference in new, ethical, antiracist ways. Distinct problems plague these works, however. Recognizing them allows a more informed movement forward in the quest to advance the project of antiracist Shakespeare.

With both *Serial* and *Othello: The Remix*, the issue of accountability looms large. Were there persons of color working alongside Koenig who could call out her white racial frame in a way the subjects of her investigation could not? Was there a diversity director or consultant at either the Chicago Shakespeare Theater or the Globe able to consider the thematic clash created by carelessly mixing hip hop, comedy, and *Othello* for colorblind aims? The approaches undertaken by these respective reanimations thus mirror a favored cultural tactic: diversity without inclusion. For some, antiracism becomes a numbers game where certain identities need only be represented, particular quotas hit, so that representation seemingly occurs. Yet representation is the bare minimum of antiracist practice. David Theo Goldberg explains that this approach to antiracism is more accurately what he terms "Racial nonracialism," which "seeks to sidestep historical legacies of racial arrangement and injustice" whereas "Anti-racism, by contrast, seeks to critically address and redress the impact of those legacies" (*Are We* 20). To use a brief illustration applicable to Shakespeare studies, racial nonracialism is what occurs when a production diversifies its cast with BIPOC actors but only places them in secondary roles, thereby ignoring how Black and brown bodies have been historically subordinated in society. Harvey Young contends, however, that if considered through "the post-black analytical framework," then "post-race" has the potential to be liberatory if conceived of as "not the end of race but rather an invitation to reflect upon and evaluate the legacy and enduring relevance of race" (68). He elaborates, "the word [post-race] could be rehabilitated to describe a clear-eyed understanding of the legacy of racial discrimination and violence within society. Post-race can help us to realize that, every day, people embody race. It can motivate us to talk about how the experience of race touches our lives." When it comes to Shakespeare, race, and re-presentation, then, true antiracist inclusion means challenging the post-racial by grappling with instead of glossing over racial differences and how, as a result, representation does not function in the same way for everybody/every body.

As a field with a large, historically embedded element of performance, such tensions between "racially neutral" and antiblack performance practices have long circulated in Shakespeare studies as Shakespeare's early modern plays get reimagined and repackaged for contemporary, multicultural audiences. This can lead to actors of color performing roles that promulgate rather than challenge historically oppressive caricatures. L. Monique Pittman observes, for instance, how a 2012 Chicago Shakespeare Theater production of *The Taming of the Shrew* for its summer Shakespeare in the Park enterprise was "disappointingly riddled with abuses of Katharina rendered decidedly uncomfortable by the color difference between Katharina and Petruchio [she was black, he was white]" ("Big-Shouldered" 261). While acknowledging that "an integrated cast affirms the many voices with which Shakespeare can and should speak," she argues that "this piece of casting did not appear 'blind' unless 'blind' is taken to mean casting without an eye to unintended interpretive consequences, namely, the visual implications of a Caucasian man imposing his will on an African American woman." Conversely, Patricia Akhimie conveys how José Esquea's 2017 work on *The Taming of the Shrew* for the Soñadores players in New York City "test[s] the possibilities of consciously racialized casting on the Shakespearean stage" ("'Fair' Bianca" 92). In his planning for a production set in a segregated twenty-first century, Esquea intended for Kate to be the "'shrewish' and darker-skinned older sister" with Bianca "her widely admired and beloved lighter-skinned younger sister'" (93, 94). For Akhimie, this decision thereby "reintroduces unspoken familial histories of miscegenation and illegitimacy, calls attention to hierarchies of racialized beauty, and questions the efficacy and even the existence of romantic love" (94). These contrasting examples of the same play demonstrate the very different representational outcomes that result when racial histories are discounted (racial nonracialism) or contemplated (antiracism) when planning and casting a Shakespearean production.

Shakespeare studies should therefore be poised to lead the charge in thinking through the widespread cultural presence of the diversity/inclusion tension across present-day performances. Mira Assaf Kafantaris provides an excellent example as she uses her early modern training to confront the Netflix series *Bridgerton*'s

(2020–present) colorblind representational problems. She focuses on a scene in which white protagonist Daphne Bridgerton (Phoebe Dynevor) and her love interest, the Black Simon Basset, a.k.a. the Duke of Hastings (Regé-Jean Page), share an erotically charged afternoon tea during which banter abounds, flirtatious glances are cast, and which culminates in Simon sensually licking his sugar spoon. Yet the series' colorblind perspective results in a seemingly sexy moment that carries troubling racial connotations, for as Kafantaris argues, "What the show does not take into account, in its impulse to imagine a world without race, are the undercurrents of cannibalism that such a triangulation of Black man, sugar, and reproductive sexuality evoke." Through an analysis that yokes her understanding of race in the premodern period with a rejection of (historical) representation as ever racially neutral, Kafantaris demonstrates how scholars in Shakespeare studies, and premodern studies more broadly, can productively assist in analyzing a wide range of racial representations in popular culture, holding them accountable for the ways they do or do not engage with the triangulation of race, power, and representation.

American Moor exposes a very different issue that bedevils racial re-presentation—that of interpersonal and institutional support. On the one hand, *American Moor* exemplifies what backing for antiracist works can achieve. Though conversations about releasing an authorized version of *American Moor* were happening behind the scenes, a Twitter campaign especially championed by the #ShakeRace community prompted Methuen Drama to accelerate their commitment to publishing the play. On the other hand, without the support of the right producers, investors, and cultural critics, *American Moor* has yet to make it to Broadway, where its antiracist re-presentation can reach much larger audiences, despite the significant academic interest the play has garnered. *American Moor* thereby illustrates what collective support can do to buoy antiracist projects, but also how far there is to go. Building stronger coalitions between BIPOC theatre practitioners and (Shakespeare) scholars, as modeled by the Red Bull Theater's "*Othello* 2020" initiative, particularly its "Exploring *Othello* in 2020" seminars, is an excellent place to start. As Daphne A. Brooks traces, such collaborative efforts have long been fruitful, such as when, in the nineteenth and early twentieth centuries, "a diverse array of political activists, stage performers, and writers utilized their work to interrogate the ironies of black identity formation" (3). This synergetic work could prove equally productive today. Not only can these distinct voices assist each other in expanding how they approach race and/in performance, but they can also work together to speak to and against the "powers that be" hoping to continue silencing the voices, contributions, and visions that these practitioners and scholars have to offer. This need to speak back, however, directs attention to the vital necessity of institutional support—whether from a particular theatre, production company, publishing house, or academic entity—in the form of time, money, creative agency, academic freedom, and promotion, to name but a few forms of institutional assistance that would go a long way toward facilitating antiracist re-presentation in Shakespeare and beyond.

I want to be honest about the suggestions I enumerate here. They are but a drop in the antiracist bucket needed to combat the siren song of the colorblind and post-racial. They are so difficult to contest that Goldberg suggests of the post-racial, "Race (as we have known it) may be over. But racism lives on unmarked, even unrecognized, potentially for ever [sic]" (*Are We* 6). Moreover, my suggestions are tied up with other forms of inequity, such as the overall precarity in academia, the still limited presence and even more limited tenured status of BIPOC scholars, and the post-COVID-19 financial pressures felt by the various industries that make up popular and fine arts culture. These recommendations are therefore not comprehensive solutions but rather a series of potential steps that create the possibility of speaking for Othello in broadly conceived ways. For even as I direct my suggestions to Shakespeare studies and the systems to which it is most intimately tied, I believe they can be applied more widely to other disciplines and in other contexts. *Reanimating Shakespeare's Othello in Post-Racial America* illustrates that reanimations of *Othello* are always in dialogue with racial ideologies pervading culture at large. To speak for Othello, then, means more than reanimating the play while employing antiracist strategies. Meeting Othello's plea takes the more expansive work of changing the anti-BIPOC, and more specifically the antiblack, racial habitus plaguing America and other global locales, those that foreclose the possibility of Othello speaking for himself in the first place.

Bibliography

"16 Years Before *Hamilton*, The Q Brothers Were Bringing Hip Hop to the Stage." *Playbill*, October 25, 2016, <www.playbill.com/article/16-years-before-hamilton-the-q-brothers-were-bringing-hip-hop-to-the-stage>. Accessed February 16, 2018.

"537: The Alibi." Transcript. *This American Life, NPR*, January 29, 2015, <www.thisamericanlife.org/537/transcript>. Accessed April 20, 2022.

"About Shakespeare Lives." *Shakespeare Lives*, British Council, May 26, 2016, <www.shakespearelives.org/about>. Accessed April 20, 2022.

Actors' Equity Association. "Equity 2020: Aggressive. Inclusive. Responsive." *Equity News*, vol. 102, no. 2, 2017.

Adams, Brandi K. "Black '(un)bookishness' in *Othello* and *American Moor*: A Meditation." *Shakespeare*, vol. 17, no. 1, 2021, pp. 49–53.

—. "The King, and not I: Refusing Neutrality—." *The Sundial*, Arizona Center for Medieval and Renaissance Studies, June 9, 2020, <medium.com/the-sundial-acmrs/the-king-and-not-i-refusing-neutrality-dbab4239e8a9>. Accessed June 9, 2020.

Adelman, Janet. "Her Father's Blood: Race, Conversion, and Nation in *The Merchant of Venice*." *Representations*, vol. 81, no. 1, 2003, pp. 4–30.

Ahmed, Leila. *Women and Gender in Islam*. Yale University Press, 1992.

Ahmed, Sara. "Affective Economies." *Social Text*, vol. 22, no. 2, 2004, pp. 117–39.

—. *What's the Use?: On the Use of Uses*. Duke University Press, 2019.

Akhimie, Patricia. "'Fair' Bianca and 'Brown' Kate: Shakespeare and the Mixed-Race Family in José Esquea's *The Taming of the Shrew*." *Journal of American Studies*, vol. 54, no. 1, 2020, pp. 89–96.

—. *Shakespeare and the Cultivation of Difference: Race and Conduct in the Early Modern World*. Routledge, 2018.

Alexander, Michelle. *The New Jim Crow: Mass Incarceration in the Age of Colorblindness*. New Press, 2010.

Alexander, Scott, and Larry Karaszewski, creators. *The People v. OJ Simpson: An American Crime Story*. FX, 2016.

"All that Glisters Is Not Gold." Transcript. *Code Switch*, NPR, August 21, 2019, <www.npr.org/transcripts/752850055>. Accessed August 10, 2021.

Alonge, AJ. "Writing Past the White Gaze as a Black Author." *Code Switch*, *NPR*, March 4, 2017, <www.npr.org/sections/codeswitch/2017/03/04/515790514/writing-past-the-white-gaze-as-a-black-author>. Accessed August 12, 2021.

Andersen, Margaret L. "The Nexus of Race and Gender: Parallels, Linkages, and Divergences in Race and Gender Studies." *The SAGE Handbook of Race and Ethnic Studies*, edited by Patricia Hill Collins and John Solomos, Sage, 2010, pp. 166–87.

Anderson, Carol. *White Rage: The Unspoken Truth of Our Racial Divide*. Bloomsbury, 2017.

Anthony, Andrew. "Jordan Peele on Making a Hit Comedy-Horror Movie out of America's Racial Tensions." *Guardian*, March 4, 2017, <www.theguardian.com/film/2017/mar/04/jordan-peele-interview-get-out-its-about-purging-our-fears-horror-film-daniel-kaluuya>. Accessed September 30, 2019.

Archer, Ina Diane. "Review: *Get Out*." *Film Comment*, March 3, 2017, <www.filmcomment.com/blog/review-get-out/>. Accessed September 30, 2019.

Asante Jr., M. K. *It's Bigger than Hip-Hop: The Rise of the Post-Hip Hop Generation*. St. Martin's Griffin, 2009.

Asian American Performers Action Coalition. *Ethnic Representation on New York City Stages, 2016–2017*.

Austin, Allan W., and Patrick L. Hamilton. *All New, All Different: A History of Race and the American Superhero*. University of Texas Press, 2019.

Bailey, Julius. *Racial Realities and Post-Racial Dreams: The Age of Obama and Beyond*. Broadview Press, 2015.

Bailey, Moya. "New Terms of Resistance: A Response to Zenzele Isoke." *Souls: A Critical Journal of Black Politics, Culture, and Society*, vol. 15, no. 4, 2013, pp. 341–43.

Banet-Weiser, Sarah, Roopali Mukherjee, and Herman Gray. "Introduction: Postrace Racial Projects." *Racism Postrace*, edited by Roopali Mukherjee, Sarah Banet-Weiser, and Herman Gray, Duke University Press, 2019, pp. 1–18.

Banton, Michael. "Race Relations." *Companion to Racial and Ethnic Studies*, edited by David Theo Goldberg and John Solomos, Blackwell, 2012, pp. 90–96.

Barlas, Asma. *"Believing Women" in Islam: Unreading Patriarchal Interpretations of the Qur'an*. University of Texas Press, 2002.

Barnes, Brendon, Ingrid Palmary, and Kevin Durrheim. "The Denial of Racism: The Role of Humor, Personal Experience, and Self-Censorship." *Journal of Language and Social Psychology*, vol. 20, no. 3, 2001, pp. 321–38.

Bartels, Emily C. "Strategies of Submission: Desdemona, the Duchess, and the Assertion of Desire." *Studies in English Literature*, vol. 36, 1996, pp. 417–33.

Barthelemy, Anthony Gerard. *Black Face, Maligned Race: The Representation of Blacks in English Drama from Shakespeare to Southerne*. Louisiana State University Press, 1999.

Bastille. "Send Them Off!" *Wide World*, Virgin, 2016.
Bates, Benjamin R., and Thurmon Garner. "Can You Dig It? Audiences, Archetypes, and John Shaft." *Howard Journal of Communications*, vol. 12, no. 3, 2011, pp. 137–57.
Bausch, Katharine. "Superflies into Superkillers: Black Masculinity in Film from Blaxploitation to New Black Realism." *The Journal of Popular Culture*, vol. 46, no. 2, 2013, pp. 257–76.
Benatar, David. "Prejudice in Jest: When Racial and Gender Humor Harms." *Public Affairs Quarterly*, vol. 13, no. 2, 1999, pp. 191–203.
Bhopal, Kalwant. *White Privilege: The Myth of a Post-Racial Society*. Policy Press, 2018.
Biden, Joseph R. "Biden: 'Scenes of Chaos at U.S. Capitol Do Not Reflect True America.'" *YouTube*, uploaded by Bloomberg Quicktake, January 6, 2021, <www.youtube.com/watch?v=Cr__YZj8V98>. Accessed August 12, 2021.
Bloom, Harold. *Shakespeare: The Invention of the Human*. Riverhead Books, 1998.
Boffone, Trevor, and Carla Della Gatta, eds. *Shakespeare and Latinidad*. Edinburgh University Press, 2021.
Bogle, Donald. *Toms, Coons, Mulattoes, Mammies, and Bucks: An Interpretive History of Blacks in American Films*. Bloomsbury, 2015.
Bommer, Lawrence. "May the Rap Be With You." *Stage and Cinema*, March 17, 2013, <www.stageandcinema.com/2013/03/17/othello-the-remix/>. Accessed February 18, 2019.
Bonilla-Silva, Eduardo. *Racism Without Racists: Color-Blind Racism and the Persistence of Racial Inequality in America*, 4th ed., Rowman & Littlefield, 2013.
Boose, Lynda E. "Othello's Handkerchief: 'The Recognizance and Pledge of Love.'" *English Literary Renaissance*, vol. 5, 1975, pp. 360–74.
Bourdieu, Pierre. *Of a Theory of Practice*. Translated by Richard Nice, Cambridge University Press, 1995.
Bovilsky, Lara. *Barbarous Play: Race on the English Renaissance Stage*. University of Minnesota Press, 2008.
Bristol, Michael D. *Shakespeare's America, America's Shakespeare*. Routledge, 1990.
British Library. "Painting of Ira Aldridge as Othello." *The British Library*, <www.bl.uk/collection-items/painting-of-ira-aldridge-as-othello>. Accessed December 1, 2020.
Britton, Dennis Austin. *Becoming Christian: Race, Reformation, and Early Modern English Romance*. Fordham University Press, 2014.
Brooks, Daphne A. *Bodies in Dissent: Spectacular Performance of Race and Freedom, 1850–1910*. Duke University Press, 2006.
Brooks, Kinitra. *Searching for Sycorax: Black Women's Hauntings of Contemporary Horror*. Rutgers University Press, 2017.
—. "What Becky Gotta Do to Get Murked? White Womanhood in Jordan Peele's *Get Out*." *The Root*, March 3, 2017, <www.theroot.com/what-

becky-gotta-do-to-get-murked-white-womanhood-in-j-1822522591>. Accessed September 18, 2019.
Brown, Jeffrey A. *Black Superheroes, Milestone Comics, and their Fans*. University Press of Mississippi, 2001.
Brydon, Diana, and Irena R. Makaryk, eds. *Shakespeare in Canada: "A World Elsewhere?"* University of Toronto Press, 2002.
Bubba-Buu. "Faux *Othello* Poster." *DeviantArt*, May 30, 2014, <www.deviantart.com/bubba- buu/art/Faux-Othello-Poster-457469373>. Accessed August 10, 2021.
Burke, Meghan. *Colorblind Racism*. Polity, 2018.
Butler, Isaac. "In the Park, an *Othello* in Which Love Conquers Little." *Vulture*, June 18, 2018, <www.vulture.com/2018/06/in-central-park-an-othello-in-which-love-conquers-little.html>. Accessed August 12, 2021.
Cahill, Patricia A., and Kim F. Hall. "Forum: Shakespeare and Black America." *Journal of American Studies*, vol. 54, no. 1, 2020, pp. 1–11.
Callaghan, Dympna. "Looking Well to Linens: Women and Cultural Production in *Othello* and Shakespeare's England." *Marxist Shakespeares*, edited by Jean E. Howard and Scott Cutler Shershow, Routledge, 2006, pp. 53–81.
Carney, Jo Eldrige. "'Being Born a Girl': Toni Morrison's *Desdemona*." *Borrowers and Lenders: The Journal of Shakespeare and Appropriation*, vol. 9, no. 1, 2014, n.p.
Césaire, Aimé. *Discourse on Colonialism*. Translated by Joan Pinkham, Monthly Review Press, 2001.
Chakravarty, Urvashi. "More than Kin, Less than Kind: Similitude, Strangeness, and Early Modern Homonationalisms." *Shakespeare Quarterly*, vol. 67, no. 1, 2016, pp. 14–29.
Charnas, Dan. *The Big Payback: The History of the Business of Hip-Hop*. New American Library, 2010.
Chatterjee, Meghna. "The Problematic Representation of Queer Masculinity in Disney Films." *Feminism in India*, September 21, 2020, <feminisminindia.com/2020/09/21/problematic-representation-queer-masculinity-disney-films/>. Accessed April 20, 2022.
Chevalier, Tracy. "A Conversation with Tracy Chevalier." *New Boy*, Hogarth Shakespeare, 2017, pp. 2014–18.
Childish Gambino. "This is America." Single. mcDJ/RCA, 2018.
Christopher, Brandon. "Paratextual Shakespearings: Comics' Shakespearean Frame." *Shakespeare/Not Shakespeare*, edited by Christy Desmet, Natalie Loper, and Jim Casey, Palgrave, 2017, pp. 149–68.
Claycomb, Ryan M. "Re-Performing Women and Reconstructing the Audience: Paula Vogel's *Desdemona* and Post-Modern Feminist Parody." *Text and Presentation: Journal of the Comparative Drama Conference*, vol. 20, 1999, pp. 87–93.
Coates, Ta-Nehisi. *Between the World and Me*. Spiegel & Grau, 2015.

—. "The Case for Reparations." *The Atlantic*, June 2014, <www.theatlantic.com/magazine/archive/2014/06/the-case-for-reparations/361631>. Accessed May 15, 2019.

Cobb, Keith Hamilton. "American Moor." 2011. Theatrical Script at the Folger Shakespeare Library.

—. "American Moor." 2018. Draft for Luna Stage.

—. *American Moor*. Methuen Drama, 2020.

—. Interview with Stephen Greenblatt. *Discussing American Moor With Stephen Greenblatt*, Fall 2017, <americanmoor.com/video/>. Accessed April 20, 2022.

—. Interview with Kojo Nnamdi. "American Moor: Race, Theater, and Shakespeare at the Anacostia Playhouse." *The Kojo Nnamdi Show*, January 15, 2019, <thekojonnamdishow.org/shows/2019-01-15/american-moor-race-theater-and-shakespeare-at-the-anacostia-playhouse>. Accessed April 20, 2022.

Cobb, Keith Hamilton, and Michael Witmore. "Playwright, Player and Partners: A Five Act Arc of *American Moor*." *Vimeo*, uploaded by Keith Hamilton Cobb, <https://vimeo.com/162091173>. Accessed April 20, 2022.

Coleman, Robin R. Means, *Horror Noire: Blacks in American Horror Films from the 1890s to the Present*. Routledge, 2011.

Collette, Matt. "To Download or Not to Download." *Slate*, November 20, 2014, <slate.com/human-interest/2014/11/serial-replaces-shakespeare-in-one-california-english-class.html>. Accessed July 19, 2017.

Collins, Patricia Hill. *Black Feminist Thought: Knowledge, Consciousness, and the Politics of Empowerment*, 2nd ed., Routledge, 2000.

—. *Black Sexual Politics: African Americans, Gender, and The New Racism*. Routledge, 2005.

Collins, Patricia Hill, and Simone Bilge. *Intersectionality*. Polity, 2016.

Conquergood, Dwight. "Performing as a Moral Act: Ethical Dimensions of the Ethnography of Performance." *Literature in Performance*, vol. 5, no. 2, 1985, pp. 1–13.

Corredera, Vanessa I. "Complex Complexions: The Facial Signification of the Black Other in *Lust's Dominion*." *Shakespeare and the Power of the Face*, edited by James A. Knapp, Ashgate, 2015, pp. 93–114.

—. "Far More Black than Black: Stereotypes, Black Masculinity, and Americanization in Tim Blake Nelson's O." *Literature/Film Quarterly*, vol. 45, no. 3, 2017, n.p.

—. "'Not a Moor exactly': Shakespeare, *Serial*, and Modern Constructions of Race." *Shakespeare Quarterly*, vol. 67, no. 1, 2016, pp. 30–50.

—. "When the Master's Tools Fail: Racial Euphemism in Shakespeare Appropriation, or, the Activist Value of Premodern Critical Race Studies." *Literature Compass*, January 2022, <doi.org/10.1111/lic3.12634>.

—. "Where Are We in the Melody of the New Scholarly Song? A Reflection on the Present and Future of Shakespeare and Race," *Exemplaria*, vol. 33, no. 2, 2021, pp. 184–96.

Crenshaw, Kimberlé Williams. "Mapping the Margins: Intersectionality, Identity Politics, and Violence against Women of Color." *Stanford Law Review*, vol. 43, no. 6, 1991, pp. 1241–99.

Crichton-Miller, Emma. "What Goes Around: The Art of Framing." *Christies*, April 30, 2015, <www.christies.com/features/Frames-in-Focus-5815-1.aspx>. Accessed July 19, 2017.

Cross, Neil, creator. *Luther*. BBC Drama Productions, 2011.

"Culture, n. 7a." *OED Online*, Oxford University Press.

Curran, Beverly. "Mingling and Unmingling Opposites: Bending Gender in Ann-Marie MacDonald's *Goodnight Desdemona (Good Morning Juliet)*." *He Said, She Says: An RSVP to the Male Text*, edited by Mica Howe and Sarah Appleton Aguiar, Fairleigh Dickinson University Press, 2001, pp. 211–20.

Dadabhoy, Ambereen. "Two Faced: The Problem of Othello's Visage." *Othello: The State of Play*, edited by Lena Cowen Orlin, Bloomsbury, 2014, pp. 121–48.

—. "Wincing at Shakespeare: Looking B(l)ack at the Bard." *Journal of American Studies*, vol. 54, no. 1, 2020, pp. 82–88.

Daileader, Celia R. *Racism, Misogyny, and the Othello Myth: Inter-racial Couples from Shakespeare to Spike Lee*. Cambridge University Press, 2005.

Davidson, Lauren. "How Serial Shook up the Podcasting Industry." *Telegraph*, April 3, 2015, <www.telegraph.co.uk/finance/newsbysector/mediatechnologyandtelecoms/11513025/How-Serial-shook-up-the-podcasting-industry.html>. Accessed February 27, 2018.

Davis, Leslie, and Richard Fry. "College Faculty Have Become More Racially and Ethnically Diverse, But Remain Far Less So Than Students." *Pew Research*, July 31, 2019, <www.pewresearch.org/fact-tank/2019/07/31/us-college-faculty-student-diversity/>. Accessed July 15, 2021.

Davis-Secord, Sarah. *Teaching a Diverse and Inclusive Premodern World*. Special issue, *Studies in Medieval and Renaissance Teaching*, vol. 27, no. 2, Fall 2020.

De Sousa, Ronald. *The Rationality of Emotion*. MIT Press, 1987.

Del Col, Anthony, and Connor McCreery. *Kill Shakespeare: Backstage Edition Volume 1*. IDW Publishing, 2015.

—. *Kill Shakespeare Volume 3: The Tide of Blood*. IDW Publishing, 2013.

—. *Kill Shakespeare Volume 4: The Mask of Night*. IDW Publishing, 2014.

—. *Kill Shakespeare Volume 5: Past is Prologue: Juliet*. IDW Publishing, 2017.

Delgado, Richard, and Jean Stefancic. "Introduction." *Critical Race Theory: An Introduction*, edited by Richard Delgado and Jean Stefancic, 2nd ed., New York University Press, 2012, pp. 1–18.

Della Gatta, Carla. "Shakespeare, Race and 'Other' Englishes: The Q Brothers' *Othello: The Remix*." *Shakespeare Survey*, vol. 71, 2018, pp. 74–87.

Denslow, Kristin N. "Guest Starring *Hamlet*: The Proliferation of the Shakespeare Meme on American Television." *Shakespeare/Not Shakespeare*, edited by

Christy Desmet, Natalie Loper, and Jim Casey, Palgrave Macmillan, 2017, pp. 97–110.

Desmet, Christy. "Recognizing Shakespeare, Rethinking Fidelity: A Rhetoric and Ethics of Appropriation." *Shakespeare and the Ethics of Appropriation*, edited by Alexa Alice Joubin and Elizabeth Rivlin, Palgrave, 2014, pp. 41–57.

"Documents: Episode 6—The Suspect." *Undisclosed*, <undisclosed-podcast.com/episodes/episode-6-the-suspect.html>. Accessed April 15, 2016.

Donnelly, Matt. "Lena Dunham to Adapt Refugee Survival Story for Steven Spielberg, J. J. Abrams." *Variety*, October 29, 2018, <variety.com/2018/film/news/lena-dunham-steven-spielberg-abrams-hope-more-powerful-than-the-sea-1202992793/>. Accessed August 12, 2021.

Due, Tananarive. "*Get Out* and the Black Horror Aesthetic." *Get Out: The Complete Annotated Screenplay*, Inventory Press, 2019, pp. 6–15.

Dyer, Richard. *White: Twentieth Anniversary Edition*. Routledge, 2017.

Dyson, Michael Eric. "Tour(é)ing Blackness." *Who's Afraid of Post-Blackness: What It Means to Be Black Now*, Free Press, 2011, pp. xiii–xx.

Edison Research. "The Podcast Consumer 2017." *Triton Digital*, n.d., <www.edisonresearch.com/wp-content/uploads/2017/04/Podcast-Consumer-2017.pdf>. Accessed February 27, 2018.

Eklund, Hillary, and Wendy Beth Hyman. "Making Meaning and Doing Justice with Early Modern Texts." *Teaching Social Justice through Shakespeare: Why Renaissance Literature Matters Now*, edited by Hillary Eklund and Wendy Beth Hyman, Edinburgh University Press, 2019, pp. 1–23.

Entman, Robert M., and Andrew Rojecki. *The Black Image in the White Mind: Media and Race in America*. University of Chicago Press, 2001.

Ephraim, Michelle. "Screwing the Bardbody: *Kill Shakespeare* and North American Popular Culture." *Upstart: A Journal of English Renaissance Studies*, 2013, n.p.

"Episode 1: The Alibi." *Serial*, NPR, October 3, 2014, <serialpodcast.org/season-one/1/the-alibi>.

"Episode 8." *Key & Peele: Season 3*. Writ. Keegan-Michael Key and Jordan Peele. Dir. Peter Atencio. Comedy Central, 2013.

"Episode 10: The Best Defense is a Good Defense." *Serial*, NPR, October 3, 2014, <serialpodcast.org/season-one/10/the-best-defense-is-a-good-defense>.

"Episode 64: Q Brothers." *Shakespeare Unlimited*, Folger Shakespeare Library, January 10, 2017, <www.folger.edu/shakespeare-unlimited/q-brothers-othello>.

Erickson, Peter. *Citing Shakespeare: The Reinterpretation of Race in Contemporary Literature and Art*. Palgrave, 2007.

—. "Images of White Identity in *Othello*." *Othello: New Critical Essays*, edited by Philip C. Kolin, Routledge, 2002, pp. 133–45.

—. "'Late has no meaning here': Imagining a Second Chance in Toni Morrison's *Desdemona*." *Borrowers and Lenders: The Journal of Shakespeare and Appropriation*, vol. 8, no. 1, 2013, n.p.

—. "The Moment of Race in Renaissance Studies." *Shakespeare Studies*, vol. 26, 1998, pp. 27–36.
Erickson, Peter, and Kim F. Hall. "'A new scholarly song': Rereading Early Modern Race." *Shakespeare Quarterly*, vol. 67, no. 1, 2016, pp. 1–13.
Espinosa, Ruben. "'Don't it make my brown eyes blue': Uneasy Assimilation and the Shakespeare-Latinx Divide." *The Routledge Handbook of Shakespeare and Global Appropriation*, edited by Christy Desmet, Sujata Iyengar, and Miriam Jacobson, Routledge, 2020, pp. 48–58.
—. *Shakespeare on the Shades of Racism*. Routledge, 2021.
"Extenuate, n. 3a and 7b." *OED Online*, Oxford University Press.
Fanon, Frantz. *Black Skin, White Masks*. Translated by Richard Philcox, Grove Press, 2008.
Fazel, Valerie M. "A Network of Our Own: Shakespeare and the Acafan." Conference Presentation. Shakespeare Association of America, April 8, 2017, Atlanta, GA.
Fazel, Valerie M., and Louise Geddes. "'Give me your hands if we be friends': Collaborative Authority in Shakespeare Fan Fiction." *Shakespeare*, vol. 12, no. 3, 2015, pp. 1–13.
—. "Introduction: The Shakespeare User." *The Shakespeare User: Critical and Creative Appropriations in a Networked Culture*, edited by Valerie M. Fazel and Louise Geddes, Palgrave, 2017, pp. 1–22.
Feagin, Joe R. *The White Racial Frame: Centuries of Racial Framing and Counter-Framing*, 2nd ed., Routledge, 2013.
Feliciano, Ivette. "'Othello: The Remix' Gives Shakespeare the Hip-Hop Treatment." Transcript. *News Hour, PBS*, December 24, 2016, <www.pbs.org/newshour/show/othello-remix-gives-shakespeare-hip-hop-treatment>. Accessed February 18, 2019.
Fernandez, Vicenc, Pep Simo, and Jose M. Sallan. "Podcasting: A New Technological Tool to Facilitate Good Practice in Higher Education." *Computers & Education*, vol. 53, 2009, pp. 385–92.
Fields, Karen E., and Barbara J. Fields. *Racecraft: The Soul of Inequality in American Life*. Verso, 2014.
Finn, Kavita Mudan, and Jessica McCall. "Exit, Pursued by a Fan: Shakespeare, Fandom, and the Lure of the Alternate Universe." *Critical Survey*, vol. 28, no. 2, 2016, pp. 27–38.
Fitchette, Dan. "5 Reasons Everyone's Obsessed with 'Serial.'" *Vulture*, November 6, 2014, <www.vulture.com/2014/11/serial-podcast-why-is-everyone-obsessed.html>. Accessed February 27, 2018.
"Frame, n. and adj. 2." *OED Online*, Oxford University Press.
Frank Ocean. "Nikes." *Blonde*, Boys Don't Cry, 2016.
Fredrickson, George M. *The Black Image in the White Mind: The Debate on Afro-American Character and Destiny, 1817–1914*. Wesleyan University Press, 1987.
Freire, Paulo. *Pedagogy of the Oppressed: 20th Anniversary Edition*. Translated by Myra Bergman Ramos, Continuum, 2005.

Friedersdorf, Conor, Tanya Basu, Katie Kilkenny, and Lenika Cruz. "Serial Episode 10: Did Racism Help Put Adnan in Prison?" *The Atlantic*, December 4, 2014, <www.theatlantic.com/entertainment/archive/2014/12/serial-episode-10-cristinas-world/383432/>. Accessed February 3, 2015.

Friedman, Sharon. "The Feminist Playwright as Critic: Paula Vogel, Ann-Marie MacDonald, and Djanet Sears Interpret *Othello*." *Feminist Theatrical Revisions of Class Works: Critical Essays*, edited by Sharon Friedman, McFarland & Co., 2008, pp. 113–34.

Gallagher, Charles A. "Color-Blind Privilege: The Social and Political Functions of Erasing the Color Line in Post Race America." *Race, Gender & Class*, vol. 10, no. 4, 2004, pp. 1–17.

Gamboa, Brett, and Lawrence Switzky. "Introduction." *Shakespeare's Things: Shakespearean Theatre and the Non-Human World in History, Theory, and Performance*, edited by Brett Gamboa and Lawrence Switzky, Routledge, 2019, pp. 1–20.

Gateward, Frances, and John Jennings. "Introduction: The Sweeter the Christmas." *The Blacker the Ink: Constructions of Black Identity in Comics & Sequential Art*, edited by Frances Gateward and John Jennings, Rutgers University Press, 2015, pp. 1–15.

Gerzic, Marina, and Helen Balfour. "Haunting Emotions: Visualizing Hamlet's Melancholy for Students in Two Recent Graphic Novel Adaptations." *Borrowers and Lenders: The Journal of Shakespeare and Appropriation*, vol. 9, no. 2, 2015, n.p.

Gillen, Katherine. "From Roman Britain to the Twenty-First Century United States: The Construction of White Masculinity in the *Cymbelines* of William Shakespeare and Michael Almereyda." *Borrowers and Lenders: The Journal of Shakespeare and Appropriation*, vol. 13, no. 2, 2020, n.p.

Gillota, David. "New Directions in African American Humor." *Studies in American Humor*, vol. 3, no. 29, 2013, pp. 17–30.

Godsey, Michael. "I'm Replacing Shakespeare with 'Serial,'" *The Skeptical Pioneer*, November 6, 2014, <www.mrgodsey.com/2014/11/im-replacing-shakespeare-with-serial.html>. Accessed February 3, 2015.

—. "Standards Based 'Serial,'" *The Skeptical Pioneer*, November 6, 2014, <www.mrgodsey.com/2014/11/standards-based-serial.html>. Accessed April 14, 2016.

Goldberg, David Theo. *Anatomy of Racism*. University of Minnesota Press, 1990.

—. *Are We All Postracial Yet?* Polity, 2015.

—. *The Threat of Race: Reflections on Racial Neoliberalism*. Wiley-Blackwell, 2008.

Goldberg, David Theo, and John Solomos. "General Introduction." *Companion to Racial and Ethnic Studies*, edited by David Theo Goldberg and John Solomos, Blackwell, 2002, pp. 1–12.

Gosling, Mya Lixian. "Shakespearean Character Spotlight: Desdemona." *Good Tickle Brain*, October 3, 2014, <goodticklebrain.com/

home/2014/10/2/shakespearean-character-spotlight-desdemona>. Accessed August 10, 2021.
—. "Stick Figure Iconography: Othello." *Good Tickle Brain*, August 2, 2018, <goodticklebrain.com/home/2018/6/21/stick-figure-iconography-othello>. Accessed August 10, 2021.
—. "Three-Panel Plays, part 13." *Good Tickle Brain*, May 5, 2014, <goodticklebrain.com/home/2014/3/5/three-panel-plays-part-13>. Accessed August 10, 2021.
Grady, Kyle. "Othello, Colin Powell, and Post-Racial Anachronisms." *Shakespeare Quarterly*, vol. 67, no. 1, 2016, pp. 68–83.
Greenblatt, Stephen, ed. *The Norton Shakespeare*, 3rd ed., W. W. Norton, 2016.
Greene, Morgan. "Holiday Video: Christmas Freestyle with the Q Brothers." *Chicago Tribune*, December 14, 2015, <www.chicagotribune.com/entertainment/theater/ct-showcase-a-q-brothers-christmas-freestyle-20151209-story.html>. Accessed February 18, 2018.
Grennan, Eamon. "The Women's Voices in *Othello*: Speech, Song, Silence." *Shakespeare Quarterly*, vol. 38, no. 3, 1987, pp. 275–92.
Grier, Miles P. "The Color of Professionalism: A Response to Dennis Britton." *Early Modern Black Diaspora Studies: A Critical Anthology*, edited by Cassander L. Smith, Nicholas R. Jones, and Miles P. Grier, Palgrave, 2018, pp. 229–38.
Gruber, Elizabeth. "Erotic Politics Reconsidered: *Desdemona*'s Challenge to *Othello*." *Borrowers and Lenders: The Journal of Shakespeare and Appropriation*, vol. 3, no. 2, 2008, n.p.
Grzanka, Patrick R. "Introduction: Intersectional Objectivity." *Intersectionality: Foundations and Frontiers*, edited by Patrick R. Grzanka, 1st ed., Westview Press, 2014, pp. xi–xxvii.
Guerrero, Ed. *Framing Blackness: The African American Image in Film*. Temple University Press, 1993.
—. "The Black Man on Our Screens and the Empty Space in Representation." *Callaloo*, vol. 18, no. 2, 1995, pp. 395–400.
Habib, Imtiaz. "The Black Alien in *Othello*: Beyond the European Immigrant." *Shakespeare and Immigration*, edited by Ruben Espinosa and David Ruiter, Routledge, 2016, pp. 135–58.
Hall, Kim F. "Beauty and the Beast of Whiteness: Teaching Race and Gender." *Shakespeare Quarterly*, vol. 47, no. 4, 1996, pp. 461–75.
—. "Can You Be White and Hear This? The Racial Art of Listening in *American Moor* and *Desdemona*." *White People in Shakespeare: Essays on Race, Culture, and the Elite*, edited by Arthur Little Jr., The Arden Shakespeare, forthcoming.
—. "Introduction." *American Moor*. Methuen Drama, 2020, pp. ix–xi.
—. "'Othello was my grandfather': Shakespeare in the African Diaspora." Shakespeare Anniversary Lecture Series Presented by the Folger Institute, June 27, 2016, Folger Shakespeare Library, Washington, DC. Keynote Address.

—. *Things of Darkness: Economies of Race and Gender in Early Modern England*. Cornell University Press, 1995.
Hall, Stuart. "Culture, the Media, and the 'ideological effect.'" *Essential Essays Vol. 1*, edited by David Morley, Duke University Press, 2019, pp. 298–336.
—. "Notes on Deconstructing 'the popular.'" *Essential Essays Vol. 1*, edited by David Morley, Duke University Press, 2019, pp. 347–61.
—. *The Fateful Triangle: Race, Ethnicity, Nation*. Harvard University Press, 2021.
Hankey, Julie, ed. *Othello (Shakespeare in Production)*, 2nd ed., Cambridge University Press, 2005.
Harrington, Louise. "'Excuse me while I turn this upside-down': Three Canadian Adaptations of Shakespeare." *British Journal of Canadian Studies*, vol. 20, no. 1, 2007, pp. 123–42.
Harris, Aisha. "The Most Terrifying Villain in *Get Out* is White Womanhood." *Slate*, March 7, 2017, <slate.com/culture/2017/03/how-get-out-positions-white-womanhood-as-the-most-horrifying-villain-of-all.html>. Accessed January 23, 2018.
Harris, Jonathan Gil. *Untimely Matter in the Time of Shakespeare*. University of Pennsylvania Press, 2008.
Harris, Jonathan Gil, and Nathasha Korda. "Introduction: Towards a Materialist Account of Stage Properties." *Staged Properties in Early Modern English Drama*, edited by Jonathan Gil Harris and Natasha Korda, Cambridge University Press, 2006, pp. 1–34.
Harris-Perry, Melissa. *Sister Citizen: Shame, Stereotypes, and Black Women in America*. Yale University Press, 2013.
Harrod, Horatia. "Chiwetel Ejiofor on Shakespeare, Race, and the Marvel Universe." *Financial Times Magazine*, October 14, 2016, <www.ft.com/content/684a4810-90d6-11e6-8df8-d3778b55a923>. Accessed August 12, 2021.
Harwell, Drew. "The Staggering Numbers that Prove Hollywood Has a Serious Race Problem." *Washington Post*, February 23, 2016, <www.washingtonpost.com/news/the-switch/wp/2016/02/23/its-too-loud-and-other-reasons-oscar-voters-ignore-black-movies/>. Accessed August 12, 2021.
Hayes, Kevin J., *Shakespeare and the Making of America*. Amberley Publishing, 2020.
Hazelrigg, Nick. "Little Progress in Diversifying Faculty Ranks, Study Finds, Particularly at Research Universities." *Inside Higher Ed*, July 2, 2019, <www.insidehighered.com/news/2019/07/02/little-progress-diversifying-faculty-ranks-study-finds-particularly-research>. Accessed July 15, 2021.
Henderson, Diana E. *Collaborations With the Past: Reshaping Shakespeare Across Time and Media*. Cornell University Press, 2006.
Hendricks, Margo. "'Obscured by dreams': Race, Empire, and Shakespeare's *A Midsummer Night's Dream*." *Shakespeare Quarterly*, vol. 47, no. 1, 1996, pp. 37–60.

—. "Visions of Color: Spectacle, Spectators, and the Performance of Race." *A Companion to Shakespeare and Performance*, edited by Barbara Hodgdon and W. B. Worthen, John Wiley & Sons, 2007, pp. 511–26.

Heng, Geraldine. *The Invention of Race in the European Middle Ages*. Cambridge University Press, 2020.

Hengen, Shannon. "Towards a Feminist Comedy." *Canadian Literature*, vol. 146, 1995, pp. 97–107.

Henry, Matthew. "'He Is a 'Bad Mother*$%@!#': 'Shaft' and Contemporary Black Masculinity." *Journal of Popular Film & Television*, vol. 30, no. 2, 2002, pp. 114–19.

Hodgson, John. "Desdemona's Handkerchief as an Emblem of Her Reputation." *Texas Studies in Literature and Language*, vol. 19, 1977, pp. 313–22.

Hoffman, Warren. *The Great White Way: Race and the Broadway Musical*. Rutgers University Press, 2014.

Holland, Peter. "Shakespeare, Humanity Indicators, and the Seven Deadly Sins." *Borrowers and Lenders: The Journal of Shakespeare and Appropriation*, vol. 7, no. 1, 2012, n.p.

hooks, bell. *Ain't I A Woman: Black Women and Feminism*. Pluto Press, 1990.

—. *Black Looks: Race and Representation*. South End Press, 1992.

—. *Teaching to Transgress: Education as the Practice of Freedom*. Routledge, 1994.

—. *We Real Cool: Black Men and Masculinity*. Routledge, 2003.

Hornaday, Ann. "In Hollywood, Must 'White' Always Equal 'Universal'?" *Washington Post*, January 26, 2016, <www.washingtonpost.com/lifestyle/style/filmgoing-after-oscarssowhite-keeping-score-vs-cultural-literacy/2016/01/26/75be6c30-c091-11e5-bcda-62a36b394160_story.html>. Accessed August 12, 2021.

Hornback, Robert. "Emblems of Folly in the first *Othello*: Renaissance Blackface, Moor's Coat, and 'Muckender.'" *Comparative Drama*, vol. 35, no. 1, 2001, pp. 69–99.

—. *Racism and Early Blackface Comic Traditions: From the Old World to the New*. Palgrave, 2018.

Hoston, William T. *Race and the Black Male Subculture: The Lives of Toby Waller*. Palgrave, 2016.

Howard, Sheena C., and Ronald L. Jackson II. "Introduction." *Black Comics: Politics of Race and Representation*, edited by Sheena C. Howard and Ronald L. Jackson II, Bloomsbury, 2013, pp. 1–8.

Huang, Eddie. "Bamboo-Ceiling TV." *Vulture*, January 2015, <www.vulture.com/2015/01/eddie-huang-fresh-off-the-boat-abc.html>. Accessed August 12, 2021.

Hutchinson, Shaun Ajamu. "*Othello: The Remix* Review." *The New Black Magazine*, September 25, 2013, <www.thenewblackmagazine.com/view.aspx?index=3183>. Accessed February 18, 2019.

"Influence, n." *OED Online*, Oxford University Press.

Iyengar, Sujata. *Shades of Difference: Mythologies of Skin Color in Early Modern England*. University of Pennsylvania Press, 2005.
—. "Woman-Crafted Shakespeares: Appropriation, Intermediality, and Womanist Aesthetics." *A Feminist Companion to Shakespeare*, edited by Dympna Callaghan, 2nd ed., John Wiley & Sons, 2016, pp. 507–19.
Jackson, Lauren Michele. "What's Missing from 'White Fragility.'" *Slate*, September 4, 2019, <slate.com/human-interest/2019/09/white-fragility-robin-diangelo-workshop.html>. Accessed September 4, 2019.
Jackson, Zakiyyah Iman. *Becoming Human: Matter and Meaning in an Antiblack World*. Duke University Press, 2020.
Jay-Z. "The Story of OJ." *4:44*. Roc Nation/Universal, 2017.
Jenkins, Henry. *Textual Poachers: Television Fans and Participatory Culture*. 20th anniversary edition. Routledge, 2021.
Johnson, Allan G. *Privilege, Power, and Difference*, 3rd ed., McGraw-Hill Education, 2017.
Jones, Chris. "Tragic Rap? 'Othello' is the Q Brothers' Best Yet." *Chicago Tribune*, March 22, 2013, <www.chicagotribune.com/ct-ent-0323-othello-review-20130322-column.html>. Accessed February 18, 2019.
Jones, Dustin. "42% in the US Can't Name a Single Prominent Asian American, a Survey Finds." *NPR*, May 16, 2021, <www.npr.org/2021/05/16/997346466/80-of-asian-americans-say-they-are-discriminated-against>. Accessed August 10, 2021.
Jordan, Julia. "The Count 2.0: Who's Getting Produced in the US?" *Dramatists Guild*, <www.dramatistsguild.com/advocacy/the-count>. Accessed March 4, 2020.
Joubin, Alexa Alice. *Shakespeare and East Asia*, Oxford University Press, 2021.
Joubin, Alexa Alice, and Elizabeth Rivlin. "Introduction: Shakespeare and the Ethics of Appropriation." *Shakespeare and the Ethics of Appropriation*, edited by Alexa Alice Joubin and Elizabeth Rivlin, Palgrave, 2014, pp. 1–20.
Kafantaris, Mira Assaf. "Sugar and Consumption," "Unsilencing the Past in Bridgerton 2020: A Roundtable." *Medium*, January 9, 2021, <kerrysinanan.medium.com/unsilencing-the-past-in-bridgerton-2020-a-roundtable-792ecffd366>. Accessed August 12, 2021.
Kang, Jay Caspian. "'Serial' and White Reporter Privilege." *The Awl*, November 13, 2014, <www.theawl.com/2014/11/white-reporter-privilege/>. Accessed February 4, 2015.
Karim-Cooper, Farah, and Eoin Price. "Shakespeare, Race, and Nation: Introduction, a Conversation." *Shakespeare*, vol. 17, no. 1, 2021, pp. 1–5.
Kauffman, Miranda. *Black Tudors: The Untold Story*. Oneworld Publications, 2017.
Kendi, Ibram X. *How to Be an Antiracist*. One World, 2019.
—. *Stamped from the Beginning: The Definitive History of Racist Ideas in America*. Bold Type Books, 2016.

Kendrick Lamar. "Fear." *Damn*. Top Dawg/Aftermath/Interscope, 2017.
"Key & Peele: 'Othello 'Tis My Shite.'" *Vimeo*, uploaded by Peter Atencio, <vimeo.com/80117015>. Accessed August 12, 2021.
Kidnie, Margaret Jane. *Shakespeare and the Problem of Adaptation*. Routledge, 2009.
Kim, Shanelle E. "'Intermission!': Reading Race in the Objects of *Key & Peele's* 'Othello 'Tis My Shite'" *Variable Objects: Shakespeare and Speculative Appropriation*, edited by Valerie M. Fazel and Louise Geddes, Edinburgh University Press, 2021, pp. 167–91.
Kimbro, Devori, Michael Noschka, and Geoffrey Way. "Lend Us Your Earbuds: Shakespeare/Podcasting/*Poesis*." *Humanities*, vol. 8, no. 2, 2019, n.p.
Kinder, Donald R., and David O. Sears. "Prejudice and Politics: Symbolic Racism versus Racial Threats to the Good Life." *Journal of Personality and Social Psychology*, vol. 40, no. 3, 1981, pp. 414–31.
Kipp-Giusti, Elizabeth. "Othello: The Remix." *The Easy*, November 28, 2016, <www.theasy.com/Reviews/2016/O/othellotheremix.php>. Accessed February 18, 2019.
Kohn, Eric. "Jordan Peele Challenges Golden Globes Classifying 'Get Out' As a Comedy: 'What Are You Laughing At?'" *IndieWire*, November 15, 2017, <www.indiewire.com/2017/11/jordan-peele-response-get-out-golden-globes-comedy-1201897841/>. Accessed August 12, 2021.
Kumar, Deepa. *Islamophobia and the Politics of Empire*. Haymarket Books, 2012.
Lanier, Douglas M. "Introduction: On the Virtues of Illegitimacy: Free Shakespeare on Film." *Shakespeare After Shakespeare: An Encyclopedia of the Bard in Mass Media and Popular Culture Vol. 1*, edited by Richard Burt, Greenwood Press, 2007, pp. 132–37.
—. "Minstrelsy, Jazz, Rap: Shakespeare, African American Music, and Cultural Legitimation." *Borrowers and Lenders: The Journal of Shakespeare and Appropriation*, vol. 1, no. 1, 2005, n.p.
—. *Shakespeare and Modern Popular Culture*. Oxford University Press, 2002.
—. "Shakespearean Rhizomatics: Adaptation, Ethics, Value." *Shakespeare and the Ethics of Appropriation*, edited by Alexa Alice Joubin and Elizabeth Rivlin, Palgrave, 2014, pp. 21–40.
—. "The Hogarth Shakespeare Series: Redeeming Shakespeare's Literariness." *Shakespeare and Millennial Fiction*, edited by Andrew James Hartley, Cambridge University Press, 2018, pp. 230–50.
LaPerle, Carol Mejia. "Race in Shakespeare's Tragedies." *The Cambridge Companion to Shakespeare and Race*, edited by Ayanna Thompson, Cambridge University Press, 2021, pp. 77–92.
—. "'Thou art translated': Peter Sellars's Midsummer Chamber Play." *Borrowers and Lenders: The Journal of Shakespeare and Appropriation*, vol. 11, no. 1, 2017, n.p.

Late Night with Seth Meyers. "Allison Williams Reveals What White People Ask Her About *Get Out*." *YouTube*, December 1, 2017, <www.youtube.com/watch?v=2AE0tMvL-aM>. Accessed February 16, 2019.

Lawrence, Derek. "Jordan Peele Says *Get Out* Can't 'be put into a genre box.'" *Yahoo*, November 15, 2017, <finance.yahoo.com/news/jordan-peele-says-em-em-232000586.html?guccounter=1&guce_referrer=aHR0cHM6Ly93d3cuZ29vZ2xlLmNvbS8&guce_referrer_sig=AQAAABeaRogaYPbybxuTBACNe8asvMogy5B2QUN-8nw7st4_6x6x6PIyPqDcyIibBCQI0eN-Pl6wTVJ1Pq9da5aos4WHJm3TGaR-cvAN7X4f2TnH3epIFl7Ii1KPzrAXgwx8ILUdIC99XDiHb89AVh8xFdi2yis20bPbUXby1VkAUAEr>. Accessed August 12, 2021.

Lehmann, Courtney. *Shakespeare Remains: Theater to Film, Early Modern to Postmodern*, Cornell University Press, 2002.

Lester, Adrian. "In Dialogue with Ayanna Thompson." *Shakespeare Survey*, vol. 70 2017, pp. 10–18.

Lewis, Reina. *Rethinking Orientalism: Women, Travel, and the Ottoman Harem*. New York: Rutgers University Press, 2004.

Little Jr., Arthur. "Re-Historicizing Race, White Melancholia, and the Shakespearean Property." *Shakespeare Quarterly*, vol. 67, no. 1, 2016, pp. 84–103.

—. *Shakespeare Jungle Fever: National-Imperial Re-Visions of Race, Rape, and Sacrifice*. Stanford University Press, 2000.

Liu, William Ming, Theodore Pickett Jr., and Allen E. Ivey. "White Middle-Class Privilege: Social Class Bias and Implications for Training and Practice." *Journal of Multicultural Counseling and Development*, vol. 35, 2007, pp. 194–206.

Londoño, Ernesto. "Hooked on the Freewheeling Podcast 'Serial.'" *New York Times*, February 12, 2015, <www.nytimes.com/2015/02/13/opinion/hooked-on-the-freewheeling-podcast-serial.html>. Accessed February 27, 2018.

Loofbourow, Lili. "The Male Glance: How We Fail to Take Women's Stories Seriously." *Guardian*, March 6, 2018, <www.theguardian.com/news/2018/mar/06/the-male-glance-how-we-fail-to-take-womens-stories-seriously>. Accessed August 12, 2021.

Loomba, Ania, and Jonathan Burton. "Introduction." *Race and Early Modern England: A Documentary Companion*, edited by Ania Loomba and Jonathan Burton, Palgrave Macmillan, 2007, pp. 1–36.

Loughrey, Clarisse. "William Shakespeare: How the UK Is Celebrating His 400th Anniversary." *Independent*, April 22, 2016, <www.independent.co.uk/arts-entertainment/theatre-dance/news/william-shakespeare-400th-anniversary-how-uk-celebrating-a6971621.html>. Accessed August 12, 2021.

Lubin, Gus. "Samuel L. Jackson Had the Perfect Response to the Writer Who Made His 'Avengers' Role Possible." *Business Insider*, April 27, 2015, <businessinsider.com/samuel-l-jackson-thanks-mark-millar-2015-4>. Accessed June 3, 2021.

MacDonald, Ann-Marie. *Goodnight Desdemona (Good Morning Juliet)*, Grove Press, 1998.

MacDonald, Joyce Green. "Acting Black: *Othello*, *Othello* Burlesques, and the Performance of Blackness." *Theatre Journal*, vol. 46, no. 2, 1994, pp. 231–49.

—. *Shakespearean Adaptation, Race and Memory in the New World*. Palgrave, 2020.

Martin, Denise. "Keegan-Michael Key and Jordan Peele on 5 Classic *Key & Peele* Sketches." *Vulture*, June 20, 2014, <vulture.com/2014/06/origins-of-5-classic-key-peele-sketches-othello-metta-world-peace-gay-health-insurance.html>. Accessed May 26, 2016.

Martinot, Steve, *The Machinery of Whiteness: Studies in the Structure of Racialization*. Temple University Press, 2010.

Marx, Nick. "Expanding the Brand: Race, Gender, and the Post-politics of Representation on Comedy Central." *Television & New Media*, vol. 17, no. 3, 2015, pp. 272–87.

Mbembe, Achille. *Necropolitics*. Duke University Press, 2019.

McCall, Leslie. "The Complexity of Intersectionality." *Signs*, vol. 30, no. 3, 2005, pp. 1771–1800.

McDonald, Soraya Nadia. "In Theater, the White Gaze Takes Center Stage." *The Undefeated*, July 2, 2019, <theundefeated.com/features/in-theater-the-white-gaze-takes-center-stage/>. Accessed March 4, 2020.

—. "The Dangerous Magical Thinking of 'This Is Not Who We Are.'" *The Undefeated*, January 14, 2021, <theundefeated.com/features/capitol-attack-trump-the-dangerous-magical-thinking-of-this-is-not-who-we-are/>. Accessed August 12, 2021.

McIntosh, Peggy. "White Privilege: Unpacking the Invisible Knapsack." *National Seed Project*, pp. 1–4, <nationalseedproject.org/Key-SEED-Texts/white-privilege-unpacking-the-invisible-knapsack>. Accessed April 20, 2022.

Mehdizadeh, Nedda. "Othello in Harlem: Transforming Theater in Djanet Sears's *Harlem Duet*." *Journal of American Studies*, vol. 54, no. 1, 2020, pp. 12–18.

Memmi, Albert. *The Colonizer and the Colonized*. Translated by Howard Greenfeld, Profile Books, 2021.

Meraji, Shereen Marisol. "Why Chaucer Said 'Ax' instead of 'Ask,' and Why Some Still Do." Transcript. *All Things Considered*, NPR, December 3, 2013, <www.kcur.org/post/why-chaucer-said-ax-instead-ask-and-why-some-still-do#stream/0>. Accessed May 11, 2019.

Miller, Ryan W. "Almost Two-Thirds of Millennials, Gen Z Don't Know That 6 Million Jews Were Killed in the Holocaust, Survey Finds." *USA Today*, September 16, 2020, <www.usatoday.com/story/news/nation/2020/09/16/holocaust-history-millennials-gen-z-cant-name-concentration-camps/5792448002/>. Accessed August 10, 2021.

Miranda, Lin-Manuel, and Jeremy McCarter. *Hamilton: The Revolution*. Grand Central Publishing, 2016.

Morey, Peter, and Amina Yaqin. *Framing Muslims: Stereotyping and Representation after 9/11*. Harvard University Press, 2011.

Morrison, Michael. "Shakespeare in North America." *The Cambridge Companion to Shakespeare on Stage*, edited by Stanley Wells and Sarah Stanton, Cambridge University Press, 2002, pp. 230–58.

Morrison, Toni. *Desdemona*. Oberon Books, 2012.

—. *Playing in the Dark: Whiteness and the Literary Imagination*. Vintage, 1993.

Mutua, Athena D. "Theorizing Progressive Black Masculinities." *Progressive Black Masculinities*, edited by Athena D. Mutua, Routledge, 2006, pp. 3–42.

Nama, Adilifu. *Super Black: American Pop Culture and Black Superheroes*. University of Texas Press, 2011.

National Endowment for the Arts. *US Patterns of Arts Participation: A Full Report from the 2017 Survey of Public Participation in the Arts*. December 2019.

Ndiaye, Noémie. "Shakespeare, Race, and Globalization: *Titus Andronicus*." *The Cambridge Companion to Shakespeare and Race*, edited by Ayanna Thompson, Cambridge University Press, 2021, pp. 158–74.

Neal, Mark Anthony. *Looking for Leroy: Illegible Black Masculinities*. New York University Press, 2013.

—. *New Black Man: 10th Anniversary Edition*, Routledge 2015.

Neill, Michael. "Introduction to *Othello*." *Othello*. Oxford Shakespeare, 2006, pp. 1–179.

—. "Response to Ian Smith." *Shakespeare Quarterly*, vol. 64, no. 1, 2013, pp. 26–31.

—. "Unproper Beds: Race, Adultery, and the Hideous in *Othello*." *Shakespeare Quarterly*, vol. 40, no. 4, 1989, pp. 383–412.

Newman, Karen. "'And wash the Ethiop white': Femininity and the Monstrous in *Othello*." *Shakespeare Reproduced: The Text in History and Ideology*, edited by Jean Howard and Marion O'Connor, Routledge, 1987, pp. 143–62.

Newton, Kim. "Finding Shakespeare in 'Serial.'" *ASC Education*, American Shakespeare Center, January 23, 2015, <asc-blogs.com/2015/01/23/finding-shakespeare-in-serial/>. Accessed July 19, 2017.

Niayesh, Ladan. "Of Pearls and Scimitars: The Shakespearean Bazaar of Oriental Props." *Société Française Shakespeare*, vol. 27, 2009, pp. 83–98.

Novy, Marianne. "Saving Desdemona and/or Ourselves: Plays by Ann-Marie MacDonald and Paula Vogel." *Transforming Shakespeare: Contemporary Women's Re-Visions in Literature and Performance*, edited by Marianne Novy, Palgrave, 1999, pp. 68–85.

Obama, Barack. "Remarks by the President at the White House Correspondents' Dinner." Opening remarks, Capital Hilton, Washington, DC, April 30, 2016.

OJ: The Musical. Dir. Jeff Rosenberg. Perf. Jordan Kenneth Kamp, Malcolm Barrett, and Larisa Oleynik, 2016.

Okri, Ben. *A Way of Being Free*. Head of Zeus, 2015.
Oluo, Ijeoma. *So You Want to Talk About Race*. Seal Press, 2019.
Orgel, Stephen. "The Authentic Shakespeare." *Representations*, no. 28, 1988, pp. 1–25.
Pande, Rukmini. *Squee from the Margins: Fandom and Race*. University of Iowa Press, 2018.
Pao, Angela C. *No Safe Spaces: Re-casting Race, Ethnicity, and Nationality in American Theater*. University of Michigan Press, 2010.
Peele, Jordan, dir. *Get Out*. Perf. Daniel Kaluuya, Alison Williams. Universal Pictures and Blumhouse Productions, 2017.
—. *Get Out: The Complete Annotated Screenplay*. Inventory Press, 2019.
Pérez, Raúl. "Racism without Hatred? Racist Humor and the Myth of 'Colorblindness.'" *Sociological Perspectives*, vol. 60, no. 5, 2017, pp. 956–74.
Perry, Imani. *Prophets of the Hood: Politics and Poetics in Hip-Hop*. Duke University Press, 2004.
Petty, Tom. "Free Fallin." *Full Moon Fever*. MCA, 1989.
Pittman, L. Monique. *Authorizing Shakespeare on Film and Television: Gender, Class, and Ethnicity in Adaptation*. Peter Lang, 2011.
—. "Big-Shouldered Shakespeare: Three *Shrews* at Chicago Shakespeare Theater." *Shakespeare Survey*, vol. 67, 2014, pp. 244–64.
—. "Color-Conscious Casting and Multicultural Britain in the BBC *Henry V* (2012): Historicizing Adaptation in an Age of Digital Placelessness." *Adaptation*, vol. 10, no. 2, 2017, pp. 176–91.
Pittman, Marvin C. "Jordan Peele Makes the Leap in 'Get Out.'" *Forces of Geek*, March 10, 2017, <forcesofgeek.com/2017/03/jordan-peele-makes-the-leap-in-get-out.html>. Accessed September 30, 2019.
Pope, Johnathan H. *Shakespeare's Fans: Adapting the Bard in the Age of Media Fandom*. Palgrave, 2020.
Porges, Seth. "Everything You Ever Wanted to Know About Listening to Podcasts." *Forbes*, January 15, 2015, <www.forbes.com/sites/sethporges/2015/01/15/everything-you-ever-wanted-to-know-about-listening-to-podcasts/#40093aaf22eb>. Accessed February 27, 2018.
Porter, Laurin R. "Shakespeare's 'Sisters': Desdemona, Juliet, and Constance Ledbelly in *Goodnight Desdemona (Good Morning Juliet)*." *Modern Drama*, vol. 38, no. 3, 1995, pp. 362–77.
Pough, Gwendolyn D. "An Introduction of Sorts for Hip-Hop Feminism." *Home Girls Make Some Noise: Hip-Hop Feminism Anthology*, edited by Gwendolyn D. Pough, Elaine Richardson, Aisha Durham, and Rachel Raimist, Parker Publishing, 2007, pp. x–ix.
Princess Weekes. "Joyce Carol Oates Asks if Othello Works Without Him Being a Moor—Um . . . Nope." *The Mary Sue*, December 27, 2017, <www.themarysue.com/joyce-caroloates-othello/>. Accessed January 18, 2019.
Q Brothers. *Othello: The Remix*. Dramatists Play Service, 2018.
—. "Othello: The Remix." Theatrical Script for The Globe. 2012.
—. *Othello: The Remix Soundtrack*. Chicago Shakespeare Theater.

Ramos, Dino-Ray. "Jordan Peele Says It Feels Like 'We're in the Sunken Place' Right Now–PGA Awards." *Deadline*, January 20, 2018, <deadline.com/2018/01/jordan-peele-get-out-stanley-kramer-award-pga-awards-norman-lear-1202264687/>. Accessed January 25, 2019.

Rankine, Claudia. *Citizen: An American Lyric*. Graywolf Press, 2014.

"Reanimate, v." *OED Online*, Oxford University Press.

Red Bull Theater. "Exploring *Othello* in 2020." October 2020, <www.redbulltheater.com/exploring-othello-2020>. Accessed August 12, 2021.

Reid, Pat. "Brain Candy." *Shakespeare Magazine*, November 27, 2017, pp. 46–52.

"Revise, v." *OED Online*, Oxford University Press.

Rich, Adrienne. "Compulsory Sexuality and Lesbian Existence." *Signs*, vol. 5, no. 4, 1980, pp. 631–60.

Richardson, Riché. *Black Masculinity and the US South: From Uncle Tom to Gangsta*. University of Georgia Press, 2010.

Rickford, John R. *African American Vernacular English*. Blackwell, 1999.

Roberts, Soraya. "Thoughts on Race, Journalism, and 'Serial,'" *Bitch Media*, November 20, 2014, <bitchmedia.org/post/thoughts-on-race-journalism-and-serial>. Accessed July 19, 2017.

Rodriquez, Jason. "Color-Blind Ideology and the Cultural Appropriation of Hip-Hop." *Journal of Contemporary Ethnography*, vol. 35, no. 6, 2006, pp. 645–68.

Romero, George A., dir. *Night of the Living Dead*. Perf. Duane Jones, Judith O'Dea, and Karl Hardman. Image Ten, 1968.

Ronk, Martha. "Desdemona's Self-Presentation." *English Literary Renaissance*, vol. 35, no. 1, 2005, pp. 52–72.

Rose, Tricia. *The Hip-Hop Wars: What We Talk About When We Talk About Hip-Hop—And Why It Matters*. Civitas Books, 2008.

Rosin, Hanna. "The Real Secret of *Serial*." *Slate*, October 23, 2014, <www.slate.com/articles/arts/culturebox/2014/10/serial_podcast_and_storytelling_does_sarah_koenig_think_adnan_syed_is_innocent.html>. Accessed July 19, 2017.

Rossing, Jonathan P. "Deconstructing Postracialism: Humor as a Critical, Cultural Project." *Journal of Communication Inquiry*, vol. 36, no. 1, 2012, pp. 44–61.

Royster, Francesca T. *Becoming Cleopatra: The Shifting Image of an Icon*. Palgrave, 2003.

—. "Rememorializing Othello: Teaching *Othello* and the Cultural Memory of Racism." *Approaches to Teaching Shakespeare's Othello*, edited by Peter Erickson and Maurice Hunt, The Modern Language Association of America, 2005, pp. 53–61.

Russo, Anthony, and Joe Russo, dir. *Avengers: Infinity War*. Marvel Studios, 2018.

Ryan, Kiernan. *Shakespeare's Universality: Here's Fine Revolution (Shakespeare Now!)*. Bloomsbury, 2015.

Salam, Maya. "Hollywood is as White, Straight, and Male as Ever." *New York Times*, August 2, 2018, <www.nytimes.com/2018/08/02/arts/hollywood-movies-diversity.html>. Accessed August 12, 2021.

Sanders, Julie. *Adaptation and Appropriation*. Routledge, 2015.

Santos, Kathryn Vomero. "Hosting Language: Immigration and Translation in *The Merry Wives of Windsor*." *Shakespeare and Immigration*, edited by Ruben Espinosa and David Ruiter, Ashgate, 2014, pp. 59–72.

Sarkar, Debapriya. "Literary Justice: The Participatory Ethics of Early Modern Possible Worlds." *Teaching Social Justice Through Shakespeare: Why Renaissance Literature Matters Now*, edited by Hillary Eklund and Wendy Beth Hyman, Edinburgh University Press, 2019, pp. 174–84.

Saucier, Donald A., Conor J. O'Dea, and Megan L. Strain. "The Bad, the Good, the Misunderstood: The Social Effects of Racial Humor." *Translational Issues in Psychological Science*, vol. 2, no. 1, 2016, pp. 75–85.

Sayet, Madeline. "Interrogating the Shakespeare System." *HowlRound*, August 31, 2020, <howlround.com/interrogating-shakespeare-system>. Accessed March 9, 2021.

Schneider, Steven Jay. "Mixed Blood Couples: Monsters and Miscegenation in US Horror Cinema." *The Gothic Other: Racial and Social Constructions in the Literary Imagination*, edited by Ruth Bienstock Anolik and Douglas L. Howard, McFarland & Co. Press, 2004, pp. 72–89.

Sellars, Peter. "Foreword." *Desdemona*, Oberon Books, 2012, pp. 7–11.

Shakespeare, William. *A Midsummer Night's Dream. The Norton Shakespeare*, edited by Stephen Greenblatt, 3rd ed., 2016, pp. 1037–96.

—. *Othello: Texts and Contexts*, edited by Kim F. Hall, Bedford/St. Martins, 2007.

—. *The Merchant of Venice. The Norton Shakespeare*, edited by Stephen Greenblatt, 3rd ed., 2016, pp. 1327–94.

—. *The Tempest. The Norton Shakespeare*, edited by Stephen Greenblatt, 3rd ed., 2016, pp. 3205–66.

—. *Titus Andronicus. The Norton Shakespeare*, edited by Stephen Greenblatt, 3rd ed., 2016, pp. 491–554.

Shakespeare Theater Association. "Shakespeare's Legacy–400." *Shakespeare Theater Association*, 2016, <www.stahome.org/2016>. Accessed August 12, 2021.

Shakespeare's Globe. "Anti-Racist Shakespeare: *A Midsummer Night's Dream*." *YouTube*, May 27, 2021, <www.youtube.com/watch?v=DkMiphOB5UA>. Accessed August 12, 2021.

Shapiro, James. *Shakespeare and the Jews*. New York: Columbia University Press, 1996.

—. *Shakespeare in a Divided America: What His Plays Tell Us about Our Past and Future*. Penguin Press, 2020.

—, ed. *Shakespeare in America: An Anthology from the Revolution to Now*. The Library of America, 2016.

Sharf, Zach. "'Get Out': Jordan Peele Reveals the Real Meaning Behind the Sunken Place." *IndieWire*, November 30, 2017, <www.indiewire.com/2017/11/get-out-jordan-peele-explains-sunken-place-meaning-1201902567/>. Accessed January 18, 2018.

Shortslef, Emily. "'A thousand several tongues': The Drama of Conscience and the Complaint of the Other in Shakespeare's *Richard III*." *Exemplaria*, vol. 29, no. 2, 2017, pp. 118–35.

Simon, Mallory, and Sara Sidner. "Decoding the Extremist Symbols and Groups at the Capitol Hill Insurrection." *CNN*, January 11, 2021, <www.cnn.com/2021/01/09/us/capitol-hill-insurrection-extremist-flags-soh/index.html>. Accessed August 12, 2021.

Singer, Marc. "'Black Skins' and White Masks: Comic Books and the Secrets of Race." *African American Review*, vol. 36, no. 1, 2002, pp. 107–19.

—. *Breaking the Frames: Populism and Prestige in Comic Studies*. University of Texas Press, 2018.

Smith, Barbara. "Racism and Women's Studies." *Intersectionality: Foundations and Frontiers*, edited by Patrick R. Grzanka, 1st ed., Westview Press, 2014, pp. 37–41.

Smith, Ian. "Othello's Black Handkerchief." *Shakespeare Quarterly*, vol. 64, no. 1, 2013, pp. 1–25.

—. *Race and Rhetoric in the Renaissance: Barbarian Errors*. Palgrave Macmillan, 2009.

—. "We Are Othello: Speaking of Race in Early Modern Studies." *Shakespeare Quarterly*, vol. 67, no. 1, 2016, pp. 104–24.

Smuts, Aaron. "The Ethics of Humor: Can Your Sense of Humor Be Wrong?" *Ethical Theory and Moral Practice*, vol. 13, no. 3, 2010, pp. 333–47.

Snook, Raven. "Theater Review: Shakespeare's Tragic Othello Set to a Hip-Hop Beat." *TimeOut*, November 16, 2016, <www.timeout.com/newyork/blog/theater-review-shakespeares-tragic-othello-set-to-a-hip-hop-beat-111616>. Accessed February 18, 2019.

Snow, Edward A. "Sexual Anxiety and the Male Order of Things in *Othello*." *English Literary Renaissance*, vol. 10, 1980, pp. 384–412.

Sollors, Werner. "Ethnicity and Race." *A Companion to Racial and Ethnic Studies*, edited by David Theo Goldberg and John Solomos, Blackwell Publishers, 2002, pp. 97–104.

—. *Neither Black Nor White Yet Both: Thematic Explorations of Interracial Literature*. Harvard University Press, 1999.

Stallybrass, Peter. "Patriarchal Territories: The Body Enclosed." *Rewriting the Renaissance: The Discourse of Sexual Difference in Early Modern Europe*, edited by Margaret W. Ferguson, Maureen Quilligan, and Nancy J. Vickers, University of Chicago Press, 1986, pp. 123–42.

Stevens, Rebecca. "Stomping on Eggshells: An Honest Discussion of Race, Identity, and Intent in the American Theater." *HowlRound*, February 2, 2014, <howlround.com/stomping-eggshells>. Accessed March 4, 2020.

Stevenson, Melanie A. "*Othello*, Darwin, and the Evolution of Race in Ann-Marie MacDonald's Work." *Canadian Literature*, vol. 168, 2001, pp. 34–53.
Sue, Derald W. "Microagressions, Marginality, and Oppression: An Introduction." *Microagressions and Marginality: Manifestations, Dynamics, and Impacts*, edited by Derald W. Sue, 1st ed., Wiley, 2010, pp. 3–25.
Syme, Rachel. "Talking to 'Serial's Sarah Koenig About Her Hit Podcast and Whether There Will Ever Be an Answer." *Vulture*, October 30, 2014, <vulture.com/2014/10/serials-sarah-koenig-on-her-hit-podcast.html>. Accessed August 17, 2017.
SZA. "Child's Play." *Z*, Top Dawg Entertainment, 2014.
Tatum, Beverly Daniel. *Why Are All the Black Kids Sitting Together in the Cafeteria? And Other Conversations About Race*. 20th anniversary edition. Basic Books, 2017.
Teague, Frances N. *Shakespeare and the American Popular Stage*. Cambridge University Press, 2006.
—. *Shakespeare's Speaking Properties*. Bucknell University Press, 1991.
Tesler, Michael. *Post-Racial or Most-Racial? Race and Politics in the Obama Era*. University of Chicago Press, 2016.
"The Color of Evil: How American Media Racializes Villains." *Sociology Lens*, March 28, 2013, <www.sociologylens.net/topics/communication-and-media/the-color-of-evil-how-american-media-racializes-villains/11636>. Accessed April 20, 2022.
The Ground We Stand On. "Statement: We See You, White American Theater." June 9, 2020, <www.weseeyouwat.com/statement>. Accessed June 9, 2020.
The Late Show with Stephen Colbert. "David Tennant Explains Why Shakespeare Still Matters." *YouTube*, April 28, 2016, <youtube.com/watch?v=nIZ_eq0vLfc>. Accessed August 12, 2021.
The Notorious B.I.G. "Juicy." *Ready to Die*. Bad Boy Records, 1994.
—. "Mo Money, Mo Problems." *Life After Death*. Bad Boy Records/Arista, 1997.
—. "Things Done Changed." *Ready to Die*. Bad Boy Records, 1994.
The Second City. "Sassy Gay Friend: Othello." *YouTube*, March 29, 2010, <www.youtube.com/watch?v=LKttq6EUqbE>. Accessed August 10, 2021.
Thomas, Ebony Elizabeth. *The Dark Fantastic: Race and the Imagination from Harry Potter to the Hunger Games*. NYU Press, 2020.
Thompson, Ayanna. *Blackface*. Bloomsbury, 2021.
—. "*Desdemona*: Toni Morrison's Response to *Othello*." *A Feminist Companion to Shakespeare*, 2nd ed., edited by Dympna Callaghan, John Wiley & Sons, 2016, pp. 494–506.
—. "Introduction." *Othello*, edited by E. A. J. Honigmann. Bloomsbury, 2016, pp. 1–116.
—. "On Protean Acting in Shakespeare: Race and Virtuosity." Centre for Renaissance and Reformation Studies, March 9, 2021, University of Toronto.

—. *Passing Strange: Shakespeare, Race, and Contemporary America*. Oxford University Press, 2011.

—. "Practicing a Theory/Theorizing a Practice: An Introduction to Shakespearean Colorblind Casting." *Colorblind Shakespeare: New Perspectives on Race and Performance*, edited by Ayanna Thompson, Routledge, 2006, pp. 1–24.

—. "The Blackfaced Bard: Returning to Shakespeare or Leaving Him?" *Shakespeare Bulletin*, vol. 27, no. 3, 2009, pp. 437–56.

—. "To Notice or Not to Notice: Shakespeare, Black Actors, and Performance Reviews." *Borrowers and Lenders: The Journal of Shakespeare and Appropriation*, vol. 4, no. 1, 2008, n.p.

Thompson, Ayanna, and Laura Turchi. *Teaching Shakespeare with Purpose: A Student-Centred Approach*. Bloomsbury, 2016.

Topham, Michelle. "Bastille's 'Send Them Off!' Is Influenced by *Othello* and It's Cool." *Leosigh*, September 4, 2016, <leosigh.com/bastilles-send-them-off-influenced-by-othello-video/>. Accessed August 12, 2021.

Touré. *Who's Afraid of Post-Blackness?: What it Means to be Black Now*. Free Press, 2011.

Tucker, Linda G. *Lockstep and Dance: Images of Black Men in Popular Culture*. University Press of Mississippi, 2007.

University of Southern California Annenberg. "Hollywood Equality: All Talk, Little Action." *USC Annenberg*, September 6, 2016, <annenberg.usc.edu/news/faculty-research/hollywood-equality-all-talk-little-action>. Accessed August 12, 2021.

Vaughan, Alden T., and Virginia Mason Vaughan, *Shakespeare in America*. Oxford University Press, 2012.

Vaughan, Virginia Mason. *Othello: A Contextual History*. Cambridge University Press, 1997.

—. *Performing Blackness on English Stages, 1500–1800*. Cambridge University Press, 2005.

Vogel, Paula. *Desdemona: A Play about a Handkerchief*. Dramatists Play Service, 1994.

Wagner, Sydnee. "Rewriting *Othello* in *Get Out*." *Racing Backwards: An Early Modern Race Studies Blog*, March 18, 2017, <racebackwards.wordpress.com/2017/03/18/first-blog-post/>. Accessed May 3, 2020.

Wallace-Wells, Benjamin. "The Strange Intimacy of 'Serial.'" *Vulture*, November 23, 2014, <www.vulture.com/2014/11/strange-intimacy-of-serial.html>. Accessed July 19, 2017.

Wanzo, Rebecca. *The Content of our Caricature: African American Comic Art and Political Beginning*. NY University Press, 2020.

Warren, Calvin L. *Ontological Terror: Blackness, Nihilism, and Emancipation*. Duke University Press, 2018.

Washington, Alesha Dominek. "Not the Average Girl from the Videos: B-Girls Defining Their Space in Hip-Hop Culture." *Home Girls Make Some Noise: Hip-Hop Feminism Anthology*, edited by Gwendolyn D.

Pough, Elaine Richardson, Aisha Durham, and Rachel Raimist, Parker Publishing, 2007, pp. 80–91.
Weaver, Simon. "Developing a Rhetorical Analysis of Racist Humor: Examining Black jokes on the Internet." *Social Semiotics*, vol. 20, no. 5, 2010, pp. 537–55.
White, Miles. *From Jim Crow to Jay-Z: Race, Rap, and the Performance of Masculinity (African American Music in Global Perspectives)*. University of Illinois Press, 2011.
Wicker, Tom. "Iqbal Khan: 'I want Shakespeare to speak urgently in a 21st-century context.'" *The Stage*, June 28, 2016, <www.thestage.co.uk/features/iqbal-khan-i-want-shakespeare-to-speak-urgently-in-a-21st-century-context>. Accessed August 12, 2021.
Williams, Nora J. "@Shakespeare and @TwasFletcher: Performances of Authority." *Humanities*, vol. 8, no. 1, 2019, n.p.
Wise, Tim. *Colorblind: The Rise of Post-Racial Politics and the Retreat from Racial Equity*. City Lights Publishers, 2010.
Wong, Julia Carrie. "The Problem with 'Serial' and the Model Minority Myth." *BuzzFeed*, November 16, 2014, <www.buzzfeed.com/juliacarriew/the-problem-with-serial-and-themodelminoritymyth?utm_term=.gaxEMdxbdL#.gexDWPX9P2>. Accessed February 4, 2015.
Worthen, William B. *Shakespeare and the Authority of Performance*. Cambridge University Press, 1997.
Wright, Bradford W. *Comic Book Nation: The Transformation of Youth Culture in America*. The Johns Hopkins University Press, 2001.
Yachnin, Paul, and Jessica Slights. "Introduction." *Shakespeare and Character: Theory, History, Performance, and Theatrical Persons*, edited by Paul Yachnin and Jessica Slights, Palgrave, 2009, pp. 1–18.
Yates, Kieran. "*Othello*—Review." *Guardian*, May 7, 2012, <www.theguardian.com/stage/2012/may/07/othello-review>. Accessed February 18, 2019.
Yim, Laura Lehua. "Reading Hawaiian Shakespeare: Indigenous Residue Haunting Settler Colonial Racism." *Journal of American Studies*, vol. 54, no. 1, 2020, pp. 36–43.
Young, Harvey. *Theatre & Race*. Palgrave, 2013.
Yurcaba, Josephine. "This American Crime: Sarah Koenig on Her Hit Podcast 'Serial.'" *Rolling Stone*, October 24, 2014, <www.rollingstone.com/culture/features/sarah-koenig-on-serial-20141024>. Accessed January 13, 2016.
Zinoman, Jason. "Jordan Peele on a Truly Terrifying Monster: Racism." *New York Times*, February 16, 2017, <www.nytimes.com/2017/02/16/movies/jordan-peele-interview-get-out.html>. Accessed January 18, 2019.

Index

adaptation, 4–5, 22, 26–7, 77, 99–100, 161–2, 171, 182, 189–90, 192–3, 226, 251, 284, 303, 311, 312–15
adaptive re-vision, 22, 161–2, 190, 192–3, 195, 196, 199, 200, 205
American Moor, (2012 play) 22, 159–205; *see also* Cobb, K. H.
antiblack(ness), 6, 9, 17, 19–20, 22, 25, 26, 27–8, 162, 204, 301–2, 304, 305, 319
  avoidance of, 23, 182, 189, 202, 209, 243; *see also American Moor* (2012 play); *Desdemona* (Morrison)
  colorblindness, 13, 316, 317
  in comics, 40, 42, 66, 67, 70, 71, 74–5, 160
  in cover art, 29–31
  in *Othello: The Remix* (2012 play), 89, 111
  stereotypes, 34, 35, 36, 125, 128, 221
  white femininity and, 208, 252
  whiteness and, 257, 310
antiracis(m)(t), 8, 10, 25, 27–8, 34, 35, 72, 73, 76, 252, 301, 304–5, 307, 308–9, 311, 315–17, 319
  in *American Moor* (2012 play), 162–3, 166, 200, 201, 204, 205
  definition, 9, 219
  in *Desdemona* (Morrison), 208, 209, 211
  in *Get Out* (2017 film), 273, 277
  hip hop, 110, 115–16
  post-racism and, 21–2
appropriation, 4, 5, 7, 17, 72, 123, 312, 313, 314, 315
  antiblack, 89, 176
  antiracist, 9, 27, 28, 162
  cultural, 21, 79, 84–5, 88, 110, 112–13, 114–15
  ethics of, 130, 135–6, 193
  feminist, 23, 213
  white, 278, 282, 288, 294, 296
audience education, 23, 162, 196, 198–201, 205, 311
authentic(ity), 4–5, 22, 33, 132, 133, 190–1, 195, 230, 251, 262–3, 264, 267
  whiteness and, 174, 191–2, 193, 256

Belanger, A. (illustrator), 33, 44, 46–7, 48, 49, 51, 57–8, 59, 61, 63, 65; *see also* Del Col, A.; *Kill Shakespeare* (comic series); McCreery, C
Bilge, S., 209–10, 220–1; *see also* Collins, P. H.; intersectional(ity)
Blackness, 9, 35, 58, 64, 66, 71, 138n14, 186, 256, 267, 270, 293–4

appropriation of, 23, 81, 84, 89, 95, 103, 110, 225
  in comics, 1, 20, 39–43, 46, 53–6, 57, 64–5, 68
  in cover art, 31
  masculinity and, 111, 222, 223, 226, 228–9, 242, 248, 272
  signifiers of, 262–3, 264, 268
  stereotyping, 3, 15, 169, 170n12, 178, 274
  white supremacy and, 173, 176, 191–2, 250, 283, 287, 289, 293; *see also Get Out* (2017 film)
  see also antiblackness
Bourdieu, P., 24–5
Britton, D., 286, 287
Bubba-Buu (fanartist), 7–9

Chevalier, T., 301–4; *see also New Boy* (2017 novel)
citation, 4, 5, 120, 122, 129–30, 313; *see also* Erickson, P.
coagula, 23, 257, 276, 277–80, 281, 283, 284–7, 296, 297; *see also Get Out* (2017 film); Peele, J.
Cobb, K. H., 22, 159–63, 167–70, 173–4, 178, 180, 182–9, 192–202, 205, 209, 298, 300–1, 308, 312, 313, 316; *see also American Moor* (2012 play)
Collins, P. H., 20, 34, 35, 36–7, 39–40, 41, 66, 85, 209–10, 220–1; *see also* Bilge, S.; intersectional(ity)
colorblind(ness), 11–15, 19, 20, 25, 27, 34, 48, 82–5, 88, 161, 166, 236, 254, 307–8, 312, 314, 316, 319
  casting, 21, 109, 200, 318
  narrative, 20, 210; *Kill Shakespeare* (comic series), 45–6, 55; *New Boy* (2017 novel), 301, 302; *Othello: The Remix* (2012 play), 80, 81, 82, 89, 95–7, 105, 106, 110, 115, 116
color line, 28, 170, 177
comics (comic books), 1–2, 20, 66, 69, 72, 73–4, 75, 301, 314
  representation of Blackness, 20, 32, 33–4, 35, 39–52, 58
Crenshaw, K. W., 23, 219; *see also* intersectional(ity)

Dadabhoy, A., 169n11, 173, 178, 188, 285, 286–7
Daileader, C., 5, 6, 26, 53, 54, 129n9, 276
DC Comics, 43, 44, 49n8
Del Col, A., 32–3, 44–5, 56–8, 59, 60, 62, 63, 65–7, 69, 72; *see also* Belanger, A.; *Kill Shakespeare* (comic series); McCreery, Conor
Desdemona (character), 1, 2, 3, 22–3, 98, 206–8, 219, 269, 276, 287–8, 290–1, 292–3, 294, 296, 299, 303
  absent but referenced: *American Moor* (2012 play), 176, 179, 194, 198, 209; *Othello: The Remix* (2012 play), 99–101, 103, 104, 107–8, 209; *Kill Shakespeare* (comic series), 54, 62–3, 64, 66–7, 67–8, 208–9
  citation in *Serial* (2014 podcast), 124, 125, 129n9, 145, 153, 209
  in *Desdemona* (Vogel), 210, 213, 215–18, 221, 222, 226–9, 251
  in *Desdemona* (Morrison), 209–11, 230–4, 236–43, 246–51
  in *Good Night Desdemona (Good Morning Juliet)* (1988 play), 210, 213–15, 218, 221–6, 251
  performance history, 211–12
  in visual art, 7–8, 31

Desdemona (2011 operetta), 22, 23, 209–11, 230–52, 305
   accessibility, 251–2
   intersectionality in, 234–41
   Sa'ran (character), 230, 234, 238–41
   toxic masculinity in, 243–6
   see also intersectionality; Morrison, T.; Traoré, R.
Desdemona (1994 play), 22, 210, 213, 215–18, 219, 221, 222–3, 226–9, 251; *see also* Vogel, P.

Emilia (character), 82, 212, 252
   in *Desdemona* (Vogel), 216, 217, 218, 221n11, 222, 226, 227–8
   in *Desdemona* (Morrison), 230, 233, 234, 236–8, 239, 240, 241, 244, 247
English (discipline), 8, 121, 150–1, 182–3, 184, 187, 198, 202
Erickson, P., 4, 6, 9, 22, 26, 120, 135–6, 148n25, 161–2, 193, 230, 234, 254, 267n10, 285, 286, 287, 290, 292, 293
Espinosa, R., 19, 28, 98, 149, 239, 306

fanart, 7–8
fandom, 35, 72–5
Fazel, V. M., 17, 72, 74, 121n6; *see also* Geddes, L.
Finn, K. M., 72, 73, 74; *see also* McCall, J.

Geddes, L., 17, 72, 74; *see also* Fazel, V.
Globe Theatre, 23, 79, 98, 113–14, 115, 197, 263, 264, 265, 308, 316
Globe to Globe Festival (2012), 77, 115
Goodnight Desdemona (Good Morning Juliet) (1988 play), 22, 210, 213, 221n11, 222, 223, 251, 252; *see also* MacDonald, A.-M.
Good Tickle Brain (webcomic, 2014–ongoing), 1–2, 3, 7, 8, 20
Gosling, M. L., 1–2; *see also Good Tickle Brain* (webcomic, 2014–ongoing)
Greenblatt, S., 197, 199–200, 312
Ground We Stand On, The (2020 protest), 203–4

Habitus, 24–6, 28, 301, 304, 313, 319; *see also* Bourdieu, P.
Hall, K. F., 5–6, 9, 16, 26, 54, 135–6, 167, 168, 183, 186, 189, 254, 285
   American Moor (2012 play), 201, 204, 205
   Things of Darkness (1995), 52, 53, 71, 100, 122n8, 137–8
Hall, S., 11, 14, 16
Hamlet (character), 3, 171, 177, 178, 191, 192
   in *Kill Shakespeare* (comic series), 33, 35, 44, 45, 55–6, 58–63, 64, 65, 66, 67, 68, 69
Hamlet (1599 play), 150, 154, 200, 267
Harlem Duet (1997 play), 213
Hendricks, M., 19, 25–6, 191–2
hip hop, 21, 37, 77–8, 79–82, 84–9, 89, 91, 92, 103, 104, 105, 107–16, 315–16; *see also Othello: The Remix* (2012 play)
hooks, b., 172, 173, 177–8, 180, 211n4, 229, 240, 249, 313, 314–15
Hornback, R., 5–6, 103, 176
Huang, Eddie, 260–1

Iago (character), 1, 2, 7–8, 19, 21, 29, 30–1, 98, 99, 207, 212, 216, 227, 275, 286, 287–8, 291, 292, 296

allusions in *Serial*, 123, 124, 126, 131–5, 154
  in *American Moor* (2012 play), 169n11
  in contemporary fiction, 300
  in the Desdemona plays, 216, 223, 224, 225, 237, 241, 243, 245
  in *Kill Shakespeare* (comic series), 33, 45, 54, 57–8, 62–5, 66
  in *Othello: The Remix* (2012 play), 77, 82, 101, 102, 103
intersectional(ity), 22–3, 209–11, 212, 219–21, 226, 229, 230, 236, 240, 241, 242, 251; *see also* Crenshaw, K. W.

Juliet (character), 33, 121
  in *Kill Shakespeare* (comic series), 44–5, 52–6, 58, 59–64, 65, 66, 67–8, 69
  in *Good Morning Desdemona (Good Night Juliet)* (1988 play), 215, 221n11, 225

Kendi, I. X., 9, 110–11, 164–5, 171, 172
Key & Peele (comedy series, 2012–2015), 23, 256–7, 262–9; *see also* Key, K. M.; Peele, J.
Key, K. M., 256–7, 262–6; *see also* *Key & Peele* (comedy series); Peele, J.
Kidnie, M. J., 4n7, 22, 161–2, 179n17, 190, 192
Kill Shakespeare (comic series, 2010–2014), 20, 32–9, 44–7, 49, 51–75; *see also* Belanger, A.; Del Col, A.; McCreery, C.
Koenig, S., 21, 119–35, 140, 141–3, 144, 145, 147, 151, 153–4, 209, 239, 302, 315, 316; *see also* podcast; *Serial* (2014 podcast)

Lanier, D. M., 4–5, 7, 15–16, 106, 120, 276, 300, 301, 303
Lee, Hae Min (*Serial*), 119, 120, 121, 123, 126, 128, 129n9, 132, 141, 144, 147, 153, 155, 209
Little Jr., A., 19, 26, 35, 54, 58, 80n6, 99, 137n13, 138, 287n18, 291, 294

McCall, J., 72, 73, 74
McCall, L,. 220–1
McCreery, C., 32–3, 44–5, 56, 57, 58, 59, 60, 62, 63, 65, 66, 67, 69, 72; *see also* Belanger, A.; Del Col, A.; *Kill Shakespeare* (comic series)
MacDonald, A.-M., 22–3, 210, 211, 212, 213–15, 216, 218, 219, 221–2, 223–6, 230, 231, 248, 252; *see also* *Goodnight Desdemona (Good Morning Juliet)* (1988 play)
MacDonald, J. G., 5–6, 26, 176, 193, 241
Marvel Cinematic Universe (MCU), 47
Marvel Comics, 43, 44, 49
masculinity, 107
  Black, 22, 111, 161, 169, 208, 221, 264, 270; in comic books, 32, 50, 51, 58, 75; in hip hop, 91, 107, 113; stereotypes, 20, 29, 87, 89, 127–8, 172, 176, 177–8, 266, 269, 299; violence and stereotypes, 30, 31, 36–9, 106, 108, 175, 265; resistance to stereotypes, 174–5, 179, 181–2, 196, 257, 262n5, 268–9, 273; sexual jealousy and stereotypes, 223, 224, 226, 227, 228
  Muslim, 128–9, 146
  toxic, 23, 209, 241, 245, 246, 248
  white, 207, 258

Mbembe, A., 250, 255
  nanoracism, 288–9
  necropolitics, 23, 278–9, 281, 282
microaggression(s), 23, 165, 184, 277, 288–94; *see also* Sue, D. W.
minstrel shows/minstrelsy, 42, 103, 105–6, 168, 171, 175–6, 177, 179, 252, 269
Miranda, L. M., 111–12
misogynoir, 108
Morrison, T., 22, 23, 148n24, 209–11, 212, 230–3, 236, 240, 241–4, 249, 250, 252, 257–8, 297, 301 308; *see also Desdemona* (2011 operetta); Traoré, R.

National Public Radio (NPR), 119, 121, 132, 259
necropolitics *see* Mbembe, A.
negrobilia *see* Quarshie, H.
New Boy (2017 novel), 301–4; *see also* Chevalier, T.; Lanier, D.

Obama, Barack (US President), 6, 9–10, 83–4, 256, 274, 289; *see also* post-racial
Okri, B., 206–8, 230, 239, 242, 244, 250
Othello (1604 play), 3–4, 94, 103, 151–2, 154, 155, 160, 241, 257, 262, 265–7, 270, 276–7, 278, 284–8, 290–4, 296, 300, 307, 319
  academic discussion of, 199–200
  antiblack interpretations of, 27–8, 34, 106, 228
  in *Serial* (2014 podcast), 120, 121, 122, 123, 125–6, 128, 129, 130–2, 135, 136, 140, 145, 153
  cover art for, 29–32
  Desdemona problem in, 206–8, 219, 227
  Iago problem in, 62n9, 98
  in *American Moor* (2012 play), 161, 166, 167–71, 173, 175, 179–80, 182, 183, 185–6, 188–9, 191, 194–6
  interracial marriage in, 53–4
  performance history, 5, 175–6, 206, 211–12, 213, 275
Othello: The Remix (2012 play), 21, 77–82, 84, 88–90, 92, 93, 94–5, 97–113, 115, 209, 316

Peele, J., 23, 256–7, 262–93; *see also Get Out* (2017 film); *Key & Peele*; Key, K. M.
Pittman, L. M., 120–1, 190, 317
podcast, 15, 21, 119, 120n5, 126–8, 130, 132–3, 140, 142, 143, 147, 315; *see also* Koenig, S.; *Serial* (2014 podcast)
post-racial, 6–7, 8–9, 27, 28, 33, 38, 72, 75–6, 139, 147, 209, 235, 299, 301, 305, 306, 316–17
  American Moor (2012 play) as, 160, 162, 170, 171, 178
  antiblackness and, 21, 304
  antiracism and, 22
  colorblindness and, 9–12, 14–18, 19–20, 25, 48, 83, 89, 115, 302, 319
  comedy, 95
  comic books and, 32, 34, 35, 43
  Desdemona (Morrison), 210, 243
  Get Out (2017 film), 23, 274, 279, 288
  Othello: The Remix (2012 play), as 112
  Serial (2014 podcast) as, 125, 130, 154
  whiteness and, 202–3, 257
Powell, Colin (US general), 135, 168–9

Q Brothers, 20–1, 77–82, 88–92, 94, 97–103, 104, 105, 106, 107, 108, 110, 114–15, 116, 209, 315
Quarshie, H., 171–2

racecraft, 17–18, 19, 25, 35, 139, 310, 315
racism, 2, 10, 18, 27, 28, 93, 123, 124, 130, 136, 142, 145, 146, 160, 169, 170, 179, 182, 199–200, 235, 310
  as violence, 278, 288–9
  colorblind, 11–14, 16, 19–20, 82–3, 110, 161, 308, 319
  humor, 94, 95–9, 102, 265n8, 274
  in comics, 41
  in education, 182–3, 185, 187, 201, 203, 254, 314–15
  in hip hop, 88
  in theatre, 189, 205, 219, 221, 222
  language, 101
  premodern, 137n13, 138, 140n17, 147–8, 170
  theorization of, 36, 38, 163–6, 171, 176
  see also antiblackness; post-racial
rap, 76, 77, 85–8, 90–1, 92, 101, 106, 107, 109, 110, 111, 114, 116, 299
reanimation(s), 5–6, 8, 16, 155, 305, 309, 313, 319
  antiblack, 19–20, 34, 35, 39, 75, 300–1, 304; see also Kill Shakespeare (comic series)
  antiracist, 22, 76, 262, 308
  colorblindness in, 11, 21, 46, 316
  feminist, 213, 307
  intersectional, 209, 210, 211, 246, 251; see also Desdemona (2011 operetta)
  theorization, 4, 25, 27–8, 73

see also adaptation; adaptive re-vision; appropriation
Romeo and Juliet (1594 play), 80n7, 120, 126
Royster, F. T., 3, 18, 23, 25, 26, 152, 267

Sa'ran (character) see Desdemona (2011 operetta)
Sassy Gay Friend (2010 webseries), 2, 3
Serial (2014 podcast), 21, 119–27, 130–6, 139–47, 150–1, 152–5, 209, 239, 302, 315–16; see also Koenig, S.; Lee, Hae-Min (Serial); podcast; Syed, Adnan (Serial)
Smith, I., 1n1, 3, 26, 31–2, 64, 74, 131n10, 137n13, 138n15, 148n24, 297, 303
stage directions, 172–4, 195–6, 202, 217
Sue, D. W., 288–90, 292–3; see also microaggression(s)
sunken place, 23, 276–8, 279, 281, 284, 294, 296–7; see also Get Out (2017 film); Peele, J.
Syed, Adnan (Serial), 119, 121, 123, 125–7, 128–9, 132, 133, 134–5, 140, 141–7, 149, 152, 153–4, 155; see also Koenig, S.; Lee, Hae-Min (Serial); podcast; Serial (2014 podcast)

Thomas, E. E., 20, 34–5, 43, 46, 66, 68, 71, 75
Thompson, A., 5–6, 7, 62n9, 82, 109, 151, 175–6, 213, 224, 251–2, 309, 314
  Passing Strange (2011), 26, 136, 137n13, 138n15, 150, 254
Traoré, R. (composer), 209, 230, 233–4, 243, 251–2; see also Desdemona (2011 operetta); Morrison, T.

Vogel, P., 22, 210, 211, 212, 213, 215–18, 219, 221, 222, 226–8, 230, 231, 236, 246, 247, 248, 252; *see also* Desdemona (character); *Desdemona* (1994 play); Emilia (character)

Wanzo, R., 41
whiteness, 10, 53–6, 58, 64–5, 85, 100, 105, 112, 169–70, 186, 223, 224, 254, 282, 285, 295, 301
   centering of, 21, 35, 71, 118, 123, 124, 130, 135–6, 184, 287, 313
   and Christianity, 285–6
   decentering, 257
   and feminism, 211n4, 223, 230, 238, 240, 246, 250
   implied audience, 174
   microaggressions and, 290
   Shakespeare as marker, 20, 33, 110, 191, 193, 196, 197, 257, 264, 268–9
   theatrical, 156–60, 161–2, 183, 201, 202, 203, 252, 299
   universality, 23, 133–4, 255–6, 257–8, 261, 298
   violence, 277, 278, 279, 280, 283, 294
white privilege, 23, 124, 130, 150, 165, 168, 203
   interrogation of, 210, 230, 234, 235, 240, 248, 250
white racial frame, 117–20, 121–2, 124–5, 128, 129, 130, 132, 133, 134, 135, 136, 155, 294, 309, 316
   theorization of, 283

EU representative:
Easy Access System Europe
Mustamäe tee 50, 10621 Tallinn, Estonia
Gpsr.requests@easproject.com

www.ingramcontent.com/pod-product-compliance
Lightning Source LLC
Chambersburg PA
CBHW051108230426
43667CB00014B/2490